Houghton Mifflin Company

222 Berkeley Street, Boston, Massachusetts 02116-3764
(617) 351-5000 Cable HOUGHTON

College Division

Dear Instructor:

In your hands you have the Instructor's Annotated Edition of READING SKILLS HANDBOOK, Sixth Edition. This ancillary provides answers to the exercises that support the instructional material in the text. For those exercises that require responses drawing on students' personal experiences or interpretations, examples of possible responses are often provided.

For the Sixth Edition of the READING SKILLS HANDBOOK, we have added Critical Thinking in Writing activities and Unit Review exercises. READING SKILLS HANDBOOK is the middle book in a three-book reading skills series; the BASIC READING SKILLS HANDBOOK, Third Edition, is the lower level book, and ALL OF US is the higher level book. Each of these texts follows the approach and format of the READING SKILLS HANDBOOK but differs in the level of instruction, the skills selected for attention, the order in which the skills are taught, and the character and level of the reading selections used for the examples, exercises, and anthology. The texts are coordinated to provide successive development of skills; they can be used separately at the appropriate level or together in sequence.

Available to adopters is a Test Package containing pre- and post-tests for most chapters in the Handbook, with complete information on the graded readability levels of the anthology readings. The Computerized Testing Program makes the tests available on disks that can be used with any word-processing software on IBM PC-compatible computers and Macintosh computers. Also available is a new Computerized Vocabulary Program keyed to the reading selections. It gives students additional opportunities to practice using the key vocabulary highlighted in the text.

Sincerely yours,

The Publishers

As part of Houghton Mifflin's ongoing commitment to the environment, this text has been printed on recycled paper.

Reading Skills Handbook

Sixth Edition

INSTRUCTOR'S ANNOTATED EDITION

Harvey S. Wiener
Adelphi University

Charles Bazerman
Georgia Institute of Technology

HOUGHTON MIFFLIN COMPANY BOSTON TORONTO

Geneva, Illinois Palo Alto Princeton, New Jersey

Cover design by Linda Manly Wade.

Cover image by Richard Diebenkorn (1922–1993), *Interior with Book,* 1959. Oil on canvas, 70″ × 64″. Courtesy: The Nelson-Atkins Museum of Art, Kansas City, Missouri (Gift of the Friends of Art), F63–15.

Sponsoring Editor Mary Jo Southern
Senior Development Editor Barbara Roth
Senior Project Editor Cathy Labresh Brooks
Associate Production/Design Coordinator Jennifer Waddell
Manufacturing Coordinator Marie Barnes
Marketing Manager George Kane

Acknowledgments begin on page 625.

Printed in the U.S.A.

Student Edition ISBN: 0-395-66145-5

Instructor's Annotated Edition ISBN: 0-395-66146-3

123456789-AM-97 96 95 94 93

Contents

Preface

Reading Skills Handbook, Sixth Edition, teaches, in clear language, the basic reading and study skills required for success in college. In this book, students read a careful explanation of a specific skill and an analysis of how that skill applies to a particular passage. Then they have a chance to test their mastery of that skill by means of numerous exercises designed for practice and review. Our step-by-step approach allows students to move from simple skills to more complex ones with confidence.

Organization

As before, the book is divided into two main parts: a *Handbook* that provides instruction in the essential reading skills and a section of *Reading Selections* that provides twenty-four reading passages and related exercises.

The *Handbook* begins with basic techniques for dealing with new words. It next examines important comprehension skills, before advancing to skills that help students interpret and evaluate what they read. Finally, the *Handbook* teaches basic study skills — techniques for taking notes, outlining, summarizing, and taking exams — that help students improve their performance in class.

Each passage in the *Reading Selections* is accompanied by comprehension, interpretation, vocabulary, and writing exercises. Each question is keyed to the appropriate section in the *Handbook;* if students have difficulty answering a question, they can easily find and review the material that covers that particular skill. For example, an **8** after a question means that a review of Chapter 8, "Making Inferences," will help students recall the techniques that readers use to make valid inferences.

Throughout the text students will find questions that guide their understanding and interpretation of specific passages.

The organization of the book allows its adaptation to specific courses in several ways. The instructor may teach the four units in the *Handbook* in the early weeks of the term, postponing the study of the *Reading Selections* until students know the basic reading skills. The brief readings in the *Handbook* allow the reinforcement of newly learned concepts, and students should be ready for the longer readings by the time they reach the *Reading Selections*. Or, the instructor may choose to further reinforce the skills taught in the *Handbook* by immediately assigning appropriate work from the *Reading Selections*. Finally, the instructor may begin with the *Reading Selections* and return to key instructional units in the *Handbook* as specific needs arise in class.

New to This Edition

For the Sixth Edition of *Reading Skills Handbook* we have made some changes in the content and organization of the text and have added materials to strengthen an already successful book.

- About one-third of the reading passages in both the *Handbook* and *Reading Selections* are new; they include lively selections of fiction and nonfiction from books, newspapers, and magazines. We have maintained the emphasis on materials from textbooks that students typically read in their college course work — texts on career planning, sociology, psychology, computers, history, business, government, and chemistry, for example.
- We have added new Critical Thinking in Writing activities to stimulate students to delve further into the ideas in selected *Handbook* readings and exercises by relating them to their own experiences and perceptions.
- We have added new Unit Review exercises to encourage students to apply all the skills they have learned in a unit to a more extensive reading.
- We have increased the number of short answer questions to allow students to demonstrate in writing the knowledge they have gained from reading.
- We have placed coverage of summarizing in the chapter with

underlining, taking notes, and outlining to reinforce the value of using all of these study techniques.

Reading Skills Handbook, Sixth Edition, is intended to be a comprehensive guidebook for students who are taking basic reading skills courses. Encouraged by the successes of students who have used previous editions, we are confident that students who use this book will make substantial improvements in their reading ability.

Acknowledgments

We have many people to thank for their ideas on the preparation of this text. Colleagues scattered around the country have made thoughtful suggestions and have guided us in writing this book. We are grateful to

Mary Boyles, Pembroke State University (NC)
Nita Drescher, Brookhaven College (TX)
Mary Alice Eastland, Hill College (TX)
Kevin Finnigan, Bunker Hill Community College (MA)
Charles Mann, Linn-Benton Community College (OR)
William A. Stanton, Jamestown Community College (NY)
Merritt W. Stark, Jr., Henderson State University (AR)
Maggie Hahn Wade, Triton College (IL)
Anne Walker, Mount San Jacinto College (CA)

We also wish to thank Sheila Byers, Dolores Shedd, Barbara Wiener, and Melissa Wiener for their help in bringing this project to fruition. To all these colleagues and friends and to our wives and families we owe much thanks and appreciation.

H. S. W.
C. B.

Correlations to Basic Reading Skills Tests

Many states require college students to demonstrate their competence in reading. In the tables below, the reading skills included in three representative state tests are correlated to the sections in *Reading Skills Handbook* where the specific skills are covered.

Texas Academic Skills Program (TASP)

Determining the Meaning of Words and Phrases	
Familiar words	1a, 1c, 1d, 2f
Words with multiple meanings	1e, 1f, 2f
Figurative language	9
Understanding the Main Idea and Supporting Details in Written Material	
Main ideas in narrative and expository writing	5a, 5b(1), 5b(2)
Stated vs. implied main idea	5b(1), 5b(2)
Supporting details	6b
Identifying a Writer's Purpose, Point of View, and Intended Meaning	
Recognizing writers' intent	12d(4), 12e
Analyzing the Relationship Among Ideas in Written Material	
Organizational patterns and relationships in written materials	7a, 7b, 7c, 7d, 7e
Drawing conclusions from written materials	10
Using Critical Reasoning Skills to Evaluate Written Material	
Steps in critically evaluating written material	8, 12a, 12b, 12c, 12d, 12e
Applying Study Skills to Reading Assignments	
Notetaking, outlining, and mapping	13a, 13b, 13c, 13d, 13e
Interpretation of information in graphic form	4b, 4d, 4e

Florida College Level Academic Skills Test (CLAST)

Reading with Literal Comprehension	
Recognize main ideas	5a, 5b(1), 5b(2)
Identify supporting details	6b
Determine meaning of words on the basis of context	1c

Florida College Level Academic Skills Test (CLAST) *(continued)*

Reading with Critical Comprehension	
Recognize the author's purpose	12d(4)
Identify the author's overall organizational pattern	7a, 7b, 7c, 7d, 7e
Distinguish between statements of fact and statements of opinion	12a
Detect bias	12b, 12d(5), 12e
Recognize the author's tone	12d(2)
Recognize explicit and implicit relationships within sentences	5a, 8
Recognize implicit as well as explicit relationships between sentences	5a, 5b(1), 5b(2), 8
Recognize valid arguments	12a, 12b
Draw logical inferences and conclusions	8, 10

Handbook

Introduction

Learning to read is not learning just a single skill. It is learning many skills that work together and build on one another. Each time you improve any one skill, it strengthens all the others. As your vocabulary improves, you will be able to understand and interpret your reading. And as you learn to comprehend and interpret better, you will gain more clues about the meaning of unfamiliar words.

The first half of this book teaches the basic skills of reading. Each skill is explained clearly in its own section. Exercises follow each section so that you can practice each skill as you learn about it. Your teacher may assign sections for the whole class to study or may assign you sections to work on individually, depending on your needs. Also, as you find areas that you want to work on personally, you can go over sections on your own.

To help you find skills that you need to study, the skills are separated into four different units: Vocabulary, Comprehension, Interpretation and Evaluation, and Basic Study Skills. The detailed table of contents and index can help you locate the exact page of any skill that you want to work on.

Each skill also is given a number, based on the chapter and section in which it is discussed. For example, finding main ideas in paragraphs is discussed in section b of Chapter 5, "Topics and Main Ideas in Paragraphs." The number **5b**, then, refers to the section that you need to look at for help in finding main ideas in paragraphs. When you are reading one section, the book may cross-refer to another section by using the number of the other section. Your teacher also may write the number on a piece of your work to suggest that you go over a particular section. Finally, the second half of this book has reading selections with questions. Each question has a reference number that lets you know which skill is needed to answer the question. If you have problems with the question, you can look at that section in the first half of the book for help.

Unit One

Vocabulary

1

Building a Strong Vocabulary

1a How to Find Out What Words Mean

To read well, you need a strong vocabulary. To build a strong vocabulary, you need to read well.

These sentences are a paradox — that is, they seem to express opposite points but, nevertheless, are both true. Together, they state the challenge facing anyone trying to improve reading skills. In order to read confidently, you have to know many words. You have to know how to figure out the meanings for new words that you discover as you read. Yet the best way to expand your knowledge of words is to read often and in varied content areas. Reading and vocabulary are strongly connected. As you improve your skills in one, you improve your skills in the other.

Most of us have vocabularies that allow us to read widely from the everyday sources of information that surround us: newspapers, magazines, computers, television, signs, posters, advertisements, credit card and job applications, instructions, and recipes. The person with the richest and most useful vocabulary, however, can read more complicated and varied sources of information easily. You may not be as confident about reading a psychology textbook, a history journal, or an encyclopedia entry as you are about reading other kinds of material. Still, supplementing your familiar and usual resources with a wide variety of materials offers you the opportunity to expand your knowledge of words as it improves your reading skills.

The first step to take in improving your vocabulary is to recognize that it is not possible for you to know the meaning of every word you see. Sometimes you may say to yourself, "I sort of know what this means" or "I can get by without figuring this one out." But often you really need to find out exactly what those words mean. In the short run, not paying attention to words you don't know may save you some work. But in the long run, you just won't know as much as you should. Here are some ways to find the meanings of difficult words:

- Learn to use the *context* — that is, clues that surrounding sentences sometimes give about the meanings of new words.
- In a word you don't know, look for parts of the word whose meanings you might know.
- Learn the difference between what a word means and what a word suggests or makes you feel.
- Learn the difference between words that mean almost the same thing but have different shades of meaning.
- Learn to use a dictionary so you can find meanings easily.
- Keep a list of words you want to add to your vocabulary.

1b How to Remember New Words

Once you've found the meaning of a new word and you think you understand it, try to make sure that you don't forget it. To remember new words:

- Write the word and its definition often, just for practice.
- Say the word. Learn to pronounce it correctly by using the pronunciation clues in your dictionary (see section **2c**).
- Try to learn the word and its meaning the first time you see it.
- Use index cards to study vocabulary. Write the word on one side of the card and its definition on the other side.
- Make up a phrase or a sentence that uses the word in a way you understand.
- Change the ending of the word: Try making it plural; try changing the tense; try adding *ly*.
- Use the word when you talk — in class, on the job, at home.
- Use the word whenever you can in your writing assignments.
- Say the word and its meaning over and over again in your mind.

- Don't try to learn long lists of new words. Study just a few words each day for several days so that you can learn by repeating.

1c Context Clues to Word Meanings

In the second paragraph of this chapter (page 5), did you notice the word *paradox*? If that word was unfamiliar to you, how could you have figured out its meaning? Let's look again at the first sentence of the paragraph and at the paragraph that comes just before it.

> To read well, you need a strong vocabulary. To build a strong vocabulary, you need to read well.
>
> These sentences are a paradox — that is, they seem to express opposite points but, nevertheless, are both true.

If you read carefully, you could have defined the word *paradox* from context clues. *Context clues* are hints provided by the words and sentences surrounding the unfamiliar word. Did you notice that the dash (—) and the words *that is* introduced a definition of *paradox*? In fact, a paradox is a statement that seems contradictory but is true. If you had checked a dictionary, you would have found a definition quite similar to that one. But you didn't really need a dictionary in this case: Surrounding sentences supplied enough hints for you to guess the meaning of the word *paradox.*

Most experienced readers try to guess the meanings of unfamiliar words through context clues. In order to make meanings clearer, good writers often provide such clues for readers. The clues are not always as clear-cut as those you just examined for the word *paradox.* Sometimes surrounding sentences do not provide enough hints, and you do have to turn to a dictionary or to some other source for the meaning of an unfamiliar word. But because context clues are so frequently available to an alert reader, it's a good idea to learn to recognize the different kinds of clues you might come across in your textbooks and other reading materials.

How to Use Sentence Hints for Word Meanings

Hint	Example	Explanation
Some sentences set off the definition of a difficult word by means of punctuation.	*Origami* — Japanese paper folding — is family fun.	Dashes — , parentheses ( ), brackets [ ].
	Fibrin, elastic threads of protein, helps blood to clot.	Commas.
Sometimes *helping words,* along with punctuation, provide important clues.	Mary felt *perturbed;* that is, she was greatly disturbed by her sister's actions.	Helping words: *that is, meaning, such as, or, is called.*
Some sentences tell the opposite of what a new word means. From its opposite, you can figure out the meaning of the word.	Parents who constantly spank their children cannot be called *lenient.*	If you are *lenient,* you do not often punish your children. *Merciful* or *gentle* would be a good guess for the meaning of *lenient.* Helping words to show opposites: *not, but, although, however, on the other hand.*
Sometimes you can use your own experiences to figure out the definition of a word.	The *cacophonous* rattling made Maria cover her ears.	A noise that would make you cover your ears would be *unpleasant* or *jarring.*

Hint	Example	Explanation
Sentences before or after a sentence containing a difficult word sometimes explain the meaning of the word.	Mozart gave his first public recital at the age of six. By age thirteen, he had written symphonies and an operetta. He is justly called a child *prodigy*.	It would certainly take a remarkably talented person to do these things. An extraordinary person, then, would be a *prodigy*.
Some sentences are written just to give the definitions of difficult words — words that readers need to know in order to understand what they are reading.	One of the remarkable features of the Nile Valley is the *fertility* of its soil. This rich earth that supported plant growth made it possible for Egyptians to thrive in a dry region.	The second sentence, which tells you that the soil was rich and that it supported plant growth, explains *fertility*.
Some sentences give examples of a new word, which allow you to build a definition.	Select a *periodical* from among the following: *Playboy, Time, Reader's Digest*, or *Seventeen*.	The sentence doesn't say that a *periodical* is a magazine, but you can figure it out from the examples.
Some sentences use a word you do know to help explain a word you don't know.	A *formidable* enemy is one to be feared.	*Formidable* — through the clues in this sentence — means *fearsome* or *dreadful*.

EXERCISES

1. Choosing Definitions from Context

Use the clues you learned about in section **1c**. Determine from the surrounding words and sentences what the words in italics mean. Then, from the choices that follow, select the word that comes closest to the meaning you've decided on. Write the letter of the correct answer in the space provided. Finally, in the space following each question, describe the clues that helped you figure out the meaning.

Student responses will vary.

a 1. The police kept the witness *sequestered* in a hotel room, hidden away from the mobsters who had threatened him.
a. secluded
b. drunk
c. tied up
d. confused

punctuation (comma precedes definition)

b 2. Rather than send his fiancee an oversized bouquet of two dozen roses, he decided to send her a delicate *nosegay* of wildflowers.
a. perfume
b. small cluster of flowers
c. painted sketch
d. artificial silk flowers

opposite ("rather than . . . oversized bouquet")

b 3. The judge tried to free herself of any bias or prejudice so that she could reach a truly *disinterested* evaluation of the case.
a. lack of interest
b. lack of bias

c. lack of skill
d. lack of thought

words you know help explain a word you don't know (bias, prejudice)

d 4. Because of the *paucity* of data, the researchers had to start all over again in order to gather enough information for the study.
a. poor quality
b. absence of thought
c. strangeness
d. lack

your own experiences

c 5. In narrow closed places like elevators, closets, and hallways, he felt scared and nervous, as if the walls were closing in on him. His was a classic case of *claustrophobia.*
a. depression
b. anxiety
c. fear of closed and narrow places
d. enjoyment of wide open spaces

sentence before explains the meaning

a 6. Regarding personality, Pedro always kept everything under tight control; Ricardo, on the other hand, was *expansive.*
a. free and open
b. happy and proud
c. foolish and annoying
d. boring

opposite ("on the other hand")

b 7. In melodramas, the evil *miscreant* who torments the other characters is always punished.
a. hero
b. villain
c. murderer
d. writer

helping words (*evil, torments, punished*)

c 8. Father Esteban said that people show their *piety* by attending church regularly, by loving God, and by giving great respect to religion.
a. happiness
b. love
c. religiousness
d. disapproval of organized religion

examples ("attending church regularly, loving God, and giving great respect to religion")

d 9. Seeing the *ford* — the place at the river where they could cross by wading — the campers rushed to the spot and waited for their leader.
a. old automobile
b. outdoor campsite
c. swift and dangerous rapids
d. shallow spot for river crossing

punctuation (dashes surround definition)

d 10. The commander's mood seemed *serene* and peaceful despite the great tragedy her troops had suffered.
a. determined
b. revengeful
c. puzzled
d. quiet

opposite ("despite the great tragedy") and

helping word (*peaceful*)

2. Your Own Definitions from Context

The words in italics in each of the following sentences may have a meaning that you do not know. Try to use hints in the sentences in order to make up a definition. In 1 through 15, write the word in the first blank and your own definition in the second blank. In 16 through 25, simply write the definition of the italicized word. Do not use a dictionary.

1. The brawl started as a small disagreement among friends but turned into a real *donnybrook* that wrecked the hall.

   donnybrook

   wild fight

2. The room contained such a *heterogeneous* group of people that it was difficult to understand what brought them together despite their differences.

   heterogeneous

   extremely varied

3. The chicken was roasted slowly over an open flame on a *rotisserie,* or revolving spit.

   rotisserie

   revolving spit for roasting meat

4. The corn seeds discovered in the ruins of the Mayan village had remained *dormant* for five hundred years but still were able to grow new plants.

   dormant

   not active

5. Chemical reactions occur when two or more *reagents* that affect one another are mixed together.

   reagents

   chemicals in a reaction

6. The class covers only the most important philosophical ideas of the nineteenth century, not the *trivial* ones.

   trivial

   unimportant; minor

7. Honesty is the most important *attribute* for a politician to possess.

   attribute

   trait; quality

8. Many fast-food restaurants operate by means of *franchises*. A franchise is permission to sell products that a manufacturer grants to a dealer.

   franchises

   permission to sell products

9. It took the scouts only a few minutes to pack up all their *paraphernalia* and move out.

   paraphernalia

   equipment and personal belongings

10. If you study your text *prior* to instead of after class, you may find the course a little easier than you do now.

    prior

    before

11. Maria bought eleven pairs of shoes, *squandering* her entire paycheck in one afternoon of shopping.

squandering

spending extravagantly or wastefully

12. The translator had difficulty finding a Russian word *equivalent* to the American word "cheeseburger."

equivalent

equal in value

13. One look at the surgeon's *grim* expression told us how badly the operation had gone.

grim

stern; unyielding

14. *Citadels,* fortresses built on high ground to defend cities, were common in many parts of the Roman Empire.

citadels

fortresses for defending cities

15. After spending three weeks alone in the woods, Henry was tired of *solitude.*

solitude

state of being alone

16. Even though Martha was not part of the fight, we know that her gossip helped to *instigate* trouble between Maria and Jane.

Instigate means **to provoke; to cause to happen**.

17. That *insecticide defoliates* most trees. Unless you want leaves on the ground instead of on branches, you'd better not use it to kill insects.

    Insecticide is **a substance that kills insects**.

    Defoliate means **to remove leaves from**.

18. Accidents are often a *consequence* of carelessness.

    Consequence means **the effect or result of something**.

19. Concert-goers are asked to *refrain* from taking flash pictures because the bright lights disturb the performers.

    Refrain means **to keep oneself from doing something**.

20. Brushing your teeth after every meal may not prevent cavities entirely, but it does *inhibit* the number of cavities you get.

    Inhibit means **to hold down; to reduce**.

21. Jason felt sick every time he had to play the violin in front of people. His mother took him to the doctor, who said that Jason's mental state was affecting him physically. His illness was *psychosomatic.*

    Psychosomatic means **relating to a physical disorder caused by the emotions or mind**.

22. A few years ago there were billboards along every highway in America. Thanks to the efforts of people who want to keep our countryside beautiful, billboards are no longer *ubiquitous.* Instead, they are widely scattered.

    Ubiquitous means **found everywhere**.

23. After the first sentence, the essay presented no new ideas; it was only a *tautology,* repeating itself needlessly.

    Tautology means **a needlessly repeating statement**.

24. Cara's mother had an elegant manner and an *urbane* wit, unlike her daughter, who told crude embarrassing jokes.

Urbane means **sophisticated**.

25. The wild horse was *fettered* at its ankles with chains and shackles so it could not escape.

Fettered means **tied up**.

3. More Context Clues

The sentences below, all written by professional writers, include clues for the words in italics. Try to determine from the surrounding words and sentences what the words in italics mean. Then select from the choices that follow the word that comes closest to the meaning you've decided on. Write the letter of the correct answer in the space provided. Do not use a dictionary.

> The Chinese led the Europeans by a *millennium* and a half or more in the use of blast furnaces, enabling them to use cast iron, and to refine *wrought iron* from pig iron.
>
> — *Joel Mokyr*

c 1. *millennium*
   a. long period
   b. economic advantage
   c. thousand years
   d. million people

b 2. *wrought iron*
   a. raw iron
   b. a relatively pure form of iron, easy to work
   c. steel
   d. ornamental ironwork

> *Physiologically*, the sight of the color red causes a rise in blood pressure, *respiration* rate and heartbeat, preparing us to take sudden physical action.
>
> — *Alison Lurie*

c 3. *physiologically*
   a. according to principles of physics
   b. now and again

c. relating to bodily functions
d. according to logical principles

b ______ 4. *respiration*
a. relaxation
b. breathing
c. eating
d. sweating

Encouraging people to speak in one manner necessarily implies that something else is not valued; *authoritative* ways of speaking are *enveloped* in *prestige* and power.

— *Kenneth Cmiel*

a ______ 5. *authoritative*
a. official
b. informal
c. writers'
d. definite

c ______ 6. *enveloped*
a. developed
b. controlled
c. surrounded
d. denied

c ______ 7. *prestige*
a. money
b. political power
c. high status
d. legal control

Everybody by now is aware that the cost of the American way is enormous, that air conditioning is an energy *glutton.* It uses some 9 percent of all the electricity produced. Such an *extravagance* merely to provide comfort is *peculiarly* American and strikingly *at odds with* all the recent *rhetoric* about national *sacrifice* in a period of *menacing* energy shortages.

— *Frank Trippett*

c ______ 8. *glutton*
a. monster
b. efficient user

c. wasteful user
d. benefit

b 9. *extravagance*
a. necessity
b. luxury
c. sacrifice
d. decision

d 10. *peculiarly*
a. usually
b. done by everyone
c. done by no one
d. special to a particular group

a 11. *at odds with*
a. opposite to
b. in agreement with
c. strange
d. betting against

b 12. *rhetoric*
a. actions
b. talk
c. legislation
d. hopes

b 13. *sacrifice*
a. hope
b. something given up
c. humor
d. product

d 14. *menacing*
a. useful
b. important
c. ridiculous
d. threatening

4. Context Clues in Long Selections

After reading the following passage from a book about prisons, define the four key terms: *retribution, deterrence, incapacitation,* and *rehabilitation.* Also define the other words listed.

At the heart of our prison system lies the belief that those who break the law should be punished. And people who believe that usually give two reasons:

Retribution. It is not unusual to want revenge when we have been hurt — to feel a need to strike back. In this same way, society wants to get back at the lawbreaker. We have all seen episodes in TV westerns where an angry mob tries to lynch a prisoner. When the sheriff holds off the crowd by saying, "He'll get what's coming to him — after the trial," he is acknowledging that he wants revenge, too. The trial is his formal, socially approved means of achieving it. . . .

Deterrence. Most defenders of the prison system argue that punishment "deters," or prevents, crime. Students know they will be punished if caught cheating on an exam; therefore, they keep their eyes on their own papers. There are those who believe that punishing the burglar or murderer brings similar results. . . .

Retribution and deterrence may provide justification for punishing the criminal. But throughout history there have been many ways to inflict punishment. Why send the lawbreaker to prison?

Defenders of the prison system offer two arguments:

Incapacitation. Someone serving a prison term can't harm society. . . .

Secondly, and most important: *rehabilitation.*

Rehabilitation, to penologists, means using prison as a means to change the criminal so he or she will no longer want to commit crimes.

— *Phyllis Clark and Robert Lehrman*

1. *Retribution* means **repayment; revenge**.
2. *Deterrence* means **prevention**.
3. *Incapacitation* means **inability to take action**.
4. *Rehabilitation* means **improvement**.
5. *Revenge* means **punishment for an injury or insult**.
6. *Episodes* means **incidents in the course of a story**.
7. *Lynch* means **execute illegally by hanging**.

8. *Justification* means **proof of right**.

9. *Inflict* means **force something on another**.

10. *Penologists* means **people who study prison management**.

> **Critical Thinking in Writing**
> Is prison the best way to punish criminals? Write a few paragraphs to explore your own thoughts on the prison system and its appropriateness as a punishment.

5. Context Clues from Your Textbooks

Using one of your textbooks from another course, locate ten sentences that provide sentence clues for words with which you are not familiar. On a separate sheet of paper, copy each of these sentences and underline the word you do not know. Circle the clues that help you determine the word meaning. Then, write your own definition of the word.

1d Word Part Clues to Meaning

Occasionally, two words may be put together to form a new word that is not familiar to you. If you look at each part (unit) of the word, though, you can sometimes recognize the new word. Then, you can try to understand the meaning. For example, look at these words:

upstage	(up + stage)
gentleman	(gentle + man)
mainstream	(main + stream)
badmouth	(bad + mouth)
paperwork	(paper + work)

Words new to you may contain certain groups of letters that have meanings you can learn. If you don't know what the word itself means, these groups of letters may help you define the word.

When a group of letters with a special meaning appears in front of a word, it is called a *prefix.*

When a group of letters with a special meaning appears at the end of a word, it is called a *suffix.*

The *root* (or *stem*) is the basic part of a word. When we add prefixes or suffixes to certain roots, we create new words. Look at the word *introspective*:

- The root *spect* means "look."
- The prefix *intro* means "within" or "inward."
- The suffix *ive* means "to tend to" or "to lean toward."

If you knew the meanings of these word parts, you might have been able to see that *introspective* means, in a very exact sense, "to tend to look inward." You would not need a dictionary to discover the definition. When we say people are introspective, we mean that they look into and examine their own thoughts and feelings. Maybe you wouldn't be able to figure out all that from the prefix, root, and suffix, but at least you would have some idea of what the word meant.

If you learn key prefixes, roots, and suffixes, you will be able to grasp the meanings of many words without looking them up in a dictionary.

1d(1) *Important Prefixes*

The following prefixes all mean "no" or "not":

Prefix	**Meaning**	**Example**
a	not, without	amoral
anti	against	antisocial
il	not	illegal
im	not	immobile
in	not	insensitive
ir	not	irresponsible
mal	badly	malformed
mis	wrongly	misdirected
non	not	nonreturnable
un	not	unattractive

These prefixes all deal with time:

Prefix	Meaning	Example
ante	before	antedated
post	after	postoperative
pre	before	prerequisite

These prefixes deal with numbers:

Prefix	Meaning	Example
auto	self	autograph
bi	two	bifocal
mono	one	monologue
multi	many	multicolored
poly	many	polygon
tri	three	tripod
uni	one	unicycle

These prefixes all deal with placement:

Prefix	Meaning	Example
ab	away from	abnormal
circum	around	circumscribe
com	with, together	committee
de	down from	descend
dis	away	discharge
ex	out of	expel
inter	among	intertwine
per	through	perceive
re	again	rebirth
sub	under	submarine
super	above	supercede
trans	across	transition

1d(2) *Important Roots*

Root	Meaning	Example
cred	believe	credible
equ	equal	equate
fac, fact	do, make	factory
graph	written	monograph

Root	Meaning	Example
mis, mit	send	missile
mor, mort	die	mortify
nomen	name	nominal
port	carry	portable
pos	place	position
spic, spec	look	spectator
tang	touch	tangible
vert	turn	subvert
vid, vis	see	vision
voc	call	vocation

1d(3) *Important Suffixes*

Suffix	Meaning	Example
able ible	able to be	manageable defensible
al ance ence ic	relating to	regal resistance independence heroic
hood ion ism ity ment	state of, quality of	brotherhood union patriotism legality puzzlement
er ite or	one who	writer Mennonite instructor
ful y	full of	wishful soapy

EXERCISES

1. Word Part Clues

Each word in the following list is made up of smaller parts. In some, two words are put together to make a new word. In others, prefixes, suffixes, and roots help make up the word. Without turning to a dictionary, use your knowledge of word part clues to write your definitions on the blank lines.

1. cradlesong **lullaby**
2. pastime **entertainment; amusement**
3. pictograph **chart using pictures**
4. transposition **state of being turned around**
5. middleman **a business person who helps people make a transaction**
6. circumvent **avoid by going around**
7. intransigence **unwillingness to give in**
8. rangefinder **an object that helps find the distance to a target**
9. mortuary **funeral parlor**
10. unsuitable **not able to serve well; inappropriate**

2. Word Part Clues

1. Look at the examples in section **1d** on page 21. Write definitions for the words listed there, using your knowledge of the words that make up the new one. Use a separate sheet of paper. After you write your definitions, check them by looking up the words in a dictionary.
2. Look at the examples of words in the right-hand columns next to the prefixes, roots, and suffixes introduced on pages 22–24. Using your understanding of the word parts, write definitions for the words. Use a separate sheet of paper. Don't check a dictionary until you are all finished.

3. Word Parts in Words You Know

Make a list of words you already know, including

1. three that begin with the prefix *un*. **Student answers will vary.**
2. three that begin with *pre*. ______
3. two that start with *ab*. ______
4. two that end with *hood*. ______
5. two that end with *al*. ______
6. two that end with *ic*. ______
7. two that end in *ity*. ______
8. two that end in *ful*. ______
9. two that begin with *bi*. ______
10. three that begin with *poly*. ______

4. Combining Word Parts

By combining prefixes, suffixes, and roots, make a word that means

1. someone who believes or trusts another. **creditor**
2. made up of many sounds. **polyphonic**
3. not capable of being believed. **incredible**
4. not capable of being placed. **impossible**
5. look at beforehand. **preview**

1e Denotation and Connotation

What we have been studying up to this point has been the *denotation* of a word — that is, what the word literally means. *Bicycle,* for instance, means "a two-wheeled vehicle." An *addax* is an animal that is like an antelope and that has two spiral horns.

But many words have other kinds of meaning beyond their surface meanings. The word *blue,* for example, denotes "the color of a clear sky." Beyond the denotation of the word, we also can find many other meanings in the name of the color. We usually do not like feeling *blue,* but we may enjoy hearing a great *blues* singer. We would like to have friends who are "true blue," to win a "blue ribbon," and to own "blue-chip stocks." But we might not like being called a "bluenose." As you see, even a simple word naming a color can have a wide range of possible meanings, depending on how it's used. This is what is meant by *connotation,* the implied (suggested) meaning of a word.

Often words with similar denotations have very different connotations. All the words in boldface type below denote a person who is not a male. Yet in each case, the connotation is different.

female a member of the sex that produces eggs or bears young

woman an adult female human being
girl a human female who has not matured into womanhood
lady a woman with refined habits and gentle manners
chick a slang word for a young woman

Knowing connotations of words helps you understand language more fully than you might otherwise. You can see from the list above, for example, that *female, woman, girl, lady,* and *chick* should not be used interchangeably, even though the words share similar denotations and even though many people ignore the differences among these words. Unless you were commenting on her social behavior, you'd be inaccurate if you referred to a physician who was not a man as a "lady" doctor. (If you *had* to signify the doctor's sex, *woman* would be much more accurate.) And most young women dislike being called *chicks,* although young men talking among themselves might not think twice about using the word.

A writer has many options in choosing words to make a point, and you have to be aware that the writer's choice of one word over a similar one can influence you when you read. In fact, writers can make you feel the way *they* want you to feel about ideas and people through connotations. Dictionaries do not usually include in their definitions all the connotations of a word. That's where your own thinking comes in. You need to be able to recognize that writers who use the word *lady* where they could have used the word *woman* may be offending some members of their audience — deliberately or not.

The more you develop a sense of connotation, the more you will understand how a writer can influence your emotional reactions to words.

EXERCISES

1. Denotation and Connotation

In the following groups of sentences, the denotations of the words in italics are very similar. However, because the connotations are different, each sentence says something slightly (or not so slightly) different. Explain the meaning of each sentence by indicating the connotations and denotations of the words in italics. Use a dictionary if necessary.

1. The *president* wanted work to begin on the project. **a person elected or appointed to lead**

   The *boss* wanted work to begin on the project. **a person in charge**

   Mr. Big Shot wanted work to begin on the project. **someone in charge who likes to throw his weight around**

2. The friends *chatted* at great length. **talked informally**

   The friends *conspired* at great length. **plotted and schemed**

   The friends *consulted* at great length. **discussed and considered each other's opinions**

3. Martin is *weird*. **odd; unusual**

   Martin is *eccentric*. **irregular; not typical**

   Martin is *mentally ill*. **abnormal psychological makeup**

4. The plan was *clever*. **mentally quick**

The plan was *slick.* **sneaky**

The plan was *devious.* **underhanded**

5. Sally seems *pleased* with her new boyfriend. **glad**

Sally seems *thrilled* with her new boyfriend. **carried away with happiness**

Sally seems *ecstatic* with her new boyfriend. **greatly joyful; delighted**

6. The guard *questioned* people entering the stadium. **asked for information**

The guard *cross-examined* people entering the stadium. **questioned closely**

The guard *hassled* people entering the stadium. **bothered; harassed**

2. Denotation and Connotation

These words all have reasonably clear denotations, but each has a number of connotations as well. Write the denotation of each word and at least one connotation. If necessary, use a dictionary.

1. shack **Student responses will vary.**

2. palace ______________________________

____

3. crush ______________________________

____

4. home ______________________________

____

5. alien ______________________________

____

1f Shades of Meaning

Some words, although they seem to mean nearly the same thing, actually mean separate, distinct things. *Boat,* for example, refers to a small craft that is usually open at the top, and *ship* refers to a large seagoing craft.

The small differences between the meanings of words help you recognize different types of similar things quickly and clearly. There are many types of boats and ships, and each type is described by a specific word. Here are a few of them:

barge a roomy flat-bottomed boat
battleship a large, heavily armed warship
destroyer a small fast warship
dinghy a small rowboat
freighter a ship for carrying freight
schooner a large sailing ship
scow a square-edged barge for carrying garbage or gravel

Not only technical words like those for ships have shades of meaning. Even when you are reading about human feelings, you will find out much more if you pay attention to the exact shades of meaning. The following words all describe some kind of unpleasant feeling, but notice how different each is:

envy a painful awareness that somebody has something you want
jealousy hostility toward a rival
suspicion distrust
resentment a feeling that someone has wronged you
grudge a long-lasting resentment
revenge the desire to hurt someone in return for what he or she has done
malice the desire to do harm for evil pleasure

The best place to find the shades of meaning of any word is in a dictionary. The use of a dictionary is discussed in Chapter 2.

EXERCISES

1. Shades of Meaning in Related Words

Each of the following words describes popular music. Explain the different shades of meaning of each word. In the blank spaces next to numbers 5 and 6, add two more words describing other kinds of music and your explanations of those words. Use a dictionary if necessary.

1. rock **popular music with a heavy beat**

2. punk rock **later form of rock emphasizing anger and pessimism**

3. country **folk-style music developed in the South and Midwest**

4. rap **a kind of rhythmic talking with a distinct beat**

5. **other possible words: jazz, bluegrass, classical, funk, disco, blues, soul, reggae**

6. ______________________________

____

2. Meanings of New Words: A Review

Using the vocabulary skills explained in this chapter, try to determine the meanings of the words in italics in the following sentences. Do not use a dictionary.

1. The *referendum* gave the state's voters the chance to decide about new environmental laws.

   Referendum means **vote**.

2. The *ambulatory* patient was allowed to wander the gardens surrounding the hospital.

   Ambulatory means **able to walk**.

3. The tribal *shaman* provided the mother of the sick child with a *talisman* to be placed beneath the child's bed.

   Shaman means **folk doctor; medicine man**.

   Talisman means **magic charm**.

4. The sudden popularity of the show's star was able to *resuscitate* the television series' dying ratings.

   Resuscitate means **bring back to life**.

5. Although we thought the professor was *omniscient*, she admitted she did not know the answers to some of our questions.

   Omniscient means **all-knowing**.

6. Is it really necessary to *cavil* and make silly complaints about this perfectly reasonable suggestion?

   Cavil means **make silly complaints**.

7. After much struggle, the climbers finally reached the mountain's *pinnacle*.

   Pinnacle means **peak; highest point**.

8. Costs for *overhead*, operating expenses for a business, usually are passed on to consumers.

   Overhead means **a business's operating expenses**.

9. The stone tablet was carved with *ideograms* that seemed to tell a story.

   Ideograms means **picture words**.

10. The judges needed several minutes to *assess* the gymnast's performance.

    Assess means **estimate; evaluate**.

11. The book was difficult and often unclear, but the professor tried to *illuminate* its main points by discussing important passages in class.

    Illuminate means **shed light on**.

12. Dieting doesn't always produce sudden weight loss. Sometimes the changes are very *gradual*.

    Gradual means **little by little**.

13. Luther was very sad when his grandfather died, but thanks to the *inheritance* his grandfather left him, he could afford to go to college.

    Inheritance means **something received by succession or through a will**.

14. One of the advantages of gold is its *malleability*, which enables jewelers to hammer, bend, and work the metal into almost any shape or design.

    Malleability means **ability to be shaped or molded**.

15. The *congruence* of these two designs makes them perfectly *interchangeable.*

Congruence means **similarity** .

Interchangeable means **able to be switched back and forth** .

16. He yawned; he glanced out the window; he drew circles on his desk — and his teacher was disturbed by his *inattention.*

Inattention means **lack of interest or attention** .

17. After thirty years, the sight of his long-lost brother was so *poignant* that Jim had to turn away for a moment to gather together his feelings.

Poignant means **appealing to the emotions; touching** .

18. Unlike Carlos, who weighs decisions very carefully and sticks to his choice, Samuel is very *fickle.*

Fickle means **changing one's mind often** .

19. After the government's *renunciation* of its debts to other nations, few countries were willing to lend it any more money.

Renunciation means **disowning** .

20. The lovers made sure their meetings were *clandestine* so that no one would suspect that they were seeing each other.

Clandestine means **secret** .

3. Vocabulary from Advertising

The selections that appear on pages 38 and 39 come from newspaper or magazine advertisements. Look at the advertisements carefully. As you read, determine the definitions of all the underlined words by using whatever clues you can. Then select the phrase that comes closest to the meaning you've decided on. Write the letter of the correct answer in the space provided. Use a dictionary only to check the accuracy of your meanings.

c 1. On page 38, the cars are called chariots because
   a. they follow ancient Roman designs.
   b. they are pulled by horses like ancient chariots.
   c. they are rapid and powerful like ancient chariots.
   d. Chariot is the name of the car model.

a 2. V-12 is a type of
   a. engine.
   b. automobile.
   c. manufacturing process.
   d. race.

d 3. The phrase two decades of refinement means the car
   a. is twenty times better than originally.
   b. is twice as expensive as it used to be.
   c. has twenty years worth of wear.
   d. has twenty years worth of improvement.

c 4. E-type, XJ-S, and S-type refer to
   a. engines.
   b. car companies.
   c. car models.
   d. performance tests.

a 5. 262 horsepower is considered potent because
   a. that is more horsepower than is found in most cars.
   b. each horse is powerful.
   c. all power is potent.
   d. the car aids in sexual reproduction.

b 6. The word impulses as used in the second paragraph refers to
   a. wanting to travel fast.
   b. power surges.
   c. sudden thoughts.
   d. horsepower.

d ______ 7. Supple leather is
a. dark in color.
b. easy to clean.
c. firm and shiny.
d. soft and flexible.

b ______ 8. In the ad on page 39, the word uniquely means
a. well.
b. singularly.
c. accidentally.
d. carefully.

d ______ 9. Adapted as used in this advertisement means
a. flexible.
b. changed.
c. borrowed.
d. matched.

a ______ 10. To forage is to
a. search for food.
b. destroy.
c. be hungry.
d. cultivate.

c ______ 11. Rhubarb is a kind of
a. tree.
b. poison fruit.
c. leafy vegetable.
d. earth-dwelling grub.

d ______ 12. Subspecies are the different
a. plants the animal eats.
b. habits of the animal.
c. habitats the animal likes.
d. varieties of the animal.

c ______ 13. Endangered species are those that
a. are thriving.
b. threaten other animals.
c. may not survive.
d. are extinct.

d ______ 14. The ecosystems mentioned in the advertisement are
a. the plants eaten by animals.
b. the different animals.
c. the physical surroundings.
d. the combination of plants, animals, and surroundings.

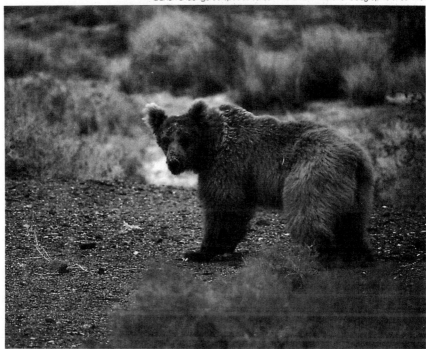

4. Finding Word Meanings in Textbooks

Each selection below comes from a college textbook. As you read each selection carefully, determine the definitions of all the words in italics by using whatever clues you can. In your own words, write definitions in the spaces provided. Use a dictionary only to check the accuracy of your meanings.

Mathematics

When money is deposited in a bank account, the bank pays the depositor for the privilege of using that money. The amount paid to the depositor is called *interest*. When money is borrowed from a bank, the borrower pays the bank for the privilege of using that money. The amount paid to the bank is also called interest.

The original amount deposited or borrowed is called the *principal*. The amount of interest is a percent of the principal. The percent used to determine the amount of interest is the *interest rate*. Interest rates are given for specific periods of time, usually months or years.

Interest *computed* on the original principal is called *simple interest*. To calculate simple interest, multiply the principal by the interest rate per period by the number of time periods.

— *Vernon C. Barker and Richard N. Aufmann*

1. *Interest* is **payment the bank makes to depositors for the privilege of using their money; payment borrowers make to the bank for the privilege of using its money**.

2. *Principal* is **original amount deposited or borrowed**.

3. *Interest rate* is **percentage used to determine the amount of interest**.

4. *Computed* means **calculated**.

5. *Simple interest* is **interest computed on the original principal**.

Philosophy

Ethics begins with our being aware that we face *alternative* possibilities in our behavior. We can either tell the truth or tell a *falsehood*. These two possibilities are presented to us as *options*. We are *capable* of doing either one. We can control our action. A stone does not face this kind of alternative because it cannot *distinguish* between different courses of action. A stone can behave only in the way an outside force makes it behave. Unlike a stone, a person can start an action by himself. The difference, then, is that a stone is not aware of options, is not *conscious* of possibilities, whereas human beings are conscious that they face *genuine* alternatives.

— *Samuel E. Stumpf*

6. *Alternative* means **other**.
7. *Falsehood* means **lie**.
8. *Options* means **choices**.
9. *Capable* means **able to achieve**.
10. *Distinguish* means **tell the difference**.
11. *Conscious* means **aware**.
12. *Genuine* means **real**.

History

During the late Roman Republic, Rome had creatively *assimilated* the Greek achievement and transmitted it to others, thereby extending the *orbit* of *Hellenism*. Rome had acquired Greek scientific thought, philosophy, medicine, and geography. Roman writers used Greek models; sharing in the *hu-*

manist outlook of the Greeks, they valued human achievement and expressed themselves in a graceful and *eloquent* style. Roman cultural life reached its high point during the *reign* of Augustus, when Rome experienced the golden age of Latin literature.

— *Marvin Perry, Myrna Chase, James R. Jacob, Margaret C. Jacob, and Theodore H. von Laue*

13. *Assimilated* means **combined; joined an existing group**.

14. *Orbit* means **range**.

15. *Hellenism* means **Greek civilization**.

16. *Humanist* means **one who studies human achievement**.

17. *Eloquent* means **well-spoken**.

18. *Reign* means **rule**.

Chemistry

Matter may exist in any of the three physical states: solid, liquid, and gas.

A *solid* has a definite shape and volume that it tends to maintain under normal conditions. The particles composing a solid stick rigidly to one another. Solids most commonly occur in the *crystalline* form, which means they have a fixed, regularly repeating, *symmetrical* internal structure. Diamonds, salt, and quartz are examples of crystalline solids. A few solids, such as glass and paraffin, do not have a well-defined crystalline structure, although they do have a definite shape and volume. Such solids are called *amorphous,* which means they have no definite internal structure or form.

A *liquid* does not have its own shape but takes the shape of the container in which it is placed. Its particles *cohere* firmly, but not rigidly, so the particles of a liquid have a great deal of mobility while maintaining close contact with one another.

A *gas* has no fixed shape or volume and eventually spreads

out to fill its container. Its particles move independently of one another. Compared with those of a liquid or a solid, the particles of a gas are quite far apart. Unlike solids and liquids, which cannot be *compressed* very much at all, gases can be both compressed and expanded.

Often referred to as the fourth state of matter, *plasma* is a form of matter composed of electrically charged atomic particles. Many objects found in the earth's outer atmosphere, as well as many *celestial* bodies found in space (such as the sun and stars), consist of plasma. A plasma can be created by heating a gas to extremely high temperatures or by passing a current through it. A plasma responds to a magnetic field and conducts electricity well.

— *Alan Sherman, Sharon J. Sherman, and Leonard Russikoff*

19. *Solid* means **matter that has definite shape and volume**.

20. *Crystalline* means **having a fixed internal form**.

21. *Symmetrical* means **having equally spaced and equally shaped parts**.

22. *Amorphous* means **having no definite form**.

23. *Liquid* means **matter that assumes its container's shape**.

24. *Cohere* means **stick together**.

25. *Gas* means **matter without fixed shape or volume**.

26. *Compressed* means **pressed into less space**.

27. *Plasma* means **matter made of charged particles**.

28. *Celestial* means **having to do with the sky**.

Broadcast Communications

Among *serialized* drama formats, the soap opera (so called because in radio days, soap companies often owned and *sponsored* them) is the classic case of *frugal expenditure* of program resources. Notorious for the snail-like pace of their plots, these daytime serials use every tactic of delay to drag out the action of each episode. Soaps exactly suit low-cost television production because entire episodes often take place in a single location, involving only camera switches from face to face as actors utter emotionally *laden* dialogue. In the 1970s, the sponsors lengthened soaps from a half-hour to one-hour (doubling episode length increases production cost relatively little).

In recent years, soap-opera writers have *accelerated* plot development and risked plots dealing with *once-taboo* topics. Contemporary viewers apparently have less patience and more tolerance than their parents did. Drugs, social diseases, and family violence, once unmentionable, have become regular elements in such soaps as "The Young and the Restless" and "General Hospital." Women and members of minority groups began appearing in more varied roles in the mid-1970s, although the *distribution* of occupations, races, and sex roles by no means reflects society's actual *norms.* More women characters in modern soaps have upper-income professions (medicine and law, with lots of free time for romantic involvements) than in society at large. Racial minorities remain underrepresented and restricted in their social interactions, though *Generations,* a *trailblazing* soap featuring close relations between a black family and a white family, emerged on NBC in 1989.

— *Sydney Head and Christopher Sterling*

29. *Serialized* means **presented in regular episodes** .

30. *Sponsored* means **paid for** .

31. *Frugal* means **cost-conscious** .

32. *Expenditure* means **amount spent; cost** .

33. *Laden* means **loaded with** .

34. *Accelerated* means **speeded up** .

35. *Once-taboo* means **previously forbidden**.

36. *Distribution* means **variation**.

37. *Norms* mean **normal pattern**.

38. *Trailblazing* means **pioneering**.

Critical Thinking in Writing

How do you account for the apparently endless popularity of soap operas? Write a few paragraphs in which you consider the success of soap operas.

2

Using a Dictionary

A dictionary is an important tool to help build your reading skills. Here is what you can find in a dictionary:

- How to spell a word or its special plural form
- Whether or not a word is capitalized or abbreviated
- How to break a word into syllables
- How to pronounce a word
- How a word fits into the English system of grammar (what part of speech it is: verb, noun, adjective, and so forth)
- Different meanings of a word, along with *synonyms* (words that have the same meaning) and *antonyms* (words that have opposite meanings)
- A sentence or an expression that uses a word correctly
- The meaning of important prefixes and suffixes
- The special uses of a word
- The history of a word
- Words made from a main word

Some dictionaries also have special sections that tell about these subjects:

- Foreign words and phrases
- Abbreviations
- Addresses of colleges or government offices
- The population of cities and countries

Depending on how complete they are and on what their purposes are, dictionaries vary in length. Unabridged dictionaries — they try to include information on all the words in our language (about half a million) — take up thousands of pages. Much of your dictionary work in class and at home, however, will involve a *pocket dictionary,* a small book designed to give only those words used most often. The example from the *Amer-*

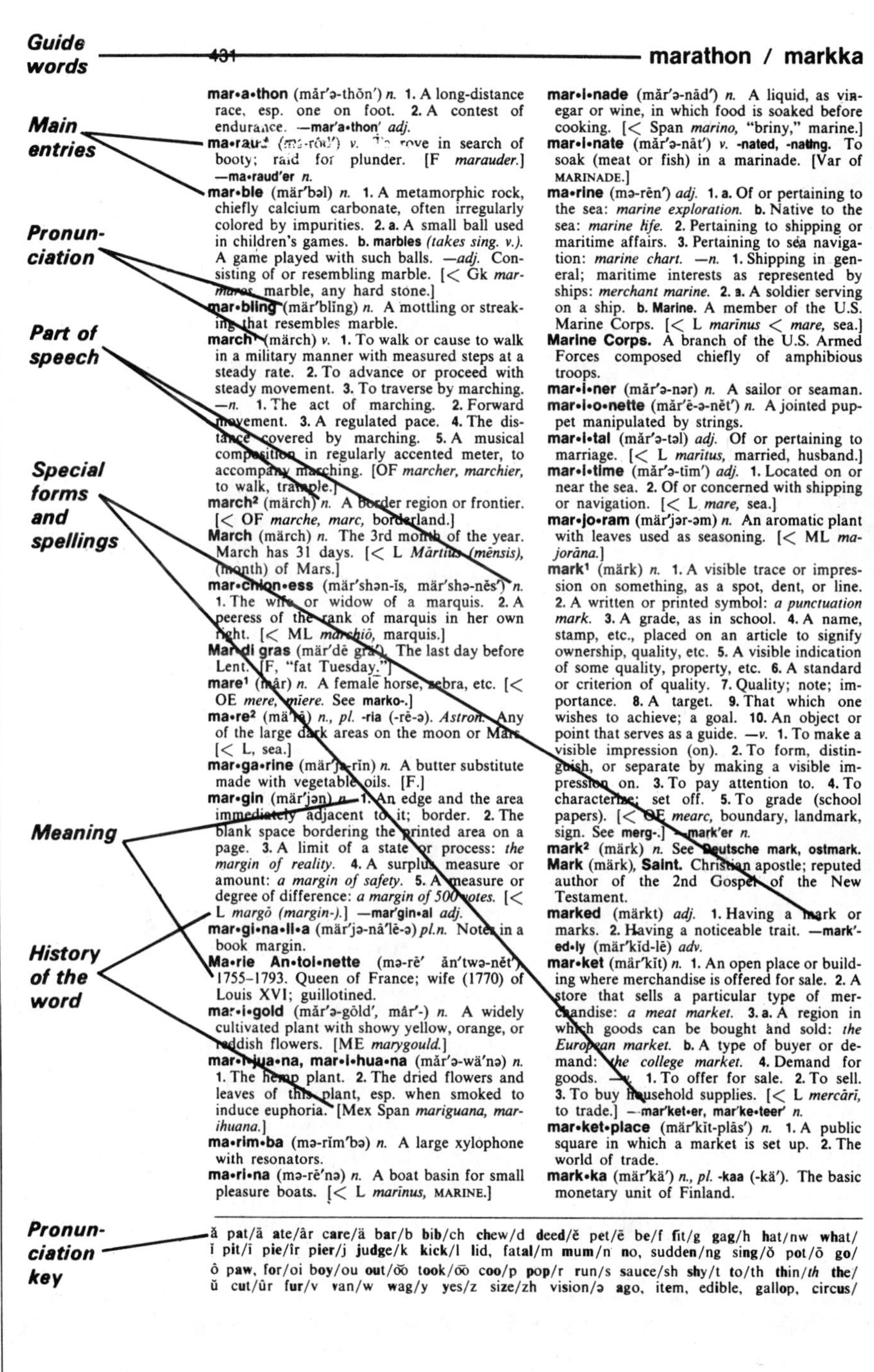

431 **marathon / markka**

mar•a•thon (măr′ə-thŏn′) *n.* **1.** A long-distance race, esp. one on foot. **2.** A contest of endurance. —**mar′a•thon′** *adj.*

ma•raud (mə-rôd′) *v.* To rove in search of booty; raid for plunder. [F *marauder.*] —**ma•raud′er** *n.*

mar•ble (mär′bəl) *n.* **1.** A metamorphic rock, chiefly calcium carbonate, often irregularly colored by impurities. **2. a.** A small ball used in children's games. **b. marbles** *(takes sing. v.).* A game played with such balls. —*adj.* Consisting of or resembling marble. [< Gk *marmaros,* marble, any hard stone.]

mar•bling (mär′blĭng) *n.* A mottling or streaking that resembles marble.

march[1] (märch) *v.* **1.** To walk or cause to walk in a military manner with measured steps at a steady rate. **2.** To advance or proceed with steady movement. **3.** To traverse by marching. —*n.* **1.** The act of marching. **2.** Forward movement. **3.** A regulated pace. **4.** The distance covered by marching. **5.** A musical composition in regularly accented meter, to accompany marching. [OF *marcher, marchier,* to walk, trample.]

march[2] (märch) *n.* A border region or frontier. [< OF *marche, marc,* borderland.]

March (märch) *n.* The 3rd month of the year. March has 31 days. [< L *Martius (mēnsis),* (month) of Mars.]

mar•chion•ess (mär′shə-nĭs, mär′shə-nĕs′) *n.* **1.** The wife or widow of a marquis. **2.** A peeress of the rank of marquis in her own right. [< ML *marchiō,* marquis.]

Mar•di gras (mär′dē grä′) The last day before Lent. [F, "fat Tuesday."]

mare[1] (mâr) *n.* A female horse, zebra, etc. [< OE *mere, miere.* See **marko-.**]

ma•re[2] (mä′rā) *n., pl.* **-ria** (-rē-ə). *Astron.* Any of the large dark areas on the moon or Mars. [< L, sea.]

mar•ga•rine (mär′jə-rĭn) *n.* A butter substitute made with vegetable oils. [F.]

mar•gin (mär′jən) *n.* **1.** An edge and the area immediately adjacent to it; border. **2.** The blank space bordering the printed area on a page. **3.** A limit of a state or process: *the margin of reality.* **4.** A surplus measure or amount: *a margin of safety.* **5.** A measure or degree of difference: *a margin of 500 votes.* [< L *margō (margin-).*] —**mar′gin•al** *adj.*

mar•gi•na•li•a (mär′jə-nā′lē-ə) *pl.n.* Notes in a book margin.

Ma•rie An•toi•nette (mə-rē′ ăn′twə-nĕt′) 1755–1793. Queen of France; wife (1770) of Louis XVI; guillotined.

mar•i•gold (măr′ə-gōld′, mâr′-) *n.* A widely cultivated plant with showy yellow, orange, or reddish flowers. [ME *marygould.*]

mar•i•jua•na, mar•i•hua•na (măr′ə-wä′nə) *n.* **1.** The hemp plant. **2.** The dried flowers and leaves of this plant, esp. when smoked to induce euphoria. [Mex Span *mariguana, marihuana.*]

ma•rim•ba (mə-rĭm′bə) *n.* A large xylophone with resonators.

ma•ri•na (mə-rē′nə) *n.* A boat basin for small pleasure boats. [< L *marinus,* MARINE.]

mar•i•nade (măr′ə-nād′) *n.* A liquid, as vinegar or wine, in which food is soaked before cooking. [< Span *marino,* "briny," marine.]

mar•i•nate (măr′ə-nāt′) *v.* **-nated, -nating.** To soak (meat or fish) in a marinade. [Var of MARINADE.]

ma•rine (mə-rēn′) *adj.* **1. a.** Of or pertaining to the sea: *marine exploration.* **b.** Native to the sea: *marine life.* **2.** Pertaining to shipping or maritime affairs. **3.** Pertaining to sea navigation: *marine chart.* —*n.* **1.** Shipping in general; maritime interests as represented by ships: *merchant marine.* **2. a.** A soldier serving on a ship. **b. Marine.** A member of the U.S. Marine Corps. [< L *marinus* < *mare,* sea.]

Marine Corps. A branch of the U.S. Armed Forces composed chiefly of amphibious troops.

mar•i•ner (măr′ə-nər) *n.* A sailor or seaman.

mar•i•o•nette (măr′ē-ə-nĕt′) *n.* A jointed puppet manipulated by strings.

mar•i•tal (măr′ə-təl) *adj.* Of or pertaining to marriage. [< L *maritus,* married, husband.]

mar•i•time (măr′ə-tīm′) *adj.* **1.** Located on or near the sea. **2.** Of or concerned with shipping or navigation. [< L *mare,* sea.]

mar•jo•ram (mär′jər-əm) *n.* An aromatic plant with leaves used as seasoning. [< ML *majorāna.*]

mark[1] (märk) *n.* **1.** A visible trace or impression on something, as a spot, dent, or line. **2.** A written or printed symbol: *a punctuation mark.* **3.** A grade, as in school. **4.** A name, stamp, etc., placed on an article to signify ownership, quality, etc. **5.** A visible indication of some quality, property, etc. **6.** A standard or criterion of quality. **7.** Quality; note; importance. **8.** A target. **9.** That which one wishes to achieve; a goal. **10.** An object or point that serves as a guide. —*v.* **1.** To make a visible impression (on). **2.** To form, distinguish, or separate by making a visible impression on. **3.** To pay attention to. **4.** To characterize; set off. **5.** To grade (school papers). [< OE *mearc,* boundary, landmark, sign. See **merg-.**] —**mark′er** *n.*

mark[2] (märk) *n.* See **deutsche mark, ostmark.**

Mark (märk), **Saint.** Christian apostle; reputed author of the 2nd Gospel of the New Testament.

marked (märkt) *adj.* **1.** Having a mark or marks. **2.** Having a noticeable trait. —**mark′ed•ly** (mär′kĭd-lē) *adv.*

mar•ket (mär′kĭt) *n.* **1.** An open place or building where merchandise is offered for sale. **2.** A store that sells a particular type of merchandise: *a meat market.* **3. a.** A region in which goods can be bought and sold: *the European market.* **b.** A type of buyer or demand: *the college market.* **4.** Demand for goods. —*v.* **1.** To offer for sale. **2.** To sell. **3.** To buy household supplies. [< L *mercārī,* to trade.] —**mar′ket•er, mar′ke•teer′** *n.*

mar•ket•place (mär′kĭt-plās′) *n.* **1.** A public square in which a market is set up. **2.** The world of trade.

mark•ka (mär′kä′) *n., pl.* **-kaa** (-kä′). The basic monetary unit of Finland.

ă pat/ā ate/âr care/ä bar/b bib/ch chew/d deed/ĕ pet/ē be/f fit/g gag/h hat/hw what/ ĭ pit/ī pie/îr pier/j judge/k kick/l lid, fatal/m mum/n no, sudden/ng sing/ŏ pot/ō go/ ô paw, for/oi boy/ou out/ŏŏ took/ōō coo/p pop/r run/s sauce/sh shy/t to/th thin/*th* the/ ŭ cut/ûr fur/v van/w wag/y yes/z size/zh vision/ə ago, item, edible, gallop, circus/

ican Heritage Dictionary on page 47 and the following discussion will help you improve your dictionary skills.

2a The Guide Words

If you wanted to look up the word *margin,* for example, the left-hand guide word *marathon* is a hint that the word is on the page, because *marg* comes after *mara* in alphabetical order. The right-hand guide word is *markka. Marg* comes before *mark,* so you know *margin* must appear between these two guide words.

2b The Main Entry

Entry words first appear in heavy black letters. (This kind of type is called *bold type.*) Centered dots mark each syllable. The main entry tells you the preferred spelling of a word and may be followed by a *variant,* the same word spelled correctly but in another way.

2c The Pronunciation Key

The groups of letters right after the main entry tell you how to say the word. (You know from words like *cough, bough,* and *through* that spelling is sometimes not helpful in telling you how to pronounce words.) The letters that appear in parentheses, or between slanted lines in some other dictionaries, stand for special sounds. To find out what sound a letter stands for in the word you are looking up, check the pronunciation key at the bottom of the page or at the front in a special section. Checking the key at the bottom of the page, you see that the *a* in *mare* (meaning "a female horse") has the same sound as the *a* in *care.* You'll notice that the *a* in *mare,* the next entry (meaning "dark areas on the moon or Mars"), has the same *a* as the word *bar,* giving *mare,* the astronomical term, a very different pronunciation.

2d The Parts of Speech

The *parts of speech* tell you how the word is placed in the system of English grammar. The *n.* after the pronouncing letters of *marinade* means "noun." The *v.* after *marinate* means "verb." The *adj.* after *marine* means "adjective." The *adv.* after *markedly* means "adverb." Sometimes a word has different meanings based on what part of speech it is. The word *march* is a verb meaning "to walk or cause to walk in a military manner." Used as a noun, *march* means "a border region or frontier." Another meaning for *March* (written with a capital letter) is "the third month of the year."

2e Special Forms and Special Spellings

Marauder is made from the word *maraud,* so it is included as part of the entry for *maraud* instead of as another main entry. Notice too that in addition to singular forms, the dictionary gives unusual plural forms, especially if they are for foreign words or words that do not simply add an *s*. The plural of *markka* is formed by adding an *a* as the final letter.

2f The Meanings of the Word

Next, the word is defined. The meanings of words that can be used in more than one sense are separated and numbered in heavy bold print. Usually the most important definitions come first. An example sometimes appears to show how the main word is used. *Syn.* is an abbreviation for *synonym*. Words that come after *syn.* have the same meaning as the main word.

2g The History of the Word

The information that appears in brackets tells the way the word has developed in our language. Many words have origins in foreign languages like Latin (L) or Greek (G). In fact, a good dictionary can be your best first source for *etymology* — the study of the origin and historical development of words. For example, *market* comes from the Latin word *mercari,* meaning "to trade." The place where goods are traded became known as a *market.*

Some Dictionary Pointers

- Review your skill with alphabetical order. Can you arrange words correctly?
- Use the guide words. They save you time.
- Check all abbreviations and symbols in the special section.
- If you look up a word and it's not where you expect it to be, don't think it's not in your dictionary! Check under several possible spellings. If you couldn't spell the word *crime,* for example, the sound of the word might suggest these spellings:

cryme	krime
kryme	krhyme
criem	crhyme

  If you couldn't spell the word correctly, you might have to check them all before you found *crime.*
- Test the meaning you find for the word in the sentence in which you found the word. You may not have picked a definition that works for the word as it is used.
- Try to say the word aloud after you look at the pronunciation key.

EXERCISES

1. Order of the Alphabet

Put the words in this list in correct alphabetical order:

1. during   dungaree
2. duplex   duo

3. duplication **duodenum**
4. duplicate **dupe**
5. duplicity **duplex**
6. duo **duplicate**
7. dupe **duplication**
8. durable **duplicity**
9. dungaree **durable**
10. duodenum **during**

2. Guide Words

The guide words at the top of one dictionary page are *selfhood* and *semaphore*. Put a checkmark beside the words you would expect to find on that page.

self
√ seltzer
seminar
√ semantic
√ seller
self-employed
√ selfish
select
√ selvage
salvage
√ self-winding
senate

3. Guide Words

Under each numbered pair of guide words appear several other words. Put a checkmark beside each word that you would expect to find on a page that shows the guide words.

1. *mum/murky*
   √ mummy
   muscle
   multiply
   √ mumbo-jumbo
   √ murder
   murmur
2. *phrase/physical*
   physics
   √ physic
   phyton
   photograph
   √ phylum
   √ phrasing
3. *shift/shipman*
   √ shiftless
   √ shine
   √ shingle
   √ shipboard
   shield
   shipyard

4. *turkey/turn*

turnip	√ Turkish	√ turmeric
Turk	turf	√ turmoil

5. *boar/body*

bluster	√ boardwalk	bogus
√ bobsled	√ boat	√ boathouse

4. One Word, Several Meanings

Each word that follows has several different meanings. Look up each word in a dictionary and write three different definitions. After each definition, write a sentence in which you use the word in that way. Study the example.

Example: book

a. *Definition:* a written work for reading
Sentence: The *book* I read was *Sissy* by John Williams.

b. *Definition:* a set of tickets bound together
Sentence: He ripped a ticket from my *book* before I entered the bus.

c. *Definition:* to engage a performer for a show
Sentence: David Merrick *booked* a Russian dance group for a U.S. tour.

Student responses will vary.

1. offer **present; volunteer; provide**

2. use **employ; consume; take advantage of**

3. fence **structure that separates areas; to separate things; person who receives and sells stolen goods**

4. temper **state of mind; tendency to get angry; moderate**

5. true **not false; genuine; accurately placed**

5. The Right Meaning

The words in italics in the following sentences have many meanings. Use a dictionary to check the definitions, and make sure you select the appropriate definition for the use of the word in the sentence. Write your meanings in the spaces provided.

1. The defendant demanded the *right* to testify.

   legal privilege

2. Carolyn decided to *audit* the course rather than take it for credit.

   attend without receiving credit

3. The store owner was afraid the economic downturn would *dash* her dreams of success.

   destroy

4. Because Adam was *independent,* he did not need to work.

   having wealth enough to support oneself

   Because Adam was *independent,* he had to get a job to support himself.

   dependent only on one's own resources

   Because Adam was *independent,* no one could tell him whether he had to work or how.

   free of the dictates of others

5. The senator took *issue* with an editorial in a recent *issue* of the newspaper.

   disagreed; one publication in a series

6. As the *pivot,* Sergeant Gomez helped turn the battle in his platoon's favor.

 one that determines a group's decision

7. The old professor returned to her *study* down the dark hallway.

 a room for reading and writing

8. In her talk about bees, she suddenly flew off on a *tangent* and complained about the poor quality of commercial honey.

 irrelevant point

9. His illness had taken its toll; his cheeks were *hollow,* his lips were dry and cracked, and his voice was weak.

 sunken

10. Although his theories are no longer *current,* Tesla's work on alternating *current* was an important contribution to American life.

 widely accepted or known; electrical flow

6. Checking Foreign Words

Many words from other languages become part of the English language. Check the numbered words in a dictionary to learn the language they come from, their pronunciation, and their meaning. Fill in this information in the following chart.

Word	*Language*	*Pronunciation*
1. de facto	**Latin**	**dēfăk'tō**

in reality

2. siesta **Spanish** **sē-ĕs′tə**

a midday rest

3. sarong **Malay** **sə-rông′**

a wrapped cloth garment

4. amok **Malay** **ə-mŭk′**

furious attack

5. rubato **Italian** **ro͞o-bä′tō**

rhythmic flexibility within a musical phrase

7. Pronouncing Words

Use your dictionary to find the correct way to pronounce these words.

1. detour **dē′toor′**
2. devisable **dĭ-vī′zə-bəl**
3. devolution **dĕv′ə-loo′shən**
4. dharma **där′mə**
5. dhoti **dō′tē**
6. dialectic **dī′ə-lĕk′tĭk**
7. diastole **dī-ăs′tə-lē**
8. diatribe **dī′ə-trīb′**

8. Same Word, Different Meanings

Each set of sentences uses a word in a variety of ways. The same word has different meanings. In the blanks write a definition for the word in italics. Use a dictionary if necessary.

1a. a *free* spirit **unfettered**

b. a *free* soda **without cost**

c. a *free* criminal **not in prison**

d. a *free* parcel of land **not built on**

e. *free* morals **loose**

2a. a *score* of five to nothing **record of points**

b. *score* a point for the team **earn**

c. a musical *score* **written form of a piece of music**

d. a *scorecard* **special form for keeping the point record**

3a. strike a *match* **wooden or paper instrument for igniting fire**

b. a shirt to *match* her sweater **go well with in color, texture, etc.**

c. a soccer *match* **game between teams**

d. make a love *match* **pair of people**

9. Practice in Dictionary Skills

Using the sample page from a dictionary on page 47, answer the following questions.

1. What is the origin of the word *maraud*?

   from French word *marauder*

2. Is the word *marginalia* singular or plural?

   plural

3. What would you use *marjoram* for?

   cooking (it's a seasoning)

4. Circle the words that have the same sound as the short *a* sound in *mark.*

   marine marinate (market) marathon marital (marjoram)

5. What color is a marigold?

   yellow, orange, or reddish

6. How did Marie Antoinette die?

   She was guillotined.

7. How does the pronunciation of *markedly* differ from the pronunciation of *marked*?

   Ed* is a separate syllable in *markedly.

8. Write the plural of the astronomical term *mare.*

   maria

9. Explain in your own words the meaning of the word *march* as used in the following sentence:

   The duke and his men guarded the *march* from invaders.

   border region or frontier

10. The symbol ə is a *schwa*. It stands for a vowel sound in a syllable that is not accented. List three words in which schwas are used to show pronunciation.

    marathon, maraud, marble, marchioness, margarine,

    marginalia, marigold

10. A Dictionary Review

Use a dictionary to find the answers to these questions:

1. What is the plural of the word *medium*, meaning "a form of communication"? **media**

2. What parts of speech can the word *run* be? **verb, noun, or adjective**

3. What language does the word *piano* come from? **Italian**

   What is its origin? **pianoforte**

4. What do the following words mean?

   a. prevaricate **lie**

   b. conflate **combine; mix together**

   c. miscible **mixable**

   d. halcyon **calm and peaceful**

   e. firkin **a small wooden barrel**

5. Write a synonym (a word with like meaning) and an antonym (a word with opposite meaning) for each of the following words.

	Synonym	*Antonym*
a. affluent	**rich**	**impecunious; poor**
b. nonchalant	**relaxed**	**anxious**
c. quiescent	**inactive; still**	**effervescent; lively**
d. ubiquitous	**everywhere**	**elusive; absent**
e. contemplative	**thoughtful**	**rash**

UNIT ONE REVIEW

Read this selection from a psychology textbook about how we find out what an infant can observe. For each word in boldface type, use the hints and clues you learned in this unit to determine definitions. Write the definitions in your own words in the blanks provided.

How Do We Know That?

(1) If psychologists want to know what adult human beings **perceive**, they can always ask their subjects to report on their
experiences. For instance, if they want to discover how soft a
sound an adult can hear, they can play loud and soft sounds
and ask the subject to report when they hear and when they
don't hear them. But infants are a different story. A psychologist cannot ask an infant, "Did you hear that?" or "Are those
two colors the same or different?" How do psychologists find
out what an infant perceives?

Developmental psychologists have invented several different techniques to find out what an infant can perceive. One is
(2) to measure the response of the **sensory organ** itself. For example, several studies of infants' ability to focus their eyes on a
(3) moving object use the **curvature** of the lenses to determine
(4) the degree of **accommodation** (Banks, 1982; Haynes, White &
Held, 1965; Aslin, 1987). These studies found that accommodation is absent at birth but develops rapidly during the first three
months of life. (Recall from Chapter 3 that accommodation is
the change in shape that takes place in the eye's lens as a
person focuses an object that is moving closer or farther away.)

Another technique focuses on infants' perceptual prefer-
(5) ences and thus involves a test of **preferential** looking, preferential hearing, or even preferential tasting. The basic technique
(6) is to offer the infant two **stimuli** and see which it looks at,
listens to, or tastes longer. One general preference that infants
have is for new stimuli. For example, infants usually look at a
(7) **novel** stimulus for a longer time than they look at a familiar
(8) one. This preference eventually **habituates**: that is, if the novel
stimulus is presented repeatedly, the novelty wears off and the
infant stops looking at it (Salapatek & Cohen, 1987).

Some researchers have used infants' fascination with the unfamiliar to determine their concepts of the world. For exam-

ple, a researcher might show an infant a series of pictures of dogs. Once the infant stops looking at the pictures, the researcher displays a picture of a cat. If looking time increases again, the researcher can assume that the infant has a concept
(9) of dogs **distinct** from his concept of cats.

Some methods for finding out what infants (even newborns) perceive make use of instrumental conditioning (Kuhl, 1987). One, the high-amplitude sucking (HAS) technique, has been widely used to test whether infants can hear differences between speech sounds before they begin to speak themselves or to understand speech (Jusczyk, 1985). The infant is given a pacifier that's been wired so that strong sucks produce a recording of a particular speech sound. When the infant has habituated to this speech sound (measured by a decrease in
(10) the quantity of **high-amplitude** sucking), a new sound is presented. If the infant responds to this new sound with an increase in high-amplitude sucking, we can conclude that the
(11) infant can **discriminate** the new sound from the old.

A variation on this technique was used by DeCasper and Spence (1986) in their study described earlier. They showed that newborns can discriminate stories that were read to them a few weeks before they were born from other similar stories.

Another technique, the head turning (HT) technique, is used with older infants (Kuhl, 1985). Here the infant sits on a parent's lap, the experimenter sits to the infant's right, and a

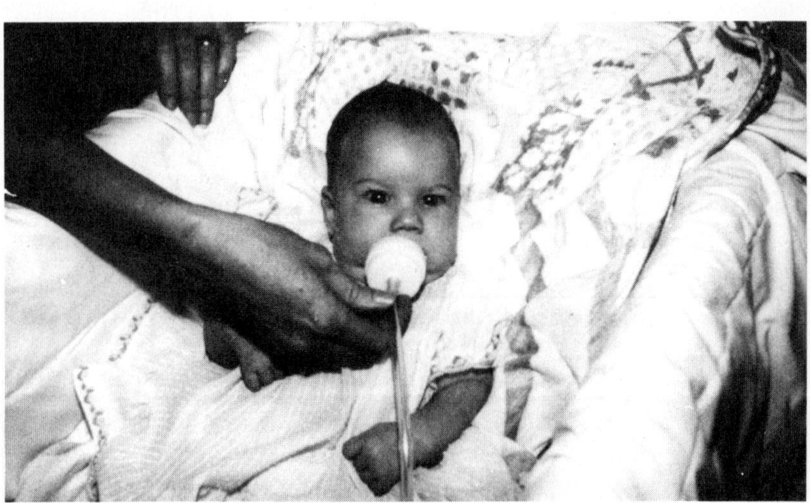

(12) **reinforcing** stimulus — let's say a toy bear tapping a drum — is placed on the infant's left. The infant is presented with a sequence of sounds and is taught that, whenever a new sound
(13) occurs, turning his head to the left will **activate** the bear. For example, the infant might be presented with a sequence of syllables beginning with the *p* sound. In this sequence, the researcher might insert a syllable that begins with a *b* sound. If the infant turns his head when he hears the *b* sound, we can conclude that the infant perceives the *b* sound as a new and different sound.

Using the head turning technique, experimenters have
(14) demonstrated that infants are able to **distinguish** more speech sounds at six months than at one year. In fact, during the second six months of life, infants actually *lose* the ability to discriminate speech sounds that are not a part of the language spoken around them (Werker & Tees, 1984).

(15) Each of these techniques has its **drawbacks** for revealing whether infants perceive a given stimulus or not (Banks & Dannemiller, 1987). Direct measurement of the sensory apparatus
(16) yields an **ambiguous** positive result. Although such measurement shows that the sense organ is responding to a stimulus, it does not necessarily show that the infant is perceiving the stimulus — that sensory information is reaching the brain and being processed there.

Preference tests and methods that rely on habituation and conditioning give ambiguous negative results because they measure only what infants are interested in, not necessarily what they could perceive if they were interested. So an infant may fail to show a preference because the differences between
(17) the stimuli are not interesting, not because they are **imperceptible**.

This is not a novel problem. Any measure of any psycho-
(18) logical **variable** has both strengths and weaknesses. And the
solution is the same here as elsewhere. When several of these
different methods are brought to bear on the same problem,
as they have been on the problem of infant speech perception,
(19) they begin to produce a pattern of **converging** results that
(20) allows us to know with some **confidence** what an infant does
or does not perceive.

— *James D. Laird and Nicholas S. Thompson*

EXERCISES

1. perceive **sense; notice**
2. sensory organ **body part that accepts stimuli from the senses (eyes, ears, nose, skin, tongue)**
3. curvature **state of being curved**
4. accommodation **change in shape of eye's lens as it focuses on objects moving closer or farther away**
5. preferential **having an advantage or preference**
6. stimuli **agents that cause responses**
7. novel **new; unfamiliar**
8. habituates **becomes routine by repetition**
9. distinct **not identical; different**
10. high-amplitude **very strong**
11. discriminate **tell differences between; make a clear distinction**
12. reinforcing **giving a reward for a certain response**

13. activate **put into motion**

14. distinguish **recognize as being different**

15. drawbacks **weaknesses; shortcomings**

16. ambiguous **uncertain**

17. imperceptible **not able to be detected**

18. variable **a characteristic in an experiment that can change**

19. converging **coming together**

20. confidence **trust or reliance; self-assurance**

Unit Two Comprehension

Handbook

3

Reading Aids

Most experienced readers use *prereading* and other strategies to make reading easier. You can use them to get a good sense of the material you plan to read. *Skimming* a selection means that you search quickly through the sentences to find facts and answers to questions you may have before you read closely. *Previewing* a selection before you read it lets you get a general idea of what you're going to be reading before you actually begin. Previewing is useful for short selections, such as book chapters, stories, articles, or essays, as well as for whole books and magazines.

3a Prereading

Reading is not just a matter of recognizing words on a page. It is a matter of what you do with those words in your mind. It is a matter of connecting what you find on the page with what you know and what you think. Certainly you learn new things from your reading, but you only learn them by building on information and ideas you already have. Aware readers always draw on their *prior knowledge,* what they know about a topic before reading the selection. When you stop to think about what you know about a topic before you read, you almost always discover that you know much more than you think you know, no matter how difficult the subject matter. It is very important to connect what you are reading with the world you are familiar with.

Prereading — thinking in advance about a topic before you read — helps you prepare for the words on the page. If you consider the topic beforehand, you'll find the writer's ideas a little more familiar than if you jump into the reading without prior thought. Your own knowledge helps you understand what the writer is saying.

For example, suppose you are ready to read a chapter called "The Nature of Motivation" in your psychology textbook. Before reading, think about motivation. What do you know and feel about motivation? How do you get motivated? What have teachers done to motivate you? How do you motivate yourself? How can you motivate a stubborn friend? As you think about these issues before you read, you remind yourself of what you already know. Also you stimulate your own interest and curiosity. You get your mind ready to take in new information.

You will find it helpful to write down your prereading efforts. As a warm-up for reading, just let your ideas about the writer's topic flow before you start reading. Make a list. Draw a word map. Use freewriting. Raise questions.

3a(1) *Making a List*

The first exercise is simply to make a list of everything that comes to mind when you think of the topic of the reading. For example, for a history class one student was required to read an article on politics during World War II. Before beginning to read, the student wrote the following list of things that came to her mind:

Politics During World War II

Who were the political leaders?
Was Franklin Roosevelt president of the U.S.?
Hitler
Nazis — took control of German government
Germany conquered most of Europe — France, Poland
D-Day — America and the allies start to regain Europe
What to do with Nazis after the war? Political problem
Pearl Harbor, Japanese bombing
Who led Japan? Didn't Japan have an emperor?
Kamikaze fighters, battles in the Pacific
Atom bomb dropped on Japan — Hiroshima
Nuclear weapons became a big political issue in the U.S.
Political alliance between Italy, Germany, and Japan

Allies — U.S., England, France, other countries
Didn't the Soviet Union switch back and forth?
Political results of the war — splitting of Europe between East and West

Notice how the student just followed her thoughts, with one idea or name leading to another. She winds up mentioning many different aspects of politics — leaders, internal politics of countries, international alliances, political consequences of the war. Sometimes she is a bit vague on facts and doesn't remember a name. Overall, however, she starts to bring back into her conscious mind much information she does know on the subject.

3a(2) *Drawing a Word Map*

A second exercise, drawing a word map, is like making a list, but it helps you organize your thoughts a bit more. In a word map you try to make some kind of visual relationship between the various thoughts you have. There is no single way to do this. Just start putting the ideas down on a piece of paper. Put related words close to each other; draw lines between connected ideas. Use boxes, circles, arrows, or any other visual symbol to show how ideas can be connected. For example, another student about to read an article on the business of sports might have put his ideas down in the word map on page 70.

3a(3) *Doing Freewriting*

A third way to warm up your thinking on a subject is freewriting. In freewriting you simply start writing about a subject and write whatever comes into your mind. Do not stop. Don't worry about complete sentences. Don't correct words or revise what you say. Even if you can't think of what to write, just keep your pen moving. You can even write things like "I don't know what this topic is all about" or "I have forgotten everything I know about this." Soon one statement will lead to the next, and you will be surprised by how much you find you know.

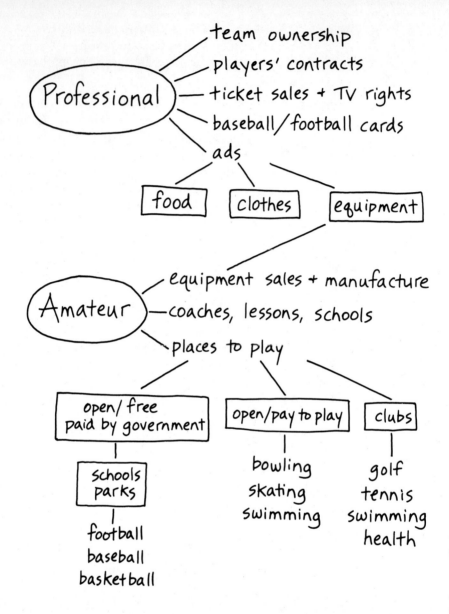

- Professional
  - team ownership
  - players' contracts
  - ticket sales + TV rights
  - baseball/football cards
  - ads
    - food
    - clothes
    - equipment
- Amateur
  - equipment sales + manufacture
  - coaches, lessons, schools
  - places to play
    - open/free paid by government
      - schools parks
        - football
        - baseball
        - basketball
    - open/pay to play
      - bowling
      - skating
      - swimming
    - clubs
      - golf
      - tennis
      - swimming
      - health

Freewriting also allows you to explore your feelings and interests, so that you can find points of connection between the subject of the reading and those things you would like or need to know about. You may also find that certain parts of the subject don't interest you. But don't give up too quickly. If you look deeply enough, you may be able to find some way

of connecting with a subject, no matter how distant it seems from your obvious interests. Consider one student's view of her own interests before reading an assigned chapter in the textbook for her biology course:

> Ugh! A chapter on flatworms. How gross. I'm just taking this course to fulfill my science requirement, and they keep giving us all this gross stuff to read about. At the very least I suppose I have to memorize the stuff in order to pass the exam. I can't get the credit if I don't pass. And if I try to skip over this chapter, I'll be lost for the rest of the term, because the teacher is making connections between simple organisms and more developed ones. Its weird to think that humans have some of the same systems as flatworms. They eat and breathe and excrete. Sometimes they do it a little differently than humans, but both flatworms and we have to solve some of the same basic problems of staying alive. It's sort of interesting to see the various ways these simple animals have developed biologically to carry out basic life functions. Maybe if I don't pay so much attention to them being disgusting worms, but instead think of them as certain ways of being alive, maybe I can understand all those details. Actually, those details are just parts of the systems that allow the thing to stay alive. Sort of amazing.

3a(4) *Raising Questions*

A final way to focus in advance on the topic of a reading selection is to write a list of questions that you would like to have answered about the subject. These questions will help you identify specific reading goals. Even if the selection does not answer your questions specifically, you might start making connections between the information in the reading and the information you are looking for. Raising questions will help stimulate your imagination and interest.

Before reading an article on violence in American history for a sociology course, one student wrote out the following questions that she was interested in:

Is America really more violent than other countries?
Do television and movies create the violence or only reflect it?
Who are the violent people and what makes them violent? Do violent people tend to come from any particular social

groups? Is the violence caused by social pressures? Is violence an individual behavior or a group's way of life?
Do the way I and my friends behave fit in with this pattern?
Are there any positive social functions of violence, or is it all negative? Do violent rock videos provide some positive entertainment and emotional release? How about violence used by the police or army? Don't they help to maintain social order?

Notice how, as the list of questions goes on, the student's special concerns appear. She moves from just blaming American society and particular groups to wondering how she might be involved in violence. From there she begins to wonder whether there might be some good to violence. She no longer sees herself as totally removed from the issue.

EXERCISES

1. Making a List

Your history teacher asks you to read a textbook chapter on the cold war. Make a list of your thoughts on the topic in advance.

2. Drawing a Word Map

You have to read an article on the automobile industry for a business management course. Make a word map on the topic.

3. Freewriting

Imagine you have to read a chapter on memory in a psychology textbook. On a separate sheet of paper, freewrite on the topic.

4. Asking Questions

Imagine you are about to read a book about race relations in the United States for a course in sociology. On a separate sheet of paper, make a list of questions about the subject that you would be interested in finding out about.

5. Prereading on Your Own

For any reading assignment in one of your other courses, explore your own interests in the topic by making a list, drawing a word map, freewriting, or asking questions. Use a separate sheet of paper.

3b Skimming

Rapid reading for facts is called *skimming*. Whenever you have to find *specific* facts in a paragraph, look for sentences that offer the needed information. When you skim a paragraph or a page, you are searching quickly among sentences for the answer to some question you have.

Here is how to skim:

- Make sure that you know what information you are looking for. Ask yourself a question. Look for a key word.
- Move your eyes quickly from line to line and from sentence to sentence.
- When you think you've found what you are looking for, *stop.*
- Slowly read the part of the line or sentence that tells you what you want to know.
- Think about the question you were trying to answer.
- Does the information you found answer the question? If not, quickly read the passage again to look for the information you need.
- Jot down the answer to the question you've asked.

EXERCISES

1. Skimming

Skim this brief biography of ragtime musical composer Scott Joplin to find out the following information: (a) his parents' background, (b) how he learned to play piano and read music, (c) how many copies of the "Maple Leaf Rag" were sold, (d) the kind of rhythm used in ragtime, and (e) the modern movie that used Joplin's music. Then write the answers below.

Scott Joplin and the "Maple Leaf Rag"

One entertainer among the hundreds who played the lively new music was to become the celebrated innovator who brought ragtime out of the disreputable sporting house and made it the respectable darling of the middle class. His name was Scott Joplin, and he was uniquely qualified to bridge the two worlds. Joplin was born in 1868 in a small town in Texas. His father had been a slave and had played the violin for plantation parties. His mother, who was free-born, had a beautiful singing voice and played the banjo. All the Joplin children were taught to play some kind of instrument.

By the time Joplin was eleven he could improvise smoothly on the piano, with a keen sense of rhythm and harmonics. Still, he could not read a note. His remarkable ability came to the attention of an old German music teacher living in the town, who gave him free lessons in technique and some sight-reading as well as an initial grounding in harmony and musical theory and classical music.

With few other outlets for his skills, Joplin became a roving pianist, working in the sporting houses and saloons up and down the Mississippi Valley. As a young adult with several years behind him as an entertainer, he took a job playing the piano in a saloon called the Maple Leaf Club in Sedalia, Missouri. While in Sedalia he also studied music at nearby George R. Smith College, which enabled him to produce technically sophisticated compositions.

Joplin began to write down the notes of ragtime pieces that he had composed. (He was not the first to do so; a number of obscure ragtime pieces had been scored a few years earlier.) He named one of his compositions the "Maple Leaf Rag," after the saloon. Then he encountered John S. Stark, a white owner of a music store in Sedalia. Stark bought the rights to the "Maple Leaf Rag" for 50 dollars in 1899 and had it printed as sheet music. Stark was an honest man and included in the agreement a royalty for the composer, just in case the piece made any money after publication. It seemed unlikely, because few outside the saloon world had ever heard of ragtime music.

As it turned out, it was the best investment Stark ever made. First, he distributed the sheet music around the region, and it caught on. Before long, the "Maple Leaf Rag" was selling briskly, even though it was an entirely new musical form, unfamiliar to those who bought it. By 1906, to Stark's and Joplin's mutual astonishment, it had sold over half a million copies. Joplin and other composers quickly produced additional ragtime pieces, and the new music began to attract an enthusiastic national following.

It is difficult to say why ragtime swept the country at the beginning of the new century. Perhaps the public had grown tired of the sentimental ballads, waltzes, and European-type music of the late nineteenth century. Ragtime was *very* different. Technically speaking, it used rhythmic forms that were not well known to the established world of music at the time.

Ragtime is based on a rhythmic form called *syncopation*. In playing the melody with the right hand, the pianist accents the weak or normally unaccented third beat of a measure while playing a precise and regularly accented bass with the left hand. Complex polyrhythms result — common enough in African drum-dominated music, but a bit startling in the Western world, particularly at the turn of this century. In fact, ragtime was far more complex and difficult to play than the ballads and waltzes that were then being published for the home piano. Nevertheless it was exciting and fun.

Scott Joplin died at a relatively young age of a serious illness. By the time of his death he had produced a number of famous ragtime compositions and had even written an opera, *Treemonisha*, but it never caught on. In 1974, decades after his death, a motion picture, *The Sting*, featured his compositions as its theme music, and Joplin's ragtime composition "The Entertainer" made the top of the charts in the same year.

— *Melvin DeFluer and Everette Dennis*

1. What was the background of Scott Joplin's parents?

   His father was born a slave; his mother was a free-born African-American.

2. How did he learn to play piano and read music?

   taught by mother at first and then by an old German music teacher

3. How many copies of the "Maple Leaf Rag" were sold?

   over half a million

4. What kind of rhythms are used in ragtime?

   syncopation

5. What modern movie used Joplin's music?

   The Sting

2. Skimming

Skim this selection from a psychology textbook to learn about high-speed decision making. Look for the six factors that influence reaction time.

High-Speed Decision Making

Imagine that, as you are speeding down a road late at night, the green traffic light you are approaching suddenly turns yellow. In an instant you must decide whether to apply the brakes or floor the accelerator. Here is a situation in which a stimulus is presented, a *decision* must be made under extreme time pressure, and then the decision must be translated into action.

Reaction Times Psychologists have studied how people make decisions like this by examining **reaction time,** the elapsed time between the presentation of a physical stimulus and an overt response. Reaction time is the total time needed for all the stages shown in Figure 9.1. In fact, the study of reaction time helped generate the information-processing approach. If cognition involves distinct stages, as the information-processing approach holds, then each stage must take some time. Therefore, one should be able to infer what stages or substages exist by examining changes in **mental chronometry,** the timing of mental events (Posner, 1978).

In a typical reaction-time task in the laboratory, a subject must rapidly say a particular word or push a certain button in response to a stimulus. Even in such simple situations, several factors influence reaction times. First, the reaction time to *intense stimuli,* such as bright lights or loud sounds, is shorter than to weaker stimuli. Second, the easier it is to *discriminate* between two or more stimuli, or the greater the difference between them, the shorter the reaction time will be.

A third factor is the *complexity* of the decision; that is, the larger the number of possible actions that might be carried out in response to a set of stimuli, the longer the reaction time. Suppose that, having cleared the yellow light, you are now scanning road signs for a turnoff to the town of Savoy. If you know that the turnoff is to the right and that the sign will say simply, "Savoy," there is only one possible stimulus-response combination, your decision will be simple, and your reaction time will be short. In contrast, if you do not know how the Savoy turnoff will be marked or in which direction the town lies, your choice will be more complex, and your reaction time will be longer.

Reaction time is also influenced by *stimulus–response compatibility.* If the relationship between a set of possible stimuli and possible responses is a natural or compatible one, then reaction time will be fast. If it is not, then reaction time will be slow. Figure 9.2 illustrates compatible and incompatible relationships.

Expectancy, too, affects reaction time. Expected stimuli are perceived more quickly than those that are surprising. Expectancy has the same effect on response time: people respond faster to stimuli that they anticipate and slower to those that surprise them.

Finally, in any reaction-time task there is a *speed–accuracy tradeoff.* If you try to respond quickly, errors increase; if you try for an error-free performance, reaction time increases (Pachella, 1974).

Knowing that these factors influence reaction time has expanded understanding of decision making under time pressure. To generate quick decisions by other drivers when an ambulance approaches, for example, designers of the warning systems on ambulances use light and sound stimuli that

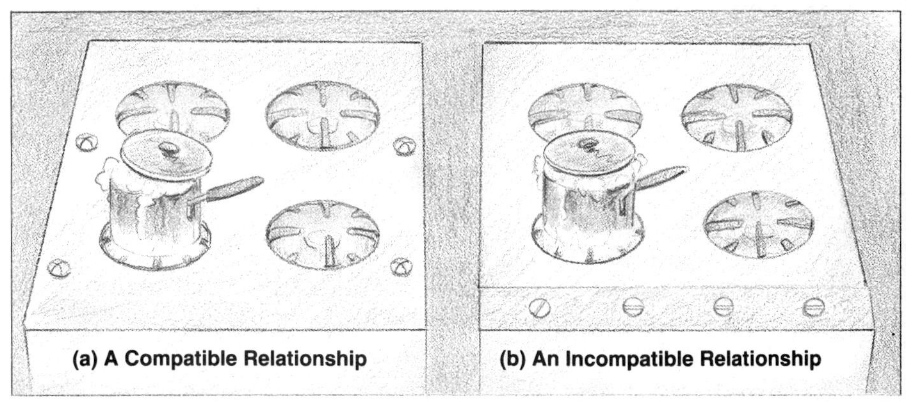

FIGURE 9.2 Stimulus–response compatibility. Suppose a cook is standing in front of the stove when a pot starts to boil over (a stimulus). The cook must rapidly adjust the appropriate dial to reduce the heat (the response). How fast the cook reacts may depend in part on the design of the stove. In the stove shown in (a), the dials are placed next to the burners, and there is a clear and visually compatible association that determines which stimulus belongs to which response. In (b), however, this compatibility does not exist, and reaction time will be much slower.

are not only very intense, but also very discriminable from any others that occur in normal traffic.

—*Douglas A. Bernstein, Edward J. Roy, Thomas K. Srull, and Christopher D. Wickens*

What are the six factors that influence reaction time?

1. **intensity of stimuli**
2. **discrimination between stimuli**
3. **complexity of the decision**
4. **stimulus–response compatibility**
5. **expectancy**
6. **speed–accuracy tradeoff**

Critical Thinking in Writing

What events in our daily lives other than decisions in a car on the road require high-speed decision making?

Write a paragraph that gives examples; then expand on the most significant high-speed decision that you believe people have to make.

3c Previewing a Selection

Other helpful steps to take in order to read for information come *before* you actually begin reading. You can *preview* — that is, look ahead to the content of a passage — in a number of ways.

Here is how to preview a reading selection:

- *Look at the title.* Does it tell what you will be reading about? If so, you can then set a purpose for your reading. Furthermore, titles often suggest the topic or the main idea of the selection. The title of the paragraphs on pages 147–148 is "20th-Century Lawsuit Asserts Stone-Age Identity." How does that help the reader set a purpose? How does it reflect the main idea?

- *Look for headings.* Essays, newspaper articles, and other longer readings sometimes offer help in finding information by inserting *headings.* Printed in bold letters or in italics, headings suggest the kind of material you will find in a small portion of the reading.
- *Look at the pictures, charts, or drawings.* Often an illustration can help you figure out beforehand what your reading will deal with.
- *Look at the first paragraph carefully.* The first paragraph usually tells what the reading will be about. Read it, and then stop to absorb the information before reading more.
- *Look at the first sentence of each paragraph.* This gives you a quick idea of what the reading involves before you begin to read carefully.
- *Look at the questions that come after the reading.* If you look at the questions *before* you read anything, you then have an idea of what's important. Questions tell you what to expect from a passage and what kind of information to look for.
- *Look for key words in different print.* Sometimes bold letters, italics, or even colored ink is used to call the reader's attention to important words or ideas. Titles of books, for example, appear in italics. Noting these in advance can give you important information.
- *Look for a summary.* At the end of a long factual piece, a writer sometimes summarizes the main points. Looking at this summary before you read can help you grasp more clearly what the selection deals with.

EXERCISE

Previewing

Before you read the following selection from an economics textbook, preview it by answering the following questions:

1. Read the title. What does it tell you about what the selection will discuss?

   Student responses will vary.

   ____

   ____

2. Read the headings. What are the major topics the selection will discuss?

____

____

3. Look at the marginal comments. What questions will be discussed in the selection?

____

____

____

4. Look at the boldface words. What are the key terms within the selection?

____

____

____

____

____

____

5. Look at the photograph. What process is illustrated and how does it relate to the concepts in the selection?

____

____

____

____

6. Look at the figure. What process is illustrated and how does it relate to the selection?

____

____

____

____

7. Look at the recap. What are the major points made in the selection?

____

____

____

____

____

____

____

____

1. What Is Economics?

What is economics?

Economics is a way of thinking about social issues and problems. It is the application of specific principles in a consistent manner. To understand economics it is necessary to discover these principles and to practice applying them. In this section, we define important terms and concepts; we then turn to the principles of economics.

1.a. The Definition of Economics

People want more *goods* and *services* than they have or can purchase with their incomes. Whether they are wealthy or poor, what they have is never enough. Neither the poor nor the wealthy have unlimited resources. Both have only so much income and time, and both must make choices to allocate these limited resources in ways that best satisfy their wants.

What is scarcity?

scarcity the shortage that exists when less of something is available than is wanted at a zero price

Because wants are unlimited and incomes, goods, time, and other items are not, scarcity exists everywhere. **Scarcity** exists when people want more of an item than is available when the price of the item is zero.

economic good any good that is scarce

free good a good for which there is no scarcity

Scarcity means that at a zero price the quantity of a good or resource is not sufficient to satisfy people's unlimited wants. Any good for which this holds is called an **economic good.** If there is enough of a good available at a zero price to satisfy wants, the good is said to be a **free good.** If people would pay to have less of a good, that good is

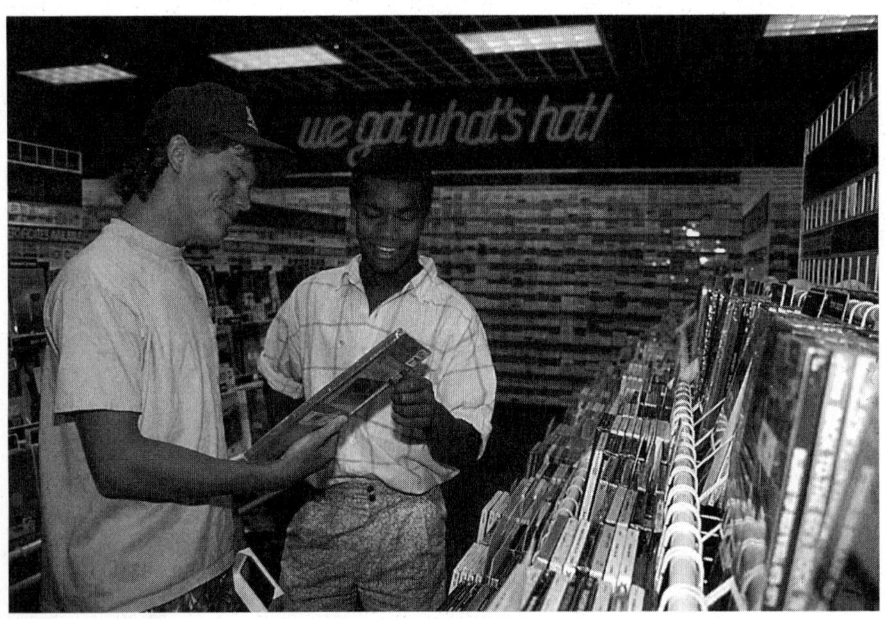

Each time you purchase a compact disk (CD), even on sale for $11.99, you give up whatever else that $11.99 could purchase. For $11.99 you could have a pizza and two soft drinks; you could purchase 2 novels; you could see two movies; you could purchase a ticket to one concert; or you could buy one tank of gas. You must make a choice. You can't have everything you want because resources are scarce; your income is limited. If you buy the CD, you have determined that it provides you more enjoyment for that $11.99 than any other use of the money.

bad any item for which we would pay to have less

called a **bad.** It is difficult to think of examples of free goods. At one time people referred to air as free, but with air pollution so prevalent, it is difficult to consider air a free good. It is not so hard to think of examples of bads: pollution, garbage, and disease fit the description.

Because people's wants are unlimited and the things they want and the income they have are scarce, individuals must make choices. But when they choose some things, they must give up or forgo other things. Economics is the study of how people choose to use their scarce resources to attempt to satisfy their **unlimited wants.**

unlimited wants boundless desires for goods and services

What is rational self-interest?

rational self-interest the term economists use to describe how people make choices

The choices people make are those they believe to be in their self-interest — that is, they believe they will receive more satisfaction from their choice than they would receive if they selected something else. **Rational self-interest** is the term economists use to describe how people make choices. It means that people will make the choices that, at the time and with the information they have at their disposal, will give them the greatest amount of satisfaction.

land all natural resources, such as minerals, timber, and water, as well as the land itself

labor the physical and intellectual services of people, including the training, education, and abilities of the individuals in a society

As illustrated in Figure 1, there are four categories of resources used to produce goods and services: land, labor, capital, and entrepreneurial ability. **Land** includes all natural resources, such as minerals, timber, and water, as well as the land itself. **Labor** refers to the physical and intellectual services of people and includes the training, education, and abilities of the individuals in a society.

capital products such as machinery and equipment that are used in production

Capital refers to products such as machinery and equipment that are used in production. Capital is a manufactured or created product used solely to produce goods and services. For example, tractors, milling machines, and cotton gins are capital; automobiles and food are goods; and haircuts and manicures are services. The word *capital* is often used to describe financial backing or the dollars used to finance a business. *Financial capital* refers to the money value of capital, as represented by stocks and bonds. In economics, *capital* refers to a physical entity — machinery and equipment and offices, warehouses, and factories.

entrepreneurial ability the ability to recognize a profitable opportunity and the willingness and ability to organize land, labor, and capital and assume the risk associated with the opportunity

Entrepreneurial ability is the ability to recognize a profitable opportunity and the willingness and

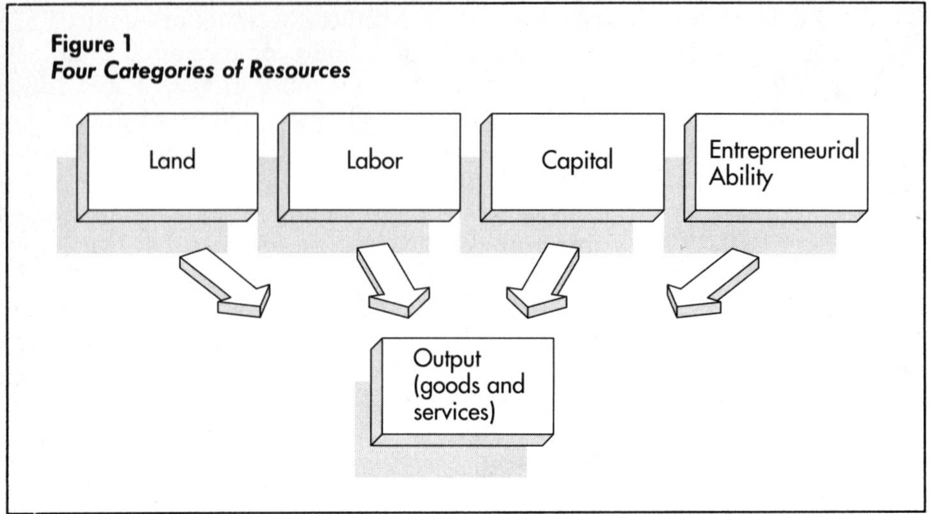

Figure 1
Four Categories of Resources

ability to organize land, labor, and capital and assume the risk associated with the opportunity. A special talent that only a few individuals have, entrepreneurial ability plays such an important role in the economy that it is considered to be a separate resource rather than just an aspect of labor. People who demonstrate entrepreneurial abilities are called **entrepreneurs.**

entrepreneur an individual who has the ability to organize resources in order to produce a product and the willingness to take the risk to pursue a profitable opportunity

People obtain income by selling the services of their resources. Owners of land receive *rent*. People who provide labor services are paid *wages* and *salaries*. Owners of capital receive *interest*, and people with entrepreneurial ability receive the *profits* from starting, running, and operating businesses. Because land, labor, capital, and entrepreneurial ability are scarce, income is limited.

durables goods that are used over a period of one or more years

nondurables goods that are used over a short period of time

services work done for others that does not involve the production of goods

Income is used to purchase goods and services. Goods that are used over a period of one or more years, such as an automobile, are referred to as **durables.** Those that are used over a short period of time, such as donuts, are **nondurables. Services** are work that is done for others that does not involve the production of goods, such as swimming lessons, haircuts, or the use of your telephone, as purchased from the telephone company.

1.b. Macroeconomics and Microeconomics

microeconomics the study of economics at the level of the individual

macroeconomics the study of the economy as a whole

Economics is usually separated into two general areas, microeconomics and macroeconomics. **Microeconomics** is the study of economics at the level of the individual economic entity: the individual firm, the individual consumer, and the individual worker. **Macroeconomics** is the study of the economy at an aggregate level. Rather than analyzing the behavior of an individual consumer or firm, macroeconomists look at the sum of the behaviors of all consumers (the *consumer sector*) and all firms (the *business sector*) as well as the government and international sectors.

Recap

1. Economics is the study of how people choose to use their scarce resources to satisfy their unlimited wants.
2. Resources are classified into four general groups: land, labor, capital, and entrepreneurial ability.
3. Scarce resources are used to produce goods and services.
4. The two main branches of economics are macroeconomics and microeconomics. Macroeconomics is the study of the economy as a whole — the consumer sector, the business sector, the government sector, and the international sector. Microeconomics is the study of economics at the level of the individual — individual consumers, individual workers, and individual business firms.

— *William Boyes and Michael Melvin*

3d Previewing the Parts of a Book

Much of what you read appears in long works. Your textbooks in biology, math, or business courses, for example, offer several hundred pages of material. One teacher may require that you read a novel or a play; another may ask you to read an article in a journal; still another may assign a new book that treats the subject of the course in a special way.

Before you read a long book for information, you can use some other effective preview techniques aside from those explained in section **3c**. Here is how to preview a book:

- *Look at the table of contents.* Found in the front of the book, the table of contents is a list of the titles of the chapters and the pages on which they begin. If the book is divided into parts, that information also appears in the table of contents. If you study the chapter titles, you can get an idea of what each section of the book deals with and how the topics relate to one another. Sometimes a table of contents is very detailed, listing the topics treated in each chapter.
- *Look at the preface.* Also located in the front of the book, the preface (or *foreword*) is a brief essay in which the author gives reasons for writing the book. The preface is a personal message to the reader. In the preface you get an idea of the kind of reader the author is writing for; of the aims of the book and just what the author expects you to learn as a result of reading it; and of the topics in the book and the best approaches to those topics. Not all books have a preface; and sometimes a preface deals with matters that interest the author but may not have much to do with specific ideas in the book. Still, it's good to look the preface over, even if you just skim it, so that you can judge for yourself whether or not to read the preface carefully.
- *Look briefly at the index.* At the end of a book you may find an index, an alphabetical listing of the topics, subjects, ideas, and names mentioned in the book. A quick look at the index suggests some of the points the writer deals with and how detailed the book is.
- *Look at one of these special features that sometimes appear in books:*

   1. After the chapters in a book a writer sometimes provides a *glossary* — a list of difficult words or terms commonly used in the subject the book deals with. The words are listed in alphabetical order along with their definitions. The fact that a book has a glossary may indicate that the subject is technical but that the author does try to explain the difficult terms.
   2. An *appendix* (plural *appendixes* or *appendices*) at the end of the book presents additional information that is interesting and useful. However, the book is complete without the appendix, and the information we find there is only

extra. An appendix may include charts and graphs, special letters or documents, or facts about the lives of the people mentioned in the book. It may just give information to explain something the author felt needed more attention. A look at the appendix, if the book has one, indicates how a writer deals with special problems.

- *Read the introduction.* Often the first chapter of the book is an introduction. The introduction gives an overview of the book and states the basic problem the author will deal with. It gives background information or discusses the history of the topic. It may summarize what others have said about the subject. It may even explain the method of research the author used. Sometimes — especially in a work of fiction (a novel, a collection of short stories, a play) — someone other than the author writes the introduction. This kind of introduction often explains the book to the readers, pointing out key scenes or ideas worth noting.
- *Look at the bibliography or references.* At the back of the book, an author sometimes gives a *bibliography* — a list, in alphabetical order, of some or all of the books that helped the author write the book. The bibliography (or works cited) indicates the author's range of knowledge and basic interests.
- *Think about what parts the book has and what parts it doesn't have.* A book with a detailed index, a long bibliography, and a number of appendixes may be more appropriate for research than a book with only a short table of contents. And books with glossaries often provide helpful introductions to difficult subjects.

EXERCISES

1. Using a Table of Contents

Look at the table of contents that appears on pages 88–89. It comes from a book entitled *Compact Disc Player Maintenance and Repair*. Read the table of contents to figure out as much as you can about the book. Then answer the following questions:

1. What aspect of compact discs is this book concerned with?

   compact disc use and maintenance

Contents

2. Who might be interested in this book and when?

   someone who has a new CD player or a broken CD player

3. In what chapter would you find out how to set up and use a CD player?

   Chapter 4

4. In what chapter would you find out how to take care of a CD player under usual conditions?

   Chapter 6

5. In what chapter would you find out how to take care of a CD player under unusual conditions?

   Chapter 7

6. In what chapters would you find out how to discover what's wrong with a CD player and how to fix it?

   Chapters 8 and 9

7. Where would you find out how CDs and CD players differ from other methods of sound reproduction?

   Chapters 2 and 3

8. Where could you find out where to go to learn more about CDs?

   Appendix B

9. Where can you find the meanings of unusual words used in the book?

   in the glossary

10. In what chapter would you find information on how to use the maintenance log presented in Appendix C?

Chapter 10

2. Using an Index

On page 92 is an excerpt from the index of the book on compact disc players whose table of contents you used in Exercise 1. Answer the following questions:

1. How does the table of contents differ from the index?

The index is alphabetical and more detailed.

2. If you wanted to find general information on how CD players work, would it be better to look at the table of contents or the index? **the table of contents**

3. If you wanted to find out quickly about oiling CD players, would it be better to look at the table of contents or the index? **the index**

4. List the pages on which you will find information about

52 a. muting errors.

97 b. lens cleaning.

81 c. lens cleaning material.

42 d. operating controls.

84 e. making test discs.

39 f. low-pass analog filtration.

8 g. the Nyquist Theorem.

3. Reading a Preface

Read the preface on page 93 from the book *Good Dirt: Confessions of a Conservationist* by Davide E. Morine. Try to determine the special qualities of the book. Then answer the questions.

1. What is the author's attitude toward conservation?

   businesslike but lighthearted

   ____

   ____

PREFACE

Conservation is my chosen profession. From 1972 to 1987 I was in charge of land acquisition for The Nature Conservancy, a nonprofit organization. During that time, we acquired three million acres of land, completed 5,000 projects, and protected 2,000 of America's most significant natural areas. We ran a good business. We raised some money. We saved some land. We had some fun.

When I started with the Conservancy, saving land was a relatively simple business. We'd look around, find some land that we liked, and buy it. Once we had acquired an area, I really believed that it would be protected in perpetuity. I, like most people, had never heard of acid rain, the greenhouse effect, or holes in the ozone layer. We didn't deal in doom and gloom. We bought land.

Today, things are different. Dire predictions seem to be the staple of the conservation movement. Most conservationists are consumed by problems for which there are no simple solutions. What good does it do, for example, to buy a forest unless you can protect it from acid rain? Why save a tidal marsh if it is going to be lost to rising oceans resulting from global warming? Who can worry about a piece of native tallgrass prairie when we are destroying the atmosphere? It is no wonder that so many of today's conservationists seem so somber. They see so many threats to the environment that they can't enjoy being conservationists. For them, humor has become a rare and endangered species.

During my tenure at The Nature Conservancy, we were generally considered to be the most businesslike of the conservation organizations. We probably were. But that didn't mean that we didn't have our share of screw-ups. Any time you undertake a major land deal, something is going to go wrong. When that happens, you can do one of two things: You can get upset, or you can laugh. More often than not, we laughed.

I believe that a large part of the Conservancy's success has been due to the fact that we never took ourselves too seriously. We never let the big issues get us down. We never spent too much time agonizing over the big picture. We attacked the problem of saving significant natural areas one piece at a time.

We weren't naive. We knew we weren't going to save the world, but we thought we could save small and important parts of it. We were focused in our work; we were happy being conservationists.

This collection of stories describes some of my more monumental foul-ups. Most are informative; a few are irreverent, and at least one is totally tasteless. Despite my having been justifiably accused of never letting the facts get in the way of a good story, these stories are, on the whole, true. I hope they will explain a little about land conservation and give conservationists a much-needed lift. With all the doom and gloom being written today, we could use a laugh.

2. How does his attitude differ from that of people today who are involved with conservation?

   They are somber.

3. What does he believe today's conservationist movement needs more of?

   humor

4. What kind of information will be presented in the book?

   stories of foul-ups

5. What do you expect the style and attitude of the book to be?

   humorous, lighthearted, not too serious

6. What kind of people do you think would find the book most interesting or useful?

   conservationists who are feeling pessimistic

Critical Thinking in Writing

Write a paragraph or two on how the activity of conservationists has affected your campus or home community.

4. Previewing the Parts of a Book

Select a book from your library. Locate the parts of the book in the following list. In your own words, write what you can find out about the book from each part. If the book does not have one of the parts, state what you think that indicates about the book.

1. Title and author's name ______________________

____

2. Table of contents ______________________

____

____

3. Preface ______________________

____

____

4. Introduction or first chapter ______________________

____

____

5. Glossary ______________________

____

____

6. Bibliography ______________________

____

____

7. Index ______

______

______

5. Previewing: Chapter 7

Preview Chapter 7 (pages 168–217) by following the guidelines given in sections **3b** and **3c.** Then answer the following questions:

1. What is Chapter 7 about? **recognizing paragraph patterns**

2. What three methods of ordering ideas are explained in Chapter 7? **time order, place order, and order of importance**

3. On what page in Chapter 7 can you find hints for seeing how paragraphs are arranged? **171**

4. What does section **7b** deal with? **listing of details**

   7c? **classification**

   7d? **comparison and contrast**

   7e? **cause and effect**

4

Visual Aids

Readings often contain more than just words arranged in sentences and paragraphs. Pictures, graphs, tables, charts, maps, and diagrams often add to the meaning of the main text. Often a *caption* — that is, a brief explanation in words — accompanies the visual aid and highlights its most important elements. Knowing how to read visual aids and how to relate them to the ideas of the selection can help you get more from your reading.

Each visual aid carries a message in itself, but the message also connects with the ideas and information in the main text in some way. Sometimes a picture or diagram simply illustrates or reinforces a point made in the writing. A newspaper article describing a meeting between the leaders of the United States and France may be accompanied by a picture of them shaking hands and smiling.

In other cases, visual aids can add new but related information that helps enrich your understanding of the points made by the main text. This is the case of the figure and photograph that accompany the selection from an economics textbook on pages 81–84 in this book.

Sometimes an essential part of the reading is visual in nature and is best represented in an illustration. Then the illustration works hand in hand with the words, as in the example on pages 99–100, a newspaper story describing research on smiles.

Finally, the visual aid may be the most important part of the selection, and the words only help explain the picture. Look, for example, at the explanation of how a zipper works on page 101. In this case the words only explain what is going on in the illustration.

Each kind of visual aid requires its own special skills for interpretation.

4a Photographs

To interpret photographs you need to be able to identify what is being represented and then to infer moods, attitudes, and relations that help give life to the pictures, particularly when they are of people. (See Chapter 8 for further discussion of inference skills.)

Thoughtful readers pause over photographs and often ask themselves a number of questions about the photographs. These questions can help connect the visual aid with the written information that goes with it.

Understanding Photographs: Questions to Ask Yourself

- Who is the person in the photograph and what is the person doing?
- What is the scene of the photograph and how does it relate to the point in the reading selection?
- What is the relation among the various people in the photograph? Why are these people (or this person) at the scene?
- What moods can I identify from the people's faces or gestures? How do I interpret — that is, explain — people's behavior?
- How does the caption relate to the photograph? What information is missing from the caption? How can I explain the information that is missing?
- Why was the photograph included with the written selection?

In the selection that follows, notice how you must look carefully at the pictures in order to understand fully what the story is saying about the differences among kinds of smiles. The caption explains the pictures, and the pictures make the visual point very well. Still, you must connect the words in the selection with the visual aids. Notice how two paragraphs in particular (paragraphs 6 and 7) point out the features revealed in the photographs.

True or False? The Anatomy of a Smile

1 The false smile, that ubiquitous social lubricant, has been unmasked by new research that has identified the different specific muscle patterns in smiles that reflect true delight and those that mask displeasure.

2 "All smiles are not the same," said Paul Ekman, a psychologist who directs the Human Interaction Laboratory at the University of California medical school in San Francisco. "A polite smile or a forced one produces a different muscle pattern than does a spontaneous smile."

3 The research may be of particular importance to those like physicians or psychotherapists who sometimes need to rely on subtle cues to know when a person is trying to hide physical pain or emotional anguish behind the mask of a smile. It holds interest for anyone who wants to tell if a smile may be lying.

4 Dr. Ekman and Wallace Friesen and Maureen O'Sullivan will publish the results of their research on smiles later this winter in the *Journal of Personality and Social Psychology.*

5 With Dr. Friesen, Dr. Ekman has developed a technique for analyzing the patterns of the more than 100 muscles of the face as a person changes expression. With their method, they have been able to determine precisely which of those muscles is at play when the face takes on a given emotional expression.

6 In the study on lying, real smiles differed from those that hid unhappy feelings on two counts. In spontaneous smiles, the cheeks move up and the muscles around the eyes tighten, making crow's feet. And, if the real smile is large enough, the skin around the eyebrow droops down a bit toward the eye.

7 In the false smiles, however, the face reveals traces of unhappy feelings behind the smile — for instance, a slight furrowing of the muscle between the eyebrows — that can be seen apart from the supposed expression of pleasure. The eyes will not develop crow's feet unless the smile is especially broad. And even then, the tell-tale droop of skin around the eyebrow, which is difficult to feign, will usually not emerge.

8 While the differences were detected using a sophisticated measuring system, Dr. Ekman said they were obvious enough to be used as social signals.

— *Daniel Goleman*

False smiles result in predictable muscle actions, apparent on face of research subject viewed on closed-circuit television. The muscle between the eyebrows tends to furrow slightly. In picture 1, a trace of sadness is apparent as the triangularis muscle pulls the lip corners down. In pictures 2 and 3, disgust is revealed by the upper lip, which is raised by the muscle levator labii superioris. *Photographs by Paul Ekman*

Critical Thinking in Writing

Write a paragraph called "Smiles" in which you classify (or group) the various smiles you have observed. Give the qualities of each group. Use concrete details.

4b Diagrams

A diagram is a drawing with labeled parts. In diagrams you need to notice the separate parts represented and to see how they work together. Labels and captions usually point out the key features and explain how the parts relate to one another. On the facing page, labels and a caption work along with the diagram to explain how a zipper works.

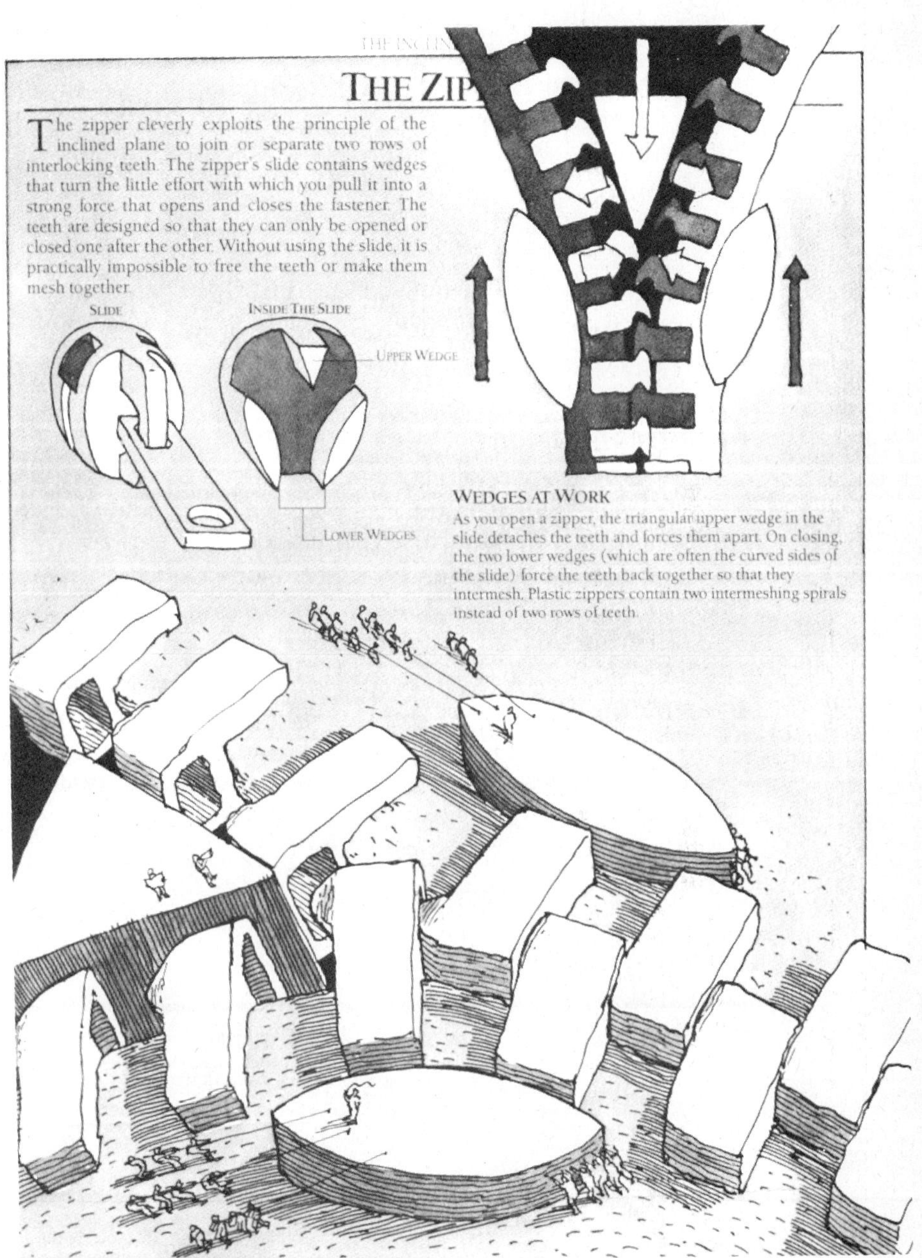

—*David Macaulay*

4c Word Charts

A word chart presents information in summary form to make material easy to find. Instead of using sentences in a paragraph, a writer can present complex information in chart form. This textbook uses word charts regularly: See pages 98 and 105, for example.

In the word chart on page 103, notice how the visual layout makes it easy to understand the examples of punctuation. At the left you see the particular kind of punctuation; at the right you read an explanation and examples of how it's used.

4d Statistical Tables

Statistical tables present numbers in chart form. Often the numbers appear in columns with headings to explain what the numbers represent. Titles also point out important information. You need to think about why the numbers in the table are interesting or what they might tell you. Compare the numbers with one another and with what you expect from the numbers in order to see what meanings you might find. Are any of the numbers significantly larger or smaller than any others? Are any surprisingly different from what you would expect?

In the following statistical table, note how the title explains the purpose of the table: to show the states that had the largest

TABLE 3.1 States With the Largest Hispanic Populations, 1990

STATE	HISPANICS (MILLIONS)	PERCENT OF U.S. HISPANICS	PERCENT OF STATE'S POPULATION
California	7.7	34.4%	25.8%
Texas	4.3	19.4	25.5
New York	2.2	9.9	12.3
Florida	1.6	7.0	12.2
Illinois	0.9	4.0	7.9
Arizona	0.7	3.1	18.8
New Jersey	0.7	3.3	9.6
New Mexico	0.6	2.6	38.2
Colorado	0.4	1.9	12.9

SOURCE: U.S. Bureau of the Census release, 1991.

A Handy Punctuation Chart

MARK	EXPLANATION AND EXAMPLES
.	To end sentences and abbreviations: Dr. Smith called.
?	To end direct questions: What time is it?
!	To show surprise or strong emotion: I don't believe it!
,	To separate words, phrases, and sentences in a series: apples, oranges, pineapples, and bananas To separate words and phrases not part of the main idea of a sentence: Fran, *the teacher's pet*, got all the answers right. To use in titles, dates, addresses: Allen Schwartz, M.D. June 30, 1945 Elk, California
—	To interrupt a sentence and to emphasize added-in phrases: Phil—*our last hope*—came to bat.
( )	To separate interrupting material: Candy Jones (*of the prominent Jones family*) invited me to a party.
[ ]	To add your own words in a quotation: "Four score [*that means eighty*] and seven years ago . . ."

Hispanic populations in 1990. Each column heading tells you what the figures mean.

4e Graphs

Graphs present statistics visually with lines, bars, or circles. The purpose of a graph is to show how statistics compare with one another. When you look at a statistical table, you have to make comparisons on your own; in a graph, the size or shape of the drawing helps you make the comparison. In reading graphs you should study the title and labels carefully.

The graphs about immigrants on this page are from a geography book. Notice how the bars allow you to see relationships among numbers. For example, the bar for 1931–1940 is much smaller than the bar directly above it, for 1921–1930. This visual comparison tells you that fewer immigrants came to the United States in the 1930s than in the 1920s. In the circle graph about immigration in the 1970s, notice the small piece for African immigrants. Even if you didn't read the low percentage of African immigrants — 1.8 percent — you could tell from the draw-

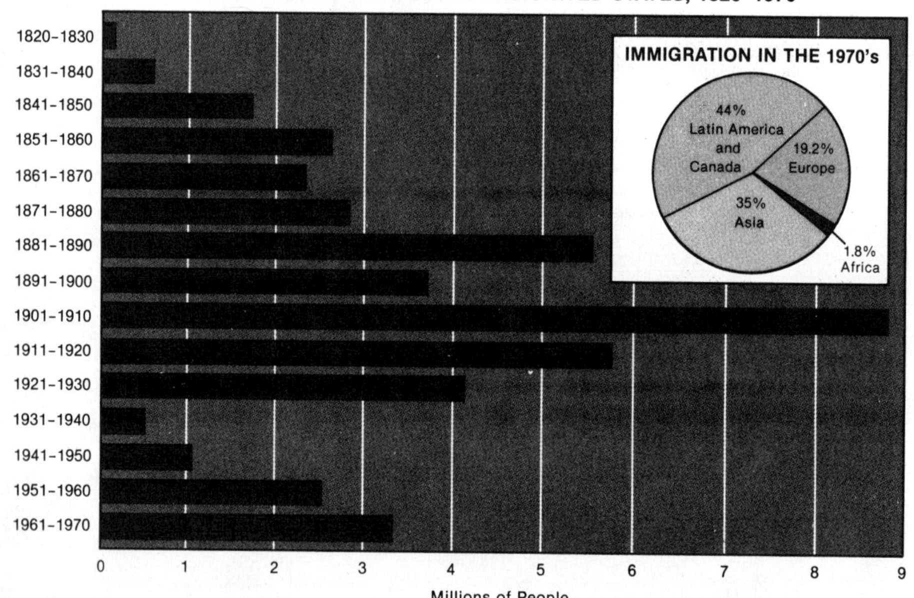

ing that the number of African immigrants was small in relation to others.

Using Visual Aids: A Review Chart

1. *Pay attention to visual aids.* Pictures, charts, graphs, and illustrations add important information to what you're reading.
2. *Examine titles, captions, or other explanations that appear with visual aids.* Accompanying words and sentences often point out the main features of the illustrations.
3. *Connect the illustrations with the sentences and paragraphs of the selection.* As you're reading, stop and ask yourself key questions. What does the illustration show? Why has it been included? What does it show that the words do not?
4. *Put visual information in your own words.* Compose sentences in your mind that explain the illustrations provided.

EXERCISES

1. Photo in a Textbook

Read this selection from a computer textbook for an introduction to government use of computers. Then answer the questions.

Local Governments

Local governments use computers for a variety of useful, if not exotic, purposes. Cities and neighborhoods use computers for budget monitoring and reporting, for police allocation, and for processing of traffic tickets, to name only a few mundane applications. They use them to prepare bills for water and power usage and to levy millage rates for property taxes. In one example of people versus machine, the homeowners of Dekalb County, Georgia, rose up in protest when they learned that the county government intended to use computers to assess annual inflationary increases in property value. Homeowners had visions of an infallible machine automatically bumping up the assessments on their homes by a horrendously accurate percentage, leading to more and more taxes. The county government was pressured into abandoning its plan and reverting to the more inefficient and inexact system of manually assessing increases.

A significant and life-saving service offered by some local jurisdictions that use computers is the *enhanced 911* emergency system. These systems use address *geocoding* that runs on a database containing the following information:

- The names and locations of all city streets, major buildings, parks, and landmarks
- Every working phone number, along with its listed address and map coordinates to pinpoint it
- The name, address, and location of every emergency service center

When a citizen calls needing help, both the name and the address of the caller appear on the operator's computer screen and are automatically routed to a dispatcher, who either radios an emergency unit or directs the computer to alert the nearest fire station, paramedic service, or police car (see Figure 16.3). The advantages of this system are obvious: even children who don't know their addresses can use it to summon help. Many lives have already been saved by enhanced 911.

— *Ronald Anderson and David R. Sullivan*

1. Why does the last paragraph of the selection say "(see Figure 16.3)"?

   This photograph illustrates the information given in the last paragraph.

2. How does the photograph provide needed information for the article?

   It shows the reader how the information from the caller is transmitted to the police.

3. What important information does the caption provide?

   It explains what the officer in the photograph is doing.

FIGURE 16.3 A police officer at a 911 answering point handles an incoming emergency call. The 911 computer system displays the caller's location on the screen, along with other important information.

2. Reading Diagrams

Look at the diagram on page 108 explaining how a car window winder works and then answer the questions.

1. What are the five main parts of the window opener?

   handle, cog, quadrant, levers, and car window

2. What does the middle diagram show that is not shown by the top diagram?

   the direction in which each part moves

3. As the handle turns to the right, what happens to the quadrant section of the large gear? What does that do to the lever? And what does that do to the window?

   The quadrant section turns to the left, raising the lever and pushing the window up.

CAR WINDOW WINDER

The handle in a car door turns a small cog that moves a toothed quadrant (a section of a large spur gear), which in turn raises or lowers levers supporting the car window. Electrically operated windows work on the same principle, but more gears are required because the speed of the motor has to be stepped down to provide a small but powerful movement.

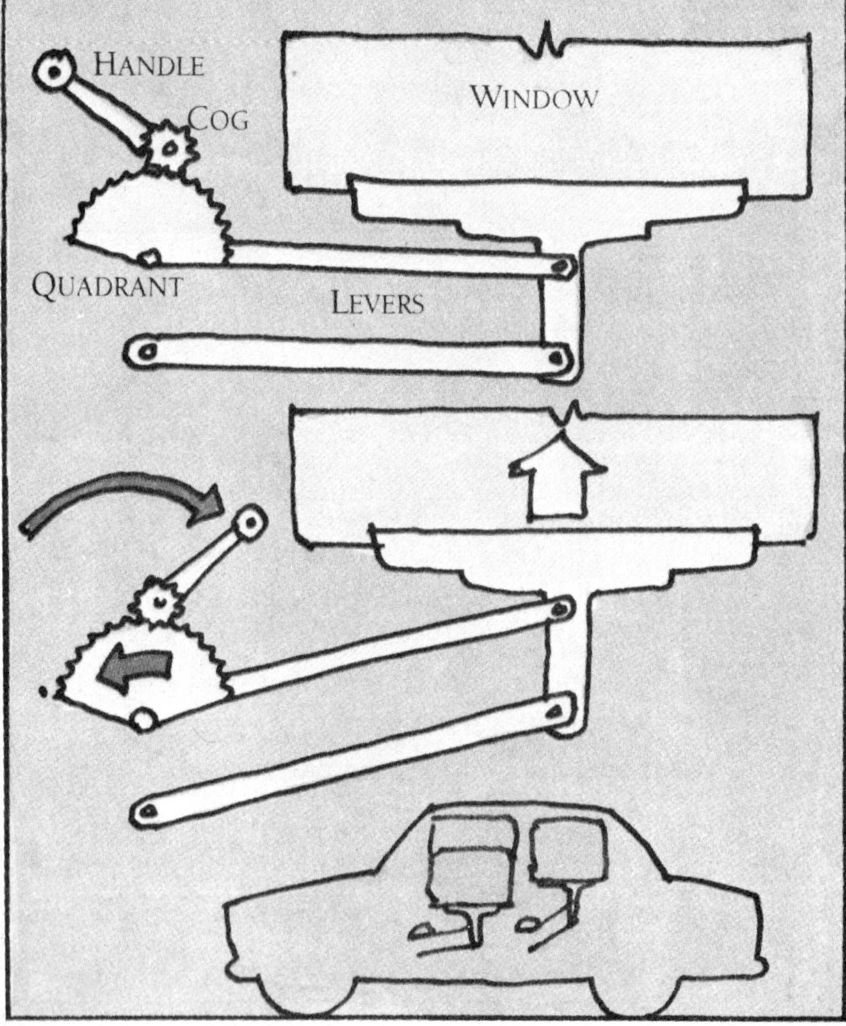

— *David Macaulay*

4. What does the bottom diagram of the car illustrate?

where the window opener is located in the car

3. Reading a Word Chart in a Textbook

Read the following chart from a geography textbook and answer the questions that follow.

Classifying Mineral Resources

METALLIC MINERAL RESOURCES

Plentiful metals: iron, aluminum, manganese, titanium, magnesium
Scarce metals: copper, iron, lead, zinc, tin, tungsten, chromium, gold, silver, platinum, uranium

NONMETALLIC MINERAL RESOURCES

Minerals for chemicals, fertilizers, and special uses: sodium chloride (salt), phosphates, nitrates, sulfur; also precious stones (diamonds, rubies) for industry
Building materials: clay, sand, gravel, gypsum, asbestos
Fossil fuels: coal, petroleum, natural gas

1. What does the chart show?

classification of mineral resources

2. What are the two main groups of information?

metallic mineral resources and nonmetallic mineral resources

3. What subcategories appear in the first group?

plentiful metals and scarce metals

In the second?

minerals for chemicals, fertilizers, and special uses; building materials; and fossil fuels

4. Give one example of each of the following kinds of resources:
   a. Fossil fuels **coal**
   b. Plentiful metals **manganese**
   c. Minerals for chemicals **sulfur**
   d. Scarce metals **uranium**
   e. Building materials **clay**

5. Why did the writers choose a word chart to present their information?

   It is easily organized and studied.

4. Word Charts

Look again at the word chart on page 109. Answer the following questions:

1. How does the title help you understand the chart?

   It tells what the purpose of the chart is.

2. How do the column headings help you understand the chart?

   They break down the information.

3. Use the chart to explain the uses of these punctuation marks:

   Brackets [ ] **to add words within quotations**

   Exclamation point ! **to show surprise or emotion**

   Parentheses ( ) **to separate interrupting material**

4. Give an example from the chart of the use of commas to separate words, phrases, and sentences.

   Fran, the teacher's pet, got all the answers right.

5. **Reading Statistical Tables**

Look at the following set of statistics and answer the questions.

1. What does the first column of statistics represent?

   total degree cost

2. What does the second column represent?

   average first-year income

3. How do the two lists of numbers relate to the words in the left-hand column?

VITAL STATISTICS

After-School Money

Graduation time is especially enjoyable for those who have jobs waiting. But some grads can afford to do more celebrating than others. A sampler:

SCHOOL ATTENDED, JOB	TOTAL COST OF DEGREE	AVERAGE FIRST-YEAR INCOME
Harvard Business School, financial consultant	**$31,300**	**$65,100**
Georgetown Law School, lawyer	**$37,800**	**$52,000**
University of Michigan (nonresident), engineer	**$20,796**	**$31,247**
UCLA (nonresident), social worker	**$6,486**	**$26,000**
Columbia University School of Journalism, newspaper reporter	**$13,308**	**$22,000**
University of Pennsylvania, media planner	**$51,000**	**$18,000**
Illinois State University College of Education, teacher	**$28,000**	**$17,000**

SOURCE: NEWSWEEK ESTIMATES; COST OF DEGREE IS BASED ON COSTS FOR 1988-89 SCHOOL YEAR

They give the degree cost and average first-year income of a person graduating from each of the schools.

4. Which education costs the most? **University of Pennsylvania**

   The least? **UCLA**

5. Which graduate earns the most? **Harvard Business School graduate**

   The least? **Illinois State teacher**

6. What can you find out by comparing the two statistical columns?

   which school's degree can provide the greatest income for the least amount of money

7. What facts of interest do you find in this chart and what do those facts mean to you?

   A University of Pennsylvania graduate may pay more to earn a degree than the first year's income as a media planner can provide. A Harvard Business School graduate will earn about $34,000 more than his or her degree cost.

6. Reading a Statistical Table in a Textbook

Look again at the data in the table on page 102. Answer these questions:

1. What percent of America's Hispanics do the nine states together contain? **86% of all U.S. Hispanics**

2. Of the states listed, which state had the highest percentage of Hispanics in America in 1990? **California**

   The lowest? **Colorado**

3. In 1990, how many Hispanics did Illinois have? **0.9 million**

4. What percent of 1990 Hispanics did New Mexico have? **2.6%**

5. Why do you think this information is offered in a table instead of in a paragraph discussion?

   The table provides comparative information at a glance.

7. Reading a Textbook Graph

Look at the circle graph on page 104. On a separate sheet of paper write a brief paragraph that explains the main point of the graph and the various statistics the graph shows.

8. Words and Diagrams Together

Read the following newspaper article about a survey of people's religious identification in the United States. Also study the accompanying figures. Then answer the questions.

Practicing or Not, Many Identify with Religion

Most Americans are religious and aren't afraid to say so, a sweeping new survey on religious affiliation shows.

The survey, commissioned by the Graduate School of the

City University of New York, found 86.5% of Americans identified themselves as Christians, 2% as Jewish and 0.5% as Muslim.

Only 7.5% of the respondents said they had no religion.

But a closer look at the data shows striking diversity. Of the Christians, 26% said they were Roman Catholic and 60% said Protestant. And respondents identified with more than 50 denominations, including Taoist and Hindu.

"The tremendous diversity of denominations shows the cross-cutting cohesive tendency of religion," says study director Barry Kosmin. "All of these groups cut across racial, ethnic, class, regional and generational lines."

The survey — of 113,000 people across the USA interviewed during a period of 13 months — is the largest and most comprehensive poll to date on religious affiliation. It was conducted because the USA "did not have a good religious profile," says Seymour Lachman, dean of community development at City University.

Despite concern that some people might be offended by questions about their religion, few refused to answer the poll.

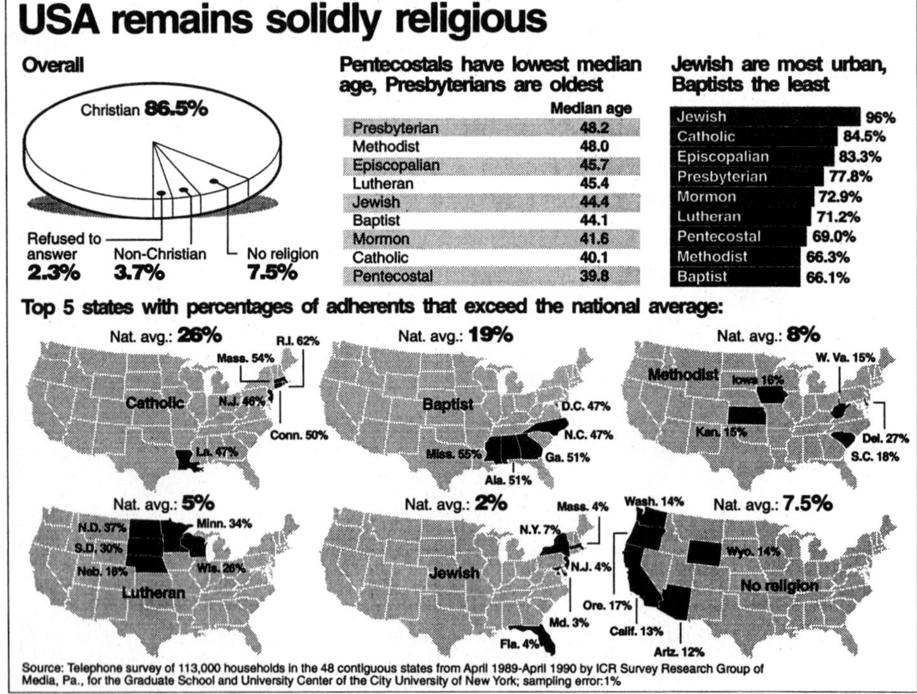

— *Julie Stacey*

"It demonstrates that for many Americans, religious identity is important, perhaps as important as their ethnic or racial identity," says Lachman.

Other findings:

- The greatest percentage of respondents who have no religion live in the West; Oregon has the highest with 17%.
- Half of all black U.S. residents are Baptists, 9% are Catholic.
- Hispanics make up 14% of all Catholics, and 65% of Hispanics are Catholic.
- Most Irish-Americans are Protestant, exploding the belief that most are Catholic.
- Most Asian-Americans and Arab-Americans are Christians.
- Mormons have the highest proportion of married adults and the most children.
- Greek Orthodox members have the lowest rate of divorce and Unitarians the highest.
- The major churches remain Roman Catholic, Baptist, Methodist and Lutheran. "In the national picture, the much publicized cults and new religions vanish into statistical insignificance," Kosmin says.

Information about the USA's religious traits has been sketchy because the Census Bureau — mindful of the nation's historic separation of church and state — does not include questions about religion on its questionnaire. However, some demographic information collected from church organizations is included in the bureau's annual yearbook, *Statistical Abstract of the United States.*

Abstract editor Glenn King says the new survey "adds to our understanding of America's religious character."

"Certainly, religion plays a role in how people view various social issues, and this kind of background helps explain those views."

The survey asked the question, "What is your religion?" and was not intended to gauge an individual's level of religious observance or commitment, says Kosmin.

But Chris Baumann, a spokesman for the U.S. Catholic Conference in Washington, D.C., says the high percentage of people who identified with a religious denomination does not contradict recent evidence of dwindling resources and flagging membership at some parishes.

"I think the findings are encouraging. Even if people don't go to church every Sunday, there is a sense of spirituality in their lives."

— *Desda Moss*

1. What is the main idea of the article?

   The vast majority of Americans identify with a religion.

2. What does the pie chart show? How does that chart illustrate information presented in the article?

   The percentage of the population that identifies with major religious groups. This shows that most Americans have a religious identity.

3. What information is displayed in the top middle figure? How does the table title summarize the information?

   The median ages of different religious groups. The headline identifies the youngest and oldest median-age groups.

4. What information is presented in the bar graph? Does this graph repeat information in the article or present additional information?

   How urban each religious group is. This information is not in the article.

5. What information is presented in the maps? How does that information relate to information in the other figures and the article?

   Top five states that have more than the average percentage of members of major religious groups. The

article mentions the geographic distribution of people who are not religious but not of people who are.

6. What facts are presented in the article that are not presented in the figures?

Racial and ethnic religious information; marriage, children, and divorce rates of different religions.

7. Overall, how do the figures and words relate to each other to present a total picture?

Together they show the diversity of religions, their different geographic and age distributions, and their ethnic composition. The two sources of information flesh out our understanding of the subject.

Critical Thinking in Writing

What role does religion play in the life of someone in your home or school community? Write a few paragraphs to explore this issue.

5

Reading for the Main Idea

5a Key Ideas in Sentences

Although a sentence may give a great deal of information, it usually offers one key idea. Readers must be able to find key ideas in order to understand sentence meanings clearly.

The key idea of a sentence usually tells

- who a person or what an object is.
- what a person or an object is doing.

> A tall girl in a white dress rushed away into the trees just beyond the gate to Stevens Park.

This sentence tells about a girl. We know that the girl rushed away. All the information about her appearance, about where she ran, and about the name of the park adds details. These are helpful in completing the scene for the reader, and very often we need to rely on details to make the main text clearer. But the key idea, the main thought, in the sentence is simply *a girl rushed away.*

Here is how to find key ideas in sentences:

- Ask *who* or *what* the sentence is about.
- Ask what the person or object is doing or what is happening to that person or object.
- Learn to separate minor details from the main idea. Many words in sentences describe things about the subject of the sentence and merely add details around it. If you ask *when, what kind, where,* or *why,* you will find details. This makes it easier to separate the key idea.

(*why*) (*what kind*) (*where*)
Because of new laws, most foreign automobiles in the United
(*when*) (*how*)
States now offer safety features at no extra charge.

Who or what is the sentence about? *automobiles*
What do the automobiles do? *offer safety features*
The key idea is *automobiles offer safety features.*

Of course, you cannot always easily decide which details are simply descriptive and which contribute markedly to the key idea. You'll have to make your own decision about how various elements influence sentence meanings. In stating a key idea, you may have to shift words in the sentence around, you may have to summarize parts of the sentence, and you may have to put some of the writer's words into your own words.

The starting point for determining the key idea in a sentence, however, is finding who or what the sentence is about and what the person or object is doing.

EXERCISES

1. Key Ideas in Sentences

In each of the following sentences, underline the words that give the key idea. Here is an example.

> Fast <u>food chains</u>, which have grown rapidly over the last twenty years, <u>have replaced</u> many <u>restaurants</u>, including the corner luncheonette.

1. In the supermarkets, **basic foods**, such as fresh vegetables and meats, **have less shelf space**, as aisles become filled with prepared foods like chips, sodas, and fancy cereals.
2. **Advertisements** on radio, television, and other media **are** constantly **tempting people to spend money**, even if they have little.
3. Because new electronics products regularly come on the market, **consumers** always **have new things to buy**.
4. Even **banks**, which used to be places to simply deposit

your money, **have become financial centers**, offering many different kinds of accounts and financial investment opportunities.

5. Although figuring out how not to waste your money has become much more complicated and difficult, **people can** still **spend their money wisely**.

2. Key Ideas in Sentences

In the space provided after each sentence, write the key idea of that sentence. Look at the example.

Although everybody has thoughts about how they might like to make their life better, changing one's life takes more work, planning, and persistence than just having a good thought.

Improving life takes work, planning, and persistence.

1. The first thing you need to do in making life changes is set specific and difficult goals that will direct your energy.

   First, set goals.

2. To be sure you are really making progress toward achieving your goals, don't rely on hunches and feelings; instead, record exactly how your situation or behavior changes in relation to your goals.

   Record changes.

3. You also need to create a situation for change — a situation that will make it easier to move in the directions you want rather than in the way you have gone in the past.

   Create a situation for change.

4. By making it more difficult and less pleasant to engage in your old way of life as well as finding a situation that will

positively reward the changes you want to make, put yourself in an environment that supports change.

Put yourself in an environment for change.

5. As you notice positive changes happening, you should reward yourself by acknowledging them and in other ways.

   Reward yourself.

6. Finally, avoid being discouraged by the inevitable setbacks through seeking the support of friends and keeping long-range goals in mind.

   Avoid being discouraged.

3. Key Ideas from Textbooks

The following sentences come from basic college textbooks. On the blank lines, write in your own words the key idea of each statement.

1. *Biology*

   Even the simplest organisms consist of many parts and each of these must do the right thing at the right time for an appropriate action to be carried out.

   — *John W. Kimball*

   Each part of an organism must work right to carry out actions.

2. *Education*

   It is an accepted fact that students are getting substantial amounts of information and developing ideas and attitudes from watching television, but very little of that technological learning is occurring in schools, despite earlier promises.

   — *Robert W. Richey*

   Students learn information from watching

television that they are not learning at school.

3. *Chemistry*

Because of its cheapness and ready availability, oxygen is one of the most widely used industrial oxidizing agents.

— *Michell J. Sienko and Robert A. Plane*

Oxygen is widely used in industry.

4. *Psychology*

Psychologist Ernest Hilgard (1986) believes hypnosis is a form of dissociation, a state of awareness in which the subject's consciousness is divided into two streams — one that is aware of everything that is going on and one that is focusing on the hypnotist's suggestions.

Hypnosis is a form of dissociation.

Social role theories stress social expectations and the relationship between hypnotist and subject; according to these theories, the subject is doing what he or she believes is appropriate in the social situation.

— *James D. Laird and Nicholas S. Thompson*

Social role theories say subjects act as they think appropriate to the situation.

5. *Economics*

A market makes possible the exchange of goods and services between buyers and sellers, and that exchange determines the price of goods and services.

A market makes possible exchanges between buyers and sellers.

Buyers and sellers communicate with each other about the quality and quantity, what the buyers are willing and able to pay, and what the sellers must receive.

— *William Boyes and Michael Melvin*

Buyers and sellers communicate.

6. *Law*

William Blackstone, an English judge and author of "Commentaries on the Laws of England" (1765–1769), defined a crime as a wrong committed against the public, a definition that is still widely recognized as appropriate.

A crime is a wrong against the public.

Defining a wrong against the public is a responsibility of the government.

The government defines wrongs.

> In a democracy, this necessarily involves a balancing of interests: society needs to protect itself and its citizens from harm, but society must also protect the rights of individuals to be free from undue government interference.
>
> — *Harold Grilliot and Frank Schubert*

A democracy balances protection and the rights of

its citizens.

5b Topics and Main Ideas in Paragraphs

A *paragraph* is a group of sentences about some related subject or topic. Each sentence states some idea about the *topic,* and all those ideas add up to an overall *main idea* of the paragraph.

A main idea is not simply a topic. A topic is just the general subject that a paragraph deals with. A main idea, on the other hand, is the statement the paragraph makes about the topic. You often can state a topic in a single word; but to state a main idea clearly, you usually need a full sentence. The topic of the following paragraph is, simply, "the escalator"; but you would have to state the main idea more fully: "Although an escalator ride may be thrilling, escalators are now a safe and unremarkable part of our daily lives."

> Who has not felt a little thrill when about to hop onto an escalator? You step onto an already moving platform that unfolds itself into a staircase to sweep you upward above your plainly visible surroundings. The ride might almost have been created as an amusement-park attraction, yet it is so safe and mild it plays an unremarked role in our daily lives. The design seems fixed and basic, but it evolved in imperfect forms over three decades before a melding of ideas in the 1920s produced the escalator we know and ride today.
>
> — *William Worthington*

In the same way, the topic of the following paragraph is "the body's use of minerals." To express the main idea, however, requires a full sentence: "Minerals are essential to the body's function." This sentence makes a statement about the topic. The statement is a general idea that covers all the specific ideas in the paragraph.

> Substances found in the environment that are essential to the body's function are *minerals.* Minerals are used to regulate a wide range of body processes, from bone formation to blood clotting. They are also important to the body's structure. Except for iron, the body does not tend to store minerals. Iron tends to be conserved by the body, except when there is blood loss. Most minerals are quickly used or lost in waste products. This means you must eat mineral-rich foods regularly to replenish your supply. Your body uses larger amounts of calcium, phosphorus, and magnesium than of iodine, iron, and zinc.
>
> — *Bud Getchell, Rusty Pippin, and Jill Varnes*

In order to understand the meaning of a paragraph, readers must identify, first, the topic of the paragraph and, next, the main idea being presented about that topic. The topic may be stated in only a word or two, naming a thing, person, or event discussed throughout the paragraph. The main idea, however, is a more complete statement that ties all the ideas and information in the paragraph together. The main idea of a paragraph may be stated directly in a sentence, or it may only be implied in the overall message of all the sentences. When the main idea is stated directly, you need locate only the main idea sentence. When the main idea is implied, you must figure out the topic of the paragraph and the idea being stated about that topic.

EXERCISE

Topic and Main Idea in Textbook Paragraphs

For each of the following paragraphs from textbooks, state the topic and main idea in the appropriate spaces.

1. Have you ever noticed that sometimes a seven- or eight-year-old can spend hours absorbed in a single activity, like doing a jigsaw puzzle or playing Nintendo, whereas a toddler seems to bound back and forth from activity to activity? Even

if your experience with children is not extensive, most of us have a sense that older children are better able to "pay attention" to a given task than younger children. Parents read brief stories to their two-year-olds but expect their adolescent offspring to read novels. Preschool teachers present their charges with only occasional brief structured tasks, like painting or coloring; high school teachers expect their students to follow their lessons for an hour or more at a time. Clearly, children's attentional processes undergo recognizable changes with development.

— *Danuta Bukatko and Marvin Daehler*

Topic **children's attention spans**

Main idea **Children's attentional processes develop with age.**

2. Early European explorers and travelers in Africa were amazed at the variety of wildlife they found there. Huge flocks of birds lived around the African lakes, while herds of elephants, giraffes, zebras, wildebeest, leopards, and lions roamed the savanna. At first the Europeans exploited these animals as they did other African resources. Both African and European hunters killed many animals, either for sport or for valuable products such as ivory from elephant tusks. Wealthy Europeans went on safaris — trips through the jungle or grasslands to hunt animals and bring home trophies.

— *Marvin Perry*

Topic **Europeans in Africa**

Main idea **Europeans exploited the great variety of wildlife in Africa.**

3. Consumers usually want to create and maintain a collection of products that satisfy their needs and wants in both the present and future. To achieve this objective, consumers make many purchasing decisions. For example, people must make several decisions daily regarding food, clothing, shelter, medical care, education, recreation, or transportation. As they make these decisions, they engage in different decision-

making behaviors. The amount of effort, both mental and physical, that buyers expend in decision making varies considerably from situation to situation. Consumer decisions can thus be classified into one of three broad categories: routine response behavior, limited decision making, and extensive decision making.

— *William Pride and O. C. Ferrell*

Topic **consumer decisions**

Main idea **Consumers make decisions to select products that satisfy their needs and wants.**

4. New storage technologies are reducing the costs of disk storage. For most personal computer systems, magnetic disks will continue to dominate, and the introduction of new recording techniques will provide improved performance at lower cost. In ten years, diskettes with capacities in the tens of megabytes and hard disks with capacities in the hundreds of megabytes to gigabytes (hundreds of millions to billions) will be commonplace. Even so, magnetic disks face stiff competition from their optical cousins.

— *Robert H. Blissmer and Roland Alden*

Topic **disks**

Main idea **Computer memory storage is increasing rapidly with improved disk technology.**

5. The Constitution gives Presidents considerable leeway in taking and using the powers of the office. Some Presidents interpret the Constitution very strictly, and are unlikely to take any powers that previous Presidents have not used. They take history as their roadmap for future actions. Such Presidents use power sparingly and are willing to let Congress take policy initiatives. Historical examples include James Madison, James Buchanan, William Howard Taft, and Dwight Eisenhower (in his first term). At the other end of the spectrum are Presidents who interpret their powers broadly. Presidents with this philosophy break with tradition and

chart their own courses by taking bold, decisive actions. Most flourish during times of crisis — war or economic hardship. Examples include George Washington, Andrew Jackson, Abraham Lincoln, Theodore Roosevelt, and Franklin Roosevelt.

— *Richard J. Hardy*

Topic **presidential power**

Main idea **Some presidents interpret their constitutional powers strictly, while others interpret them more broadly.**

6. Creative thinking and critical thinking are as essential to effective thinking as a good offense and defense are to a winning football team. Both are essential in all areas of human activity. To put a new product on the market, the manufacturer must first "create" the idea for the new product. But if he has good business sense, he will not market the product until it has been thoroughly "criticized" by testing and evaluation. In solving a crime, a good detective "creates" possible explanations and then tests them with all the evidence he can get. If he fails to "create" the right explanations, he cannot possibly solve the crime. If he is careless in "criticizing" the explanations he has created, his "solution" of the crime may be the wrong one. In diagnosing an illness, the physician first "creates" possible diagnoses that seem to fit the symptoms and then "criticizes" these by further examination of the patient or by laboratory tests. His final diagnosis cannot be right unless the possible diagnoses he has "created" include the right one. Even when his possible diagnoses do include the right one, he may still make a mistake if he is careless in "criticizing" his possible diagnoses.

— *W. Edgar Moore*

Topic **creative and critical thinking**

Main idea **Creative and critical thinking is essential to all human activities.**

5b(1) *Stated Main Ideas*

Often one sentence in the paragraph tells the reader exactly what the rest of the paragraph deals with and therefore gives the main idea. This *main idea sentence* (it is often called a *topic sentence* or *topic statement*) may appear in one of several places.

Main Idea in the Beginning

> *As the sun went down, the scene from the bridge was beautiful.* It had been a perfect day. Up and down on either side of New York the bright blue water lay gently rippling, while to the south it merged into the great bay and disappeared toward the sea. The vast cities spread away on both sides. Beyond rolled the hilly country until it was lost in the mists of the sky. All up and down the harbor the shipping, piers, and buildings were still gaily decorated. On the housetops of both Brooklyn and New York were multitudes of people.
>
> — *David McCullough*

— ***Main idea at beginning***

The main idea of this passage is *the scene from the bridge was beautiful.* All the sentences in the paragraph illustrate that idea by providing many details.

Main Idea in the Middle

> There are 74.5 million television sets in the United States, at least one set for 98 percent of all American homes. Forty-eight percent of all U.S. homes have more than one set, and some families even have a set for every person in the house. *Yet, despite the fact that the number of sets in the United States has virtually reached a saturation point, the amount of time spent watching television has declined steadily since 1976.* Explanations vary from the increasingly poor quality of network shows to the rising popularity of home video equipment, but the fact remains that we are owning more sets but enjoying them less.

— ***Main idea in middle***

The main idea of this paragraph is *despite the fact that the number of television sets in the United States has virtually reached a saturation point, the amount of time spent watching television has declined steadily since 1976.*

Main Idea at the End

Although the buildings are tall, none of them blots out the sky. People rush about as in New York, but someone always stops to answer a question about directions. A person will listen when he or she is asked a question. Often a sudden smile will flash from the crowds of strangers pushing down State Street. It is a smile of welcome and of happiness at the same time. And the traffic: it is tough, noisy, active; but a person never feels as if he takes his life in his hands when he crosses the street. Of course, there is always the presence of the lake, the vast, shimmering lake that shines like an ocean of silver. Something about that lake each time it spreads out around a turn on Lakeshore Drive says, "Hello. It's good to see you again." *Chicago is a fine, friendly city.* — ***Main idea at end***

The main idea in the paragraph is *Chicago is a fine, friendly city*. All the sentences in the paragraph support that idea with details. By stating the main idea at the end, the author summarizes the point of the paragraph.

Main Idea in More Than One Sentence

Dogs make warm, friendly pets. But they can also be very troublesome. — ***Main idea in two sentences*** No one will deny the feeling of friendship when, after a long day's work, a wet pink tongue of greeting licks a master's hand at the door. And watching television or reading a book, a man or woman can reach down over the side of the couch and feel a warm furry patch of life, hear the quiet contented breathing of a good friend. However, try to plan a trip without your faithful pet and your life is very difficult. Where will you leave him? Who will feed him? Further, leaving a cozy house in the midst of winter and facing a howling frozen wind so the dog may take his walk is no pleasure at all. I often wonder why people put up with such demands upon their time and energy.

The main idea in this paragraph appears in two sentences. Although the first sentence of the selection says that dogs are warm, friendly pets, only part of the paragraph gives details to support that idea. Other details in the paragraph show that dogs are troublesome. An accurate statement of the main idea would have to include the information in both of the first two sentences: *Dogs make friendly pets, but they can also be troublesome.*

EXERCISE

Stated Main Ideas

For each of the following paragraphs, underline the sentence that tells the main idea. In the blank space write the main idea in your own words.

Student responses will vary.

1. Surprisingly, many liars are betrayed by their words because of carelessness. It is not that they couldn't disguise what they said, or that they tried to and failed, but simply that they neglected to fabricate carefully. The head of an executive search firm described a fellow who applied to his agency under two different names within the same year. When asking the fellow which name should he be called, "The man, who first called himself Leslie D'Ainter, but later switched to Lester Dainter, continued his prevaricating ways without skipping a beat. He explained that he changed his first name because Leslie sounded too feminine, and he altered his last name to make it easier to pronounce. But his references were the real giveaway. He presented three glowing letters of recommendation. Yet all three 'employers' misspelled the same word."

   — *Paul Ekman*

2. Ropemaking required room, lots of it, because rope was made in a straight line, and a rope made in one continuous length was much stronger than a rope pieced together from

many smaller lengths. To avoid space constraints, ropemaking was at first done outdoors. When the need to produce rope on a regular schedule came up against the vagaries of the weather, the earliest enclosed work spaces were constructed. Built to be longer than the longest rope that would be made, they often stretched for more than a thousand feet. These buildings were called ropewalks, because workers had to slowly pace the length of the building backward during the early phase of the ropemaking operation.

— *Barbara A. Merry and Ben Martinez*

3. I may be more upsettable than most, but during the years I was involved with carriages and strollers and wagons and tricycles, I was always getting bugged. Why wasn't there, even in the children's section of a department store, a high chair so you could deposit your child and spend your money in some sort of comfort? Why did it have to be a major struggle to get a stroller or a shopping cart across a street; would it cost so much to rake the curbs? And why did the entrance to the playground offer the steepest curb of all? Small enough problems, but enough to clue in to the fact that the last people anyone in charge of planning the city are concerned with are mothers and children.

— *Joanna Clark*

4. A strand of spider's silk is capable of holding five times more weight than a similar strand of steel, making it one of the strongest substances in the world. The silk is also extremely elastic: a strand only four-millionths of an inch in diameter can stretch to twice its original length before breaking. So if it were practical to harvest webs or to milk spiders, the diaphanous material would be ideal for industrial use.

— *Discovery*

____

____

5. Triumph in battle offers twin trophies to the victors. Their writers can impose on history their version of the war they won, while their statesmen can impose the terms of peace. In each case the opportunity was missed after the 1914–18 conflict. Ernest Hemingway later called it "the most colossal, murderous, mismanaged butchery that has ever taken place on earth," and the treaty-making assumptions of Allied leaders almost all proved falsely based. Those leaders, gathered around Paris in 1919 to draft the security they had pledged the world, found themselves trapped by secret promises they had made one another and by slogans they had uttered to hearten their mud-bound troops. When the machine guns subsided in November 1918, there was actually less chance of a safe and democratic earth than when the slaughter started, more than four years earlier.

— *R. L. Sulzberger*

____

____

6. America owes its progress as an industrial nation in large part to its ability to produce tremendous quantities of steel. Railway rails and cars, automobiles, all sorts of machinery, and huge buildings are only a few of the things which are made from steel. For centuries, steel was known to have qualities of strength and toughness not found in iron. But steel was too expensive to be widely used. Impurities had to be removed from iron to make steel, and no cheap method of removing these impurities was known. Then, in the 1850s, an Englishman, Henry Bessemer, and an American, William Kelly, each discovered a startling fact. Working on the same problem separately, they found that a blast of air directed at melted iron would remove its impurities. This new process of making steel was so cheap and easy that steel could be produced in large quantities and at low cost.

— *Wilder, Ludlum, and Brown*

7. People, as we know, have strong preferences for right or left, for clockwise versus counterclockwise movement. Is this true in the rest of the natural world? The answer is *yes:* animals and plants, even minerals, show clear preferences for the left or for the right in terms of growth and motion. "Hand" preference in nature — since rocks, plants and animals do not possess hands — expresses itself most basically in terms of the helix, a spiral curve through a cylindrical or conical shape. The helix may turn to the right, in a clockwise direction, or to the left, counterclockwise. The news is that Mother Nature isn't biased.

— *James Bliss and Joseph Morella*

8. Once beyond the age of two, Roadville boys and girls do not play together, but are sex segregated if there are playmates of the appropriate sex and age available. Friendships tend to develop between young mothers who have girls or boys of the right age to play together. Roadville divides its behaviors sharply into male and female, and this division begins for toddlers. Beyond rattles, stuffed animals, early ABC books, and books on basic objects, toys and games are sharply differentiated for boys and girls. Preschool girls are given Raggedy Ann dolls; boys are given Raggedy Andy. Girls are given metal tea sets; boys, plastic soldiers. Girls are given dollhouses and doll furniture; boys are given toy trucks, tractors, campers, and jeeps. Girls are given books about little girls, babies, and baby animals living in a human family-like setting; boys are given books about trucks, ballgames, and boys and their animals.

— *Shirley Brice Heath*

9. For the most part we think of portable radios as a post–World War II phenomenon. From the cheap plastic models of the 1950s to today's elaborate Walkmans, they have been among the most visible examples of the electronics revolution. But portable radios did not start with the invention of the transistor; their history stretches back more than two decades earlier. The 1920s gave birth to the boom box, but the boom box boom quickly went bust.

— *Michael Brian Schiffer*

5b(2) *Implied Main Ideas*

Sometimes paragraphs do not state exactly what the topic is. Instead, you must decide on the main idea yourself. In order to do that, you must add up all the details the writer gives and then state the main idea in your own words.

When the writer has not stated a main idea exactly, but instead *suggests* the idea to you through information in the paragraph, the idea is *implied*. An *implied main idea* is one that is suggested. Here is an example:

> The first boring task is to prepare breakfast. Johnny, Cathy, and Jed need juice and eggs before a day at school; my husband, Bill, coffee and toast before he speeds off to the office. When everyone is finally away, doing something he or she enjoys, I scrape the dishes off into the garbage, then wash them in the sink. I hate it! Afterwards I look forward to making beds, washing the kitchen floor, cleaning the rug in the living room. If I'm lucky the mailman rings the bell so I talk to another human being in the flesh for ten seconds or so. I put up the roast, find some other things to do, all along thinking of the adventures my children meet in the classroom while their homemaker-mother watches the house in the suburbs. And Bill, the people he meets, the glamorous lunches, the excitement he sees on the streets every day; these are things I'll never know from this position. I sweep floors, sew buttons, clink pots and pans — that's my work for the world.

One way to state the main idea of the paragraph is *My life as a homemaker is filled with dull, meaningless tasks.* No one sentence makes this point. Furthermore, the writer never tells us exactly that her life is filled with dull chores. Instead we add up the details she gives us in order to state the main idea in our own words. She finds making breakfast dull, washing dishes boring, and cleaning the house lonely and tiresome. She envies the excitement that her husband finds in his work. Putting all this information together, we conclude that this writer is trying to show us that she leads a dull life as a homemaker.

Here is how to state the main idea in your own words:

- Try to figure out what *all* the details in the paragraph are trying to show, not just a few of them.
- Make a complete sentence that (1) names a person or an object and (2) tells what the person or object is doing.
- Do not look at just a few sentences in the paragraph in order to find out the main idea. Even though the first few sentences of this paragraph express the idea that giving breakfast to the family is dull, it would not be correct to say that the sentence *Serving breakfast is a dull task* is the main idea of the paragraph. The sentence is true; we know that from statements in the paragraph. But the sentence is not the *main* idea; it is only one narrow idea that helps us build the main idea sentence: *My life as a homemaker is filled with dull, meaningless tasks.*
- Do not offer a statement that is *too general* as the main idea. For example, it would be incorrect to say that the main idea of the paragraph is *The job of the American homemaker is dull and meaningless.* The author of the paragraph might agree with this statement. But no details in the paragraph suggest that the writer is talking about the American homemaker in general. The author is talking about *herself;* she is showing that *her* job is dull and meaningless, so the main idea should be stated in these terms: *My life as a homemaker is filled with dull, meaningless tasks.*

EXERCISES

1. Implied Main Ideas

In each of the following paragraphs the main idea is implied. In your own words write the implied main idea in the blanks.

1. Wednesday was the day we had planned to go fishing. Tuesday afternoon we took the fishing tackle out of the closet, checked it over, and untangled the lines. In the evening we dug up worms from the garden and put them in a bait box. We checked the weather reports and set the alarm for 5:00 A.M. In the morning we trudged out the door, bleary eyed, with coffee mugs in one hand and gear in the other.

We had many things to do in order to prepare for our next day's fishing trip.

2. My little brother has seen all the Star Trek and Star Wars movies. He regularly watches all the science fiction series on television. He even made me buy him model spaceships for his birthday.

My brother loves the idea of outer space.

3. After the teacher handed out three pages of instructions for the assignment, he left no time for us to ask questions, and he wasn't available in his office. When I asked my classmates if they understood what we had to do, they all gave different explanations. Even my friend who had taken the course the previous semester couldn't help me.

I was very confused about my homework assignment.

4. The beach was crowded, the parking lot was full, and the highway was backed up. But there was no swimming or sun bathing or volleyball going on. From one edge to the other, the beach was lined with people carrying signs, among them "Keep our beaches free," "How much should a sunset cost?" and "No parking fees." The town council heard the message.

Citizens crowded the beach area to protest fees to the town council.

2. Implied Main Ideas

Read the following brief passages. Add up all the details in your mind in order to figure out the implied main idea. Write a sentence that tells the main idea of the paragraph.

1. Third Avenue. As far as the eye could see, the cobblestone street was saddled by a great, black, spider-like iron monster called the "Third Ave. El." It cast a checkerboard shadow, alternating with shafts of sunlight like a huge web draped across the wide boulevard waiting for unsuspecting victims. I remember sitting on the curb, staring across to the east side of the street, the ominous, forboding presence of the "El" weighing on my 8-year-old mind and giving more substance to the taboo that Third Avenue was for the Puerto Rican kid in East Harlem.

   — *Humberto Cintrón*

   The "El" made Third Avenue seem ominous.

2. Understanding stepfamilies is important to businesses simply because so many Americans are involved in them. But stepfamilies also have unique needs for products and services. Children who travel between families need duplicate supplies, from toothbrushes to clothes and teddy bears. Some stepfamilies plan their summer vacations around custody considerations, and even small children with divorced parents sometimes travel great distances alone. And the physical needs are only part of the story. Psychological strains on stepfamilies influence their financial position, their need for family counseling, their requirements for health insurance, and their legal rights.

   — *Jan Larson*

   Stepfamilies have special needs, physical and psychological.

3. A pair of identical snowflakes was the last thing cloud physicist Nancy Knight expected to find. Everyone knows that no two snowflakes are alike. Yet there they were, collected on an oil-coated glass slide; the slide had been suspended from

an airplane flying through a snow cloud on a routine run for the National Center for Atmospheric Research in Boulder. Knight had two snow crystals that, as she cautiously puts it, "if not identical, are certainly very much alike." Her husband, Charles Knight, also a cloud physicist at the center, is more than cautious. "When my wife showed me the slide I said, 'Impossible.' I still think it's impossible."

Impossible, that is, that the two crystals should be precisely identical. The Knights are loath to dispute the old adage, because they know the extraordinary odds against two snow crystals — not to speak of snowflakes, which are usually clumps of crystal — being even strongly similar.

— *Shawna Vogel*

Despite many impressions to the contrary, two snow crystals were found to be exactly alike.

4. Pollyanna was right, new research shows. Optimism — at least reasonable optimism — can pay dividends as wide-ranging as health, longevity, job success and higher scores on achievement tests. Pessimism not only has the opposite effect but also seems to be at play in such psychological disorders as extreme shyness and depression.

— *Daniel Goleman*

One's outlook toward life can influence health and happiness.

5. Psychologists are tracking the importance of how people explain their failures to themselves. People tend to have a habitual explanatory style, a typical way of explaining the events that befall them, according to work by Martin Seligman, a psychologist at the University of Pennsylvania. Pessimists, Dr. Seligman has found, tend to construe bad events such as flunking an exam or giving a party that flops as resulting from a personal deficit that will plague them forever in everything they do. Others see the same setbacks more optimistically, as being due to mistakes that can be remedied. They feel they can make the necessary changes.

— *Daniel Goleman*

People have different ways of explaining their failures.

6. Working with the dean of admissions at the University of Pennsylvania, Dr. Seligman and Leslie Kamen tested 500 members of the incoming freshman class in 1984. Using a composite of the student's high school grades and college entrance examination scores, the Dean's office is able to predict what each student's freshman year grades should be. The test of explanatory style, however, was able to predict which freshmen would do better than expected and which would do worse. "College entrance exams measure talent, while explanatory style tells you who gives up," Dr. Seligman said. "It is the combination of reasonable talent and the ability to keep going in the face of defeat that leads to success. What's missing in tests of ability is a measure of motivation. What you need to know about someone is whether they will keep going when things become frustrating."

— *Daniel Goleman*

Not only test scores and grades predict college success; explanatory style also is important in making predictions about college freshmen.

Critical Thinking in Writing

The selection above says that what leads to success is "the combination of reasonable talent and the ability to keep going in the face of defeat." Do you agree? Why or why not? How would you define success?

3. Implied Main Ideas

In each of the following selections, the main idea is implied. Read the selection and the statements that follow. Then put a checkmark next to the statement that you think best gives the main idea most clearly. Be prepared to explain why the other choices are not correct.

1. This Alaska river we're crossing pours out of a nearby glacier and braids its way down a gravel floodplain nearly a mile wide. The water is rock stew, so thick and gray you can't tell whether your next step is going to be a few inches deep or a few feet. Bet on a few feet. The flow is very high just now, swollen from several days of unusually hot June weather, and very strong. When you lift your leg, the current tries to toss it downstream; when you don't, the current eats away the gravel you're standing on and you sink by degrees. Larger rocks roll against your legs in the meantime, threatening to bowl you down. Their tumbling makes the whole river growl.

— Douglas H. Chadwick

_______ a. You can't tell the depth of the river.

√______ b. The river is filled with dangers.

_______ c. Alaskan rivers are the most treacherous in the United States.

_______ d. Rocks and currents cause rivers to growl.

2. The other day I came across some old record albums. One of them was a Nat King Cole, and I would have loved to play it, but I have not owned a functioning record player for years. For a time I had some broken or malfunctioning ones, but there seemed no reason to have them repaired since I was moving into compact discs. So, inevitably, inadvertently and just plain somehow, the phonographs disappeared and so did almost my entire record collection, which included, should you be interested, a Beethoven's Fifth in a green jacket that featured a bust of an extremely stern-looking Beethoven. It was the first album I ever bought.

— Richard Cohen

_______ a. Nat King Cole is one of my favorite singers.

_______ b. I no longer own a record player.

_______ c. My first record was of Beethoven's Fifth Symphony.

√______ d. Compact discs have made my record collection outdated.

3. The idea *happiness*, to be sure, will not sit still for easy definition: the best one can do is try to set some extremes to the idea and then work in toward the middle. To think of happiness as acquisitive and competitive will do to set the materialistic extreme. To think of it as the idea one senses in, say, a holy man of India will do to set the spiritual extreme. That holy man's idea of happiness is in needing nothing from outside himself. In wanting nothing, he lacks nothing. He sits immobile, rapt in contemplation, free even of his own body. Or nearly free of it. If devout admirers bring him food he eats it; if not, he starves indifferently. Why be concerned? What is physical is an illusion to him. Contemplation is his joy and he achieves it through a fantastically demanding discipline, the accomplishment of which is itself a joy within him.

— *John Ciardi*

______ a. Happiness as an idea exists in avoiding extremes.

______ b. We can define happiness by seeing what makes us happy.

√ ______ c. The definition of happiness exists between two extremes.

______ d. Only people who are extreme are happy.

4. There are times when I find myself spending the night in the home of another. Frequently the other is in a more reasonable line of work than I and must arise at a specific hour. Ofttimes the other, unbeknownst to me, manipulates an appliance in such a way that I am awakened by Stevie Wonder. On such occasions I announce that if I wished to be awakened by Stevie Wonder I would sleep with Stevie Wonder. I do not, however, wish to be awakened by Stevie Wonder and that is why God invented alarm clocks. Sometimes the other realizes that I am right. Sometimes the other does not. And that is why God invented *many* others.

— *Fran Liebowitz*

______ a. The author does not like Stevie Wonder's music.

√ ______ b. The author does not like to be awakened by music.

_______ c. The author does not like to wake up in the morning.

_______ d. The author believes that God invented the alarm clock.

5. The last inch of space was filled, yet people continued to wedge themselves along the walls of the Store. Uncle Willie had turned the radio up to its last notch so that youngsters on the porch wouldn't miss a word. Women sat on kitchen chairs, dining-room chairs, stools and upturned wooden boxes. Small children and babies perched on every lap available and men leaned on the shelves or on each other.

— *Maya Angelou*

_______ a. There was little room left in the store for the people who wanted to be there.

_______ b. Uncle Willie made sure that everyone heard the radio.

√_______ c. Crowds of people gathered in the store to listen to important news on the radio.

_______ d. Children and young babies sat on their parents' laps.

4. Main Ideas in Paragraphs: A Review

In the following paragraphs, the main idea is either stated or implied. [See sections **5b(1)** and **5b(2)**.] Try to determine the main idea of each selection. Write the main idea in your own words in the space provided.

1. Almost 240 years earlier, another Ben sent his kite up into a thunderstorm in a flashy experiment that still burns bright in the memory of schoolchildren. While not the first to use kites in the service of meteorology, Benjamin Franklin captured widespread public attention with his shocking exploits. After the invention of the box design in 1893, the U.S. Weather Bureau adopted kites as a meteorological tool, flying them from a network of stations for the next 30 years. But with improvements in scientific balloons and the growing importance of airplanes, the popularity of research kites plummeted in the years following World War I. In 1933, the Weather Bureau finally closed its last station dedicated to this task. In recent decades, kites have served in a mere handful of atmospheric experiments.

— *Richard Monastersky*

Kites have been used in meteorological experiments since the time of Benjamin Franklin.

2. Richard Lazarus (1981), another well-known stress researcher, has concluded that our "everyday hassles" may play an even larger role in the development of physical and emotional illness than do major life events. Indeed, recent research underscores the relationship between daily **hassles** and common health problems such as headaches, backaches, sore throats, and flu (DeLongis et al., 1988). Even depression and a negative sense of well-being have been strongly linked to an accumulation of daily hassles (Holahan & Holahan, 1987). Losing things, running short of money, having car trouble, and working late are among the common offenders. Lazarus suggests that you need to balance daily hassles with daily **uplifts,** such as visiting with friends, completing a job, eating out, and getting a good night's rest. A two-to-one ratio of uplifts to hassles should keep stress at a manageable level.

— *Robert Williams and James Long*

Hassles can cause stress and illness.

3. When you watch a bird over the beach or a fish along the reef you realize how ill-adapted man is to this environment anyway. Physically there is nothing he can do that some other creature cannot do better. Only his neocortex, the "thinking cap" on top of his brain, has enabled him to invent and construct artificial aids to accomplish what he could not do by himself. He cannot fly, so he has developed airplanes that can go faster than birds. He is slower than the horse, so he invented the wheel and the internal combustion engine. Even in his ancestral element, the sea, he is clumsy and short of breath. Without his brain, his artificial aids, his technology, he would have been unable to cope with, even survive in, his environment. But only after so many centuries is his brain dimly realizing that while he has managed to control his environment, he has so far been unable to protect it.

— *A. B. C. Whipple*

Humans are ill-suited physically to survive, but

thanks to their brains they have created artificial aids to cope with the environment.

4. The demand to "make something of yourself" through work is one that Americans coming of age hear as often from themselves as from others. It encompasses several different notions of work and of how it bears on who we are. In the sense of a "job," work is a way of making money and making a living. It supports a self defined by economic success, security, and all that money can buy. In the sense of a "career," work traces one's progress through life by achievement and advancement in an occupation. It yields a self defined by a broader sort of success, which takes in social standing and prestige, and by a sense of expanding power and competency that renders work itself a source of self-esteem. In the strongest sense of a "calling," work constitutes a practical ideal of activity and character that makes a person's work morally inseparable from his or her life. It subsumes the self into a community of disciplined practice and sound judgment whose activity has meaning and value in itself, not just in the output or profit that results from it. But the calling not only links a person to his or her fellow workers. A calling links a person to the larger community, a whole in which the calling of each is a contribution to the good of all. . . . The calling is a crucial link between the individual and the public world. Work in the sense of the calling can never be merely private.

— *Robert Bellah*

A person's work has meaning or value in his or her life; it is not simply a means of production or profit.

5. As with so many problems that overwhelm our sensibilities, the facts about child abuse have become mind-numbing: over 50,000 killed since 1965; at least 2.5 million children victimized each year; thousands afflicted with neurological and physical handicaps and life-long emotional scars. The US Advisory Board on Child Abuse and Neglect was not overstating the case in a recent report when it called the situation "a

national emergency" and concluded that "the system the nation has devised to respond . . . is failing."

— *Jetta Bernier*

Child abuse has reached mind-numbing proportions.

Critical Thinking in Writing

Write a letter to the editor of your local newspaper outlining the steps you believe we should take to reduce child abuse in this country.

5. Main Ideas from Textbooks: A Review

The paragraphs below come from college texts. After you read each selection, try to determine the main idea. Then, from the choices given, put a checkmark next to the statement that best states the main idea. Remember: Some main ideas are stated; others are only implied.

1. *Marketing*

Eastman Kodak Co., one of the world's leading photographic companies, makes innovation a part of its everyday company strategy. Recently, Kodak introduced a line of single-use, or disposable, cameras. These cameras are very simple to operate: all one needs to do is aim and push a button. There are no adjustments for light level, exposure time, or focusing. After shooting all the exposures, the customer turns in the entire camera to the film processor. Depending on the model, these cameras retail from $8.35 for the Fling, to around $14 for the more specialized models. One model is a modified wide-angle camera; another can take pictures up to twelve feet underwater. They all use 35mm color film. Very inexpensive to produce, these cameras are basically just a role of film in an encasement of plastic that has an elementary lens on the front and a minimum of internal parts. Kodak executives hope that the disposable cameras (Kodak prefers the name "single-use" cameras) become highly profitable.

— *William Pride and O. C. Ferrell*

______ a. Eastman Kodak is an innovative company.

______ b. Single-use cameras come in a variety of types, but they are all simple to use.

______ c. Disposable cameras are inexpensive to produce and will prove profitable.

√_____ d. The single-use camera is an example of Kodak's innovative strategy.

2. *Psychology*

Who decides what is maladaptive or abnormal? When is treatment required? In large measure, the society or culture shapes the answers to such questions. If you live in a tolerant society and do not upset other people too much, you can behave in some rather unusual ways and still not be officially diagnosed or treated for psychopathology. For example, our collection of recent news clippings contains stories about (1) a man in Long Beach, California, who moved out of his apartment, leaving behind sixty thousand pounds of rocks, chunks of concrete, and slabs of cement neatly boxed and stacked in every room; and (2) a Richmond, California, woman whose unexplained habit of opening all her faucets (some connected to garden hoses hanging from trees) regularly consumed over twenty thousand gallons of water a day until a judge ordered a flow restrictor placed on her meter. In a less tolerant country, these individuals might be taken into custody and subjected to treatment or imprisonment.

— *Douglas A. Bernstein, Edward J. Roy, Thomas K. Srull, and Christopher D. Wickens*

______ a. The United States is tolerant of unusual behavior.

√_____ b. What is considered psychologically abnormal varies from culture to culture.

______ c. More people should receive treatment for psychopathologies.

______ d. People who do not harm anyone else should be allowed to do as they wish.

3. *History*

The population of a given place can grow in three ways: by extension of its borders to include nearby land and people; by natural increase — an excess of births over deaths; and by migration — an excess of in-migrants over out-migrants. Between the Civil War and the early 1900s, many cities annexed nearby suburbs, thereby increasing their populations. The most notable consolidation occurred in 1898 when New York City, which had previously consisted only of Manhattan, merged with four surrounding boroughs and grew overnight from 1.5 million to over 3 million people. Although annexation did increase urban populations, its major effect was to enlarge the physical size of cities. As death rates declined in the late nineteenth century, the populations of most cities increased naturally. But urban birthrates also fell steadily throughout the nineteenth century. As a result, natural increase did not account for very much of any city's population growth. Migration and immigration made by far the greatest contribution to urban population growth. In fact, migration to cities nearly matched the migration to the West that was occurring at the same time. Each year millions of people were on the move, many of them lured by the cities' promise of opportunity. Urban newcomers arrived from two major sources: the American countryside and Europe. Asia, Canada, and Latin America also supplied immigrants, but in smaller numbers.

— *Mary Beth Norton, David M. Katzman, Paul D. Escott, Howard Chudacoff, Thomas G. Paterson, and William M. Tuttle, Jr.*

______ a. In the late nineteenth century, many cities increased in size.

______ b. In the late nineteenth century, both death- and birthrates declined.

______ c. In the late nineteenth century, most immigration to the cities came from rural areas and Europe.

√_____ d. In the late nineteenth century, American cities grew mostly because of immigration and only secondarily because of expansion.

4. *Ecology*

Certain terms are used in ecology to provide a consistent description of conditions and events. A *population* refers to all of the members of a given species that live in a particular location. For example, a beech-maple forest will contain a population of maple trees, a population of beech trees, a population of deer, and populations of other species of plants and animals. All of the plant and animal populations living and interacting in a given environment are known as a *community*. The living community and the nonliving environment work together in a cooperative ecological system known as an *ecosystem*. An ecosystem has no size requirement or set boundaries. A forest, a pond and a field are examples of ecosystems. So is an unused city lot, a small aquarium, the lawn in front of a residential dwelling, or a crack in a sidewalk. All of these examples reflect areas where interaction is taking place between living organisms and the nonliving environment.

— *Gabrielle I. Edwards*

_______ a. An ecosystem is an area several miles across.

√______ b. Ecologists use terms like *ecosystem*, *population*, and *community* to describe conditions and events in a consistent way.

_______ c. Nonliving things are not important to ecologists' work.

_______ d. In ecology it is very important always to count the number of animals, plants, and nonliving elements found in a location.

5. *Economics*

The purpose of markets is to facilitate the exchange of goods and services between buyers and sellers. In some cases money changes hands; in others only goods and services are exchanged. The exchange of goods and services directly, without money, is called **barter.** Barter occurs when a plumber fixes a leaky pipe for a lawyer in exchange for the lawyer's work on a will; when a Chinese citizen provides fresh vegetables to an American visitor in exchange for a pack of American cigarettes; and when children trade baseball cards. Most markets involve money because goods and services can be exchanged more easily with money than without it. When IBM purchases microchips from Yakamoto of Japan, IBM and Yakamoto do not engage in barter. One firm may not have what the other wants. Barter requires a **double coincidence of wants:** IBM must have what Yakamoto wants, and Yakamoto must have what IBM wants. The **transaction costs** (the costs involved in making an exchange) of finding a double coincidence of wants for barter transactions are typically very high. Money reduces these transaction costs. To obtain the microchips, all IBM has to do is provide dollars to Yakamoto. Yakamoto accepts the money because it can spend the money to obtain the goods that it wants.

— *William Boyes and Michael Melvin*

______ a. Barter is exchange without the use of money.

√_____ b. Markets allow the exchange of goods and services through either money or barter.

______ c. Money is more convenient than barter.

______ d. Double coincidence of wants rarely occurs in international trade.

6

Reading for Information

The first step in reading for specific information is to look for the main idea. In a one-paragraph selection, you add up all the sentences to find the main idea. In a longer work, you add up the main ideas of the various paragraphs in order to figure out the main idea of the whole selection.

But the main idea does not give you all the information you need. Facts and details appear within the paragraphs you read that help develop the main ideas of the paragraphs. These facts and details may paint a more complete picture, give examples to help you understand the ideas better, prove a point, or show how the idea relates to other ideas. To make the best use of these facts and details, you have to be able to

- find important facts and remember them.
- separate major facts and details from minor facts and details.

For a particular course, you can have a better sense of how to use a book if you know how your instructor *expects* you to use it. Often your syllabus or course outline tells you just how to approach a book; sometimes your instructor explains what you are to do with a text.

Do you need to understand ideas or memorize facts from the book? Are you supposed to take the book as absolute truth or as something to think about? Will you be asked to relate the concepts or facts from this book to other material you have read? A course that requires several books may demand different kinds of reading for those several books. Is one book the basic text for the course? Is another book just a supplement, something added to flesh out instruction? Does a third book repeat the lectures you hear each day? If you ask yourself — and your instructor — some of these questions, you'll know what to do with your text for a given class.

6a Fact-Finding

To find and remember important facts, you must be an active, aware reader. Here are nine ways to locate facts:

- Have a definite purpose for reading. Are you reading a page of your biology book to find out how the eye works? Are you reading a chapter of a political science text to learn the meaning of *democracy*? Are you reading the newspaper out of general interest or for a specific research project?
- Learn to read for the main idea. If you recognize the main idea easily, the facts to support that idea will stand out.
- Know that all facts and details are not equal in importance. Look only for the facts that relate to the main idea.
- Look for information in groups or units. Facts often appear together in clumps.
- Look for the way the paragraph is put together. How is the information arranged? Has the writer organized the material in terms of a pattern that is easy to see?
- Learn to keep an author's *opinions* apart from the *facts* offered in the writing.
- Question yourself as you read. Stop to think and to let facts sink in before you rush on to other information. Ask yourself, "What does that mean?" or "What does that information tell me?" or "Why is this information here?"
- Use the five *W*s when you read in order to ask yourself specific questions about the facts.

    1. Ask yourself "Who?" Then look for the name of someone or something.
    2. Ask yourself "When?" Then look for a date (a day, a month, a year) or a time of day or year.
    3. Ask yourself "Where?" Then look for words that show a location or name a place.
    4. Ask yourself "What?" or "What happened?" Then look for some action.
    5. Ask yourself "Why?" Then look for an explanation of some act or event.

- Think about the kinds of questions someone might ask you about the information you have read. Go back after you have finished to reread quickly and review any facts you have learned. Try to summarize the important facts in your mind.

Look at the following selection about an unusual court case in the Philippines to find the main idea, to see how the information is organized, and to answer the five *W*s. The comments in the margin illustrate fact-finding.

20th-Century Lawsuit Asserts Stone-Age Identity

Members of a primitive tribe claiming a jungle cave — ***Who?***
for its home took a giant step into the 20th century — ***When?***
this week by filing a lawsuit against two anthropologists who say they are a hoax. — ***What happened?***

"We are the forest," the tribeswoman Dul said gravely before affixing her thumbprint to the complaint. "We are the Tasaday." — ***More information on the people in the story***

"We are as real as the forest and the flowers and the trees and the stream," she said through an interpreter. "We are as strong as the stone of the cave of Tasaday."

The suit was filed Monday by four members of the group known as the Tasaday, who were first described in 1971 as a Stone Age tribe of forest gatherers who dressed in orchid leaves and bark and had no word for war, enemy or ocean. — ***Where are they from?***

Visits by Journalists

Since 1986 they have been in the news again after visits by several journalists who found them to possess bits of clothing, knives and trinkets and proclaimed them to be a fraud perpetrated by Ferdinand E. Marcos when he was President. — ***More information on the conflict that led to the court case***

The group's complaint names the two anthropologists who are among their most insistent debunkers, Jerome Bailen and Zeus Salazar of the University of the Philippines, and asks that the Tasaday be left in peace in the forest preserve set aside by Mr. Marcos on Mindanao Island. — ***Who are the opponents in the conflict?***

The four tribespeople were joined in their complaint by their protector, Manuel Elizalde Jr., the — ***Who?***

man accused of concocting the fraud in his role as Mr. Marcos's Minister for Tribal Minorities.

Mr. Bailen has called the Tasaday "the most elaborate hoax perpetrated on the anthropological world" since the Piltdown man, human skeletal remains discovered in England in 1908, falsely attributed to the Lower Pleistocene epoch and then proved a hoax in 1950.

— ***What is the conflict about?***
— ***What does one side believe?***

Persuaded to Wear Leaves

He and Mr. Salazar say Mr. Elizalde, for his own reasons, persuaded members of another more advanced tribal group to wear leaves, make stone implements and pose as cave-dwellers.

The legal complaint insists that the Tasaday are "a separate ethnic community" with their own language and forest home who until this generation had believed that they were the only people in the world.

— ***What does the other side believe?***

It cites a still-unreleased report by a committee of the Philippine Congress that reverses that body's position and declares the group to be genuine. According to the report, those who cry fraud have failed to prove their case.

— *Seth Mydans*

Did you have a purpose in reading? Did you use the words *unusual court case in the Philippines* in the instructions to help you read for special information? Did you ask yourself these questions as you read: What is the main idea? How is the information arranged? Which facts are most important? What questions might someone ask about this selection?

EXERCISES

1. Fact-Finding: A Review

Reread the selection beginning on page 153.

1. What is the main point of the selection? **A primitive tribe is suing two anthropologists who claim the tribe is a fake.**

2. What are two questions someone might ask about the selection?

   Who are these tribal people? What is their life like?

   How could the tribe be fake? Why do some anthropologists think the tribe is fake? What does the tribe want?

3. Write down three of the most important facts.

   The Tasaday were first described in 1971 and were called a "Stone Age tribe." Recently they have been found to have modern objects. Some anthropologists claim that a government official persuaded members of a more advanced tribe to fake being cave-dwellers. The tribe wants to be left alone.

4. At what paragraph does the writer start to give you less important facts about the incident? **paragraph 6**

2. Reading for Facts

Read the following paragraphs about the modern kitchen to find the main idea and to discover some of the major facts about the uses people have for their kitchens. Then answer the questions.

> Kitchens are for more than just cooking. Most Americans also use them as places to eat, talk, entertain, work, and relax. Americans are also fond of kitchen-oriented products and services that have more to do with self-image than with food.

That's why a recent advertisement for General Electric appliances says, "You may call it a kitchen, but we know it's your living room."

In 1991, Americans spent $88 billion to redesign their kitchens. Almost every dollar went toward the goal of creating a larger, more complex space.

Three out of four people who come to kitchen designers say that family socializing in the kitchen is an extremely or very important part of their lives, according to a survey of designers conducted by the Maytag Corporation. Two-thirds say that entertaining in the kitchen is important enough that their new kitchens must have a bar. Six in ten want their kitchens to include a place to study or work. And more than one-third (39 percent) of kitchen redesign clients want to do their laundry in the place where they prepare food.

In the 1990s, televisions, stereos, and even pool tables are showing up next to the refrigerators and coffeemakers. "It's hard to tell how big kitchens are getting," says Leslie Hart, editor of *Kitchen and Bath Business,* "because kitchens are opening into family rooms."

— *Susan Krafft*

1. What is the main idea of this selection?

   Kitchens serve many functions.

2. How much did Americans spend in 1991 to redesign kitchens, and what was most of the money spent on?

   $88 billion, to create a larger, more complex space

3. What fraction of Americans say that socializing in the kitchen is important to their family life?

   three-fourths

4. What percentage want a bar in their kitchen? What percentage want a place to study? What percentage want a laundry?

   bar: 67 percent; study: 60 percent; laundry: 39 percent

5. What are some unusual items that are now being located in kitchens?

   televisions; stereos; pool tables

Critical Thinking in Writing

How does the kitchen function in your home? Write a paragraph to describe the different uses your family members make of your kitchen.

3. Reading with a Purpose

Read the following explanation about two sports used for self-defense to learn their differences and similarities. Then answer the questions that follow.

Judo and Karate

Judo and karate are sports for self-defense. They began in the eastern part of the world, but now many Americans enjoy them too. In fact, schools for teaching them have been opened all over the United States and Canada.

Players in both sports use only their hands, arms, legs, and feet. Aside from that, the two sports are quite different. In karate, players hit each other with the open hand and with the closed fist. They also use the foot for kicking. In judo, players are more likely to throw one another. Then they try to pin each other down. In judo, then, players touch each other. They also move their arms and legs in large circles. Karate moves, on the other hand, are short and quick. Players stand away from each other. They only touch one another with quick punches and kicks.

Can a karate player beat a judo player? It depends on the players. One sport is not better than the other. They are both very good forms of self-defense. Both aim toward control of the mind and body. A wise old man in Japan had a good answer to the question. He said, "We do not say the other martial arts are bad. The mountain does not laugh at the river because it is lowly, nor does the river speak ill of the mountain because it cannot move about."

— *Jeannette Bruce*

1. What is the main idea of the selection?

   to compare and contrast judo and karate

2. Which details help you understand how to do karate?

   Players hit each other with open hands and closed fists; they also kick. Moves are short and quick; players touch with quick punches only.

3. Which details help you understand how to do judo?

   Players throw each other and then try to pin each other down; they touch and move their arms and legs in large circles.

4. Suppose a friend asked you for advice about which sport was better than the other. Which information would help you answer the question?

   Student responses will vary.

6b Major Details, Minor Details

It's obvious that not all facts in a paragraph have the same importance. In the selection on pages 153–154, for example, the names of two anthropologists and the report of the Philippine Congress are among the less important details. Because you do not need these details to understand the selection, the information they give is minor. Minor details help round out a paragraph and often hold our attention to make the material we are reading more interesting. Still, we can ignore minor details if our goal is a quick understanding of what we've read. Details that give major information about the main idea, however, are very important.

Here is how to find major details:

- State the main idea in your own words.
- Look only for information that supports the main idea.
- Read quickly over the words or sentences that give information that is not important to the main idea.
- Look for signal words like *most important, first, finally, the facts are,* and so on.
- Underline the major details when you locate them.

Here is how one student separated the major details from the minor details in a passage she was reading to learn about *culture shock* for her course in sociology.

> Anthropologists use the term "culture shock" to describe the impact of a totally new culture upon a newcomer. In an extreme instance such shock will be experienced by the Western explorer who is told, halfway through dinner, that he is eating the nice old lady he had been chatting with the previous day — a shock with predictable physiological if not moral consequences. Most explorers no longer encounter cannibalism in their travels today. However, the first encounters with polygamy or with puberty rites or even with the way some nations drive their automobiles can be quite a shock to an American visitor. With the shock may go not only disapproval or disgust but a sense of excitement that things can *really* be that different from what they are at home. To some extent, at least, this is the excitement of any first travel abroad. The experience of sociological discovery could be described as "culture shock" minus geographical displacement. In other words, the sociologist travels at home — with shocking results. He is unlikely to find that he is eating a nice old lady for dinner. But the discovery, for instance, that his own church has considerable money invested in the missile industry or that a few blocks from his home there are people who engage in cultic orgies

Main idea: sociologists, like anthropologists, get shocked by a culture, but the sociologist looks at his own culture instead of foreign ones

> may not be drastically different in emotional impact. Yet we would not want to imply that sociological discoveries are always or even usually outrageous to moral sentiment. Not at all. What they have in common with exploration in distant lands, however, is the sudden illumination of new and unsuspected facets of human existence in society.
>
> — *Peter Berger*

Notice that by underlining, the student focuses only on details that help explain the main idea directly. Some of these details are the concept of culture shock, the reaction to shocking events, and the kinds of shocking things that a sociologist can find in the United States.

Notice, too, those details the student passes over as not so important. Some unimportant details are the nice old lady being served for dinner, the decrease in cannibalism today, and the experience of the first trip abroad. These minor details make the main idea more vivid, but the main idea can be understood without them.

EXERCISES

1. Separating Major Details from Minor Details

Read this paragraph about how Napoleon was inspired by a pyramid. Then answer the questions that follow.

> The grandeur of the Great Pyramid at Giza challenged the young Napoleon's imperial imagination. When the ambitious 29-year-old general led his ill-starred expedition to Egypt in 1798, he visited Giza where he was awed by what he saw. Some of his officers climbed all 450 feet to the top of the Great Pyramid, but Napoleon remained below, drawing and calculating. We still have his sketches of the Giza pyramids and his notes. Napoleon reportedly informed his generals, after their descent, that the three pyramids contained enough stone to build a wall 10 feet high and one foot wide around all of France. Recalling Alexander the Great before him, Napoleon asked to be left alone in the King's Chamber inside the Great Pyramid. On coming out he was said to be pale, as though he had witnessed a mysterious vision. Napoleon never told what he had seen, but he repeatedly hinted at an epiphany that revealed his destiny. Seventeen years later,

while a prisoner on St. Helena, he was tempted to reveal this experience to Emmanuel Las Cases, to whom he was dictating his memoirs, but he stopped abruptly, saying, "What's the use? You'd never believe me."

— *Daniel Boorstin*

1. Copy the sentence that gives the main idea of the paragraph, and then rewrite the main idea in your own words.

   a. **The grandeur of the Great Pyramid at Giza challenged the young Napoleon's imperial imagination.**

   b. **Napoleon was inspired in his conquests by the Great Pyramid at Giza.**

2. Below, write the three most important details that support this idea.

   Student responses will vary.

   He visited Giza at age 29.

   He asked to be left alone in the King's Chamber.

   He broke off a description of the incident in his memoirs.

3. Below, write the three least important details from the paragraph.

   Student responses will vary.

   The pyramid is 450 feet tall.

   Napoleon's officers climbed to the top.

   Emmanuel Las Cases took dictation of Napoleon's memoirs.

2. Finding Major Details in a Textbook

Read the following selection from a textbook in developmental psychology. It describes how people in earlier periods of history had different attitudes toward childhood than we have now. Then answer the questions.

Children in Medieval and Renaissance Times

Europe during the Middle Ages and through premodern times fostered an attitude toward children strikingly different from our contemporary society's. Though their basic needs to be fed and clothed were attended to, children were not coddled or protected in the same way that infants in our society are. As soon as they were physically able, usually at age seven or so, children were incorporated into the adult world of work, in which they harvested grain, learned craft skills, and otherwise contributed to the local economy. In medieval times, Western European children did not have special clothes, toys, or games. Once they were old enough to shed swaddling clothes, they wore adult fashions, played archery and chess, and even gambled, all common adult pastimes (Ariès, 1962).

At the same time, premodern European society regarded children as vulnerable, fragile, and unable to assume the full responsibilities of adulthood. Medical writings alluded to the special illnesses of young children, and laws prohibited marriages of children under age twelve (Kroll, 1977). Religious movements of this era proclaimed the innocence of children and the need for educating them. Children's souls were also worth saving, said the clerics, and on this notion was founded the moral responsibility of parents to provide for their children's spiritual well-being. Parents also recognized that children needed to be financially provided for and helped them to set up their own households as they approached adulthood and marriage (Pollock, 1983; Shahar, 1990). Thus, even though medieval children were incorporated quickly into the adult world, they were also recognized both as different from adults and as possessing special needs.

REFERENCES

Ariès, P. (1962). *Centuries of childhood: A social history of family life* (R. Baldick, Trans.). New York: Vintage.

Kroll, J. (1977). The concept of childhood in the Middle Ages. *Journal of the History of the Behavioral Sciences, 13,* 384–393.

Pollock, L. A. (1983). *Forgotten children: Parent-child relations from 1500–1900.* Cambridge: Cambridge University Press.

Shahar, S. (1990). *Childhood in the Middle Ages.* London: Routledge.

— *Danuta Bukatko and Marvin Daehler*

1. What is the overall main idea of this passage?

   Medieval and Renaissance children had lives different from those of modern children.

2. What is the main idea of just the first paragraph?

   Children were incorporated into the adult world at a young age.

3. What are the major details supporting the main idea of the first paragraph?

   not coddled; worked at harvest and crafts; no special clothes or toys

4. What is the main idea of just the second paragraph?

   Children were recognized as vulnerable and not ready for full responsibilities.

5. What are the major details supporting the main idea of the second paragraph?

   special illnesses recognized; marriage prohibited before age twelve; parental financial support

6. List three minor details from each paragraph.

   Grain was what was harvested; children played archery; Ariès did research. Kroll's work was

published in 1977; illnesses appeared in medical writings; religious movements occurred in the period.

Critical Thinking in Writing

How were you treated as a child? How are children today treated in our society? Write a few paragraphs about how the treatment of children now compares and contrasts with the treatment of children in medieval and Renaissance times.

3. Finding Major Details

Read the following case study from a marketing textbook about how an American motorcycle manufacturer turned its business around. Then answer the questions on major details and minor details.

Harley-Davidson Shifts into High Gear

Harley-Davidson Motor Co., Inc., the Milwaukee-based maker of big, heavy motorcycles (often called "hogs"), led the U.S. heavyweight motorcycle market until the late 1970s. The company's market share slipped largely because of competition from Japanese motorcycles. (Harley owners refer to Japanese bikes as "rice burners.") Harley-Davidson's reputation also suffered because their products were of inferior quality. At one point, the company's biggest competitor, Honda Motor Co., Ltd., held more than half of the U.S. market, whereas Harley-Davidson held on to a tiny 4 percent. The Japanese bikes are often cheaper; Honda's comparably sized motorcycles cost about $500 less than Harley-Davidson's. Harley received help from the U.S. government in 1983 in the form of a five-year tax on heavy motorcycles imported from Japan, but Harley had to solve its other problems alone.

2 The company focused first on improving old products and developing new ones. Customers had been complaining

about the deteriorating quality of Harley bikes, and many people called Harley's flagship V engine an antique. The company updated the V engine and eliminated many of its problems. Harley-Davidson also turned to Japanese manufacturing and management techniques to cut costs and improve product quality. It introduced several midsized bikes with lower price tags. Its Sportster model sells for $3,995, although top-of-the-line Harley-Davidson road cruisers still fetch up to $12,000.

3 In the past, Harley-Davidson aimed its bikes at two main groups: the "bikers" and the "towers." The bikers fit the popular conception of motorcycle riders, with their leather jackets, tattoos, and Harley insignia. The towers are conventional blue-collar workers who tend to take longer trips than do owners of smaller motorcycles. The company has survived the last few years largely because of these loyal customers and dedicated dealers. Some of Harley-Davidson's better known customers include Malcolm Forbes (publisher of *Forbes* magazine) and members of the Hell's Angels and the California Highway Patrol.

4 However, more white-collar professional people are now riding hogs. In fact, 10 percent of hog riders are women. The white-collar market particularly values the luxury, durability, and classic image that Harley represents. Harley-Davidson is expanding its marketing activities to include these consumers, although they will not forget the loyal bikers and towers. The company promotes its hogs to these groups with a new all-American image and by sponsoring motorcycle rallies.

5 The company's shift in marketing strategy resulted in an increase in market share, to almost 40 percent of the U.S. heavy and midsized motorcycle market. The company's situation improved so much that it asked the government to withdraw the tariff on heavy Japanese bikes one year early. The company will not compete with the Japanese for the small-bike market, but it plans to compete head-on in the heavy and midsized bike markets, where its hogs have a quality edge.

6 Harley-Davidson achieved its return to success through dedication to its customers and emphasis on durability and high quality. Although Harley-Davidson is the last of more than 150 U.S. motorcycle manufacturers, its chance for success in the future is enhanced because they are following one of the company's oldest axioms: Harley-Davidson sells more than just motorcycles, they sell a special loyalty and image to their customers.

SOURCES: Michael Oneal, "Full Cycle," *Continental*, November 1987, pp. 20–24; Rod Willis, "Harley-Davidson Comes Roaring Back," *Management Review*, March 1986, pp. 20–27; John A. Conway, "Follow Through: Harley Back in High Gear," *Forbes*, April 20, 1987, p. 8.

— *William M. Pride and O. C. Ferrell*

1. In your own words state the main point of this selection.

   Harley-Davidson improved its business through dedication to its customers and emphasis on durability and quality.

2. What are the major details of the problems Harley-Davidson faced?

   Competition with Japanese motorcycles increased because of the Japanese companies' superior manufacturing and management techniques and better-quality products.

3. What are the major details of the company's new products?

   The company has updated the V engine, uses a new "all-American image," and has manufactured new mid-sized bikes at lower costs.

4. What are the major details of the company's new marketing strategy?

   It has expanded its marketing activities to include white-collar consumers, while maintaining products for bikers and towers as well.

5. What major details best indicate the new strength of the company?

The new strategy brought an increase in market share to almost 40 percent of the U.S. heavy and mid-sized motorcycle market.

6. For each paragraph list two minor details.

Paragraph 1 **Harley owners often refer to Japanese bikes as "rice burners." Big, heavy motorcycles are called "hogs."**

Paragraph 2 **People called Harley's V engine an antique. The Sportster model sells for $3,995.**

Paragraph 3 **"Bikers" fit the popular conception of motorcycle riders. Malcolm Forbes was one of Harley-Davidson's more well-known customers.**

Paragraph 4 **Ten percent of hog riders are women. White-collar consumers value luxury, durability, and classic image.**

Paragraph 5 **Harley-Davidson asked the government to withdraw a tariff one year early. Harley will not compete with the Japanese for the small-bike market.**

Paragraph 6 **Harley-Davidson is the last of more than 150 U.S. motorcycle manufacturers. Harley-Davidson sells loyalty and an image to its customers.**

7

Recognizing Paragraph Patterns

Paragraphs are important units of thought in your reading. Each paragraph fits together ideas and information into a connected web of meaning. To understand a paragraph, you must see how its parts create an overall pattern of meaning. Writers often help you discover this pattern of meaning by the way they arrange information or ideas in paragraphs. Paragraph thoughts often appear in patterns that are easy to recognize. If you miss a paragraph's pattern and don't see how the details fit together, the paragraph will seem a jumble of confused ideas or facts to you. Once you are familiar with these patterns you will be able to spot them when you read.

For example, when you are able to recognize that a story is being told in time order, you will immediately know how to put the details together in your mind. You will also know that each new sentence will answer the question "What happens next?" When you recognize a comparison-contrast pattern, you will know that the writer is presenting two sets of information — details for each of the two things being compared. You will then be careful to match up every detail with its proper subject. You will also look to see how the sets of details match up with each other, point by point.

However, writers rarely use basic paragraph patterns in a straightforward way. They often shift, overlap, and combine patterns. Sometimes they invent new ones. A paragraph that begins by following place order to set a scene may shift to time order to let the writer tell a story. When an order of importance emerges, the writer is conveying opinions about the material.

Recognizing straightforward paragraph patterns will help you see how writers use them in complex or flexible ways. Get in the habit of looking for patterns in everything you read.

Soon you will be able to figure out any paragraph pattern, no matter how original. The writer's information and ideas will then become clear in your mind.

7a Ordering of Ideas

7a(1) *Time Order (Chronology)*

Some paragraph ideas are put together so that we see them in the time order in which they happened. You must keep in mind the *sequence:* One idea follows another and relates to an event or idea that comes before. This order is often used to tell a story or to explain how to do or make something.

> A small, hand-propelled German submarine, the *Brandtaucher*, sank in 1851 in sixty feet of water, with her captain, Wilhelm Bauer, and two crew members aboard. Her hull immediately began to collapse under the pressure of the sea. Captain Bauer, who had built the tiny craft, knew that if he could keep his two companions from panicking while allowing the water to rise steadily inside her, the interior and exterior pressure would equalize and they would be able to open the hatch and get out. They did. As Bauer wrote later, "We came to the surface like bubbles in a glass of champagne." The world made little note of this first escape from a sunken submarine.
>
> — *Ann Jensen*

7a(2) *Place Order*

Some paragraph details are put together so that we see them in terms of their place in a room, a building, or an outdoor scene. These details follow a direction that traces movement from one part of a scene to another. A writer, especially when describing something, may give details from left to right, from near to far, from east to west, or in some other clear place order.

> As I look around this room in this third-rate boarding house, my eyes are greeted first by the entrance to its gloomy inte-

rior. The door is painted a dirty cream color. There is a crack in one panel. The ceiling is the same dingy color with pieces of adhesive tape holding some of the plaster in place. The walls are streaked and cracked here and there. Also on the walls are pieces of Scotch tape that once held, I presume, some sexy girls, pictures of *Esquire Magazine* origin. Across the room runs a line; upon it hang a shirt, a grimy towel, and washed stump socks belonging to my roommate, Jack Nager. By the door near the top sash juts a piece of wood on which is hung — it looks like an old spread. It is calico, dirty, and a sickly green color. Behind that is a space which serves as our closet; next to that is the radiator, painted the same ghastly color. The landlady must have got the paint for nothing. On top is Jack's black suitcase, his green soap dish, and a brightly colored box containing his hair tonic. Over by the cracked window are a poorly made table and chair. On top of the table, a pencil, shaving talcum, a glass, a nail file; one of my socks hangs over the side. Above the table is our window, the curtains of cheese cloth held back by a string. There is also a black, fairly whole paper shade to dim such little sunlight as might enter.

— *John J. Regan*

7a(3) Order of Importance

Some paragraph details are put together so that we know which ideas the writer thinks are more important. In this kind of paragraph the least important idea comes first, and the writer tells the other details in order of growing importance. Of course, the most important idea comes last.

Robert Hooke's work in science was varied and important through the 1700s in England. In the first place he served as the head of the Royal Society, a group of the day's leading men of science; there he urged new tests and experiments to advance knowledge. He helped provide a means by which people could discuss their ideas with others who shared their concerns. Hooke was also a well-known architect whose advice about the design of buildings was welcome. He designed a large beautiful house in London where the British Museum now stands. Unfortunately Hooke's building burned down; the six long years of work he did on it were wiped out by a careless servant. Of all Hooke's gifts to humanity, however, the most important was his own research in science. He studied the movement of planets and improved tools for looking at the heavens. He invented the spiral watch spring. And, of course, it was Hooke who first described the cell as a basic part of plant tissue.

Once you know the way the writer orders details, you can follow the sequence more easily. In time order, events come one after the other. In place order, objects appear in relation to other objects. In order of importance, you learn the writer's opinion about which ideas are more crucial than others.

How to See the Order of Details in a Paragraph

- Certain words in paragraphs give you hints about how the ideas are arranged.
- For *time order* look for words that tell time, such as *when, then, first, second, next, last, after, before, later, finally.*
- For *place order* look for words that locate, such as *there, beside, near, above, below, next to, under, over, alongside, beneath, by, behind, on.*
- For *order of importance* look for words that help us judge importance, such as *first, next, last, most important, major, greatest, in the first place.*

EXERCISES

1. Ordering of Ideas

1. In the example of *time order* (page 169), circle the words that help you see that paragraph details are arranged in time order.
2. In the example of *place order* (page 169), circle the words that help you see that paragraph details are arranged in place order.
3. In the example of *order of importance* (page 170), circle the words that help you see that paragraph details are arranged in order of importance.

2. Understanding Sequence

Look at the following details from the example of time order (page 169). Arrange the details in correct chronological order by putting a 1 in front of the first event that happened, a 2 in front of the second, and so on.

4 ______ a. The water rose inside the submarine.

9 ______ b. The world paid little attention to the escape.

1 ______ c. Wilhelm Bauer built a submarine.

6 ______ d. The trapped people opened the hatch.

2 ______ e. Wilhelm Bauer and the two crew members entered the submarine.

7 ______ f. Wilhelm Bauer and his companions escaped from the submarine.

5 ______ g. The interior and exterior pressure equalized.

3 ______ h. The submarine sank.

8 ______ i. The three people rose through the water like bubbles of champagne.

3. **Understanding Sequence**

1. Reread the example of place order (page 169). Put a 1 next to the item described first in the paragraph, a 2 next to the item described second, and so on.

4 ______ a. things hung on the wall

2 ______ b. the ceiling

10 ______ c. the window

1 ______ d. the entrance

5 ______ e. the closet

3 ______ f. the walls

8 ______ g. the table

7 ______ h. items on top of the radiator

6 ______ i. the radiator

9 ______ j. things on top of the table

d ______ 2. In what order are the details arranged?
a. Top to bottom
b. Left to right
c. Around the room
d. From big things like walls to small personal items

b ______ 3. What kind of picture does the writer give of the room?
a. Hopeful and cheery
b. Run-down and gloomy
c. Poor but proud

4. Understanding Sequence

The following details all come from the example on page 170. Put a checkmark next to the statement that is most important in the paragraph. Then circle the statement that comes last in the paragraph.

______ a. Robert Hooke was a scientist.

√ ______ (b.) Hooke's own research in science included the invention of a watch spring and a description of the cell as a basic part of plant tissue.

______ c. Hooke was a well-known architect.

______ d. A building Hooke designed was burned by a careless servant.

______ e. Hooke served as head of the Royal Society.

5. Understanding Sequence

Read this paragraph to discover what one researcher has found by digging through garbage. Then answer the question about the sequence of information in the selection.

After 20 years of sorting through garbage cans and landfills, the archaeologist William L. Rathje has accumulated precious memories. There are the 40-year-old hot dogs, perfectly preserved beneath dozens of strata of waste, and the head of lettuce still in pristine condition after 25 years. But the hands-down winner, the one that still makes him shake his head in disbelief, is an order of guacamole he recently unearthed. Looking like it had just been mixed, it sat next to a newspaper apparently thrown out the same day. The date was 1967.

— *William Grimes*

1. How long has William Rathje been sorting through garbage?

   twenty years

2. What three items did Rathje find that he considers especially memorable?

   forty-year-old hot dogs; twenty-five-year-old lettuce;

   guacamole from 1967

3. Which one does he consider most amazing?

   the guacamole

4. Do you agree that it is the most amazing? Why?

   Student responses will vary.

6. Understanding Sequence

Read this paragraph to learn how an ancient vending machine worked. Then answer the questions that follow.

A coin-operated vending machine was invented by the Greeks 2000 years ago. It stood in a temple, and when a worshiper put a coin in the slot, it automatically produced a measured amount of holy water. The coin fell onto a small pan hung from one end of a delicately balanced beam. Its weight caused the beam to dip; the beam's opposite end rose, opening a stopper valve and allowing the holy water to flow out. When the pan carrying the coin had been tilted enough, the coin slid off. Free of its weight, the down end of the beam bobbed upward again and the up end swung down, closing the valve and cutting off the holy water. Surprisingly, the device closely parallels one used in today's flush toilets.

— *Murray Rubenstein*

d 1. What action starts the machine in motion?
   a. The balance beam moving
   b. The valve closing
   c. The pan tilting too much
   d. The coin dropping in the slot

c 2. What causes the valve to open to let out water?
   a. The coin dropping in the slot
   b. The end of the beam with the pan going up
   c. The end of the beam without the pan going up
   d. The coin sliding off the pan

a 3. What causes the coin to slip off the pan?
   a. The end of the beam with the pan dipping too low
   b. The water pushing the coin off the pan
   c. The water ceasing to flow
   d. The machine shaking

b 4. What closes the stopper valve and turns the machine off?
   a. The coin weighing down the pan
   b. The beam swinging back to its original position
   c. The pan tilting too much
   d. The coin falling off the pan

b 5. The balance beam moves like what playground device?
   a. A merry-go-round
   b. A seesaw
   c. A swing
   d. A jungle gym

7. Understanding Sequence

Read this paragraph about what one man visualizes when he works. Then answer the questions that follow.

As I sit at my desk, I know where I am. I see before me a window; beyond that some trees; beyond that the red roofs of the campus of Stanford University; beyond them the trees and the roof tops which mark the town of Palo Alto; beyond them the bare golden hills of the Hamilton Range. I know, however, more than I see. Behind me, although I am not looking in that direction, I know there is a window, and beyond that the little campus of the Center for the Advanced Study in the Behavioral Sciences; beyond that the Coast Range; beyond that the Pacific Ocean. Looking ahead of me again, I know that beyond the mountains that close my present horizon, there is a broad valley; beyond that a still higher range of mountains; beyond that other mountains, range upon range, until we come to the Rockies; beyond that the Great Plains and the Mississippi; beyond that the Alleghenies; beyond that the eastern seaboard; beyond that the Atlantic Ocean; beyond that is Europe; beyond that is Asia. I know, furthermore, that if I go far enough I will come back to where I am now. In other words, I have a picture of the earth as round. I visualize it as a globe. I am a little hazy on some of the details. I am not quite sure, for instance, whether Tanganyika is north or south of Nyasaland. I probably could not draw a very good map of Indonesia, but I have a fair idea where everything is located on the face of this globe. Looking further, I visualize the globe as a small speck circling around a bright star which is the sun, in the company of many other similar specks, the planets. Looking still further, I see our star the sun as a member of millions upon millions of others in the Galaxy. Looking still further, I visualize the Galaxy as one of millions upon millions of others in the universe.

— *Kenneth Boulding*

1. What place is the author describing? **the view from his window, extending to the Galaxy**

2. The author is sitting (circle one)
   a. at his desk.
   b. near a window.
   c. on the campus of Stanford University.
   d. in Palo Alto, California.
   (e.) All of the above
3. The author can see the (circle one)
   a. Center for the Advanced Study of Behavioral Sciences.

b. Pacific Ocean.
(c.) Hamilton Range.
d. Coast Range.
e. Rockies.

4. What details of the planet can he not visualize too clearly?

where Tanganyika is located; the shape of Indonesia

5. His most distant visualization is of the (circle one)
a. earth.
b. galaxy.
c. Atlantic Ocean.
(d.) universe.
e. solar system.

8. Ordering of Ideas

1. Of the three sample paragraphs on pages 174–176, which paragraph places details in space order? **paragraph 7 on the author's location, page 176**

2. Which paragraph places details in order of importance?

paragraph 5 on archaeological "finds," page 174

3. Which paragraph places details in time order? **paragraph 6 on the vending machine, pages 174–175**

9. The Ordering of Ideas Through Several Methods

The following selections show the arrangement of details in a variety of ways. On the blank lines after each selection, explain the order that the writer has selected.

1. Once in a long while, four times so far for me, my mother brings out the metal tube that holds her medical diploma. On the tube are gold circles crossed with seven red lines each — "joy" ideographs in abstract. There are also little flowers that look like gears for a gold machine. According to the scraps of labels with Chinese and American addresses, stamps, and

postmarks, the family airmailed the can from Hong Kong in 1950. It got crushed in the middle, and whoever tried to peel the labels off stopped because the red and gold paint came off too, leaving silver scratches that rust. Somebody tried to pry the end off before discovering that the tube pulls apart. When I open it, the smell of China flies out, a thousand-year-old bat flying heavy-headed out of the Chinese caverns where bats are as white as dust, a smell that comes from long ago, far back in the brain. Crates from Canton, Hong Kong, Singapore, and Taiwan have that smell too, only stronger because they are more recently come from the Chinese.

Inside the can are three scrolls, one inside another. The largest says that in the twenty-third year of the National Republic, the To Keung School of Midwifery, where she has had two years of instruction and Hospital Practice, awards its Diploma to my mother, who has shown through oral and written examination her Proficiency in Midwifery, Pediatrics, Gynecology, "Medecine," "Surgary," Therapeutics, Ophthalmology, Bacteriology, Dermatology, Nursing, and Bandage.

— *Maxine Hong Kingston*

The overall structure here is one of time order, although the spatial arrangement of details plays a major part. One might also argue that because the contents of the tube are more important than the outside, the author is using order of importance as a controlling device.

2. In 334 B.C. with an army of 35,000 men, Alexander crossed into Asia Minor. In addition to soldiers, the former student of Aristotle brought along scientists to study plant and animal life and to chart the terrain. After capturing the coast of Asia Minor, Alexander marched into Syria and defeated the Persian army at the battle of Issus. Rather than pursuing the fleeing Persian king, Darius III, Alexander stayed with his master plan, which included the capture of coastal ports in order to crush the Persian navy. He captured Tyre, thought

to be an impregnable city, and advanced into Egypt. Grateful to Alexander for having liberated them from Persian rule, the Egyptians made him pharaoh. Alexander appointed officials to administer the country and founded a new city, Alexandria.

Having destroyed or captured the Persian fleet, Alexander in 331 B.C. moved into Mesopotamia in pursuit of Darius. The Macedonians defeated the numerically superior Persians at Gaugamela, just east of the Tigris River, but Darius escaped. After a stopover at Babylon and at Persepolis, which he burned in revenge for Xerxes' destruction of Athens more than 150 years earlier, Alexander resumed the chase. When he finally caught up with Darius, the Persian king was dead, killed by Persian conspirators.

Alexander relentlessly pushed deeper into Asia, crossing from Afghanistan into north India where he defeated the king of Pontus in a costly battle. When Alexander announced plans to push deeper into India, his troops, exhausted and far from home in a strange land, resisted. Yielding to their wishes, Alexander returned to Babylon in 324 B.C. In these campaigns, Alexander proved himself to be a superb strategist and leader of men. Winning every battle, Alexander's army had carved an empire that stretched from Greece to India. Future conquerors, including Caesar and Napoleon, would read of Alexander's career with fascination and longing.

— *Marvin Perry*

Time and space order fit together throughout most of the passage. The last few sentences continue to follow time order; the discussion of the spatial expansion of Alexander's territory stops in the middle of the last paragraph.

3. Inland from the Gulf of Mexico's languid, lapping waters, beyond Mississippi's blinding white coastline and across its serpentine bayous, a dark edge of trees marks the beginning of the great southern pine forest. On my uncle's farm near the fringe of that forest I spent every summer of my youth

milking cows and traipsing the woods, as near to heaven as a barefoot boy can be.

In the hour before sunrise a mist breathed from sleeping fields scented with animals and hay. Thunderheads laced with snakes' tongues of lightning rose over the Gulf to the south and emerged from the dawn, blue and scarlet and egg-shell white, huge stalking gods that spoke to me of horizons of the sea.

One morning of my 13th summer, in 1966, a new cloud rose over the trees: a thin, billowing mushroom of steam sent skyward by Saturn V rocket engines at the National Aeronautics and Space Administration's test site, newly constructed in coastal Mississippi to help send man to the moon.

NASA's arrival spelled the end of 150-year-old Logtown, which lay within a safety zone cleared of habitation. Twenty-five years later Roy Baxter drives me through vine-hung woods where the hamlet once stood. Mossy live oaks mark the abandoned site of the house where he was born and lived his first 47 years.

"But I'm not bitter in any shape or form," he says. "We didn't want 'em. We were getting along without 'em. But when NASA came, it was the biggest thing that ever happened here."

He is silent for a while as we ride the sandy roads. "Nobody wanted to move, though. Some of the older people couldn't stand the shock. They died within six months."

At the John C. Stennis Space Center three monolithic structures of steel and concrete stand as out of place as teleported pyramids in the flat, wooded swampland. Inside the B-1 stand, NASA technicians are preparing a space shuttle main engine for testing.

— *Douglas Bennett Lee*

The selection starts with a space-order description of the region and farm, and then goes into a time-order memory of childhood that leads into the space age. It then returns to a space-order account of a trip to the space center.

Critical Thinking in Writing

Modern technology, with its buildings and energy needs, often challenges nature and disrupts people's lives, as the selection above shows. Where have you seen the impact of modern technology on the environment? What should be the relation between nature's world and the world of science and high technology? Write your views on these issues in a few paragraphs.

7b Listing of Details

Information in a paragraph sometimes appears just as a series of facts or details. Though all statements relate to the main idea, each fact is not expanded. The paragraph presents a listing of information.

In the following paragraph about conditions in America during the Great Depression, notice how the writer lists a series of details to support the topic.

> In 1935 the depression in America was five years old and deepening. America had over 19,000,000 people on relief, one in every six or seven of the population. As FERA administrator, Harry Hopkins had spent $323,890,560 on relief in the first ten months of 1934, almost a third more than in 1933. In 1935 Congress appropriated $4,880,000,000 for the Work Relief Bill. *Time* estimated uncomfortably that of the 19,000,000 on relief, 20 percent were unemployables, or "chronic dependents." Over the country the debate ran, "Most people out of work couldn't hold jobs if they had them." For the first time since 1911, marriages had fallen in 1932 below the one-million mark, though the population had risen from 93,000,000 in 1911 to 125,000,000 in 1932. In 1935, according to the President's inaugural statement of 1937, one-third of American families were "ill-fed, ill-clothed, and ill-housed." The mean income of 13,000,000 families was $471 annually, including income from gardens and part-time labor. For these families the average expenditure for food was

$206 annually. The middle third of American families received a mean income of $1,076; the upper third received an average of $2,100.

— *Don M. Wolfe*

EXERCISES

1. Listing of Details

Reread the preceding paragraph and answer these questions:

1. What is the main idea? **In 1935 the depression in America grew worse.**

2. List five details the writer gives to support the main idea.

   19 million on relief

   almost $5 billion for Work Relief Bill

   20 percent on relief unemployable

   marriages under 1 million

   mean income for 13 million: $471

2. Listing of Details

Read the following paragraph and answer the questions that follow. Pay particular attention to the details the writer lists.

I know how a prize watermelon looks when it is sunning . . . among pumpkin vines and "simblins"; I know how to tell when it is ripe without "plugging" it; I know how inviting it looks when it is cooling itself in a tub of water under the bed, waiting; I know how it looks when it lies on the table in the sheltered great floor space between house and kitchen, and the children gathered for the sacrifice and their mouths watering; I know the crackling sound it makes when the carving knife enters its end, and I can see the split fly along in front of the blade as the knife cleaves its way to the other end; I can see its halves fall apart and display the rich red meat and

> the black seeds, and the heart standing up, a luxury fit for the elect; I know how a boy looks behind a yard-long slice of that melon, and I know how he feels; for I have been there. I know the taste of the watermelon which has been honestly come by, and I know the taste of the watermelon which has been acquired by art.
>
> — *Mark Twain*

1. What experience is the writer trying to capture by listing all the details? **the experience of enjoying a watermelon**

2. List the main details that capture this experience.

   the watermelon sunning; telling whether it is ripe; the melon cooling in a tub of water; the children standing around; the cutting; the sight of the meat and seeds; the eating

3. The details in lines 3 through 11 are arranged in a kind of time order. Explain what happens in those lines to show the time sequence.

   We go through all the steps, from cooling the watermelon to serving and eating it.

3. Listing of Details

Read the following paragraph about working conditions in meat-packing plants and answer the questions that follow. Notice the many details the writer uses to back up his main idea.

> It is 81 years since Upton Sinclair's "The Jungle" described the brutal working conditions of the Chicago slaughterhouses. But here in Sioux Falls — and in places like it throughout the Midwest — history is quietly repeating itself.
>
> Modern machinery has changed the look and the sound of a packing house. But the meatpacking industry, which employs about 100,000 people, remains today the most haz-

ardous industry in America. Meatpackers work in extreme heat or refrigerated cold, often standing shoulder to shoulder, wielding honed knives and power saws. Grease and blood make the floors and the tools slippery. The roar of the machines is constant. Occasionally, an overpowering stench from open bladders and stomachs fills the air.

The workers cut themselves. They cut each other. They wear out their insides doing repetitive-motion jobs. They are sliced and crushed by machines that were not even imagined when Sinclair published his book in 1906.

— *William Glaberson*

1. What is the main idea of the paragraph?

   Meat packers today endure extremely hazardous working conditions.

2. What details reveal the danger of the working conditions?

   Workers use honed knives and power saws while standing close together. Grease and blood make the floor and tools slippery.

3. What details reveal the unpleasantness of the working conditions?

   extreme heat or cold; machines roaring; unpleasant smells

4. What details reveal how workers get injured?

   They cut themselves and each other; repetitive motion wears out workers' insides; machines slice and crush workers.

5. How are the kinds of details (see questions 2, 3, and 4) related?

They all contribute to the brutal working conditions of the meat-packing industry.

6. In what ways are the details presented here compared to the details in Upton Sinclair's novel *The Jungle*?

   The conditions in today's meat-packing houses are like those in Chicago's slaughterhouses, but now there are dangerous machines that did not exist in 1906.

Critical Thinking in Writing

Conditions on many jobs today are unsafe and uncomfortable. In what jobs do you think safety and comfort could be improved? What steps can employers and employees take together to make the workplace safer and more comfortable?

4. Listing of Details

Read the following selection describing children's behaviors. Then answer the questions about lists of details within the paragraphs.

> We've all known children like this: They stand too close and touch us in annoying ways; they laugh too loud or at the wrong times; they make "stupid" or embarrassing remarks; they don't seem to get the message when given a broad hint or even told outright to behave differently; they mistake friendly actions for hostile ones, or vice versa; they move too slowly, or too fast, for everyone else; their facial expressions don't jibe with what they or others are saying; or their appearance is seriously out of step with current fashions.
>
> These are children who don't seem to fit in, ones whom other children often label as "nerds," "geeks" or "weirdos," children who are often last to be chosen for a team or group, if they are chosen at all. They have trouble making or keeping friends and tend to become loners or sometimes bullies.

But underneath the "out-of-sync" exterior are intelligent, well-meaning children who are baffled by their peers' rejection. Often their equally baffled parents go out of their way to foster friendships, inviting other children over to play, spend the night or join the family on special outings. Yet their youngsters repeatedly fail to make lasting friends.

According to two renowned child psychologists from Emory University in Atlanta, these children are misfits for reasons that are both identifiable and correctable. Dr. Stephen Nowicki Jr. and Dr. Marshall P. Duke say such children have a form of learning disability that prevents them from properly using or understanding nonverbal communication. The psychologists call the problem "dyssemia," from the Greek "dys," for "difficulty," and "semes," for "signals." In testing several thousand children with an evaluation scale they developed to identify various aspects of dyssemia, the Atlanta psychologists found that 10 percent of children have one or more problems in transmitting or receiving nonverbal signals.

— *Jane E. Brody*

1. In the first paragraph how many different children's behaviors are listed? In your own words, repeat three of the items from the list.

   At least nine. Student responses will vary.

   their laughter doesn't fit the situation

   they don't follow hints

   they misinterpret others' actions

2. Overall, how would you describe these behaviors?

   socially awkward

3. From the second paragraph, give several examples of the ways children don't fit in.

called names; not chosen for teams; lack of friends;

loners or even bullies

4. In the second paragraph, overall, what kind of things are listed?

   names and characterizations of the children

5. The third paragraph lists different solutions that parents have tried. What are they?

   inviting other children to play; having other children

   for overnights; taking other children on trips

6. In the fourth paragraph, what explanation is given for the unhappy situations described in the lists of the previous paragraphs?

   a learning disability that has to do with sending and

   receiving nonverbal signals

5. Listing of Details in Longer Passages

Read this passage of several paragraphs from an American history textbook to discover some recent changes in American social behavior. Then answer the questions that follow.

> In the 1970s Americans turned their gaze inward and concentrated on self-expression and personal improvement. As a popular beer commercial proclaimed, "You only go 'round once in life and you've got to grab for all the gusto you can get." That gusto ranged from recreational vehicles to roller skates, disco to punk rock, *The Godfather* to *Star Wars*. Social commentator Tom Wolfe branded the 1970s the Me Decade, a time of diversion and material consumption designed to make Americans' private worlds, in the midst of public confusion, at least tolerable.
>
> *Human Potential Movement*
>
> In the self-centered new decade, suggestions for realizing one's full potential were consumed as readily as jogging

shoes and health foods. Transactional Analysis (TA), a form of psychotherapy emphasizing interpersonal relationships, was popularized in Eric Berne's *Games People Play* (1969) and Thomas Harris's *I'm OK — You're OK* (1969). Transcendental Meditation (TM), a yogic discipline, drew 350,000 adherents and spawned over two hundred teaching centers. Est (Erhard Seminars Training), a system of encounters meant to enable people to "get in touch with themselves," was grossing $10 million a year in 1975. In addition to these fads, Zen, yoga, the Sufi, Hare Krishna, and other new therapies and exotic religions flourished.

Spiritual Revival

As millions of Americans sought to fill spiritual and emotional voids through esoteric movements, millions more were drawn to more traditional beliefs. According to a 1977 survey, about 70 million Americans defined themselves as born-again Christians, and 10 million claimed to have had the experience since 1975. President Jimmy Carter, singers Pat Boone and Johnny Cash, professional football player Roger Staubach, former Black Panther Eldridge Cleaver, and Watergate defendants Jeb Stuart Magruder and Charles Colson all counted themselves among the saved. Religious revivals and evangelical sects were not new, of course, but by the mid-1970s they were a growth industry. In the latter years of the decade evangelicals were grossing $2 million annually in sales of religious books, and the Virginia-based Christian Broadcast Network was earning nearly $60 million from its four stations and 130 affiliates.

Messianic Cults

Besides the relatively harmless human potential movements and the traditional religious enthusiasms, a dark undercurrent of cult-like adherence to charismatic leaders ran through the 1970s. In 1973 and 1974, the Reverend Sun Myung Moon, founder of the Unification Church, toured the United States and converted young Americans to his religion, a curious blend of Christianity, anti-Communism, and worship of Moon as a messiah. "Moonies" disposed of their possessions, moved into communes, and raised funds for the church by selling ginseng tea, candles, flowers, and peanuts. Critics charged that Moon and his disciples had brainwashed their converts, and soon worried parents were attempting to rescue their children from the influence of the church by kidnapping them.

For most of those who followed the Reverend Jim Jones to Guyana, attempts at rescue came too late. Jones's California cult, the People's Temple, had begun as a church committed to social reform and civil rights. But in 1977 stories began to surface alleging death threats, beatings, and extortion. Jones moved the cult to Guyana, where he established a colony named Jonestown. In November 1978, convinced that the United States was about to destroy the colony and embark on an apocalyptic race war, the crazed leader ordered his followers to poison their children and then kill themselves with a mixture of Kool-Aid and cyanide. The mass murder and suicide of almost nine hundred people at Jonestown added a satanic headline to the history of cults in the United States.

Yet another facet of "me-ness" was the phenomenon called "Roots." The 1977 television series, based on a best-selling book by Alex Haley, dramatized the author's family history beginning with his ancestor, Kunta Kinte, a Gambian boy sold into slavery. "Roots" spawned an interest in family trees that touched all races and ethnic groups. More important, the sheer numbers of Americans exposed to the book and television series (130 million watched the eight-part series) helped to sensitize the public to the agonies of slavery and racism.

Physical Fitness Craze

If Americans went running to libraries to research their family trees during the 1970s, they probably did so in an expensive pair of Nikes, Pumas, or Adidas, for this was the decade of the jogger. James Fixx's *Complete Book of Running* (1977) enjoyed tremendous popularity, and literature on running, physical fitness, diet, and health jammed book shelves and magazine racks. Perhaps America was no longer the best nation it could be, but Americans were determined to make themselves the best, or at least the healthiest, individuals they could be. Saunas, hot tubs, and Jacuzzis became popular, and membership in tennis and racquet-ball clubs, health centers, and diet and suntanning clinics boomed. At the supermarket, consumers kept a careful eye out for products marked "no preservatives" or "all natural."

— *Mary Beth Norton, David M. Katzman, Paul D. Escott, Howard Chudacoff, Thomas G. Paterson, and William M. Tuttle, Jr.*

1. What is the main idea of the entire passage? **During the 1970s Americans were concerned with self-expression and personal improvement.**

2. What is the main idea of the second paragraph? **The human potential movement attracted many followers.**

   What are some of the details in the paragraph supporting that idea? **Transactional Analysis, Transcendental Meditation, est, Zen, yoga, Sufi, Hare Krishna**

3. What is the main idea of the third paragraph? **A spiritual revival emerged.**

   What are some of the supporting details listed in the paragraph? **statistics about born-again Christians; names of celebrity born-agains; money earned by evangelicals**

4. In what order are the details about the Jones cult presented under the heading *Messianic Cults*? **time order**

5. What are some of the details supporting the idea of an American fitness craze? **brand names of athletic shoes; books and magazines on running, fitness, diet, and health; hot tubs etc.; clubs and clinics; natural products**

Critical Thinking in Writing

Were the 1980s in America still a Me Decade? What about the 1990s? How have we moved away from the sense that our private worlds are more important than anything else? Write a few paragraphs in which you consider whether we are still in a Me Decade.

7c Classification

In some paragraphs different details relating to a topic are arranged in categories, or groups. This paragraph pattern identifies categories, shows how various examples in the same category are alike, and shows how the separate categories are different. Classification can also show how a large subject may be broken up into different parts. In reading paragraphs organized according to classification, notice what kinds of categories separate the specifics into groups.

The following paragraph, for example, classifies the courts in the United States into two categories, depending on whether the courts correspond to government level or to kind of case.

> There are several different kinds and levels of courts in the United States. Some correspond to the different branches of government. These include municipal (or city) courts, county courts, state courts, and federal courts, all the way up to the Supreme Court of the United States. Specialized courts deal with specific kinds of cases. There are divorce courts, for example, as well as traffic courts, small claims courts, and courts that do nothing but handle appeals from the decisions of other courts.
>
> — *Michael Kronenwetter*

EXERCISES

1. Classification

Reread the preceding paragraph and answer these questions:

1. What is the first category of courts and what are some examples of it? **those corresponding to the branches of**

government (municipal, county, state, and federal courts)

2. What is the second category of courts and what are some examples of it? **courts for specific cases (divorce courts, traffic courts, small claims courts, and appeals courts)**

3. What is the difference between the two categories?
The first category is more general than the second.

2. Classification

Read the following two paragraphs that continue the discussion of courts of the United States. Then answer the questions.

> The basic function of all these courts can be stated very simply: It is to resolve disputes. But that simple statement masks an extremely complicated reality. Just as there are many kinds of courts, those courts are called upon to resolve many kinds of disputes. Some disputes are between private individuals, as when one person sues another for breaking a contract. Other disputes may be between a branch of government and a private person, as when a citizen is sued for underpayment of taxes, or when an individual sues the government for violation of his or her rights. Still other disputes may be between governments — the government of a state, for example, and the federal government — or even between different agencies of the same level of government.
>
> Many disputes have to do with business matters, particularly with the interpretation of contracts. Some have to do with public questions, such as the application of the Constitution or of lesser laws. Another large category of disputes consists of criminal matters, cases in which the government

of a particular state, or the federal government, accuses an individual of committing a crime.

— *Michael Kronenwetter*

1. What is the main idea of both paragraphs? **The function of all courts is to resolve disputes.**

2. What overall subject do both paragraphs classify?
disputes

3. According to what principle is the subject classified in the first paragraph? **The disputes may be between individuals, governments, branches of government, or a mix.**

4. According to what principle is the subject classified in the second paragraph? **There are many different kinds of disputes.**

7d Comparison and Contrast

The technique of relating one object to another by showing how they are alike and how they are different is called *comparison and contrast*.

In order to describe an unfamiliar object or idea, an author often relates the unfamiliar object to a familiar one. Not many of you, for instance, know what a *bowler* in the game of cricket does. If you learned that a bowler is much like a pitcher in baseball, however, you would understand the bowler's job. Then, by also considering how a bowler is *not* like a pitcher, you would get an even better idea of what a cricket bowler does.

In the following paragraph, the writer compares the usefulness of learning to lie for natural liars and for those without natural skill in lying. First the writer describes how natural liars don't need training, and then he shows that the rest of us could not make use of the training. So, for different reasons for the two contrasting cases, the writer concludes that a school for lying is not a very good idea.

> While there could be a school for lie catchers, a school for liars would not make sense. Natural liars don't need it, and the rest of us don't have the talent to benefit from it. Lying well is a special talent, not easily acquired. One must be a natural — ***Natural liars*** performer, winning and charming in manner. Such people are able, without thought, to manage their expressions, giving off just the impression they seek to convey. They don't need much help. Most people need that help, but lacking a natural — ***Most people*** ability to perform, they will never be able to lie very well. Lying can't be improved by knowing what to do and what not to do. And I seriously doubt that practice will have much benefit. A self-conscious liar, who planned each move as he made it, would be like a skier who thought about each stride as he went down the slope.
>
> — *Paul Ekman*

Another type of comparison and contrast allows the writer to state one point and discuss *both* objects in regard to that idea; then to state another point and discuss both objects in regard to *that* idea; and so on. See how the features of high school and college are discussed in this paragraph.

> While there are many differences between high school and college, I'd have to say that the most important ones all involve freedom. Everyone has — ***One point*** to attend high school, at least until tenth grade, so very often you find classes where the students aren't serious about learning. College is exactly the opposite. People are there voluntarily because they want to learn and improve themselves. As a result college students are much more serious and interested. Another major difference is that col- — ***A second point*** leges don't enforce arbitrary rules. In high school you need a pass to be in the hallway during class,

and you can't leave a classroom without permission. On the other hand, college students can go where they please. No one asks them for passes and, if they need to leave a class to make a phone call or go to the bathroom, they just leave. Finally, in high school classes are assigned and the same classes are held every day. However, in college, most classes only meet two or three days a week, and students have many options about which classes to take. — ***A third point***

Here are some tips for understanding comparison and contrast:

- Look for key words that help relate the two objects or ideas. These words point to like ideas:

similarly	in addition	in the same way
also	further	likewise

These words point to ideas that differ:

but	on the other hand	still
although	in contrast	in spite of
however	yet	even so
nevertheless	conversely	nonetheless

- Look for a sentence or two that tells just what is being compared to what.
- As you read, keep in mind the two ideas that the writer is comparing or contrasting. Ask yourself: "What things are being compared? Why are they being compared? How are the things alike or different?"

EXERCISES

1. Comparison and Contrast

Reread the paragraph about learning to lie on page 194 and answer the following questions:

1. Underline the sentence that directly contrasts how the two groups would relate to lying lessons.

2. Explain why natural liars would not gain from lessons.

They already know and use all of the techniques.

3. Explain why poor liars would not benefit from lessons.

To lie well one must have some natural ability.

4. In what ways do natural liars differ from poor liars?

Natural liars can perform with a winning and charming manner without thinking much about it; poor liars cannot.

5. Why would a school for liars not make sense?

According to the writer, lying cannot be improved with practice, and natural liars don't need the lessons.

2. Comparison and Contrast

Reread the paragraph about high school and college on pages 194–195 and answer the following questions:

1. What is the main idea? **The main difference between high school and college is increased freedom.**

2. In what three ways does the writer compare high school and college?

attendance; rules; choice of classes

3. Which students are more serious and why? **Students are**

more serious in college because they are there voluntarily.

4. How do rules compare between high school and college? **In college, there are few arbitrary rules, such as rules about needing a pass to leave a classroom.**

5. How does the selection of courses differ in high school and college? **In high school, you have no choice about classes, which meet every day; in college, you have choices, and classes meet only two or three times a week.**

3. Comparison and Contrast

Read the following paragraph from a communications textbook and answer the questions. Pay attention to the similarities and differences that the writers explore.

> Books obviously have distinctive characteristics that set them apart from other media. Certainly, they differ from other print media, such as newspapers and magazines, in that they are bound and covered and are consecutive from beginning to end. Because books often take a year or more to produce, they are less timely than newspapers and magazines. Nevertheless, like other mass media, they are produced by professional communicators and generally distributed to relatively large and diverse audiences. One obvious difference from several other media is that, like movies, they are not basically supported by advertising (although some publishers are experimenting with this idea). Thus, books have to earn profits for their producers on the basis of their content. More than other media, moreover, books are made to last, and their form lends itself to in-depth, durable exploration and development of a topic or idea.
>
> — *Melvin DeFluer and Everette Dennis*

1. What are the two things that are being compared and contrasted?

   books and other media

2. In what way are books like other media?

   produced by professionals; widely distributed

3. In what way are books like movies but not like some other media? **not supported by advertising; profits dependent on content**

4. In what other ways do books differ from other media?

   bound and covered; consecutive material; longer to produce; less timely; lasting; in-depth exploration

5. Overall, does the author present books as more like or more unlike other media? **more unlike**

4. Comparison and Contrast in a Long Selection

Read this selection comparing the experiences of boys and girls growing up. Then answer the questions that follow.

> Even if they grow up in the same neighborhood, on the same block, or in the same house, girls and boys grow up in different worlds of words. Others talk to them differently and expect and accept different ways of talking to them. Most important, children learn how to talk, how to have conversations, not only from their parents but from their peers. After all, if their parents have a foreign or regional accent, children do not emulate it; they learn to speak with the pronunciation of the region where they grow up. Anthropologists Daniel Maltz and Ruth Borker summarize research showing that boys and girls have very different ways of talking to their friends. Although they often play together, boys and girls spend most of their time playing in same-sex groups. And, although some of the activities they play at are

similar, their favorite games are different, and their ways of using language in their games are separated by a world of difference.

Boys tend to play outside, in large groups that are hierarchically structured. Their groups have a leader who tells others what to do and how to do it, and resists doing what other boys propose. It is by giving orders and making them stick that high status is negotiated. Another way boys achieve status is to take center stage by telling stories and jokes, and by sidetracking or challenging the stories and jokes of others. Boys' games have winners and losers and elaborate systems of rules that are frequently the subjects of arguments. Finally, boys are frequently heard to boast of their skill and argue about who is best at what.

Girls, on the other hand, play in small groups or in pairs; the center of a girl's social life is a best friend. Within the group, intimacy is key: Differentiation is measured by relative closeness. In their most frequent games, such as jump rope and hopscotch, everyone gets a turn. Many of their activities (such as playing house) do not have winners or losers. Though some girls are certainly more skilled than others, girls are expected not to boast about it, or show that they think they are better than the others. Girls don't give orders; they express their preferences as suggestions, and suggestions are likely to be accepted. Whereas boys say, "Gimme that!" and "Get outta here!" girls say, "Let's do this," and "How about doing that?" Anything else is put down as "bossy." They don't grab center stage — they don't want it — so they don't challenge each other directly. And much of the time, they simply sit together and talk. Girls are not accustomed to jockeying for status in an obvious way; they are more concerned that they be liked.

— *Deborah Tannen*

1. What aspect of growing up is being compared between boys and girls?

   the way boys and girls play and learn to use words

2. From whom do children learn to talk?

   from parents and peers

3. From the second and third paragraphs select five points on

which the play and talk of boys and girls contrast. Describe the contrasts by filling in the following sentences.

Student responses will vary.

a. Boys **play in groups**,

while girls **play in small groups or in pairs**.

b. Boys **play in hierarchical groups**,

while girls **play in intimate groups**.

c. Boys **give orders**,

while girls **make suggestions**.

d. Boys **are boastful**,

while girls **downplay inequalities**.

e. Boys **seek status**,

while girls **want to be liked**.

4. Write one sentence summarizing the overall difference between boys' and girls' talk.

Boys' play and talk are about power, while girls' are about friendship.

5. Comparison and Contrast in a Long Selection

Read this selection discussing how people express individuality even when they seem to be following the same style of dressing. Then answer the questions that follow.

> The cliché outfit may in some cases become so standardized that it is spoken of as a "uniform": the pin-striped suit, bowler and black umbrella of the London City man, for instance, or the blue jeans and T-shirts of high-school students. Usually, however, these costumes only look like uniforms to

outsiders; peers will be aware of significant differences. The London businessman's tie will tell his associates where he went to school; the cut and fabric of his suit will allow them to guess at his income. High-school students, in a single glance, can distinguish new jeans from those that are fashionably worn, functionally or decoratively patched or carelessly ragged; they grasp the fine distinctions of meaning conveyed by straight-leg, flared, boot-cut and peg-top. When two pairs of jeans are identical to the naked eye a label handily affixed to the back pocket gives useful information, identifying the garment as expensive (so-called designer jeans) or discount-department-store. And even within the latter category there are distinctions: in our local junior high school, according to a native informant, "freaks always wear Lees, greasers wear Wranglers, and everyone else wears Levis."

Of course, to the careful observer all these students are only identical below the waist; above it they may wear anything from a lumberjack shirt to a lace blouse. Grammatically, this costume seems to be a sign that in their lower or physical natures these persons are alike, however dissimilar they may be socially, intellectually or aesthetically. If this is so, the opposite statement can be imagined — and was actually made by my own college classmates thirty years ago. During the daytime we wore identical baggy sweaters over a wide variety of slacks, plaid kilts, full cotton or straight tweed or slinky jersey skirts, ski pants and Bermuda shorts. "We're all nice coeds from the waist up; we think and talk alike," this costume proclaimed, "but as women we are infinitely various."

— *Alison Lurie*

1. What is the main idea of the first paragraph?

   Although the "cliché outfit" may seem like a uniform to outsiders, members of the group can detect subtle differences.

2. What two views of the cliché outfit are being contrasted in the paragraph? How does each see the cliché outfit?

   Members of each group see significant differences in

the outfit, while outsiders see identical clothing.

3. What two examples are given of the insider's view in the first paragraph?

the London businessman's tie; the high school student's jeans

4. How is classification used in the first paragraph? **Jeans wearers are classified into freaks, greasers, and "everyone else."**

5. What two groups are being contrasted in the second paragraph? **what college students wear today versus what college students wore thirty years ago**

6. What is the difference between the two groups, and what is the meaning of that difference? **Today's students all wear jeans but different tops. Students thirty years ago wore the same tops but different lower garments. Meaning: Today's students are alike in their lower natures while dissimilar in their higher natures; older students proclaimed similarity in their higher natures but dissimilarity in their lower natures.**

7. What is the main idea of the second paragraph? **Clothes**

make statements, but the statements often seem to

contradict one another.

7e Cause and Effect

In this kind of paragraph, you learn either *why* something happened or what happened *as a result* of something. The writer may explain conditions or events that *cause* a certain situation or may discuss conditions or events that *result* from a situation. The following selection tells about a common effect in humans, and then it explains the causes that scientists have found.

> Have you ever had the experience of putting money into a soda machine or a pay phone and, instead of getting soda or a dial tone, you get nothing? Even though you know it's just a machine, how many of you find yourselves kicking the machine or giving it a frustrated shake? It may interest you to know that scientists have studied this behavior, which is called the *pain-attack mechanism.* Pigeons were trained to peck at a disk mounted on a wall and to expect the reward of some grain every time they did so. Scientists found that, when they didn't reward the pigeon as it expected, the bird became very agitated, attacking the wall disk and even other pigeons in the same box. In similar experiments, monkeys, rats, and pigeons also reacted violently when they were given an electric shock for no reason. From these results, scientists decided that animals, and in a sense this includes us, will respond to a painful event by fighting back. The event can be physical pain, such as an electric shock, or emotional pain, such as expecting a reward and not getting it. But it also seems that getting yelled at or being fired, like losing a lover or losing money in a soda machine, will trigger anger or aggression in humans.

Cause and effect are important in much of the scientific and technical material you will read in college. As those of you who study science already know, many scientific discoveries were made because a scientist studied cause and effect in natural events. In the passage you just read, you saw how behavioral psychologists studied an *effect*, aggression, to see if they could discover some possible *causes* for it. The pain-attack mechanism provides an explanation for an important cause-and-effect relationship.

- If the writer tells why something happened, what happened because of something, or what might happen because of something, you can expect reasons to explain causes or effects.
- Look for word clues: *because, since, as a result, therefore, consequently, so.*
- Remember that many causes can contribute to a single effect and that many effects can stem from a single cause.

In our everyday life we frequently respond to causes. For instance, we avoid eating food that smells bad or touching something that is glowing hot because we know what effect tainted food or red-hot objects will have on us. So also, when we read a passage, we can look for reasons (causes) behind events described (effects).

EXERCISES

1. Cause and Effect

Reread the paragraph on page 203 and answer these questions:

1. What situation will the writer try to explain by giving causes?

   why animals lash out when they are frustrated or hurt

2. What cause did scientists find for the type of angry, violent behavior described in the article?

   frustration and pain

3. In what situations and in what way does the pain-attack mechanism apply to pigeons and other animals?

   When pigeons expected a reward and did not get

one, they became angry and violent. Monkeys and other animals reacted violently when they were given an electric shock for no reason.

4. How does the pain-attack mechanism apply to humans?

   Humans sometimes react violently to a machine that thwarts them or become angry when they go through a painful experience.

5. On a separate piece of paper, describe any personal experiences you have had that might relate to the pain-attack mechanism. Do your experiences support or contradict the cause-and-effect pattern described in the article?

2. Cause and Effect

Read the following selection about who gets killed by lightning strikes. Then answer the questions that follow.

> It seems a deadly form of sex discrimination: When the National Weather Service tallies up the deaths caused by lightning each year in the United States, an overwhelming number of the victims are male. Of 74 lightning-related deaths in 1990, females numbered only seven. Little research has focused on the causes of the disparity. But it's acknowledged that men tend to be outdoors more than women, at work or at play, and are thus more vulnerable to a strike. Examining lightning fatalities from 1968 through 1985, the Centers for Disease Control found that 85 percent were male and that a third of them died on the job. The victims included farm laborers, construction workers, nurserymen, and a land surveyor. Since 1959 Florida has led the nation in lightning deaths and injuries. Apart from those killed at work, many are struck while fishing from boats, others while at the beach or on the golf course. "There's probably that old macho ego," says Roger Tanner, a weather researcher. "A male may not be cautious and take cover readily."
>
> — National Geographic

1. What effect is being explained in this selection?

   why more men than women are killed by lightning

2. Is the cause definitely known why men are killed more often by lightning than women?

   no

3. What is the main reason offered for the higher male mortality?

   Men are outdoors more.

4. What evidence is offered in support of this reason?

   lists of male occupations and recreations that keep them outdoors

5. What further reason does the closing quotation suggest?

   Men are too stubborn to come in during a storm.

3. Cause and Effect

The paragraph below explains how women's clothes in the nineteenth century actually weakened them. Read the paragraph and then answer the questions that follow.

> By the 1830s, female fashions offered somewhat more protection from the climate, but they continued to suggest — and to promote — physical frailty. Early-Victorian costume not only made women *look* weak and helpless, it made them

weak and helpless. The main agent of this debility, as many writers have pointed out, was the corset, which at the time was thought of not as a mere fashion but as a medical necessity. Ladies' "frames," it was believed, were extremely delicate; their muscles could not hold them up without assistance. Like many such beliefs, this one was self-fulfilling. Well-brought-up little girls, from the best motives, were laced into juvenile versions of the corset as early as three or four. Gradually, but relentlessly, their stays were lengthened, stiffened and tightened. By the time they reached late adolescence they were wearing cages of heavy canvas reinforced with whalebone or steel, and their back muscles had often atrophied to the point where they could not sit or stand for long unsupported. The corset also deformed the internal organs and made it impossible to draw a deep breath. As a result the fashionably dressed lady blushed and fainted easily, suffered from lack of appetite and from digestive complaints, and felt weak and exhausted after any strenuous exertion. When she took off her corset her back soon began to ache; and sometimes she still could not breathe properly because her ribs had been permanently compressed inward.

— *Alison Lurie*

1. For what effect is the writer explaining a cause?

   the weakness and helplessness of females in the 1830s

2. What is the main example the writer uses to show how clothes caused weakness?

   the corset

3. Why did people think women needed corsets?

   They believed women's frames were so delicate that they needed support.

4. In what two main ways did the corset harm women's bodies?

It weakened their back muscles from lack of use; it deformed internal organs.

5. List five harmful consequences of corsets.

Women could not breathe deeply.

They suffered from eating and digestive problems.

They suffered from backaches.

They could not sit or stand unsupported.

They blushed and fainted easily.

4. Combined Paragraph Patterns from Textbook Selections

Read each of the following excerpts from college textbooks on law and history. Then answer the questions that follow each selection.

Criminal and Civil Law

The distinction between criminal and civil law is a very important concept in our legal system. . . . This text deals primarily with civil law. A civil suit involves a dispute between private individuals involving either a breach of an agreement or a breach of a duty imposed by law. A criminal action is brought by the government against an individual who has allegedly committed a crime. Crimes are classified as treason, felonies, and misdemeanors, depending on the punishment attached to the crime. *Treason* is a crime defined only by the Constitution, article III, section 3, clause 1. To commit treason — levying war against the United States, or adhering to or giving aid or comfort to its enemies — there must be an overt act and the intent to commit treason. A *felony* is a crime that is classified by statute of the place in which it is committed. That is, the severity of the punishment for a felony varies from place to place. A felony is generally regarded as being any criminal offense for which a defendant may be imprisoned for more than one year, or executed. One determines whether a crime is a felony according to the sentence that might lawfully be imposed, not according to the sentence actually ordered. Felonies do not include *misdemeanors,* which are offenses that are generally punishable by a maximum term of imprisonment of less than one year.

In a civil suit, the court attempts to remedy the dispute between individuals by determining their legal rights, awarding money damages to the injured party, or directing one party to perform or refrain from performing a specific act. Since a crime is an act against society, the criminal court punishes a guilty defendant by imposing a fine or imprisonment or both.

In a criminal prosecution, the rules of court procedure differ. In order to meet the burden of proof to find a person guilty of a crime, guilt must be proved beyond a reasonable doubt, a stricter standard than the preponderance of evidence usually required in a civil case.

— *Harold Grilliot and Frank Schuber*

1. What is the overall pattern of the three paragraphs?

   comparison and contrast

2. What two types of law are being compared in the selection?

   civil and criminal

3. What is the main difference between these two types of law?

   Civil law concerns disputes between individuals over a breach of an agreement. Criminal law concerns crimes done by individuals.

4. What aspect of these two kinds of law is being compared in the second and third paragraphs?

   how the courts handle civil and criminal cases

5. What are the main differences in how the courts treat civil and criminal cases?

In civil cases, the courts determine rights, award damages, and direct actions as remedies. In criminal cases, once guilt is proved, the court may order the individual to pay a fine or to serve time in jail, or both.

6. In the second half of the first paragraph, what paragraph pattern is used to tell more about types of criminal law?

   classification

7. What are the three types of criminal law and what distinguishes each?

   Treason — intentional attack on the United States or support of its enemies.

   Felony — any crime with a possible prison sentence of a year or more or execution.

   Misdeameanor — a crime punishable by less than a year's prison sentence.

An Age of Adversity

In the Late Middle Ages, Latin Christendom was afflicted with severe economic problems. The earlier increases in agricultural production did not continue. Limited use of fertilizers and limited knowledge of conservation exhausted the topsoil. As more grazing lands were converted to the cultivation of cereals, animal husbandry decreased, causing a serious shortage of manure needed for arable land. Intermittent bouts of prolonged heavy rains and frost also hampered agriculture. From 1301 to 1314, there was a general shortage of food, and from 1315 to 1317, famine struck Europe. Throughout the century, starvation and malnutrition were widespread.

Other economic problems abounded. A silver shortage, caused by technical problems in sinking deeper shafts in the mines, led to the debasement of coins and a spiraling inflation, which hurt the feudal nobility in particular. Prices for manufactured luxury goods, which the nobility craved, rose rapidly. At the same time, the dues that the nobility collected from peasants diminished. To replace their revenues, lords and knights turned to plunder and warfare.

Compounding the economic crisis was the Black Death, or bubonic plague. This disease was carried by fleas on brown rats, and probably first struck Mongolia in 1331–32. From there it crossed into Russia. Carried back from Black Sea ports, the plague reached Sicily in 1347. Spreading swiftly throughout much of Europe, the plague attacked an already declining and undernourished population. The first crisis lasted until 1351, and other serious outbreaks occurred in later decades. The crowded cities and towns had the highest mortalities. Perhaps twenty million people — about one-quarter to one-third of the European population — perished in the worst human disaster in recorded history.

Deprived of many of their intellectual and spiritual leaders, the panic-stricken masses drifted into immorality and frenzied forms of religious life. Hysteria and popular superstition abounded. Flagellants marched from region to region beating each other with sticks and whips in a desperate effort to please God, who they believed had cursed them with the plague. Black magic, witchcraft, and sexual license found eager supporters. Dress became increasingly ostentatious and bizarre; art forms concentrated on morbid scenes of decaying flesh, dances of death, and the torments of Hell. Sometimes this hysteria was directed against the Jews, who were accused of causing the plague by poisoning the wells. Terrible massacres of Jews occurred despite the pleas of the papacy.

— *Marvin Perry*

1. In the first paragraph, which pattern of meaning is used?

   cause and effect

2. In the second paragraph, what details are listed to add to the economic details in the first paragraph?

silver shortage; rising inflation and increased prices;

decreased revenues; plunder and warfare

3. In the second paragraph, what cause is explained?

   the cause of the silver shortage

   What are the several effects of this cause? **debasement of coins; inflation; rising prices; decreased revenues; plunder and warfare**

4. In the third paragraph, what order is used to list the details of the Black Death? **time order**

5. What two paragraph patterns are combined in the fourth paragraph? **cause and effect; listing of details**

Critical Thinking in Writing

What events similar to those in the Middle Ages do we still note today? Agricultural problems? Inflation? Plagues? Religious hysteria? Acts against Jews and other minorities? How do problems today compare and contrast with those in the Late Middle Ages, as described in the selection above? Write your response in a few paragraphs.

UNIT TWO REVIEW

Read the following selection about how Americans like to eat chicken in restaurants, and study the accompanying graph. Then answer the questions in the space provided.

Fried Chicken Still Rules the Roost

In these fat-conscious times, you might think that fried chicken wouldn't fly with consumers. Batter-dipped, deep-fried, and oozing with calories, it is clearly a no-no for people who crave lean physiques. So why is the venerable fried bird gaining market share?

Of all poultry entrees ordered by restaurant customers last year, 52 percent were for fried chicken, up from 48 percent in 1988, according to the National Restaurant Association. Kentucky Fried Chicken (KFC) posted a 20 percent increase in sales worldwide last year, and sales have increased by 8 percent at Al Copeland Enterprises, owners of Popeye's Famous Fried Chicken and Church's Fried Chicken. Copeland is riding a 28 percent sales increase for the first quarter of this year, says Ernest Renaud, vice president. That's a lot of greasy fingers.

What is causing Americans to go greasy in the health conscious 1990s? Hard times, for one thing. "In a recession, the pocketbook will win out over the calorie counter every time," says Wendy Webster, spokeswoman for the National Restaurant Association. "People like to feel they're getting more for their dollar."

Discount coupons and other special deals account for a significant share of sales at KFC and Copeland eateries. Renaud agrees that the recession has affected consumer behavior. But he also says that Americans tend to eat differently when they go out.

"I've been in this business for 39 years. In my experience, Americans talk a great game about nutrition. But when they go out to eat, they eat as they were programmed by their parents," he says. "When they get take-out, they buy for the flavor and the experience."

Conventional wisdom about fried-food consumption is way off, says KFC spokesman Dick Detwiler. "One of the great

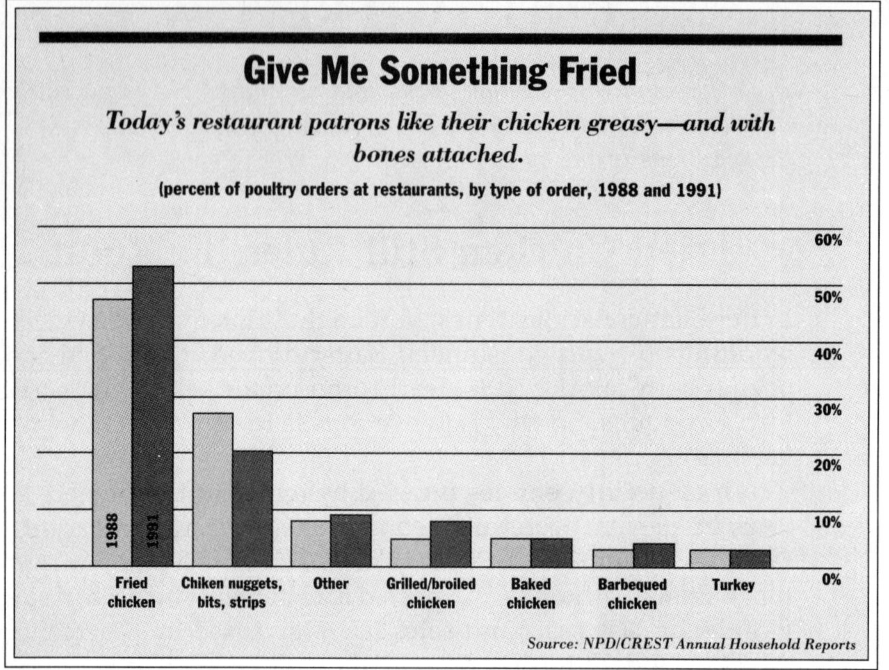

myths is that no one eats fried food any more,'' he says. ''If that were true, fast food wouldn't be a $60 billion industry.''

Another reason for the fried-chicken resurgence is the spending power of families with children. One-tenth of fried-chicken orders at restaurants are for children under age 6, while 12 percent are for children aged 6 to 17, according to the National Restaurant Association.

A final reason is psychological. ''Fried chicken is a comfort food,'' says Bill Roenigk, vice president of the National Broiler Council in Washington, D.C. When life is rough, he says, a bargain bucket of fried chicken and biscuits can soothe stressed-out souls.

— Franklin Crawford

1. What is the main idea in the article?

Fried chicken is the most popular restaurant poultry meal.

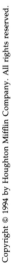

2. What sentence or phrase best represents the main idea?

   the first sentence of the second paragraph

3. In the second paragraph, what are the two most important details?

   52 percent fried chicken orders, up from 48 percent in 1988

4. Who is Wendy Webster and is her identity a major or minor detail?

   spokeswoman for the National Restaurant Association; minor

5. How much money does the fast food industry earn each year?

   $60 billion

6. Which paragraph gives a listing of details?

   paragraph 2

7. Which paragraphs give causes for the main effect reported in the article?

   paragraphs 3–8

8. What are the reasons given for the popularity of fried chicken?

   the recession; discount coupons and deals; flavor and experience; the spending power of families with children; psychological comfort

9. What two things are compared in the fifth paragraph?

how people talk about nutrition and what they do about it

10. On the graph what do the light and dark bars represent?

light: 1988 percentage of orders; dark: 1991 percentage of orders

11. What are the different kinds of poultry products compared on the graph?

fried chicken; nuggets, bits, and strips; grilled/broiled chicken; baked chicken; barbequed chicken; turkey; other

12. Which poultry products had increased sales between 1988 and 1991?

fried chicken; grilled/broiled chicken; barbequed chicken; other

13. Which poultry products had decreased sales between 1988 and 1991?

chicken nuggets, bits, strips

14. Which are the four least popular products?

turkey; barbequed chicken; baked chicken; grilled/broiled chicken

15. In what way does the graph support the article?

It shows that fried chicken is far more popular than any other poultry products.

16. What kind of information does the article provide that is not represented in the graph?

    sales figures for KFC, Popeye's and Church's; causes; the size of the fast-food industry; figures for children

17. What kind of information does the graph provide that is not presented in the article?

    figures for other poultry products

Unit Three

Interpretation and Evaluation

Handbook

8

Making Inferences

Inference is a process by which readers use hints to gather information. In making inferences, you go beyond surface details and "read between the lines" to reach information logically. When you read, certainly, you develop ideas from the exact information you have before you. Factual details in what you read provide the basis of your knowledge. But not every bit of information is easily apparent or clearly stated. Hints or suggestions may appear that you have to build on with your own knowledge and experience in order to understand something fully. Because information is not always stated in exact terms, we must supply our own information from details or ideas that are only suggested by the writer. We can't always be certain that what we supply is absolutely right. But if we follow hunches that are based on evidence, we can be fairly sure about some things, even if they are only hinted at.

Of course, a page of writing does not offer the only opportunity you have to learn more about something by means of hints or suggestions. In understanding human behavior, you've been using your inference skills for most of your childhood and adult lives.

How? Let's take an example. Your supervisor comes to work one Monday morning at 9:30. (She's usually there waiting for you as you punch in at 9:00 sharp.) She mumbles to herself under her breath and shakes her head from side to side, biting her lip. She doesn't say "Hello" as she usually does. Instead, staring straight ahead of her, she storms past your desk and the desks of your co-workers. At her office she turns the doorknob roughly, throws open the door forcefully, and then slams it loudly behind her.

What do you *infer* from her behavior? Clearly she's angry about something. You conclude that she's angry by adding up all that you see and by relying on what you know about her

usual behavior. No one had to tell you that she was angry. From her appearance, her actions, her body language, and her behavior, it was safe for you to infer that she was irritated about something.

In making inferences, you have to be careful not to go too far beyond the information at hand. Otherwise your inferences might not be correct. For example, could you assume that the supervisor we have described was angry because she had had a fight with her son? Not at all. Nothing in what you saw or observed suggested that. On the other hand, you might have heard her mumble an angry remark to herself about her son as she passed by you. Or you might know for a fact that she fights with him often and that when she does, her behavior resembles the behavior she displayed that morning. Then you might safely say to yourself, "Well, I guess she's been at it with Pepé again!" The point, of course, is that inferences must be based on valid available information, not simply on vague suspicions or wild guesses.

Look at the picture above. In a sentence explain the point of the picture — that is, what you think the picture is about.

You probably wrote something like *A man is sitting on a park bench holding an umbrella,* which pretty much states the subject of the picture. Now look back at it to answer these questions.

b 1. The person in the picture is about
   a. twenty years old.
   b. forty years old.
   c. eighty years old.

c 2. The picture was taken on a
   a. hot summer day.
   b. snowy winter evening.
   c. rainy spring day.

b 3. The scene takes place
   a. on a crowded city street.
   b. in a quiet city park.
   c. near a country farm.

If you picked answer *b* for question 1, how did you know that the person is about forty? If you picked answer *c* for question 2, how did you know that the scene probably took place on a rainy spring day? If you picked answer *b* for question 3, how did you know that the picture was taken in a quiet city park? None of the answers you picked is stated by the main idea of the picture: *A man is sitting on a park bench holding an umbrella.*

To answer the first question, you looked at the man's face and inferred that he is about forty. The hints from the picture enabled you to reject the extremes.

For the second question, you had to look at what the man was wearing. You knew that in a sweater and suit coat, he is dressed too warmly for a hot summer day but not warmly enough for a snowy winter one. You inferred that it is spring by the leaves in the background, and you inferred that it is raining by the presence of the man's open umbrella.

For the third question you eliminated answer *a* easily. The presence of a brick walk and several benches allowed you to infer that the scene is not a farm but a park. And the length of the bench, long enough for many people to sit on, tells you that the park is located where many people need a place to sit, probably in a city.

In reading, too, inference is an important skill because it helps us fill in information a writer only suggests. Look at the following paragraph to see if you can understand Diane's behavior. Answer the questions that follow.

> After lunch Diane took her bike and sneaked quietly into the yard. She moved carefully to the plot of soil under the oak in back of the house as she checked to see that nobody watched her. She leaned her bicycle against the tree and bent down. All around dark clouds rumbled noisily in the sky; a streak of yellow zig-zagged far away, and she trembled. Digging swiftly in the hot earth, she made a small hole and quickly took a crushed ten-dollar bill from her pocket. After she slipped the money into the ground and covered it, she breathed deeply and smiled. She was glad *that* was over! Now no one would find it or know how she got it. Certainly it would be there later when she wanted it.

a ______ 1. Diane is probably a
- a. nine- or ten-year-old child.
- b. young mother.
- c. three- or four-year-old child.

c ______ 2. About the money, Diane probably
- a. got it as a gift from her father.
- b. earned it.
- c. got it in a suspicious way.

b ______ 3. This event probably took place
- a. on a snowy winter afternoon.
- b. before a summer rainstorm.
- c. one night during Easter vacation.

b ______ 4. After she hides the money, Diane feels
- a. very guilty and sorry.
- b. relieved.
- c. worried that someone saw her.

To answer all these questions about this deliberately oversimplified paragraph, you needed to use inference skills. The sentences about Diane give only hints about the questions asked. No one answer is stated exactly in the paragraph.

You know Diane is probably a nine- or ten-year-old child from her actions and thoughts, which are too advanced for her to be three or four. Further, a young mother would *generally* not bury money in the ground. Answer *a* is correct for question 1.

Because she sneaked into the yard and because she looked to see if anybody watched her, you infer that Diane has done something wrong. When she thinks that no one will know how she got the money, you guess that she received it in a suspicious way. Answer *c* is correct for question 2.

The noisy clouds and the streak of yellow — thunder and lightning, surely — suggest that a storm is coming. *Hot earth* suggests the summer. Besides, Diane goes out after lunch, so the scene is not a nighttime one. Answer *b* is correct for question 3.

You can infer from Diane's deep breath and from the statement "She was glad *that* was over!" that she is relieved after she hides the money. Answer *b* is correct for question 4.

Building Inference Skills

- Try to read beyond the words. Fill in details and information based on the writer's suggestions.
- Question yourself as you read. "Why is this person doing what she is doing?" you might ask as you read. "What can I infer from the scene?" Supply the answers on the basis of the writer's hints and your own experience.
- If a writer describes a person, try to understand the person from how she moves, what she says, what she looks like. You can infer things about character from the way a person behaves. Try to build a picture of the person in your mind; base your picture on the writer's description of action and appearance.
- If you find that you cannot easily answer a question about what you have read, remember to use inference skills. Return to the part of the reading where you expect the answer. Then see if the writer suggests something that you yourself have to supply in clearer terms.

EXERCISES

1. Inferring Details from Cartoons

A. Look at the cartoon below. Use your inference skills to answer the following questions.

c 1. The cartoon takes place in a(n)
   a. movie theater.
   b. city square.
   c. amusement park.
   d. television studio.

b 2. We can infer that the people on stage are
   a. in an Elvis look-alike contest.
   b. in a "don't look like" Elvis contest.
   c. workers in an amusement park.
   d. professional entertainers.

"I think the Elvis business has just about run its course."

3. List the clues that helped you infer the answer to question 2. **the wording of the banner above the stage; the appearance of the contestants**

d 4. We can infer that the words at the bottom were spoken by
   a. the contestants.
   b. the master of ceremonies.
   c. a member of the audience seated in the front row.
   d. the male onlooker standing at the back.

c 5. We can infer that the speaker believes that
   a. this is a new and interesting contest.
   b. an amusement park is a place for fun.
   c. there have been too many Elvis activities.
   d. any business is good business.

Critical Thinking in Writing

How do you account for the ongoing popularity of Elvis Presley and for the look-alike contests and conviction that Elvis still lives? Write a few paragraphs on the Elvis phenomenon.

B. Look at the cartoon below. Use your inference skills to answer the following questions.

Cheng/China Daily/Beijing

b
_____ 6. The person in the middle
a. is the boss of the two people at the sides.
b. works for the two people at the sides.
c. is talking bluntly to the two people at the sides.
d. has two heads.

c
_____ 7. From the appearance of their heads, we can infer that the two people at the sides
a. are not pleased with the person in the middle.
b. think alike.
c. think differently.
d. cannot see the reports.

a
_____ 8. We can infer from the person's smile that he
a. is interested in being agreeable to his bosses.
b. is pleased with his work.
c. finds the way of thinking of the two people amusing.
d. is a practical joker.

d
_____ 9. From the appearance of the reports, we can infer that the
a. reports are the same.
b. reports will not please the people receiving them.
c. person in the middle has worked hard on the reports.
d. person in the middle gives his two bosses what they want to read in his reports.

2. Inferring Details from an Advertisement

Use your skills at inferring information to answer these questions about the advertisement (on page 229). Think about what this advertisement is trying to suggest about change and diversification.

b
_____ 1. The statement that best reflects the main idea of this advertisement is:
a. Change is always difficult and painful, even when necessary.
b. The more options we have, the better off we are.
c. The future belongs to athletes.
d. The future belongs to ballerinas.

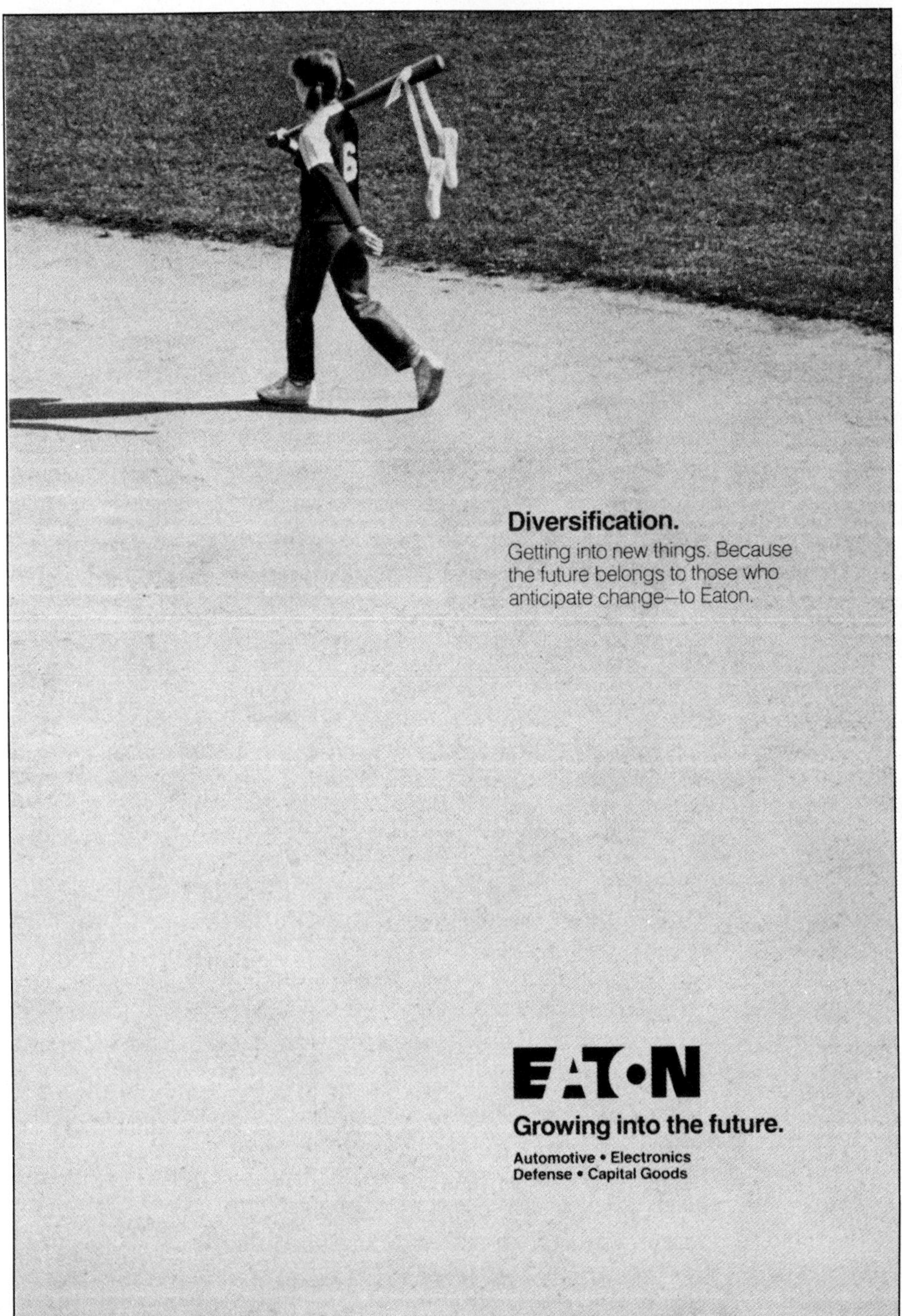
6
Diversification.
Getting into new things. Because the future belongs to those who anticipate change—to Eaton.
EATON
Growing into the future.
Automotive • Electronics
Defense • Capital Goods

b ______ 2. We can infer from the picture that the person shown is a
a. boy.
b. girl.
c. woman.
d. worker for Eaton.

a ______ 3. We can infer that the child in the picture
a. belongs to Little League.
b. is just out for a walk.
c. is carrying someone else's bat.
d. is carrying someone else's ballet shoes.

d ______ 4. What does the picture have to do with the advertiser?
a. Nothing
b. The company supports Little League.
c. The company believes that dancers make better infielders.
d. The child in the photo is a good illustration of diversification.

c ______ 5. Which of the following is a valid inference from the picture?
a. The advertiser disapproves of coed sports.
b. The advertiser believes that women can't fix automobiles.
c. The child in the picture enjoys both ballet and baseball.
d. The child in the picture is too shy to be photographed from the front.

b ______ 6. What is the connection between the child's interests and the Eaton Corporation?
a. They both like ballet.
b. They both do a variety of things.
c. By trying to do several different things, they are no good at any of them.
d. They can't decide what to concentrate on.

c ______ 7. What view of the future is suggested by the ad?
a. Only the strong will survive.
b. The future belongs to strong women.

c. The future belongs to those who are prepared for change.
d. The future belongs to business.

c ______ 8. We can infer that the child in the photograph will
a. grow up to be the first woman major leaguer.
b. grow up to be a famous ballet dancer.
c. be prepared to change with the future.
d. work for Eaton.

3. Making Inferences

Read the following selection, in which a former migrant worker describes the treatment he received. As you read, try to use inference skills. Then answer the questions after the selection.

> I began to see how everything was so wrong. When growers can have an intricate watering system to irrigate their crops but they can't have running water inside the houses of workers. Veterinarians tend to the needs of domestic animals but they can't have medical care for the workers. They can have land subsidies for the growers but they can't have adequate unemployment compensation for the workers. They treat him like a farm implement. In fact, they treat their implements better and their domestic animals better. They have heat and insulated barns for the animals but the workers live in beat-up shacks with no heat at all.
>
> — *Roberto Acuna*

1. Write in your own words the main idea of this selection (see section **5b**).

The way migrant workers are treated by the growers

is worse than it ought to be.

b ______ 2. We can infer that the author believes that
a. migrant workers should stop complaining and get back to work.
b. farm owners are mistreating workers.
c. veterinarians are better than medical doctors.
d. workers should be treated like farm tools.
e. growers are unable to figure out how to supply migrant workers with running water.

a 3. The attitude of farm owners toward migrant workers is one of
   a. neglect.
   b. fairness.
   c. hostility.
   d. favoritism.

a 4. What inferences can we draw from the passage about what motivates the farm owners?
   a. Workers can be replaced easily at no cost to owners.
   b. Farm owners are cruel people who like to make others suffer.
   c. The government causes farm owners to mistreat their help by paying them money to do so.
   d. Farm owners can't distinguish between humans and animals.

4. Making Inferences from Poetry

Read the following poem, using your inference skills to determine who is speaking in the poem, who the speaker is speaking to, and what the other person is saying. Then answer the questions after the selection.

Sure You Can Ask Me a Personal Question

How do you do?
    No, I am not Chinese.
No, not Spanish.
    No, I am American Indi-uh, Native American.
No, not from India.
    No, not Apache.
No, not Navajo.
    No, not Sioux.
No, we are not extinct.
    Yes, Indin.
Oh?
    So that's where you got those high cheekbones.
Your great grandmother, huh?
    An Indian Princess, huh?
Hair down to there?
    Let me guess. Cherokee?

Oh, so you've had an Indian friend?
    That close?
Oh, so you've had an Indian lover?
    That tight?
Oh, so you've had an Indian servant?
    That much?
Yeah, it was awful what you guys did to us.
    It's real decent of you to apologize.
No, I don't know where you can get peyote.
    No, I don't know where you can get Navajo rugs real cheap.
No, I didn't make this. I bought it at Bloomingdale's.
    Thank you. I like your hair too.
I don't know if anyone knows whether or not Cher is really Indian.
    No, I didn't make it rain tonight.
Yeah. Uh-huh. Spirituality.
    Uh-huh. Yeah. Spirituality. Uh-huh. Mother.
Earth. Yeah. Uh'huh. Uh'huh. Spirituality.
    No, I didn't major in archery.
Yeah, a lot of us drink too much.
    Some of us can't drink enough.
This ain't no stoic look.
    This is my face.

— *Diane Burns*

1. Who is speaking in this poem?

   a Native American

2. With whom is the speaker speaking? In what kind of situation?

   a stranger who does not know much about present-day American Indians and has developed stereotypes about them

3. What are some of the statements you can infer the other person makes?

   Student responses will vary. Some possibilities: My great-grandmother was an Indian Princess. I've had an

Indian friend, lover, and servant. We did awful things to the Indians. Where can you get peyote? Cheap Navajo rugs? I like your hair. Is Cher really an Indian? Is alcohol a problem for Indians?

4. What do you infer is the attitude of the other person to the speaker?

   ignorance, but also curiosity about and insensitivity toward the Native American's feelings

5. What do you infer the speaker feels in reaction to what the other person says?

   tolerance at first and then impatience with the person's blunt questions

6. Look up the word *stoic* in a dictionary. What feelings of the writer do you infer from the closing lines:

   This ain't no stoic look.
       This is my face.

   The speaker wants the person to see that she is an individual, to look at her without making assumptions about what she is like.

7. What is the implied main idea of the poem?

   Stereotypical assumptions about an individual in a minority group ignore individuality and often are ridiculous.

Critical Thinking in Writing

Write your own poem called "Sure You Can Ask Me a Personal Question," in which you explore your own heritage by asking and answering questions as Burns has.

5. Making Inferences

Read the following selection about the development of magazines and newspapers in America. Answer the questions that follow.

> The impact of the American periodical press also has been technological and social. The large, mass-circulation magazines have influenced the smaller magazines, which in many instances seek to imitate their appearance and to emulate the high quality of their printing, layout, and make-up. They also have influenced magazines around the world. Europe, for example, is given to publishing magazines resembling *Life* and *Look,* and almost no heavily industrialized country is without its imitator of *Time* (*The Link* in India, *Elseviers* in the Netherlands, *Tiempo* in Mexico, *Der Spiegel* in Germany, and *L'Express* in France, for example). The social effect has to do with the discharge or failure to discharge its social responsibilities. These responsibilities the magazine press shares with all communications media, printed or electronic. They include the obligation, in a political democracy such as in the U.S.A., to provide the people with a fair presentation of facts, with honestly held opinions, and with truthful advertising. All but the subsidized periodicals hold — or seek to hold — to these goals within a certain framework: that of the business order, the private initiative, profit-making system.
>
> — *Roland E. Wolseley*

1. In your own words write the point that the writer makes about the impact of American magazines and newspapers (see section **5b**).

   The American periodical press has had a technological and social impact on the rest of the world.

c

______ 2. We can infer about news magazines like *Life, Look,* and *Time* that
a. they are resented in European countries.
b. they sell very well throughout the world.
c. they are respected as models for foreign magazines.
d. they do not discharge social responsibilities.
e. their production costs are extremely high.

e

______ 3. The writer believes that magazines
a. must make a profit at any cost.
b. should not compete with television for advertising.
c. should be subsidized.
d. should imitate European models.
e. should not accept untruthful advertising.

b

______ 4. We can infer about the author's knowledge of the subject that
a. he knows very little about Asian or African periodicals.
b. he knows a great deal about European and American magazines.
c. he knows a great deal about European magazines but not much about American magazines.
d. he has worked as a magazine layout editor.
e. None of the above

6. Making Inferences

Read the following selection about the ocean, using inference skills. Then answer the questions after the selection.

> The ocean cannot be dissociated from any of our problems. Though not always properly "billed," it is nonetheless a vital actor in the "production" of climate, storms, agriculture, health, war and peace, trade, leisure, and creative art. It is not merely a weather-regulating system and a source of food, cattle feed, fuel, and minerals. More generally, it absorbs vast quantities of the carbon dioxide generated by the combustion of fossil fuels, it releases a major part of the oxygen we breathe, and it acts as a powerful buffer to slow down or to avoid such calamities as quick variations in the sea level. Moreover, the human body is made up of much more water than all its components combined. A dehydrated human being would weigh little more than 30 pounds. Our flesh is composed of myriads of cells, each one of which contains a

miniature ocean, less salty than today's ocean but comprising all the salts of the sea, probably the built-in heritage of our distant ancestry, when some mutating fish turned into reptiles and invaded the virgin land.

— *Jacques Cousteau*

1. What main point is the author trying to make about the ocean (see section **5b**)?

   The ocean affects every part of the world.

a 2. We can infer that the author believes that
   a. the ocean does not always get the attention it should as human beings try to solve their problems.
   b. the ocean is polluted.
   c. people should do more to investigate the ocean's resources.
   d. the ocean is not a weather-regulating system.
   e. oceans cause a number of problems for humanity.

e 3. Between the physical makeup of the ocean and the human body, Cousteau believes that
   a. there is not much of a relationship.
   b. there is no evidence to suggest a relationship.
   c. we must study the possible relationships.
   d. there is much confusion.
   e. there is a very close relationship.

e 4. According to the author, which of the following can we infer are affected by the ocean?
   a. Paintings
   b. Tourism
   c. Hurricanes
   d. Hunger
   e. All of the above

9

Understanding Figurative Language

To make language clearer, more interesting, and more vivid, we all use expressions that are not literally true. We make comparisons in speaking and writing. *Figurative language* — language that compares — paints a picture.

People frequently use figurative expressions when they speak:

1. "I worked *like a dog* last night!"
2. "Either spend that fifty dollars or put it in the bank. You can't *have your cake and eat it too.*"
3. "I told him to stop *bugging me.*"

None of these expressions is *literal* — that is, not one means exactly what it says. The speakers are not really talking about dogs, cake, or bugs.

In example 1, the speaker tries to show how hard she worked. She compares herself to a dog to achieve the effect she wants.

In example 2, the person is saying that you cannot both use something up and keep it to use later. He states a familiar figurative expression. With it he compares the person he's talking to with someone who wants to eat a piece of cake and, at the same time, to save it for later — an impossible thing to do.

In example 3, the speaker compares someone to an insect, even though she is really talking about a person. The expression *bugging me* suggests that the person is behaving like an annoying bug — a mosquito, perhaps, or an ant.

With informal and familiar figurative expressions like these, you rarely see a picture in your mind as a result of the comparisons being made. But writers who use *original* figurative language expect you to picture the comparisons they make so that you can see something more easily. Look at these two statements:

4. A yellow light was slanting over the high walls into the jail yard.
5. A sickly light, like yellow tinfoil, was slanting over the high walls into the jail yard. (George Orwell)

In example 4, the writer certainly has painted a picture for the reader. You can see the jail yard, the high walls, and the yellow light slanting over it. There are no figurative expressions here; the description is literal. But in example 5, because of *figurative language,* the picture is much more vivid. You know that light cannot be ill (only living things like people or animals can get sick). Yet by calling the light *sickly* — comparing it to a living thing — Orwell makes us see unhealthfulness in the scene. Then he makes the picture even clearer by comparing the light to yellow tin foil. Of course, there is no tin foil here: You would not expect there to be any on the walls outside a prison. But by means of the comparison, the writer is trying to paint an original picture in your mind. If you have ever seen (or can imagine) yellow tin foil, you can picture the kind of light Orwell wants you to see as it slants over the jail yard walls.

Writers have many different ways of using figurative language to create vivid pictures. Sometimes nonhuman things are given human features (a kind of comparison called *personification*):

6. The sun *yawned* through the trees. (The sun is being compared to a person yawning.)
7. An idea *spoke* to him, *racing through* his mind. (The idea has the quality of a living thing: it speaks and races.)

Sometimes we make comparisons using the word *like* or the word *as* (a kind of figurative expression called a *simile*):

8. The tree bent in the wind *like an old man praying.* (A tree is compared to an old man at prayer.)
9. The moon looked *as white as a skull.* (The moon's color is being compared to the color of a skull.)

Some comparisons are only suggested. One of two objects being compared is said to *be* the other object, but the things compared are usually quite different from each other. (Implied comparisons like those that follow are called *metaphors.*)

10. His *blackberry* eyes darted nervously. (The eyes are being compared to blackberries — small and black.)

11. A brown, withered *leaf of a hand* fluttered gently on her lap and then lifted up to wipe a tear away. (The hand is being compared to a leaf to suggest frailty and the approaching end of life.)

For special effects, we exaggerate some comparisons (a figurative expression that exaggerates is called *hyperbole*):

12. He roared with the force *of a thousand lions.* (The force of his roar is exaggerated by being compared to the roars of lions.)

In newspapers, magazines, and textbooks, you can expect to find figurative language to make a point clearer or more lively, or often both. In poetry and other forms of creative writing, writers often use figurative language in subtle and complex ways. As a reader, you must recognize figurative expressions so that you can understand a writer's point fully.

Understanding Figurative Language

- Make sure that you are aware that the writer is making a comparison. In example 11, the writer is talking about a woman's hand, not a leaf. The writer has not changed the topic suddenly to a discussion of leaves. The writer is simply making the description more vivid by comparing the hand to something else.
- Keep in mind just what is being compared to what. Don't lose the basic point by getting confused about the comparison and forgetting what the writer is explaining in the first place. In example 8, you are supposed to see the tree better because it looks like an old man at prayer; you should not, however, expect to read anything further about religion or praying. (There are, however, *extended metaphors,* which carry the implied comparisons further. Especially in poetry, you should watch for additional words that continue and extend a simple comparative theme.)
- Look for the words *like* and *as,* which often introduce comparisons.
- Try to figure out why the writer has made the comparison. Why, in example 6, is the sun compared to a person yawning? Why, in example 9, is the moon compared to a skull?

EXERCISES

1. Understanding Figurative Language

Each of the following sentences makes a comparison. Explain in your own words what the comparison means. Tell also why you think the writer makes the comparison. Use a separate sheet of paper to record your answers. **Student responses will vary.**

1. An aged man is but a paltry thing,
   a tattered coat upon a stick . . .

   — *William Butler Yeats*

2. Sailing through silent seas of thought, alone.

   — *William Wordsworth*

3. Blow, blow thou winter wind
   Thou art not so unkind
   As man's ingratitude . . .

   — *William Shakespeare*

4. Hope is the thing with feathers
   That perches on the soul,
   And sings the tune without the words,
   And never stops at all.

   — *Emily Dickinson*

5. A wicked whisper came and made my heart as dry as dust.

   — *Samuel Taylor Coleridge*

6. Last summer you left
   my life quivering
   like a battlefield.
   I wore headaches like garments.

   — *Colleen McElroy*

7. When Duty whispers low, *Thou must,*
   The youth replies, *I can.*

   — *Ralph Waldo Emerson*

8. My father's body was a globe of fear
   His body was a town we never knew . . .

   — *Michael Ondaatje*

2. Common Figurative Expressions

The figurative language in the following sentences appears often in everyday talk and conversation. On a separate sheet of paper, explain the meaning of the figurative expressions that appear in italics. **Student responses will vary.**

1. You may not like this, but *the bottom line* is that unless your grades improve, you can't buy a television.
2. We'd like to get *feedback* and *input* from you on this project.
3. Jason's mother gave him a lot of *static* about his coming home late last night.
4. My brother Kevin *eats like a horse* and *sleeps like a log.*
5. After the checkup, the doctor declared Mr. Shapiro to be *strong as an ox.*

3. Figurative Language in Poetry

The poem "Year's End" by Brother Antoninus uses figurative language to describe Antoninus's feelings about the end of the year. As you read the poem think about how each figurative expression helps you understand the poet's feelings and thoughts. Then answer the questions.

Year's End

The year dies fiercely; out of the north the beating storms,
And wind at the roof's edge, lightning swording the low sky:
This year dying like some traitored Norse stumbling under
 the deep wounds,
The furious steel, smashing and swinging.

From the northern room I watch in the dusk,
And being unsocial regard the coming year coldly,
Suspicious of strangers, distrustful of innovations,
Reluctant to chance one way or another the unknown.
I leave this year as a man leaves wine.
Remembering the summer, bountiful, the good fall, the
 months mellow and full.
I sit in the northern room, in the dusk, the death of a year,
And watch it go down in thunder.

— *Brother Antoninus*

1. Why is the year described as dying?

 It is the end of the year.

2. What is the weather like?

 It is windy with a lightning storm.

3. Explain the meaning of "lightning swording the low sky."

   Lightning bolts cut across a cloud-covered sky.

4. In what way is the year's end like a dying Norse warrior?

   It grows angry and violent.

5. How does the weather compare to the poet's own mood and attitudes?

   The poet's mood is gloomy and angry like the weather.

6. Explain the meaning of "I leave this year as a man leaves wine."

   He is unwilling to let the year go.

7. The poet says he is "distrustful of innovations." What does the word *innovations* mean? How is the new year like an innovation?

   An innovation is something new; and a new year brings new things.

8. What are the poet's general feelings about the old year and the new?

   He is angry and brooding about leaving the old year behind and having to face a new year.

4. Figurative Language in Prose

Read the following passage about what a young woman named Esperanza thinks about her name. As you read the selection notice the many ways the writer uses figurative language to express her feelings about her name. Then answer the questions.

> In English my name means hope. In Spanish it means too many letters. It means sadness, it means waiting. It is like

the number nine. A muddy color. It is the Mexican records my father plays on Sunday mornings when he is shaving, songs like sobbing.

It was my great-grandmother's name and now it is mine. She was a horse woman too, born like me in the Chinese year of the horse — which is supposed to be bad luck if you're born female — but I think this is a Chinese lie because the Chinese, like the Mexicans, don't like their women strong.

My great-grandmother. I would've liked to have known her, a wild horse of a woman, so wild she wouldn't marry until my great-grandfather threw a sack over her head and carried her off. Just like that, as if she were a fancy chandelier. That's the way he did it.

And the story goes she never forgave him. She looked out the window all her life, the way so many women sit their sadness on an elbow. I wonder if she made the best with what she got or was she sorry because she couldn't be all the things she wanted to be. Esperanza. I have inherited her name, but I don't want to inherit her place by the window.

At school they say my name funny as if the syllables were made out of tin and hurt the roof of your mouth. But in Spanish my name is made out of a softer something like silver, not quite as thick as my sister's name Magdalena which is uglier than mine. Magdalena who at least can come home and become Nenny. But I am always Esperanza.

I would like to baptize myself under a new name, a name more like the real me, the one nobody sees. Esperanza as Lisandra or Maritza or Zeze the X. Yes. Something like Zeze the X will do.

— *Sandra Cisneros*

1. How can a name that means "hope" also mean "sadness" and "waiting"?

   One waits in a sad condition until hopes come true, if they ever do.

2. What does having too many letters have to do with sadness and waiting?

   Neither is crisp, clear, or over quickly.

3. What feelings does calling her name "a muddy color" convey?

   uncertainty; unhappiness

4. Why does Esperanza think of her name as like her father's records?

   They are both sad, like sobbing.

5. Who else has the name Esperanza?

   her great-grandmother

6. What associations do people make with her and her great-grandmother being born in the year of the horse? Does Esperanza accept those associations?

   Strength, which is bad luck for a woman. Yes, but Esperanza likes her wildness and strength.

7. What new associations does she make between her great-grandmother and a wild horse? Why?

   The great-grandmother's strength was like that of a wild horse because she would not give in to the great-grandfather except by force — and she still kept an independent spirit.

8. What does it mean that the great-grandmother "looked out the window all her life?"

   She could not do anything; she could only look out on what others did.

9. What does it mean that "women sit their sadness on an elbow"?

   They don't act; they only sit thinking about their sadness, with head resting on a bent arm.

10. What does it mean that at school they say her name "as if the syllables were made out of tin"?

    They make her name sound harsh and ugly.

11. What does she compare her name spoken in Spanish to? Why?

    Her name in Spanish is soft, as though made of silver. She thinks the name is beautiful in Spanish because of the vowels and sibilants.

12. What other names would she like? What do those names convey?

    Lisandra, Maritza, Zeze the X. Student responses will vary.

Critical Thinking in Writing

If you could change your name, would you? To what? Why? Write a few paragraphs in which you explain why you would either change your name or keep it the same.

10

Drawing Conclusions and Predicting Outcomes

Careful readers *interpret* what they read; that is, they try to explain and to understand ideas brought out by their reading. One way to build your skill at interpreting is to try to draw conclusions from what a writer tells you.

A reading selection gives you information about a topic. Good readers are able to use that information on their own in order to know what to expect next. Paragraphs or larger readings present information to support a topic, but they do not always state all the possible results of the events the writer discusses. In fact, if you must answer questions after you read, those questions often involve conclusions you must draw on your own.

But before you think of larger units like paragraphs or whole essays, it's useful to think about drawing conclusions from parts of individual sentences. Sometimes you can predict the outcome of a sentence — that is, you can make a reasonably accurate guess about how the sentence will end. You can use this skill to help you see how to draw conclusions and to predict outcomes in longer works.

Which word group from the choices given would you select to complete the following sentence?

> If you keep reading books with small print in such dim light,
>
> a. you'll never pass your exam.
> b. you may not learn the meaning of important words.
> c. you may strain your eyes.
> d. you should play some music on the radio.

We can reasonably guess that *c* is the correct ending of the sentence. In fact, the only logical selection we can make from the choices given here is *c*.

We can tell from the word *if* that the writer is setting up conditions that will affect the outcome of the sentence. From the words in the sentence and from our own experiences, we know that small print and dim lighting can indeed lead to eyestrain. Although we cannot be absolutely certain that the writer had that point in mind, choice *c* would be a safe one.

Even though there may be some truth in the other choices, not one logically develops from the rest of the sentence. Choice *a* is not as good a choice as *c* because some people could pass an exam even though they read small print in poorly lit rooms. Similarly, you'd have to reject *b;* although you might have to squint, you could determine word meanings even if you read under poor conditions. Also, nothing in the first part of the sentence helps us predict that music would satisfy the meaning that the writer is aiming for. True, dim lighting and music sometimes go together, but in this example playing music is not a logical outcome, so choice *d* would be incorrect.

If you followed the preceding explanation, you have some idea about how to draw conclusions or to predict outcomes even in paragraphs and longer selections. You have to put together facts and details logically in your own mind in order to draw the right conclusions. You have to think ahead to events or ideas that might come from information the writer gives, information that forces you to *predict* how things come out. Even though you might not know for sure, you have to use evidence you find in your reading to forecast what will happen.

Read this selection about birds following a ship at sea. Answer the questions after the selection, which involve drawing conclusions.

> Ever since our departure, the seagulls have been following our ship, apparently without effort, almost without moving their wings. Their fine, straight navigation scarcely leans upon the breeze. Suddenly, a loud plop at the level of the kitchens stirs up a greedy alarm among the birds, throwing their fine flight into confusion and sending up a fire of white wings. The seagulls whirl madly in every direction and then with no loss of speed drop from the flight one by one and dive toward the sea. A few seconds later they are together again on the water, a quarrelsome farmyard that we leave behind, nesting in the hollow of the wave, slowly picking through the manna of the scraps.
>
> — *Albert Camus*

c ______ 1. The seagulls are following the ship because
a. the men are playing with them.
b. they are angry at the noises from the ship.
c. they are hungry.
d. they are confused.

d ______ 2. The "loud plop at the level of the kitchens" is probably
a. the sound of a dead bird falling from the sky.
b. the drop of the engine or anchor to slow the ship down.
c. a man falling overboard.
d. the sound of leftover food hitting the waves.

a ______ 3. The men probably throw scraps overboard because
a. they have to get rid of unwanted garbage and leftovers.
b. they like the seagulls.
c. the seagulls are hungry.
d. the seagulls annoy them.

b ______ 4. The men will probably
a. try to shoot one of the birds.
b. travel on, leaving the gulls to their meal.
c. feed the birds whenever the birds are hungry.
d. shout and make noises to keep the annoying birds away.

We can tell from the way the birds behave at the end that they were probably hungry and are following the ship for food; therefore answer *c* is correct for question 1.

From the plopping sound near the kitchen, we conclude that someone has thrown food overboard and pick answer *d* for question 2.

In question 3, we can reach a conclusion from the way the men behave. Nothing in the paragraph suggests how they feel about the gulls; we don't know if the men like the birds or are annoyed by them. We also do not know whether the men know if the seagulls are hungry or even whether the men *care* that the birds may be hungry. The only safe conclusion is that the men want to dispose of their garbage: Answer *a* is correct for question 3.

In like manner, the only thing we can predict about a future event is that the men will leave the birds behind as the ship moves forward. For question 4, only *b* is an appropriate conclusion to draw.

How to Form Conclusions and Predict Outcomes

- Be sure you know the main idea of the selection.
- Be sure you understand all the facts or details that the writer gives to support the idea.
- Check on difficult vocabulary. Did you use context *clues* (section **1c**) to figure out that *manna* had something to do with food? (Food supplied as if by a miracle — like the food that came to the Jews in the wilderness — is called *manna*.)
- Look out for the logic of action. Did you follow the sequence (section **7a**)? Did you put events together in the right order of time or place to help you predict what would happen?
- Look at the way people are described. Can you tell from their personalities — from the way they think and feel — just how they might act?
- Ask yourself after you read: What will happen as a result of these actions or events?
- Be careful to build your conclusion on evidence you find in what you read and not exclusively on your own opinions, likes, and dislikes. Of course you need to rely on your own experience to help you figure out how things may happen. But most of your conclusions must be based on what you read in the selection.

EXERCISES

1. Predicting Outcomes of Sentences

Try to determine the outcome for the following statements. In your own words, state what you feel would be a logical ending to finish each sentence. Be prepared to defend your choice. Write your sentence ending in the space provided. **Student responses will vary.**

1. If baseball players keep getting more expensive contracts, then the price of tickets ______________________________

____.

2. If Janice keeps arguing with the boss about every rule and procedure she has to follow on the job, she ____.

3. If Bob keeps up with the assignments and keeps asking questions, even though he is not the top student in the class, he will probably ____.

4. When the building's owner discovered six cats, two dogs, three parakeets, a duck, a small alligator, and a snake in Leo Ito's apartment, she ____.

5. People who do not smoke or drink, who exercise regularly, and who eat healthful foods probably ____.

2. Drawing Conclusions and Predicting Outcomes

Read the following selection to see what kind of instruction children may need in order to learn to read. Answer the questions that follow.

A child takes great pleasure in becoming able to read some words. But the excitement fades when the texts the child must read force him to reread the same word endlessly. Word recognition — "decoding" is the term used by educational theorists — deteriorates into empty rote learning when it does not lead directly into the reading of meaningful content. The longer it takes the child to advance from decoding to meaningful reading, the more likely it becomes that his pleasure in books will evaporate. A child's ability to read depends unquestionably on his learning pertinent skills. But he will not be interested in learning basic reading skills if he thinks he is expected to master them for their own sake. That is why so much depends on what the teacher, the school, and

> the textbooks emphasize. From the very beginning, the child must be convinced that skills are only a means to achieve a goal, and that the only goal of importance is that he become literate — that is, come to enjoy literature and benefit from what it has to offer.
>
> — *Bruno Bettelheim and Karen Zelan*

d ______ 1. As the writers use it, the word *decoding* means
a. figuring out secret languages.
b. empty rote learning.
c. educational theorists.
d. learning to read individual words.

c ______ 2. From the writers' point of view we can conclude that a child who reads mainly by rote decoding will
a. learn how to read intelligently.
b. never learn how to read.
c. not gain much joy and satisfaction from reading.
d. come to enjoy literature later in life.

b ______ 3. We can conclude from this selection that as a skill, decoding is
a. worthless.
b. important only as a part of a larger effort to enjoy literature.
c. supported by teachers, schools, and textbooks as the most important reading skill.
d. still being explored as a new area for teaching reading.

a ______ 4. If the writers examined a children's reading text that read "Run, Jim, run. Run to Tim. Tim and Jim run to Tom," we could predict that they would
a. disapprove quite strongly.
b. approve enthusiastically.
c. have no real opinion one way or the other.
d. want teachers and parents to read the text aloud to children.

3. Drawing Conclusions and Predicting Outcomes

Read the following selection about changing male behavior and answer the questions that follow.

> Here's a portrait of the American man, circa 1992. He is romantic and self-centered, family-oriented and individualistic,

hard-working and leisure-loving. In other words, he is a mass of contradictions. . . .

Women have spent the last three decades behaving more like men in certain ways. In the 1990s, men are adapting to these changes. Women have enjoyed significant advances in educational attainment, labor force participation, career involvement, and economic independence. They have also endured significant increases in smoking, divorce, and single-parent families. The overwhelming result has been stress, as women try to play multiple roles, and increasing conflict, as women demand more from men.

"Men were thrown a curve ball," says Michael Clinton, publisher of *GQ* magazine. "The patterns they had established in terms of interacting with women were no longer relevant."

In response, men started helping out more with housework and child care. Nurturing became a manly thing in the 1980s; it was celebrated in movies like *Three Men and a Baby* and television programs like "Full House." Advertisers became infatuated with the image of a handsome towelled man dandling a baby on his knees. But many women see these images of men as desirable though unattainable fantasies.

In reality, men can't move fast enough to meet women's expectations. As men have come to respect women more, women have become less satisfied with men. In 1970, 40 percent of men said they thought women were better respected than they had been in the past, according to the Roper Organization. In 1990, this share had risen to 62 percent. In 1970, women were most likely to describe men as "basically kind, gentle, and thoughtful." In a similar Roper survey 20 years later, women were most likely to say that men only value their own opinions, that men find it necessary to keep women down, that they immediately think of getting a woman in bed, and that they don't pay attention to things at home.

As torrents of negativity wash over them, men are beginning to reach out to one another — just as women learned to do with the women's movement, social networks, and magazines like *Working Mother.* The first issue of *Full-Time Dads* was published in April 1991. This bimonthly publication serves men who are isolated, in both a physical and psychological sense, as full-time parents. Their stories about the joys and frustrations of child-rearing are not new to women, but they are new to many men.

Men who are full-time homemakers are still rare. But for whatever reason, men are taking on more of the everyday responsibilities of running a household. That includes shopping, child care, and cooking.

— *Dianne Crispell*

c 1. From this selection we can conclude that men's behavior in the last few decades has
a. not changed at all.
b. grown further from that of women.
c. started to develop in traditionally female areas.
d. followed a straightforward pattern of development.

a 2. In the same period, women's behavior has
a. taken on some aspects of male patterns.
b. become more feminine.
c. led to greater happiness.
d. rejected interaction with men.

b 3. Men have found that
a. women like being treated in the old ways.
b. they need to find new ways of interacting with women.
c. they no longer need to respect women.
d. showing that they are nurturing is a sure way to meet women.

d 4. We can conclude that women today
a. do not appreciate the changes in men.
b. have found that men are fulfilling new ideals.
c. would like men to be more powerful and masculine.
d. demand more respect from men than in the past.

d 5. We can conclude that modern men are
a. hopelessly confused.
b. finding housework and child raising too difficult to cope with.
c. becoming more isolated and lonely than ever.
d. starting to learn to cope with new roles.

a 6. Overall from this selection we can conclude that
a. men's lives are changing, as are their relationships.
b. men have successfully adopted a new ideal of tenderness.

c. men all share equally in housework and child rearing.
d. men no longer know how to keep women happy and so do not try.

4. Drawing Conclusions from Textbook Selections

Read each of the following selections from textbooks and answer the questions afterward by drawing conclusions and predicting outcomes.

Science

The *resolving power* of an optical instrument, such as a telescope or a microscope, is the measurement of its ability to distinguish clearly between two different things. Anton van Leeuwenhoek (1632–1723) is listed in the *Biographical Dictionary of Outstanding Men* because he was the first to arrange simple lenses as a primitive microscope and call the attention of the Royal Society of London to living forms in a drop of water. Up to that moment, his usefulness to society had been as a family man and custodian. Leeuwenhoek's invention helped the human eye to distinguish clearly among living protozoa, very small single cell animals. This was a simple beginning that led to more sophisticated generations of instruments and incredible advances in science and medicine.

— *John W. Harrington*

b ______ 1. The main point in this selection is to
a. define *resolving power.*
b. discuss Leeuwenhoek's contribution to improving the resolving power of optical instruments.
c. explain the ability of the human eye to see one-celled animals.
d. call the attention of the Royal Society of London to living forms in a drop of water.

a ______ 2. We can conclude from this selection that the better the resolving power of a microscope or telescope, the
a. more sophisticated the instrument.
b. more important Leeuwenhoek's family life.
c. less we need to rely on the human eye in scientific observations.
d. more protozoa in a drop of water.

d 3. It is correct to assume that a direct outcome of Leeuwenhoek's primitive microscope was
a. the growth of the Royal Society of London.
b. his increased usefulness as a family man and custodian.
c. his improved ability to arrange simple lenses.
d. the high-powered microscopes and telescopes in use today.

Government

Ending Sex Discrimination

Bans on Job Discrimination

As in other areas of civil rights, the first major legislative efforts to prohibit job discrimination based on sex came in the 1960's. The Equal Pay Act of 1963 forbids using different pay scales for women and men who do equal work under similar conditions. The bill's coverage, though, effectively excluded millions of women and permitted wage differences for a number of reasons. Until it was amended in 1972, the law applied only to large interstate companies.

Many of these shortcomings were addressed in the Civil Rights Act of 1964. . . . Title VII of this act prohibits sex (as well as racial) discrimination in employment. This provision was not in the bill first introduced in Congress. Southern Congressmen — the principal opponents of the Civil Rights Act — introduced an amendment on sex discrimination in hopes of weakening its chances of passage. Both the act and the amendment passed, bringing about the first comprehensive legislation on sex discrimination.

Following these new laws, many cases of sex discrimination in the workplace came before the Supreme Court in the 1970's. For example, it ruled against a corporation that would not hire women with preschool-age children, though it employed men with young children (*Phillips* v. *Martin Marietta Corp.*, 1971). The Court also rejected arbitrary height and weight requirements that effectively barred women from jobs as prison guards (*Dothard* v. *Rawlinson*, 1977). It also outlawed company policies in which maternity leave was treated differently from other types of leave in calculating seniority benefits (*Nashville Gas* v. *Satty*, 1977).

— *Mary Beth Norton, David M. Katzman, Paul D. Escott, Howard Chudacoff, Thomas G. Paterson, and William M. Tuttle, Jr.*

d 1. We can conclude from this selection that sex discrimination now
   a. no longer occurs.
   b. has been declared illegal in all its forms.
   c. is a political issue.
   d. has been declared illegal in some specific ways.

b 2. We can conclude that the Supreme Court has
   a. actively banned sex discrimination throughout this century.
   b. been concerned with sex discrimination in recent decades.
   c. not been concerned with sex discrimination as a problem.
   d. been the only government branch concerned with sex discrimination.

a 3. We can conclude from this selection that sex discrimination
   a. in large part has been eliminated from the workplace.
   b. is only a matter of job discrimination.
   c. has been eliminated in many areas of life.
   d. is a simple matter to eliminate.

Critical Thinking in Writing

What instances of sex discrimination on the job can you identify today? What efforts are we making individually and as a nation to reduce the differences between men and women in the work force?

11

Generalizing

Another way to help you interpret what you read and to get deeper meanings from it is to develop skills in generalizing. When you *generalize,* you extend meanings beyond the specific ideas you read about. Generalizing allows you to apply information you've learned in a broader, less specific sense. You add up facts and details and draw from that particular information some general ideas or principles.

In Chapter 10 you learned about drawing conclusions and predicting outcomes. These skills are closely related to generalizing. *Generalizing* carries you a step beyond a conclusion you can draw about a specific set of details. It's almost as if *you* develop a concept or a rule based on material you've read.

Read the following selection about an eventful drive through the rain. Then examine the questions and discussion that follow.

> One rainy morning . . . Harry Van Sinderen left his home in Washington, Connecticut, to drive to his office in New York, about a hundred miles away. The rain turned into a downpour — the heaviest he could remember. Switching on the car radio, he learned that he was in the midst of a tropical storm that had swung inland from the coast, and that streams were flooding all through northern Connecticut. A few minutes later he got worse news: a dam on the Shepaug River above Washington had broken, and the resulting flood had wiped out the center of the town, with considerable loss of life and property.
>
> Harry drove on to New York, walked into his office, and wrote out his resignation as chairman of the board of the export-import company he had managed for many years. He then drove back to Washington, through the still-pouring rain, and appointed himself Chief Rebuilder of the town. He was sixty-six years old at the time.
>
> — *John Fischer*

a ______ 1. Harry Van Sinderen was probably
a. interested in urban planning.
b. interested in tropical storms.
c. somewhat unstable mentally.
d. not making enough money on his job.

d ______ 2. Van Sinderen's actions suggest that
a. people should never go outdoors in tropical rainstorms.
b. a manager's job is often dull.
c. driving a car to and from work every day is a great drain on one's energy.
d. people late in life can change careers to find more meaningful work.

b ______ 3. Van Sinderen would agree that
a. personal success in business and finance is a person's key aim.
b. service to the community in a time of crisis is more important than personal goals.
c. people should carry heavy insurance in case of disasters like flooding.
d. unexpected storms in Connecticut are violent.

Based on Van Sinderen's concern for damage to the city from the rainstorm, and based on the statement that he made himself "Chief Rebuilder" of the town, the idea that he has an interest in urban planning is clear. Even though he may have acted strangely in giving up his job with his company, and even though people often leave jobs for work that pays more, we have no evidence to make us believe that he is either mentally unstable or underpaid for the work he does now. And just because he found himself in the midst of a heavy downpour, we cannot conclude that he had a special interest in tropical storms. Only answer *a* is a fair conclusion for question 1.

In question 2, however, we must be able to go beyond the conclusions we have drawn from the paragraph. Van Sinderen, a man of sixty-six, suddenly resigned one job to take on another that he thought was important. We can generalize from his actions and say that they suggest that age does not have to stop a person from making major changes in his or her life's work. Based on Harry Van Sinderen's action, we've developed a general rule: People late in life can change their careers to find more meaningful work. This is not a general statement that everyone would agree with, but information in the paragraph supports the generalization. For question 2, only answer *d* is correct.

All the other statements in question 2 are generalizations too, but there is no reason to believe that they are true based on information given in the selection. It's a general rule that people should not go out in tropical storms. But the word *never* here is too strong; it does not allow any exceptions. Van Sinderen really benefited from his ride in the heavy rains — it helped him make an important decision. And although it's often generally true that driving each day drains energy, nothing in the paragraph supports that idea. Further, even though Van Sinderen quit his job, and even though we suspect, in general, that a manager's job often has moments of dullness, we cannot support that idea from information in this paragraph. For question 2, then, we would have to reject choices *a*, *b*, and *c*.

Question 3 also asks us to make some rule based on information we have in the paragraph. Although we know generally that financial and business success is a key aim for many people, we do not know that Van Sinderen would agree. (In fact, his quitting a high-level job suggests that these forms of success are not essential to him.) Choice *a*, then, is not correct. Choice *c* is also a generalization, and a reasonable one at that. Many people would agree that heavy insurance can help in times of disaster. But there's nothing in the passage to show that Van Sinderen agrees with the idea. Therefore we have to rule out choice *c*. Choice *d* also is not correct. It is much too broad. It suggests that any unexpected storm in Connecticut is violent. How can we make that generalization from this paragraph, which talks about only one storm?

For question 3, then, only answer *b* is correct. Van Sinderen did make a personal sacrifice by giving up his secure job as chairman of the board; he made that sacrifice in order to help rebuild his town after a very serious storm. His actions suggest that he would agree that in times of crisis, people should give up their personal goals to serve their communities. That is a fair generalization from this paragraph.

How to Generalize

- Make sure that you understand the main idea and key details from the reading.
- Make sure that you can draw conclusions or predict outcomes based on information you have read.
- Think about how you might apply the writer's ideas in different situations.
- Don't go *too* far beyond the information the writer gives when you try to generalize. Otherwise you face the problem of making statements that are too broad in scope.
- As you state a generalization, be particularly careful of words that do not allow exceptions. Words like *always, never, must, certainly, absolutely,* and *definitely* can rule out possibilities for any challenge to the general statement.

EXERCISES

1. Practice with Generalizing

Read the following passage about how different mice are treated differently. When you finish, examine the statements after it and put a checkmark next to those that are correct generalizations on the basis of the passage.

> The University of Tennessee's Walters Life Sciences Building is a model animal facility, spotlessly clean, scrupulous in obtaining prior approval for experiments from an animal-care committee. Of the 15,000 mice housed there in a typical year, most give their lives for humanity. These are "good" mice and, as such, warrant the protection of the animal-care committee.
>
> At any given time, however, some mice escape and run free. These mice are pests. They can disrupt experiments with the pathogens they carry. They are "bad" mice, and must be captured and destroyed. Usually, this is accomplished by means of "sticky" traps, a kind of flypaper on which they become increasingly stuck. Mice that are not dead by morning are gassed.
>
> But the real point of this cautionary tale, says animal behaviorist Harold A. Herzog, Jr., writing in the June issue of

American Psychologist, is that the labels we put on things can skew our moral responses to them. Using sticky traps or the more lethal snap traps would be deemed unacceptable for good mice. Yet the killing of bad mice requires no prior approval. "Once a research animal hits the floor and becomes an escapee," writes Herzog, "its moral standing is instantly diminished."

In Herzog's own home, there was a more ironic example. When his young son's pet mouse, Willie, died recently, it was accorded a tearful, ceremonial burial in the garden. Yet even as they mourned Willie, says Herzog, he and his wife were setting snap traps to kill the pest mice in their kitchen. With the bare change in labels from "pet" to "pest," the kitchen mice attained a totally different moral status. Something of the sort happens with so-called feeders — mice raised to be eaten by other animals. At the Walters facility, no approval is needed for feeding mice to laboratory reptiles that subsist on them. But if a researcher wants to film a mouse defending itself against a predator, the animal-care committee must review the experiment, even though the mouse will often survive. The critical factor in the moral regard of the mouse is whether it is labeled "subject" or "food."

— *David Gelman*

_____ 1. Some mice are more deserving of good treatment than others.

√_____ 2. We treat mice differently depending on the label we attach to them.

_____ 3. Animal laboratories have too many restrictions on how they treat experimental animals.

_____ 4. We need to treat all animals better.

√_____ 5. Some mice get treated better by humans than do others.

_____ 6. Our principles of morality are always fair and well thought through.

_____ 7. "Bad" mice ought to be exterminated.

√ 8. "Bad" mice are unwanted mice, and they are exterminated.

_______ 9. Labels are silly and of no importance.

√ 10. Labels affect how we treat animals.

2. Generalizing

What does people's behavior mean? Read the following selection that shows how we often come away with false impressions when we observe what other people do. Then answer the questions.

As the clutch of mourners files out of the cemetery, they pass a neatly attired man approaching a grave. He kneels by the headstone, pulls a rubber chicken from his overcoat and props it against the burial marker. A strained chuckle escapes from the pit of his stomach.

Puzzled looks cross the mourners' faces. By the time they reach their cars, each has an explanation for the bizarre scene.

"What a disrespectful young man," says one woman. "How would you like someone to throw a dead chicken on your grave and then laugh about it?"

Her husband nods. "He did look a little funny. Could have been gloating over the death of a business competitor."

Another woman shakes her head. "Who knows, the chicken might have meant something to the dead person. Still, that guy was odd, wasn't he?"

Meanwhile, the mysterious poultry bearer pays his last respects to his departed friend, a comedian whose favorite prop was a rubber chicken.

This tombside tale may seem a bit unusual, but it offers a glimpse of the ease with which someone's behavior gets transformed by others into misjudgments about his or her intentions and character, asserts psychologist Daniel T. Gilbert of the University of Texas at Austin. Emerging evidence suggests that ruminations about social encounters — whether pondering the meaning of a foreign guest's unfamiliar body language or mentally rehearsing one's behavior for an upcoming meeting with the boss — can create major misreadings of why others act as they do.

"We may strive to see others as they really are, but all too often the charlatan wins our praise and the altruist our scorn," write Gilbert and University of Texas colleague Patrick S. Malone in an article reviewing research on such judgmental mishaps, slated for publication later this year in *Personality and Social Psychology Bulletin.* "People are drastically overconfident about their judgments of others," Gilbert adds.

— *Bruce Bower*

1. What do the woman and her husband conclude about the mourner with the rubber chicken?

   The mourner was disrespectful and possibly a business competitor.

2. What two generalizations does the second woman make?

   The chicken might have meant something to the dead person; the mourner was odd.

c 3. From the information in the article you can generalize that
   a. the mourner with the chicken likes to play practical jokes.
   b. you should always respect unusual customs.
   c. we can easily misunderstand the unusual acts people perform.
   d. you should never take a comedian too seriously.

a 4. From the opening paragraphs we can generalize that when presented with unusual behavior, people
   a. make judgments about the intentions and character of the individual performing the act.
   b. let the unusual behavior pass without comment.
   c. always think negatively about the person performing the act.
   d. always misunderstand what is happening.

5. What two major generalizations does Daniel Gilbert make about how we think about others' behavior?

   We are often wrong about other people; we are

drastically overconfident about our judgments of others.

Critical Thinking in Writing

Write about a moment in which you misunderstood or misjudged someone's actions or behavior — or when someone misunderstood or misjudged you.

3. Generalizing from Textbooks

The following passages come from textbooks you might use in your courses. Read the selections and then answer the questions, most of which are based on your ability to generalize.

Marriage and the Family

Exploration of bodies, "playing doctor," and other forms of sex play are quite common in childhood, but they seem to have more to do with curiosity about oneself and the parts adults regard as taboo than they do with satisfying a primordial urge. A good deal of behavior concerning sex roles is learned during childhood. But sexual experience as such begins at adolescence with the biological events of puberty. The timing of puberty varies, but girls generally undergo these changes between the ages of 12 and 14, and boys go through puberty about two years later. The complex changes of puberty begin in the brain with the signal to release certain hormones. Over a period of about two years, the reproductive organs mature, and adolescents develop sex characteristics, which give them the physical attributes of men or women. Although the physical events and sexual experiences of adolescence are quite different for male and female, the sense of oneself as a sexual being — a *sexual identity* — is part of the overall sense of individual identity that develops during the teenage years. The experience of socializing with the opposite sex and feeling desirable or undesirable, the events that surround sexual arousal, and the combination of guilt, anxiety, and satisfaction that accompanies such feelings — these are some of the elements that shape this new sense of sexual identity.

— *Diane I. Levande, Joanne B. Koch, and Lewis Z. Koch*

d
_____ 1. The main idea of this selection is to
a. provide a comprehensive view of puberty.
b. outline the requirements of socializing with the opposite sex.
c. define "playing doctor" among young children.
d. explain the elements of sexual identity.

b
_____ 2. It is safe to generalize from this passage that a young child who engages in sex play
a. will develop an abnormal sexual identity.
b. is merely exploring.
c. may require psychiatric counseling in adulthood.
d. is following a normal biological urge to satisfy sexual feelings.

b
_____ 3. We can generalize that a girl who undergoes puberty at the age of fifteen is
a. abnormal.
b. not typical of most girls but not abnormal.
c. never going to catch up fully with her peers in terms of sexual development.
d. generally more mature and therefore more attractive to the opposite sex.

4. Examine the statements below and put a checkmark next to those that, on the basis of the passage, are correct generalizations.

_____ a. Girls are more dependable than boys.

√ _____ b. Guilt and anxiety are normal consequences of early sexual arousal.

√ _____ c. Boys and girls are alike in that they form sexual identities in their teens.

_____ d. Only girls develop adequate sexual identities.

_____ e. Adolescent boys and girls generally have similar sexual experiences.

_____ f. People develop a sense of sex roles with the onset of puberty.

√ _____ g. Sexuality involves both physical and emotional changes.

_____ h. Children should not socialize too early with the opposite sex.

√ _____ i. The start of sexual experiences is related to biological events.

√ _____ j. Sexual identity is an important part of a larger individual identity.

Data Processing

Many problems of interest to scientists involve converting data into useful information by solving mathematical equations. The first computers were used in solving scientific problems because of their capacity to do arithmetic at great speeds. For example, one of the first problems computers solved, in the late 1940s, was where a shell shot from a cannon would land if it were fired with a certain force and in a certain direction, given a certain wind velocity, and so on. What were the data? The data here might include the design and weight of each shell, the amount of powder used to propel it, and the design of the bore of the cannon. We could use a manual or a mechanical system to solve the equations that needed solving — but the work would take so long that the shell would long since have reached its target.

— *Gary S. Popkin and Arthur H. Pike*

c _____ 5. In general, mathematical equations help us turn data into
a. facts.
b. computer resources.
c. practical knowledge.
d. scientific problems.

a _____ 6. Complex mathematical equations like those that can tell where a shell shot from a cannon might land
a. can be solved by humans.
b. require computers to provide solutions.
c. are no longer of any use in current warfare.
d. None of the above

b
______ 7. In general, according to this passage you would turn to a computer to help solve a complex problem because the computer is

a. smarter than human beings.
b. quick.
c. relatively inexpensive.
d. important in determining the data needed to solve problems.

12

Evaluating Ideas

The skills described in Chapters 1 through 11 can help you understand and interpret what you read. But effective reading is more than just understanding. You must be able to read in a *critical* way — which means that you have to *evaluate* ideas once you understand them. When you *evaluate* a writer's ideas, you judge the worth of what you read.

Here are some important questions to ask yourself in evaluating what you read:

- Does the author carefully separate objective fact from opinion?
- Does the passage present the facts completely, specifically, and accurately?
- Does the author seem reliable? Can you see what strengths or experiences make the author qualified to write about a topic?
- Does the author make any claims that seem outrageous or unsupportable?
- Does the author make his or her intent or point of view clear?
- Does the author take into account other points of view on the topic?
- Does the author try to appeal more to your emotions than to your reason and common sense?
- Do your emotions get in the way of your ability to judge an author's statements fairly?
- Does it seem that the author is slanting information in such a way as to prejudice your ideas? Is the author using propaganda?

The following sections will help you sharpen your critical reading.

12a Fact and Opinion

Most reading samples contain ideas based on fact *and* opinion. Of course it's not always easy to keep the two apart. A writer can combine the two in such a way that you do not notice where fact ends and opinion begins. In a philosophy course you may spend much time discussing just what is a fact or an opinion. Here you want to be able to distinguish between two types of statements as you read.

Facts are statements that tell you what really happened or really is the case. A fact is based on direct evidence. It is something known by actual experience or observation.

Opinions are statements of belief, judgment, or feeling. They show what someone thinks about a subject. Solid opinions, of course, are based on facts. However, opinions are still somebody's view of something; they are not facts themselves.

Look at the following statements, which come from Dee Brown's *Bury My Heart at Wounded Knee: An Indian History of the American West:*

1. In 1848 gold was discovered in California.
2. In 1860 there were probably 300,000 Indians in the United States and Territories, most of them living west of the Mississippi.
3. Now, in an age without heroes, the Indian leaders are perhaps the most heroic of all Americans.

In sentence 1 we read a statement of fact. We have evidence of the discovery of gold in California in 1848. If we checked sources, we would see that the statement is true.

The use of numbers, dates, and geography in sentence 2 creates a sense of fact. But the word *probably* suggests some doubt, so we cannot accept the statement as completely factual. That doesn't make it wrong or untrue. It just makes it partly an opinion. Because Dee Brown is a scholar in American Indian history, most people would accept his statement as fact. But it is still his educated judgment that 300,000 Indians lived in the United States in 1860. The writer's education and background tell us to rely on his statement, and we accept it as true without much thought. It is possible, though, that some people have other views on this subject.

In sentence 3 we have a clearer example of the author's opinion. The statement is not wrong; it is just clearly not a statement of fact. The word *perhaps* tells us that the author himself believes other ideas are possible. It is true that many people would agree that Indian leaders are the most heroic. Others might say, however, that the leaders of World War II or the leaders of countries in times of crisis were the most heroic. Others would say that the leaders on the battlefields of Vietnam were the most heroic. None of these statements is incorrect. All, however, are opinions.

To judge a writer's work you have to be able to tell opinion from fact. Often writers mix fact and opinion even within the same sentence, with some words representing facts and others representing opinions. Think about the following sentences:

> Compact discs reproduce truer sound than records. They cannot skip or scratch the way records do. Despite this, there will always be a market for record players because people don't like to change things they're used to for new gadgets they can't understand.

The first part of this statement is true. Compact disc players use digital computers, which do reproduce sound more faithfully than records do. Because compact disc players use lasers, not needles, they can't damage discs or cause scratches or skips.

The next part of the statement is a prediction based on two beliefs that may or may not be true. First, "People don't like to change things they're used to" is not a fact. It isn't true in all cases. For instance, one hundred years ago people traveled by horse and buggy, but today hardly anyone would consider it more practical to travel by horse than by automobile. New inventions take time to become accepted. Elevators, computers, televisions, and airplanes have all been accepted by most people, and someday maybe everyone will own a compact disc player. The second opinion expressed, that people can't understand new gadgets, is invalid for similar reasons. Years ago people were unfamiliar with calculators, automatic teller machines, microwave ovens, and many other "gadgets." While some people avoid objects they find difficult to operate or understand, many people discard old devices and adapt themselves to new gadgets. The fact of the matter is, no one knows for certain whether "there will always be a market for record players."

When you have a mixture of fact and opinion in a single statement, you must decide whether the main point of the statement is essentially fact or opinion. In the last example, the main point of the statement was to make a prediction, so it basically offers an opinion, even though it contains many facts.

Consider another example:

> Dressed in a beautiful ten thousand dollar dress, Mary Foley looked elegant and serene on her wedding day as she marched down the aisle beside her father. She said, "I must be the happiest woman alive."

Even though the words *beautiful, elegant,* and *serene* state the writer's opinion, the sentence states many facts. The woman's name is Mary Foley; she was getting married; her dress cost $10,000; her father escorted her down the aisle. Yet the writer's main point is to give an opinion about how Mary looked wearing a particular dress on a particular occasion. Thus the first sentence basically presents an opinion.

The second sentence reports what Mary said. Mary stated her opinion, but that she said it is a fact. So the second sentence is basically factual.

Keeping Fact and Opinion Apart

- Look for words that *interpret.* In the first of the following sentences, we have details that describe facts — without any evaluation of these facts. In the second sentence, the writer interprets the details for us.

  1. The man leaning against the fence had brown eyes and black hair touching his shoulders.
  2. A handsome man leaned against the fence.

  It's somebody's opinion that the man is handsome. Other words that interpret — there are countless examples — are *pretty, ugly, safe, dangerous, evil, attractive, well dressed, good,* and so on.

- Look for words that serve as clues to statements of opinion. Some words like *probably, perhaps, usually, often, sometimes,* and *on occasion* are used to limit a statement of fact and to indicate the possibility of other opinions. Other words — *I believe, I think, in my opinion, I feel, I suggest* — say clearly that an opinion follows.
- Before you accept a statement of fact and before you agree with a statement of opinion, question the credibility of the author. Is he or she reliable? Why should you take his or her word?
- Test the writer's opinion by asking whether a different opinion is possible. You do not have to agree with the different opinion (or with the author's, for that matter). You just have to be able to see if there is another point of view.
- Some authors include statements from other writers or authorities in order to illustrate their own ideas. Make sure you can tell the source of any statement that appears in what you read.

EXERCISES

1. Fact and Opinion

In the following sentences, underline the words that present facts and circle the words that present opinions. Write F before each sentence that basically represents a fact; write O before each statement of opinion.

O ______ 1. Baseball is the most American of all sports.

F ______ 2. Baseball is based on the British game of rounders.

F ______ 3. More Americans enjoy baseball than soccer or tennis.

O ______ 4. Japanese professional baseball players are good enough to play in the American big leagues.

F 5. Taiwan has won more Little League World Series championships than any other country in recent years.

F 6. Most big league ballparks use artificial turf.

O 7. Baseball should be played on natural grass, not on an artificial surface.

2. Clues to Fact and Opinion

Write F before each statement of fact and O before each statement of opinion. Then circle any words that help tell you whether the statement expresses a fact or an opinion.

F 1. Over twenty years ago, child labor laws were passed to protect children under eighteen years of age from being injured and exploited.

O 2. Children under sixteen should not work at all.

F 3. Over 5 million children between the ages of twelve and seventeen worked in 1990.

O 4. Work is usually unpleasant and dangerous.

F 5. Fast-food chains like McDonalds and Burger King have developed policies to protect the safety and interests of school-age employees.

O 6. Young people often feel they need to earn money for themselves when I think they really don't need to.

F 7. In 1990, 139 children were killed and 71,660 were injured in work-related accidents in the United States.

O 8. It seems we need stricter enforcement of existing child labor laws and passage of new laws.

3. Fact and Opinion

Read the following selection to learn Barbara Kerbel's thoughts about schoolwork assignments that require parents' involvement. Then answer the question, which is based on your ability to tell fact from opinion.

Schoolwork: The Student's Job

I'm doing a slow burn about homework, and I don't even go to school. It's my daughters' homework that's keeping me up nights. And it's my daughters' homework that led me to open my mouth at Open House this year — specifically, in the social studies class.

Right before the dismissal bell, several parents asked questions about a recently completed assignment. "Who won in the class trial of Edwards vs. the Supreme Court?" "Did anyone argue that people can't be considered goods in interstate commerce?" "Was anyone brave enough to represent the unpopular view and argue against Edwards?"

I didn't raise my hand; I raised my voice. And as I heard it, I was aware of the hostility with which it was laced. "How come we all know so much about this case?" I asked.

The fact is that our children are bringing home homework assignments whose requirements they cannot fulfill without parental assistance. Assignments whose completion is *predicated* on parental assistance. My daughter's social studies teacher said, "When you're working with your children on their writing assignments . . ." and my anger clogged my ears so I didn't even hear the rest of the sentence.

I don't want to work with my children on their homework assignments. Don't get me wrong. I'm happy to help with an equation. I don't mind listening to a speech or helping to define a good composition topic. And I love talking with my kids about what's going on in school.

But I don't like trying to make sense of rivers and valleys and plateaus on an unreadable ditto. I don't like having to call lawyer friends to determine how a legal brief should be written. I don't like having to use in cogent sentences words that only belong in dictionary games.

A very good friend of mine can recite, chapter and verse, precisely what's going on in each of her children's classes. She knows when her kids' papers are due, what they've scored on every test and quiz, what story they're reading in their reading books. That's OK for her; she chooses to be so involved. It would not be my choice even if I didn't work all day.

What I don't like is not having the choice. I don't like being put in a situation where my anger at a teacher metamorphoses into anger at my child, and I hear myself yelling things like, "If you're not in bed in two minutes, I'm tearing up Europe and the whole Mediterranean and throwing them in the garbage." Where I find myself giving answers instead of direction because it's more expeditious. Where I feel like a crummy mom for wanting some time in the evening — after work, dinner, dishes — for me.

Last year, one homework assignment stated: "Read and react to the editorial, in writing, and then have one of your parents do the same." No misinterpretation here. Mom had an assignment.

When two parents work, they have very little time with their children on weekdays. Single parents have even less, which makes the hours between dinner and bedtime very important.

When I'm cleaning up, my daughters are at the kitchen table doing homework. If I take the paper into my room, my bed becomes their desk. Too often, this important time together becomes a battleground.

I believe in homework. In nine years of teaching high school English, I assigned it almost every night. But I also believe that homework is kids' work, and they should be able, for the most part, to handle it on their own. It should invite independent thinking, not parental involvement. And parents should resist the urge to convert creative assignments into artistic feats.

One Halloween, the fifth graders at my daughter's school had a witch-making competition. Prizes were promised for the ugliest, the funniest, the scariest, the prettiest. My daughter worked for days and created a pretty good witch. Not necessarily a prize-winning witch, but a solid competitor fashioned from old stockings and glitter and fabric scraps and ingenuity. When she dragged her witch home Friday afternoon after the judging, she was less disappointed in not winning than she was in the judges' choices. The winners were too high-tech, too perfect to have been done by kids her age. The prizes, in effect, were won by parents. And what did the children — winners and losers alike — learn?

What should a parent's involvement be? Should she silently suffer her child's groans of frustration? Give away the answers wholesale? Suggest that an 11-year-old garner the courage to tell her teacher she gave up after two hours?

School is our kids' first employment. They are subject to

constant on-the-job evaluation, frequent overtime and significant frustration with their bosses. They are also in the perfect position to accrue ample bonuses in the form of self-satisfaction if they are given well-thought-out assignments they can complete themselves. And if, as parents, we let them.

— *Barbara Kerbel*

1. Put an F next to the facts of Barbara Kerbel's situation, and an O next to her opinions. After you have finished putting a letter next to each statement, place a checkmark before the one statement that you think best sums up Kerbel's opinions.

F ______ a. Kerbel taught high school English for nine years.

O ______ b. Parents should never become involved in their children's homework.

F ______ c. Kerbel's daughters' social studies homework involved parental help.

O ______ d. Some subjects are pleasant to work on and others are unpleasant.

O ______ e. School dittos are unreadable.

F ______ f. Kerbel asked a question at the school Open House.

O ______ g. The question was hostile.

O ______ h. No parents like working on legal questions with their children.

F ______ i. Kerbel and her daughter were assigned to write a response to an editorial.

O ______ j. Working parents have little time to spend with their children on weekdays.

O ______ k. Homework should invite independent thinking.

F l. Kerbel's daughter worked for days on a Halloween contest.

O m. The winners of the Halloween contest had been helped by their parents.

√ O n. Parents should be able to choose whether to get involved with homework.

O o. Too much homework is no good.

O p. Schoolwork is the job of children, not parents.

Critical Thinking in Writing

Write a letter to the editor of your local newspaper in which you argue the opposite of Kerbel's point. That is, explain why you think it is a good idea for parents to work with their children on homework.

4. Separating Fact and Opinion on a Controversial Topic

In the numbered spaces write down four statements that you have heard or read concerning racism in the United States. Then read over the statements, and in the small space before each write F or O depending on whether it is a statement primarily of fact or opinion. **Student responses will vary.**

_____ 1. ______________________________

____

_____ 2. ______________________________

____

_____ 3. ______________________________

____

_____ 4. ____

____

12b Evidence

Sometimes when writers state their opinions, they just assert their points of view without providing any support. In such cases you have no particular reason to believe their opinions unless you trust them as authorities or experts. Any writer (even an "expert") who states opinions without giving supporting evidence probably should not convince you.

More often, writers try to convince readers to share their opinions by presenting various facts or evidence, just as a lawyer presents evidence in a court case to support the opinion that the accused is innocent or guilty of a crime. Just as a jury must evaluate the evidence carefully to decide whether to accept a lawyer's opinion about the accused, so must you evaluate the evidence presented in what you read to decide whether to accept a writer's opinion. The following questions will help you to evaluate any evidence offered in support of an opinion you find expressed in your reading:

- Can the facts be trusted?
- Are the facts given in an objective way?
- Do the facts really support the opinion being expressed?
- Are the facts relevant to the point being made?
- Have unfavorable or negative points been left out?
- Do the facts prove the writer's opinion, or do they only suggest that the opinion is reasonable?

If two writers give opposite opinions, you should judge which one gives the better evidence. Whose facts are more reliable, are more complete, are expressed more objectively? Whose facts support the opinion more fully?

Many times, writers try to convince you to share their opinions. They may use all their persuasive skills to try to make you believe that tall people make better presidents, or that Michael Jackson is the greatest male vocalist, or even that people who use crack should be shot. Only a careful reader can avoid falling for an emotional or poorly reasoned argument.

EXERCISES

1. Evidence Backing Up Statements

Before each of the following statements, write E if the statement is backed up properly by evidence, write N if there is no supporting evidence, and write I if there is evidence but it is improperly used.

N 1. Anyone who studies a foreign language in college is just wasting time.

I 2. Because English is the most commonly used language in international business, there is no business advantage to be gained by learning a foreign language.

I 3. Because college courses in computer programming are more popular than language courses, computer programming is far more useful to learn than any foreign language.

N 4. Oriental languages, like Japanese and Chinese, will be important to learn in the future.

E 5. Because French and German contributed so many words to English, studying these languages can develop your English vocabulary.

N 6. You learn a foreign language best when you have a real need to use it every day.

E 7. The fact that more American students study Latin than Russian, Chinese, and Japanese combined shows that Americans are not preparing themselves to communicate in the modern world.

2. Evidence in a Longer Selection

Read the following article about Americans' work patterns. Determine the author's main opinions and think about the evidence she uses. Then answer the questions.

Americans Work Too Hard

Americans suffer from an overdose of work. Regardless of who they are or what they do, Americans spend more time at work than at any time since World War II.

In 1950, the U.S. had fewer working hours than any industrialized country. Today, it exceeds every country but Japan, where industrial employees log 2,155 hours a year compared with 1,951 in the U.S. and 1,603 in the former West Germany.

Between 1969 and 1989, employed Americans added an average of 138 hours to their yearly work schedules. The workweek has remained at about 40 hours, but people are working more weeks each year. Moreover, paid time off — holidays, vacations, sick leave — shrank by 15 percent in the 1980's.

As corporations have experienced stiffer competition and slower growth in productivity, they have pressed employees to work longer. Cost-cutting layoffs in the 1980's reduced the professional and managerial ranks, leaving fewer people to get the job done. In lower-paid occupations, where wages have been reduced, workers have added hours in overtime or extra jobs to preserve their living standard. The Government estimates that more than seven million people hold a second job.

For the first time, large numbers of people say they want to cut back on working hours, even if it means earning less money. But most employers are unwilling to let them do so. The Government, which has stepped back from its traditional role as a regulator of work time, should take steps to make shorter hours possible.

First, it should require employers to give employees the opportunity to trade income for time. Growth in productivity makes it possible to raise income or reduce working hours. Since World War II, we have "chosen" money over time; one reason is that companies give annual raises but rarely offer more free time. But California municipalities have offered this option successfully.

Second, standard hours should be required for all salaried jobs. Salaried workers often work 50 or 60 hours a week. When annual pay is fixed, an employer has a powerful motive to induce ever-longer hours of work, since each added hour is "free." This incentive would disappear if companies were obliged to set a standard workweek for salaried jobs. Employees who worked beyond the standard would be entitled to paid time off.

Congress should legislate an annual four-week vacation regardless of a worker's length of service. Nearly all Western European workers get four- to six-week vacations. Americans struggle to hold on to their two weeks.

Other reforms are long overdue. Paid parental leave is necessary. Fringe benefits should be pro-rated by hours of work to give bosses a reason not to overwork employees. Time-and-a-half pay for overtime should give way to compensatory time off, and mandatory overtime should be eliminated. Wages of adults who earn less than $10 an hour should be raised so they can avoid overwork.

Citing Japanese competition and other pressures, many employers would complain that they cannot afford such measures. But trading income for time is cost-free. And guaranteed vacations are likely to improve employees' performance: The fatigue and inefficiency resulting from long hours are a major reason why Japan's productivity remains lower than ours.

The growing scarcity of leisure, dearth of family time and horrors of commuting all point to the need to resume an old but long-ignored discussion on the merits of the 30-hour or even the four-day week.

— *Juliet B. Schor*

1. What is Schor's main opinion about American workers?

They work too hard.

2. What evidence does she present to back up this opinion?

They work harder today than at any time since World War II; they work longer hours than workers in any country except Japan; 138 hours of work per year were added between 1969 and 1989; paid time off decreased by 15 percent in the 1980s.

3. In the author's opinion, what has caused this situation to develop?

   stiffer competition and slower productivity growth

4. What evidence does she provide to support her explanation of the cause?

   cost-cutting layoffs; wage reductions in lower-paid occupations

5. What is the author's opinion about what should be done? Name at least four points. **Student responses will vary.**

   1. Allow workers to trade income for time.

   2. Require standard hours for all salaried jobs.

   3. Legislate a four-week annual vacation.

   4. Require paid parental leave.

6. For which of these points does she offer evidence in support?

   1. Municipalities in California have tested this successfully.

   2. No evidence

   3. Western European workers get four to six weeks.

   4. No evidence

Critical Thinking in Writing

Many critics believe that Americans do not work hard enough. They believe that Americans are lazy and unproductive and produce goods and services inferior to those produced in Europe and Japan. What do you think? Do Americans work too hard? Or are they lazy? Drawing on people you know for examples, write a few paragraphs to explore your views.

12c Your Opinion

Whether you accept a writer's opinions depends also on your own opinions — both your opinions about the subject and your opinions about the piece of writing. Before you read a particular selection, you may have such strong beliefs on the subject of the selection that any author would have a very hard time trying to change your mind. On the other hand, you may be so unfamiliar with the subject that you are ready to believe whatever a writer says. As you read the piece of writing, you may be so bored or so amused that your attitude toward the ideas presented may change. In order to evaluate fairly the ideas expressed in a piece of writing, you need to become aware of your own opinions and reactions.

As you read, you usually respond with some reactions and ideas of your own. Some of the thoughts that pop into your head may be good — that is, they can be developed further and supported convincingly. At other times, your thoughts may turn out to be unsupportable — perhaps the result of a prejudgment or bias or perhaps the result of not thinking carefully enough. Until you stop to write your thoughts down and think them through with care, you won't know which of your ideas are worth keeping. Much of your opinion, whether positive or negative, will depend on these moment-to-moment thoughts, and you'll need to sort them out.

One way to sort out your thinking is by keeping a reading journal, a kind of diary of your thoughts about your reading. Every time you finish reading a selection, write out your thoughts and reactions to it. You should not summarize or simply repeat what the reading stated. Instead you should say whether you liked or agreed with the passage and why. If there were any ideas you objected to, you might give reasons for your objections. If the reading reminds you of something you have experienced, describe that experience and how it is related to the reading. If other facts you know or ideas you hold support the writer's opinions, discuss them. If you dislike the writer's attitude or manner of looking at the subject, explain exactly what is wrong with the writer's approach.

It does not matter exactly what you say about the reading in your journal as long as you put down your ideas and develop them. Do not be satisfied with expressing an opinion in a single sentence or two. Go on to explain your ideas further, to give examples, to explain why you feel as you do. Think your thoughts through in any way that strikes you. After writing your ideas down and discussing them for a while, you may end up changing your mind — or you may find yourself even more firmly committed to your original position.

This sample from a reading journal presents a student's reactions to the selection on pages 263–264, which describes how people misjudge other people's behavior.

> A rubber chicken at a funeral! That is pretty weird. But some of my friends have done pretty weird stuff too. And I first thought they were crazy. Only when I got to understand what was going on did I see that what they did made a lot of sense. I remember in elementary school my friend Karen would stand by the tray return in the cafeteria to collect empty soda cans. All of us thought that she must be preparing to be a bag lady. We used to tease her a lot about that. It turns out that she was really into recycling before anybody in our town paid attention to it. By high school, there were recycling bins in the cafeteria, and anybody who didn't recycle was just trying to act bad. Sometimes when you understand more, too, you find out very painful things in people's lives. At first we all thought Janice was trying to be too stylish by always wearing scarfs and hats. After all, what kind of high school student always wears her head covered. But she went along with what we were thinking and pretended that she wanted to be a fashion designer or a model. She wanted to hide the fact that the medical treatment she was getting caused her hair to drop out. But finally we all did find out. We stopped thinking weird things about her, but we

> never let her know we knew, because she seemed to want it that way.

This student's personal experiences support and develop the idea presented in the selection, helping her understand her reading more deeply and personally. Notice how she begins by repeating a key incident and key point from the selection. But then she immediately starts exploring her own experiences. The journal should connect what you read with what you feel and think.

Next, read this reading journal entry that another student wrote about the selection on page 162 on childhood during the medieval and Renaissance periods.

> It sounds as though children were treated as much more grown up in earlier times. I think I would have liked that — taking on adult tasks, playing adult games, even gambling. I can't remember how many times I was frustrated by being told, "You're not old enough to do that." There were lots of things I wanted to try before I was an adult. Actually, I did try most, but I had to hide them from parents, teachers, and other adults. Kids want to do everything adults do, so they try everything they can, even if they are not allowed.
>
> Of course, even in the medieval period they recognized that children under twelve needed protection. I could live with financial support from my parents up until the age of twelve, and even not have to get married until after that age. I wasn't much interested in jobs or girls till about that time anyway.
>
> But on the other side, treating children as adults means that there won't be all that great kids' stuff we have in our society — like summer camp, baseball cards, candy bars, cartoons, and Nintendo. I'm not sure I am willing to give all that stuff up. Besides, I needed my parents to pay for my support all those teenage years when I went to school, and even now to help out with college. Maybe one reason they could treat kids as adults back then is that kids didn't go to school that long — in fact, most probably didn't go to school at all. That doesn't sound bad either, but maybe not.

Do you see how the writer of this reading journal didn't just summarize the material he read, but started to think about his reactions to the way of life described in the selection? Notice, also, how the student writer related the situations described in the selection to his own experiences and feelings about growing up. By thinking about what growing up would be like in the medieval world, he started to understand both the positive and negative aspects of living then and now. He started out with a simple, one-sided view of what he would like. At the end of the journal entry, however, he saw some of the complex issues presented in the reading.

EXERCISES

1. Set aside a notebook to be used as a reading journal for the rest of the semester. Every time you have a reading assignment, write down and develop your thoughts in response to your reading by making an entry in the journal. At the end of the semester, read through your entire journal and write down as a final entry your observations on how the journal helped you, how your thinking developed through the journal, or how your use of the journal changed throughout the semester.
2. Read the following passage about the pressures put on men as they grow up. Then write down your own thoughts in your journal. You may want to write about similar experiences you or someone you know had. You may want to discuss whether the experiences are as common as the author seems to say. You may want to discuss how these experiences influence male character. Or you may want to discuss whether young women go through anything similar.

When I was young, there was a story that all boys knew. It went something like this. On his way home from school, a boy is attacked by the neighborhood bully. He runs crying to his mother who comforts him and cleans his wounds, but when his father comes home, the boy is told he must fight back like a man. Then begins a period of surreptitious training in self-defense, a process which culminates with the ignominious and glorious defeat of the bully.

That was the myth, and, as every boy knows, it's a barefaced lie. In real life, the bully kills you.

But the truth is not important. What counts is that at some time and in some way a boy is told to be a man, and he simply doesn't know how. Whether it's as blatant as being given boxing gloves for Christmas, as I was, or being pushed to play unwanted games, or urged to try one more time, or any of a thousand coercions, all he knows is that somehow he has failed and he hasn't even taken the test.

There are two ways a boy can go at this critical moment in his life. He can become fearful and quit, get out of the game, or begin to create his own little swagger and try to start winning. In my case, I combined the two. Deep inside I was scared to death, and I knew it well, but I was big and a pretty fair mimic, and I developed an image that got me by. When physically confronted, I blustered and posed and did my imitation of tough and usually bluffed my way through. When that didn't work, I "chickened out" and suffered the torments of the damned.

As I grew older, the rules were modified, but the game remained the same. Being a man was still about winning, and when, in my early 20s, I dropped out of the race, it was a rejection of all that I was "supposed" to be. Later, when I became ambitious, it was acceptance of the very same things, and in each case I measured myself against the definition of manhood that I had carried since I was 3 or 4 or 5.

Though the game was not of my devising, when I chose to play, I did it well and accumulated the trophies that come with success. But the catch was that for a real man there is never enough. There's always a bigger prize, a greater challenge, a tougher test, and to stop winning is to lose.

Now all of us know that this is ridiculous — crazy, in fact — and no one need be so great a fool as to step into such a self-destructive trap. But I'm not talking about what makes sense. I'm talking about feelings, particularly the insidious feeling that is a part of every American male no matter how sane or intelligent or gentle or wise. The feeling deep in the pit of his stomach that says, "I'm not a man."

— *Robert Ragaini*

12d The Writer's Technique

An important way to develop critical skills is to be aware of the writer's technique in any selection you read. Once you know what the writer is doing with his or her material — once you know the effect he or she is trying to create — you can judge what is said more fairly and clearly.

12d(1) *Style*

In general, *style* is the way a writer picks words and puts them together. Style usually tells you whom the writer expects to read the work. If the sentences are long and the words are difficult, the writer expects an educated reader. If the language is rich in slang expressions and current phrases, the writer is talking to a more general group. If the words are very technical, the writer is aiming for a special audience that knows the language of the subject being discussed. Some writers pick words with deep emotional appeal in order to urge their readers to act. Other writers choose a more impartial style.

A writer who wants to convince you of how urgent his or her problem is might use short sentences so that as you read along, you become wrapped up in the fast pace. During World War II, Winston Churchill said, "We shall fight them on the beaches. We shall fight them street by street. We shall never give up." Here he used repetition and short sentences effectively to show how committed England was to keep fighting. If he had said, "We shall fight them on the beaches and in the streets and never give up," the basic message would have been the same, but the style would not have fired up his listeners' appreciation.

12d(2) *Tone*

Tone is the attitude a writer takes toward a subject. An author may write about something he or she respects or about something he or she hates. A writer may be angry. A writer may be impatient. A writer may take a humorous view of a subject. Or a writer may be ironic — saying one thing but really meaning the opposite.

Oscar Wilde was asked by a judge during his trial, "Are you trying to show contempt for this court?" and Wilde replied, "On the contrary, I'm trying to conceal it." The tone of his response was much more effective than if he had said, "Yes, I am."

12d(3) *Mood*

Mood is a state of mind or feeling at a particular time. Often writers create a mood so that they can make you respond in a certain way.

Edgar Allan Poe said that sibilants (words that contain the *s* sound, like *snake, sinister,* and *shadow*) help create a mysterious mood, and he used sibilants often: "And then did we, the seven, start from our seats in horror, and stand trembling, and shuddering and aghast."

12d(4) *Purpose*

Writers write for a *reason*. Some want to give information. Some want to persuade you to believe something. Others try to push you into taking some action related to a subject of deep meaning to them. Some writers write to amuse or entertain.

Advertising is a good example of writing with a purpose — that is, writing to make you buy a certain product. Another example is editorials in newspapers. Editorials aim at gaining public support for a political position.

12d(5) *Point of View*

A writer's own beliefs and ideas often determine how he or she looks at a given subject. In this sense, *point of view* means "opinions" or "attitudes," although there are a number of other meanings that make it a complex term to use. Our concern here is for the way a writer's own interests and beliefs influence the writing we read. A communist, for example, would look at the Cuban government in a very different way from a man or woman who believes in democracy. A Catholic would not look at religious ceremonies in the same way as a Protestant or a Jew. A black person might have much stronger views on the treatment of sickle-cell anemia than a white person. Sometimes an author's point of view forces him or her to *slant* the writing. Slanted writing leans toward one way of looking at a problem and leaves out ideas that might conflict.

Of course, these techniques often blend together in any

sample of writing. Style and tone are often impossible to separate, and they both clearly relate to purpose and point of view. Also, the writer's style often creates a mood.

Furthermore, an author's technique often yields many results. Writing may be both humorous and ironic. An author may want to give information in order to persuade you to do something, and in so doing he or she may write in a style that is very emotional.

Mark Twain once said, "Man is the only animal that blushes, or needs to." This is a much more effective way to communicate his point of view than if he had said, "People, unlike animals, do things that they are ashamed of." As Twain and other humorists have discovered, people listen to any argument if it is put in a humorous or entertaining way.

The point in seeing a writer's technique is to help you notice that what an author says relates to *how* the author says it. What we discuss here is just a beginning of the study of writing technique. In literature courses you may go much further into the subject.

EXERCISES

1. The Writer's Technique

Read the following statements. After all the statements you will find a series of questions. In the blank space, write the letter of the statement that answers the question. You may use the same letter more than once, and you may use more than one letter for each answer.

a. For nearly 400 years Americans have spent their history getting from There to Here and usually found Here unsatisfactory after they arrived. Sometimes, as now, they have been so disenchanted with Here that they want to go back to There and start over again.

— *Russell Baker*

b. **Introducing Achieva by Oldsmobile.** The Achieva™ is so intelligently engineered, you'll wonder why you ever looked at Honda Accord or Toyota Camry. **Start with a well-thought-out cockpit.** One with controls and analog gauges designed precisely where you need them. **Four-wheel anti-lock brakes come standard.** In fact, the ABS VI system in

Achieva has been awarded "Technology of the Year" by *Automobile Magazine.* **Its High-Output Quad 4® engine** delivers 180 horsepower, in a machine that gets over 30 highway miles per gallon. **The Oldsmobile Edge,℠** the industry's most comprehensive owner satisfaction program, also comes standard. You can drive other cars. But none as well-thought-out as Achieva. Or as fun.

c. **Instructions to the Patient**

Follow these simple steps to optimize your vision care benefits:

- Make sure the patient name, member I.D. number, and group name are correct. **This benefit form can only be used by the person whose name appears as patient.**
- Pay close attention to the Exam, Lens, and Frame boxes. **Information in the boxes indicates if you are eligible for those services.**
- Make an appointment with a Plan Member Doctor. (Selecting a Plan Member Doctor will assure that you receive the maximum benefit of your plan. Please see your group plan brochure regarding availability of service from a doctor who is not a panel member.)
- Take this form to the doctor at the time of your appointment.

d. The Santa Monica Farmers' Market is more orderly, perhaps, than outdoor produce markets elsewhere in the world. Prices, by regulation, must be posted, and there is very little bargaining. Shoppers make at least a minimal effort to stand in line or wait their turn at the produce to pick, squeeze and buy. But the market is still a lively place. Strains of live music — Peruvian pipes, a mellow alto sax, Dixieland jazz — filter through the morning air. The occasional selling cry can be heard above the hubbub: "Free samples. Taste 'em first!" exhorts one woman, cutting a wedge off a large Fuji apple. "Sweet and juicy!" advertises a citrus grower. "Fresh eggs. One day old!" This is certainly not the fluorescent-lit, Muzak-steeped produce section of your local supermarket.

— *Stanley Young*

e. Your new bicycle is guaranteed by the manufacturer to be free from defects in material and workmanship under normal use in accordance with the Manufacturer's Installation and Use Instructions. All items shipped from the manufacturer on a warranty claim will be freight collect. This warranty does not apply to damage resulting from accident, misuse or abuse of the product, or alteration or modification of the product after your purchase.

f. Editors and teachers share a number of similar professional responsibilities, including being both enablers and gatekeepers. For instance, both editors and teachers have a responsibility to enable writers to learn how to prepare the best possible documents that they can. One way editors can do this is by providing an author with their comments and the comments of reviewers. Teachers can do this by helping authors think clearly about such concerns as audience and purpose and by providing authors with opportunities to write a variety of documents for particular purposes and audiences. However, editors and teachers also serve as gatekeepers who make decisions about the quality of a writer's work; editors accept and reject manuscripts, and teachers grade students.

— *Bruce Speck*

b,c,d,e 1. Which statements are designed to make you do something?

a 2. Which statement is written from a critical point of view?

b,d 3. Which statements are written from an approving point of view?

f 4. Which statement is written from a personal point of view?

c,e,f 5. Which statements are written in an objective style?

f 6. Which statement is written in a style appropriate for specialists?

d 7. Which statement is written in a vivid style?

a 8. Which statement is written with humor?

c,e 9. Which statements give instructions?

c,e,f 10. Which statements are written with a precise tone?

b,d 11. Which statements are written in an informal tone?

2. The Writer's Technique

Read the following opening sentences of short stories. Then complete the statement that follows each with the best answer.

> The thousand injuries of Fortunato I had borne as I best could, but when he ventured upon insult I vowed revenge.
>
> — *Edgar Allan Poe*

c _____ 1. The tone of the person speaking is
a. matter-of-fact.
b. ironic.
c. angry.
d. sad.

> One view called me to another; one hill top to its fellow, half across the country, and since I could answer at no more trouble than the snapping forward of a lever, I let the country flow under my wheels.
>
> — *Rudyard Kipling*

b _____ 2. This opening sentence sets a mood of
a. quiet peacefulness.
b. hurried discovery.
c. uncertain fear.
d. friendliness.

> In the Bureau of . . . but it might be better not to mention the Bureau by its precise name. There is nothing more touchy than all these bureaus, regiments, and government offices, and in fact any sort of official body.
>
> — *Nikolai Gogol*

a _____ 3. The point of view of the teller of this story is that of a person who is
a. afraid of getting officials upset.
b. an outspoken enemy of the government.
c. an army officer.
d. a criminal.

> "If I was setting in the High Court in Washington," said Simple, "where they do not give out no sentences for crimes, but where they give out promulgations, I would promulgate.

Up them long white steps behind them tall white pillars in the great marble hall with the eagle of the U.S.A., where at I would bang my gavel and promulgate."

— *Langston Hughes*

c ______ 4. Simple speaks in the style of someone who
a. knows a great deal.
b. is very powerful.
c. is impressed by power and big words.
d. is very old.

"My dear fellow," said Sherlock Holmes, as we sat on either side of the fire in his lodgings at Baker Street, "life is infinitely stranger than anything which the mind of man could invent. We would not dare to conceive the things which are really mere commonplaces of existence. If we could fly out of that window hand in hand, hover over this great city, gently remove the roofs, and peep in at the queer things which are going on, the strange coincidences, the plannings, the cross-purposes, the wonderful chains of events, working through generations, and leading to the most *outré* results, it would make all fiction with its conventionalities and foreseen conclusions most stale and unprofitable."

— *Arthur Conan Doyle*

c ______ 5. The point of view portrayed in this paragraph is of a(n)
a. unhappy critic of human folly.
b. concerned leader of a public service organization.
c. serious but amused observer of humankind.
d. comedian, looking to make fun of people.

Day had broken cold and gray, exceedingly cold and gray, when the man turned aside from the main Yukon trail and climbed the high earth-bank, where a dim and little-travelled trail led eastward through the fat spruce timberland. It was a steep bank, and he paused for breath at the top, excusing the act to himself by looking at his watch. It was nine o'clock. There was no sun nor hint of sun, though there was not a cloud in the sky. It was a clear day, and yet there seemed an intangible pall over the face of things, a subtle gloom that made the day dark, and that was due to the absence of sun.

— *Jack London*

b 6. The opening lines of this story set a mood of
   a. quiet hope.
   b. possible threat.
   c. stark natural beauty.
   d. heroic conquest.

3. Style

As you read each of the following selections, figure out from the writer's style what kind of person is writing and who the intended audience is. Write your answers in the space after each selection, and then write your impressions of the style.

1. **Understanding Hard and Floppy Disks**

Both hard and floppy disks store information so you and your computer can have access to it.

Hard disks are sealed inside a disk drive (which in turn may be sealed inside your computer).

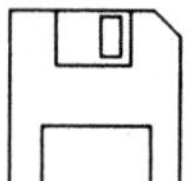

Floppy disks can be inserted into and ejected from a disk drive.

Both hard disks and floppy disks show up as icons on your desktop. You look at, work with, and add to the information on both kinds of disks in exactly the same way.

The major difference between hard and floppy disks is their *capacity* — the amount of information they can hold.

Author: a computer expert

Audience: computer beginners wanting to learn

2. If a mother nags in a house full of kids, does she make a sound? Probably not. Children, like all of us, have selective hearing, and a constant barrage of commands and directives is likely to be tuned out. So how do you keep your kids' feet off the table, stop your daughter from biting your son, or save the family car from a midnight rendezvous on the local strip? Well, let's talk about it.

Author: **a parent or an expert on parent-child relations**

Audience: **other parents**

3. You're trying to find your car in a crowded parking lot. You remember what your car looks like, the appearance of the lamppost you parked beside, and glancing at that lamppost over your shoulder as you walked off the parking lot. How can you piece these bits of information together to find your car?

If you'd parked just a few hours before — to go shopping, for example — a new experiment indicates that you would use a banana-shaped region of your brain called the hippocampus to navigate your way back to your car. But if you'd parked weeks before — say, at an airport before embarking on a month-long trip — the study suggests that you would have to retrieve the information about your car's whereabouts from another part of your brain, probably the neocortex, where longer-term memories are stored.

Author: **a science journalist**

Audience: **nonscientists looking for the latest science news**

4. Happiness, then, being an activity of the soul in conformity with perfect goodness, it follows that we must examine the nature of goodness. When we have done this we should be in a better position to investigate the nature of happiness. There is this, too. The genuine statesman is thought of as a man who has taken peculiar pains to master this problem, desiring as he does to make his fellow-citizens good men obedient to the laws. Now, if the study of moral goodness is a part of political science, our inquiry into its nature will clearly follow the lines laid down in our preliminary observations.

   Well, the goodness we have to consider is human goodness. This — I mean human goodness or (if you prefer to put it that way) human happiness — was what we set out to find. By human goodness is meant not fineness of physique but a right condition of the soul, and by happiness a condition of the soul. That being so, it is evident that the statesman ought to have some inkling of psychology, just as the doctor who is to specialize in diseases of the eye must have a general knowledge of physiology.

   Author: **a philosopher (Aristotle)**

   Audience: **one who wants to examine the nature of human goodness**

4. Tone and Purpose

Look at the cartoon on page 299 and answer the following questions:

1. What is the difference in tone between the critical comments of a national commission on education and the critical comments of the boy in the principal's office?

"It's one thing for the National Commission to comment on the quality of teaching in our schools. It's another thing entirely for you to stand up and call Mr. Costello a yo-yo."

DRAWING BY STEVENSON; © NEW YORKER MAGAZINE, INC.

The national commission's comments were phrased as a careful judgment; the boy's comments were phrased as an insult. The commission's comments were formal and respectful in tone; the boy's were informal and disrespectful.

2. What is the commission's purpose in making its comments, and what is the boy's purpose in calling his teacher a name?

The commission wants to improve education; the boy wants to insult his teacher.

3. Why are the commission's criticisms but not the boy's, acceptable to the principal?

   The commission's comments were respectfully constructive; the boy's were disrespectfully destructive.

4. Judging from the principal's tone, what is his purpose in speaking to the boy?

   The principal wants to reprimand the boy and improve the boy's behavior.

5. What moods do you think are expressed by the commission, the boy, and the principal?

   The commission was serious; the boy, mischievous; the principal, stern.

Critical Thinking in Writing

Put yourself in the position of either the principal or the child in the cartoon on the previous page. Write a few narrative paragraphs explaining the events that led up to the moment in the principal's office.

12e Techniques That Twist the Truth

As a critical reader, you have to be able to judge unfair writing. Sometimes a piece of writing will not use truthful methods if its purpose is to force you to have a certain opinion about a subject. *Propaganda* (particular ideas forced on the public by organizations with special interests) is often developed by the use of unfair writing and logic. Any information that leaves out or alters facts in order to press a special point of view is called *biased, prejudiced,* or *slanted.*

Be on your guard for propaganda.

- Look out for words used for emotional effect: *commie, bleeding heart, right-winger, hippie, geek, airhead, druggie.*
- Look for words that have special connotations (see section **1e**).
- Try to recognize the following methods of propaganda.

1. The writer tries to combine a famous person's name with an idea so that people, liking the person, will like the idea too.

   Reggie Jackson plays the field in Murjani jeans.

2. The writer quotes a famous person who approves of or agrees with an idea so that the reader will approve of it too.

   Jacques Martin, the famous French chef, says, "Margarine is just as good as butter." Why are *you* still using butter?

3. The writer says that everyone is doing something (or thinking in some way), so you should do it too.

   Every farmer, every hard-working city resident knows the dangers of the welfare system.

4. The writer uses very positive words in regard to an idea so that only general statements appear.

   Every driver loves this stunning, efficient, and completely safe automobile. Add a bit of sunshine to your life — take a ride in a glamorous, high-fashion car!

5. "Stacking the cards" is a technique whereby the writer presents only facts that tend to make you agree with him or her.

   There's nothing wrong with drinking before driving. Not one person at our party was hurt on the way home — and believe me not too many people there were sober!

6. The writer uses bad names about a person or product.

   Only a nitwit like Lorna would buy an imported car. Those things look like wind-up toys.

We can see the effect of slanted writing in the following statements:

> There is no point in working. The money just goes to the no-good government and the cheating landlord. You break your back to make the boss rich.
>
> Look, you do the best you can. Taxes are high and rent is impossible. But if you do not work, you give up your pride and the few comforts you have. Of course, the boss has to make a fair profit from your work; otherwise, you would not be hired. You just have to live on what is left over.
>
> Every American should be proud to work and support the system. Your taxes go to making this country great. And by helping the landowners and the factory owners make money, you are strengthening the backbone of the nation. Hard work makes good Americans.

The first version is slanted against work by telling only part of the story and by name-calling — making it appear that everybody is out to take advantage of the poor worker. The third version slants the case in the opposite direction by "stacking the deck" in favor of those who benefit from the worker's labor, by using only positive language and by pressuring the reader to follow a group. Only the second version gives a balanced view, expressed truthfully.

EXERCISES

1. Slanted Writing

Read the following sentences. Write T before those sentences that use only truthful methods. Write S before those sentences that use slanted writing techniques.

S 1. All politicians are the same, only out for themselves and their friends.

T 2. Jason Steele, the downtown real estate developer, contributed $10,000 to State Representative Jameson's campaign;

and after the election Jameson introduced a bill that would provide tax breaks on the kind of project Steele specializes in.

S 3. I hear that State Representative Jameson has been seen having lunch with some of the worst crooks in the city.

S 4. Candidate Robinson is in the great tradition of John F. Kennedy and Franklin Roosevelt.

S 5. Robinson has done only good for this city, providing services for each and every neighborhood, while never harming a single individual or ever doing anything that could be seen as dishonest.

T 6. Robinson, on the whole, offers a more specific program for improving the city than does Jameson, who tends to talk only in generalities.

S 7. Everyone is voting for Robinson, so join in and vote for a real winner.

2. Persuasive Techniques in Advertisements

Describe the methods of propaganda from pages 301–302 used in each of these slogans from advertisements to persuade you to use a product that you might not otherwise use.

1. "Accept no cheap imitations."

   portraying the other brands negatively (6)

2. "The ultimate driving machine."

   using positive words (4)

3. "Join the Pepsi generation."

   saying that everyone is doing it (3)

4. "In touch with Tomorrow."

   using positive words (4)

5. "The commanding presence of champion Nancy Lopez. And her Rolex."

   associating a famous person's name with the

   brand (1)

3. Slanted Writing and Persuasion

From your reading of advertisements and articles in newspapers and magazines, find five examples of slanted writing intended to persuade you of something. On a separate sheet of paper, write each of them down. After each, explain how the writing is slanted.

UNIT THREE REVIEW

Read this discussion from a business communication textbook about how international and intercultural issues affect business communication. Then answer the questions that follow.

International and Intercultural Dimensions

The United States is a major participant in international business — both as a buyer and seller. We are the world's largest importer of goods and services and the world's second largest exporter. The dominant role that the United States thus plays in the global economy does not, however, mean that international business matters are handled "the American way." Some years ago a book called *The Ugly American* condemned Americans abroad for the attitude of "Let 'em do it our way or not at all."

Ethnocentrism is the belief that one's own group is superior. Such an attitude hinders communication, understanding, and goodwill between trading partners. An attitude of arrogance is not only counterproductive but also unrealistic, considering the fact that the U.S. population represents less than 5% of the world population. Moreover, of the world's countries, the United States is currently fourth in population and is expected to drop to seventh place by the year 2100.[1]

Another fact of life in international business is that comparatively few Americans speak a foreign language. Although English is the major language for conducting business worldwide, it would be naive to assume that it is the other person's responsibility to learn English. As a matter of fact, only 8.5% of the world's population speaks English. This means that English-only speakers cannot communicate one-to-one with more than 90% of the people in this world.[2]

When we talk about **culture,** we mean the customary traits, attitudes, and behaviors of a group of people. International business depends very heavily on communicating effectively with people of different cultures. Competent communicators are aware of the implications of language differences, they learn to interpret nonverbal messages appropriately, and they recognize the importance of group-oriented behavior in different cultures.

The following discussion provides useful guidance for communicating with people from different cultures. Although it is helpful to be aware of cultural differences, you should also recognize that each member of a culture is an individual, with individual needs, perceptions, and experiences, and should be treated as such.

Language Differences

Unless you will actually be located overseas in the same country for an extended period of time, it may not be reasonable for you to learn the host language. Most of the correspondence between American firms and foreign firms is in English; in other cases, the services of a qualified interpreter may be available. However, even if you do not learn the host language, you should try to learn a few common phrases, such as "Good morning," "Good afternoon," "please," and "thank you." Doing so is a form of courtesy that shows personal interest, respect, and acceptance.

Even with the services of a qualified interpreter, some problems can occur. Consider, for example, the following marketing blunders:[3]

- In Brazil, where Portuguese is spoken, a U.S. airline advertised that its Boeing 747 had "rendezvous lounges," without realizing that *rendezvous* in Portuguese implies prostitution.
- In China, Kentucky Fried Chicken's slogan "Finger-lickin' good" does not have a poetic Chinese translation. The slogan was translated literally: "So good you suck your fingers."
- In Puerto Rico, General Motors had difficulties advertising the Chevrolet Nova automobile because the name sounds like the Spanish phrase "No va," which means "It doesn't go."
- In Thailand, the slogan "Come Alive with Pepsi" was translated, "Bring your ancestors back from the dead with Pepsi."

To ensure that the exact meaning is not lost during translation, legal, technical, and all important documents should be translated into the second language and then retranslated into English.

Interpreting Nonverbal Messages

Even if both parties are fluent in the same language, differences in interpretations will occur, because of the different cultures. Each person interprets events through his or her mental filter, and that filter is based on the receiver's knowledge, experiences, and viewpoints. As a result, several of the nonverbal forms of communication discussed in Chapter 1 have different meanings in different cultures.

Time The language of time is as different among cultures as the language of words. Americans and Germans are very time conscious and very precise about appointments. As a rule, Japanese are too (although they will expend much time trying to reach agreement within the group). In Tokyo, it's better to be 15 minutes early than 5 minutes late.

South Americans and Arabs, however, are often more casual about time. For example, your Egyptian host would not be considered rude if he made you wait 30 minutes for an appointment while he took care of some family matter. It should be noted, however, that the increasing complexity of international business is making all countries, including Latin and Arab countries, more time conscious.

Business people in both Asian and South American countries tend to favor long negotiations and slow deliberations. Pleasantries will be exchanged at some length before getting down to business.

Body Language Body language, especially gestures, also varies among cultures. For example, a nod of the head means "yes" to most of us, but in Bulgaria and Greece a nod means "no" and a shake of the head means "yes." Likewise, our sign for "okay" — forming a circle with our forefinger and thumb — means "zero" in France, "money" in Japan, and a vulgarity in Brazil.

Waving or pointing to an Arab business person would be considered rude, because that is how Arabs summon dogs. Folded arms signal pride in Finland but disrespect in Fiji. The number of bows that the Japanese exchange on greeting each other, as well as the length and depth of the bows, signals the social prestige each party feels toward the other. Italians might think you're bored unless you use your hands animatedly during discussions. Many American men sit with their legs crossed, with one ankle resting over the opposite knee. However, such a stance would be considered an insult in Moslem countries, where one would never show the sole of the foot to a guest.

Likewise, Americans consider eye contact very important, often not trusting someone who is "afraid to look you in the eyes." But in Japan and many Latin American countries, keeping the eyes lowered is a sign of respect; to look a partner full in the eye is considered a sign of ill breeding and is felt to be irritating.

Touch Touching behavior is very culture-specific. In Thailand, people do not touch in public, and to touch someone's head would be a major social error. The Chinese are a very reserved people and do not like to be touched, other than by a brief handshake in greeting. However, handshakes in much of Europe tend to last much longer than in the United States; pumping the hand five to seven times is normal. Europeans also tend to shake hands every time they see each other, perhaps several times a day. Similarly, in much of Europe, men often kiss each other upon greeting; unless an American businessman is aware of this custom, he might react inappropriately.

Space Our feelings about space are partly an outgrowth of our culture and partly a result of geography and economics. For example, Americans are used to wide-open spaces and tend to move about expansively, using hand and arm motions for emphasis. But in Japan, which has much smaller living and working spaces, such abrupt and extensive body movements are not typical. Likewise, Americans tend to sit face to face, so that they can maintain eye contact, whereas the Chinese and Japanese (to whom eye contact is not important) tend to sit side by side during negotiations.

In the United States, office size is related to status, with top executives having the largest offices. In other parts of the world, however, the "bigger is better" mentality gives way to logic: not much space is needed for thinking and planning, so top executives do not need large offices.

The sense of personal space — the distance from others at which we feel comfortable interacting — also differs among cultures. In the United States, a person's social zone is between 4 and 12 feet, with most business exchanges occurring at about 5 feet. However, in both the Middle East and Latin American countries, this distance is too far. Business people there tend to stand close enough to feel your breath as you speak. Most Americans tend to back away unconsciously from such close contact.

Group-Oriented Behavior

The business environment in a capitalistic society such as the United States places great value on the contributions of the individual toward the success of the organization. Individual effort is often stressed more than group effort, and a competitive atmosphere prevails. In other cultures, however, originality and independence of judgment are not valued as highly as teamwork. There is a frequently quoted Japanese saying, "a nail standing out will be hammered down."[4] Thus, the Japanese go to great lengths to reach decisions through consensus, wherein every participating member, not just a majority, is able to agree.

Closely related to the concept of group-oriented behavior is the concept of saving face. The desire to "save face" simply means that neither party in a given interaction should suffer embarrassment. Human relationships are highly valued in such cultures and are embodied in the concept of *wa,* or the Japanese pursuit of harmony. This concept makes it difficult for the Japanese to say "no" to a request because it would be impolite. They are very reluctant to offend others — even if they unintentionally mislead them instead. Thus, a "yes" in Japanese might mean "Yes, I understand you" rather than "Yes, I agree." Likewise, a strongly negative reaction to an American proposal might prompt only a mild response, such as "I will try my best." Latin Americans also tend to avoid an outright "no" in their business dealings, preferring a milder, less explicit, response.

One business executive compared negotiating with the Japanese to studying a Japanese ink painting: "Ink painting creates an effect by the use of blank spaces, and unless one is able to read those empty areas, one cannot understand the work. The same is true, they say, of Japanese speech. One always has to figure out the parts that have been left unsaid."[5] In other words, one has to read between the lines, because what is left unsaid or unwritten may be just as important as what was said or written.

Strategies for Communicating Across Cultures

To hasten final acceptance and to enhance your chances for achieving your objectives when communicating with business people abroad, use the following strategies.

Maintain Formality Much more than the United States, most other countries value and respect a formal approach to business dealings. Call others by their titles and family names unless specifically asked to do otherwise. By both verbal and nonverbal clues, convey an attitude of propriety and decorum. Most other cultures do not equate formality with coldness.

Show Respect Withhold judgment, accepting the premise that attitudes held by an entire culture are probably based on sound reasoning. Listen carefully to what is being communicated, trying to understand the other person's feelings. Learn about your host country — its geography, form of government, largest cities, culture, current events, and the like.

Be Flexible In terms of cultural differences, assume the attitude that there are no right ways or wrong ways — only different ways. Be adaptable, willing to change your behavior, attitudes, and eating habits. (As one seasoned traveler has said, "Anything tastes like chicken if you slice it thinly and swallow it quickly.") Patience and a sense of humor will help you adapt to your host country.

Communicate Clearly To ensure that your oral and written messages are understood, follow these guidelines:

- Avoid slang, jargon, and other figures of speech. Expressions such as "They'll eat that up," "out in left field," or "a Catch-22 situation" are likely to confuse even a fluent English speaker.
- Be specific and illustrate your points with concrete examples.
- Provide and solicit feedback. Summarize frequently; provide a written summary of the points covered in a meeting; ask your counterpart to paraphrase what has been said; encourage questions.
- Use a variety of media — handouts (distributed before the meeting to allow time for reading), audiovisual aids, models, and the like.
- Avoid attempts at humor; humor is likely to be lost on your counterpart.
- Speak plainly and slowly (but not so slowly as to appear to be condescending), choosing your words carefully.

Intercultural Diversity in the United States

Perhaps the (unintended) implication up to this point has been that you must leave the United States in order to encounter cultures different from the one with which you are comfortable. Nothing could be farther from the truth. Consider, for example, the following:[6]

> *Fact*: Today blacks, Asians, and Hispanics make up 21% of the American population. More than 30% of New York City's residents are foreign born. Miami is two-thirds Hispanic. Detroit is 63% black. San Francisco is one-third Asian.
>
> *Projection*: In ten years, minorities will make up 25% of the population of the United States. English will be the second language for the majority of California's population by the year 2000; by 2020, the majority of that state's entry-level workers will be Hispanic. Sometime in the next century, whites will become the minority in the population of the United States.
>
> *Implication*: Diversity will have a profound impact on our lives — and will pose a growing challenge for most human resources managers. Those who view diversity among employees as a source of richness and strength for the company can help bring a wide range of benefits to their organizations.

Whether you happen to belong to the majority culture or to one of the minority cultures in the United States, you will share your work and leisure hours with people different from yourself — people who have values, mannerisms, and speech habits different from your own. This is true today, and it will be even truer in the future. The same strategies given earlier — showing respect, being flexible, and communicating clearly — apply whether the cultural differences are at home or abroad.

A person who is knowledgeable about, and comfortable with, different cultures is a more effective manager because he or she can avoid misunderstandings, avoid poor performance, and tap into the greater variety of viewpoints a diverse culture provides. In addition, such understanding provides personal satisfaction.

References

1. *The World Almanac and Book of Facts: 1989,* pp. 522, 532; *The 1989 Information Please Almanac,* p. 139.
2. Retha H. Kilpatrick, "International Business Communication Practices," *Journal of Business Communication,* 21 (Fall 1984): 36; *The 1989 Information Please Almanac,* pp. 225, 522.
3. Stephen Karel, "Learning Culture the Hard Way," *Consumer Markets Abroad,* 7 (May 1988): 1, 15.
4. Martin Rösch and Kay G. Segler, "Communication with Japanese," *Management International Review,* 27 (December 1987): 56.
5. Koreo Kinosita, "Language Habits of the Japanese," *Bulletin of the Association for Business Communication,* 51 (September 1988): 36.
6. Lennie Copeland, "Making the Most of Cultural Differences at the Workplace," *Personnel,* 65 (June 1988): 52.

— *Scot Ober*

EXERCISES

1. Place a checkmark before each of the statements about ethnocentrism that can be inferred from this selection.

_____ a. Ethnocentrism does not hurt business.

√ b. Americans have conducted business ethnocentrically in the past.

_______ c. European companies also operate ethnocentrically.

√_______ d. Our economic power in the world in the past let us get away with enthnocentrism.

_______ e. People in other countries who want to do business with Americans always learn English.

_______ f. Americans today are as ethnocentric as in the past.

√_______ g. The book *The Ugly American* was opposed to ethnocentrism.

2. In your own words, give the meaning of each of the figurative expressions in the selection.
   a. "A nail standing out will be hammered down."

      People who are different will be made to conform.

   b. "One always has to figure out the parts that have been left unsaid."

      People do not speak directly.

   c. "Anything tastes like chicken."

      You can get by if you don't worry about strange appearances.

   d. "They'll eat that up."

      People will like that.

   e. "Out in left field."

      not understanding the obvious

   f. "A Catch-22 situation"

      a trap where you always lose

3. Put a checkmark before the statements you can reasonably conclude from the selection.

____ a. Every member of a different culture follows the rules of that culture.

√ b. If international business continues to increase, people will be more time conscious throughout the world.

____ c. Americans use more hand signs and gestures than other people.

√ d. Americans consider office space a sign of status, but people in other cultures often do not.

√ e. Being sensitive to other people's cultures is good business.

____ f. Even if you are not sensitive to other people's cultures, you will usually be understood.

____ g. Because all Americans are alike, you need not worry about cultural difference inside this country.

4. Based on the article, state in your own words
   a. a generalization about the effect of ethnocentrism on business:

   Student responses will vary.

   b. a generalization about the relation between individual differences and cultural patterns:

   c. a generalization about the use of foreign languages in international business:

d. a generalization about body language and hand gestures:

____

e. a generalization about individuality and group orientation:

____

f. a few general rules to follow in doing international business:

____

____

____

____

g. a generalization about cultural diversity in the United States.

____

5. What opinion does each of the following sets of facts support in the selection?
   a. Statistics about U.S. imports, exports, and population

   Although we are important in the world, other countries are important too.

   b. Stories about marketing Pepsi, Kentucky Fried Chicken, and other products

   It is easy to be misunderstood if you are not careful.

c. Statistics about minorities in the United States today and in the future.

We need to appreciate the intercultural diversity in this country.

6. Overall, what is the writer's purpose in this selection? What effect does he want to have on you?

He wants to sensitize you to diversity and the need to pay more attention to communicating more carefully in intercultural situations.

7. Overall, how would you describe the writer's style? In what ways is this written like other textbooks? In what way is it different?

Student responses will vary.

Critical Thinking in Writing

What did you learn from this selection about the connection between cultural issues and international business communications? Write a brief summary of the selection (see **13**); and then evaluate the author's points. Do you agree with Ober? Why or why not? How do your experiences support or challenge his points?

Unit Four

The Basic Study Skills

Handbook

13

Underlining, Taking Notes, Outlining, and Summarizing

For your course work you will often need to look back at what you learned from your reading. To study for exams, to refresh your memory for class discussions, and to prepare papers and projects, you will need to go over information you gathered from assigned readings as well as from your personal extra readings. If you had the time and energy, you could just reread all the material from beginning to end. But reviewing the material is easier and quicker if you identify and mark important information the first time you read it. Then later you can go right to the parts you need.

There are several ways to locate and record important information as you read. *Underlining* the material on a page is quickest, but *taking notes* makes you reorganize the reading material into an easily understood form. *Outlining* helps you record the structure of the ideas in your reading. *Summarizing* — restating the meaning in a concise way — helps you grasp the meaning of what you read most fully.

Each of these study techniques does more than create a record of what you think is important in the reading for later review. By making you work actively to get at the important facts or ideas, each of these techniques helps you understand the material better the first time you read it. Because you have to use your mind to identify ideas and facts in what you read and your pencil to mark them, you are more likely to remember what you are supposed to learn. The more active a study technique is, the more it helps you understand and remember what you read.

13a Underlining

If you underline the most important ideas and details in a reading assignment, you can rapidly find what you need when you reread the passage. You can also add special marks and comments in the margin about the main ideas and major details you underline. These extra marks and comments can help you remember your thoughts and interpretation of the passage.

A Method for Underlining

- Underline only reading material that belongs to you. Do not mark up library books, borrowed books, or books that belong to your school. Underlining is a personal process. Your underlining may interfere with other readers' use and enjoyment of a book.
- Mark the main ideas and the major details differently. Underline the main ideas with a double line and the major details with a single line. Or use a different color highlighter pen for each.
- Find main-idea sentences by following the suggestions in section **5b**. Underline the sentences or the parts of sentences that state the main idea of a paragraph. If the main idea is only implied, write your own main-idea sentence in the margin.
- Find major details by following the suggestions in section **6b**. Underline these major details.
- Circle key words. Use brackets ([ ]), asterisks (*), or any other symbol to mark parts that are especially interesting or important to you.
- Write notes or comments to yourself in the margin. The margins are good places to put down your own thoughts as you read. Margin notes can help you connect ideas from different parts of the selection. They can also help you connect a passage with other material you have read, comments your teacher has made, or your own experience.

Read the following passage describing how coins came to be used to see how one student used the technique of underlining and making margin notes to highlight important points.

Where Does Money Come From?

Stages
1. Cattle

From the earliest agricultural times some 9000 years ago people used cattle for currency, a practice that has carried into the present in our word "pecuniary," from the Latin *pecus,* meaning "cattle."

2. Metal ingots

Metallic money appeared considerably later, about 2000 B.C., in the form of bronze ingots, often shaped like cattle and traded on the open market according to their weight. Not only were amulets of cattle infinitely more convenient to exchange than the real thing, but the intrinsic brilliance of the metallic pieces heightened their esthetic appeal. Exchanging money then, however, always required the presence of an honest balance-beam scale and often was accompanied by a fiery dispute when the honesty of one of the parties was impugned. cheating easy

3. Rare metals

By about 1000 B.C. bronze had been superseded by the purer, rarer metals, silver and gold, and cattle shapes had given way to heads of cats (particularly in Egypt, where cat worship reached obsessional heights), statuettes of rulers, deities, or merely ornamental medallions. These pieces, too, derived their worth from weight, a troublesome standard that would survive only a few hundred years longer. new shapes

4. Protocoins

The first protocoins were produced by the Lydians of Anatolia about 800 B.C. Made of electrum, a natural alloy of gold containing as much as 35 percent silver, these pieces were crude, bean-shaped ingots that bore a punchmark signifying their worth, thus obviating the need for a scale.

5. True coins

Around 640 B.C., the Lydians began producing the first true coins (the word "coin" is a Latin derivative from *cuneus,* or "wedge"). They were made by a smith hammering a punch through a sheet of electrum as it lay on his anvil. Being a malleable alloy, electrum made possible the imprinting of a figure of a man or an animal on the coin's face; a particular relief signified a coin's value, which almost immediately led to cheating on the ratio of gold to silver in the currency.

Coins, of course, allowed payment for goods to be made by count instead of weight, a great boon to commerce and convenience, but one that opened the possibility of counterfeiting. Facsimiles of coins were fashioned of cheaper metals; precious gold and silver were shaved off the edges of real coins; and bunches of coins were shaken for hours in leather bags so that the cheater could collect the dust produced by friction — a tedious procedure to be sure, but one that yielded more dust than we might imagine, since coins then were made of purer, and hence softer, metals. The introduction in the late 17th century of *milling*, or serrating the edge of a coin, finally put an end to the profitable practice of coin shaving. And today's more solid coins shaken for hours in a bag might leave a wisp of dust, but it would be more copper and nickel than silver, and definitely not worth the time and energy.

new cheating

— *Charles Panati*

EXERCISES

1. Underlining

1. Read the article about Robert Hooke on pages 170–171. Use underlining to show important information.
2. Review Chapter 6, "Reading for Information," by underlining important ideas.

2. Underlining

1. Read a chapter in a textbook assigned for another one of your courses. Underline and make other marks to highlight important information.
2. Read the following material from a textbook on organizational management. Underline and mark to highlight important information.

Individual Creativity

Individual creativity is a core requirement for organizations whose aim is to introduce new and exciting products and services into the marketplace. What makes a person creative? How do people become creative? How does the creative process work? Although psychologists have not yet discovered complete answers to these questions, examining a few general patterns can help us understand the sources of individual creativity within organizations.

The Creative Individual

Numerous researchers have focused their efforts on attempting to describe the common attributes of creative individuals. These attributes generally fall into three categories: background experiences, personality traits, and cognitive abilities.

Background Experiences and Creativity Background experiences are the events that people live through during childhood and young adulthood. Researchers have noticed that many creative individuals were raised in an environment in which creativity was perceived and rewarded. Mozart, one of the greatest composers of all time, was raised in a family of musicians and began composing and performing music at age 6. Pierre and Marie Curie, great scientists in their own right, also raised a daughter, Irene, who won the Nobel Prize in Chemistry. Thomas Edison's renowned creativity was nurtured by his mother.

However, people with background experiences very different from theirs have also been creative. The African-American abolitionist and writer Frederick Douglass was born into slavery in Tuckahoe, Maryland, and had very limited opportunities for education. Nonetheless, Douglass became one of the most influential figures of the Civil War era. His powerful oratory and creative thinking helped lead to the Emancipation Proclamation, which outlawed slavery in the United States.

Personality and Creativity Various personality traits have been linked with individual creativity. As listed in Table 9.1, the personality traits shared by most creative people are broad interests, attraction to complexity, high levels of energy, independence and autonomy, strong self-confidence, and a strong belief that one is, in fact, creative. Individuals who have these personality characteristics are more likely to be creative than people who do not have them.

TABLE 9.1 Personality Traits Shared by Most Creative People

1. Broad interests	4. Independence and autonomy
2. Attraction to complexity	5. Strong self-confidence
3. High levels of energy	6. Belief in personal creativity

Different industries tend to attract different numbers of highly creative people. One industry that seems to attract a large number of these people is the fashion industry. Indeed, the fashion industry thrives on the creativity of individuals. . . .

Cognitive Abilities and Creativity **Cognitive abilities** are an individual's power to think intelligently and to analyze situations and data effectively. Research suggests that intelligence may be a precondition for individual creativity, which means that although most creative people are highly intelligent, not all intelligent people necessarily are creative. Creativity is also linked with the ability to think divergently and convergently. **Divergent thinking** is a skill that allows people to see differences between situations, phenomena, or events. **Convergent thinking** is a skill that allows people to see similarities between situations, phenomena, or events. Creative people are generally very skilled at both divergent and convergent thinking.

Some of the decisions made by Lee Iaccoca after he assumed the presidency of Chrysler illustrate the interplay between divergent and convergent thinking. As he joined Chrysler, the company was losing millions of dollars, laying off numerous employees, and on the verge of bankruptcy. Once the organization was stabilized financially with the help of government loans, Iaccoca turned to improving the products available to potential Chrysler customers. The first task was to catalog what a range of different customers might want in a car in terms of size, performance, cost, and styling. Describing these diverse and sometimes contradictory customer needs is an example of divergent thinking. One of Iaccoca's insights was that it might be possible to meet all these different customer needs by manufacturing different versions of one basic automobile design. This design became known as the "K-car." It was the result of using convergent thinking to find a common solution to numerous problems.

— *Jay Barney and Ricky Griffin*

Critical Thinking in Writing

Write a few paragraphs in which you define creativity from your own perspective. Give examples of creative people you know or have studied about in order to explain what you think creativity is.

13b Taking Notes

To take notes on your reading, you must identify the main ideas and major details, and then write them down in an organized list. You may choose to list the information on one line after another down the page. The items may or may not be numbered. If you decide that some points are more important than others, you can indent the less important information underneath the main points it supports.

As you write down the information, you pay active attention to it, making it easier to remember. Also indenting the less important information underneath the more important helps you see how the parts of the reading fit together.

The following notes are based on the passage about the origin of coin money (pages 321–322). Go back and reread the passage quickly. You may find it useful to compare these notes with the sample underlining in the original.

First money — cattle, 9000 years ago
First metal money — bronze ingots in shape of cattle, 2000 B.C. Had to be weighed.
By 1000 B.C. silver and gold in shape of cat heads
800 B.C., first protocoins of gold alloy, bean-shaped ingots with punchmark of value
640 B.C., first real coin by Lydians, value given by figure punched on. Replacing weighing with counting made counterfeiting, dust stealing, and coin shaving possible.

These notes help bring out the time-order organization of the passage. Each main point lists a new stage in the development of coin money. The importance of the switch from weighing to counting is also noted.

A Method for Taking Notes

- Find the main ideas following the suggestions in section **5b**. Write these main ideas down on notebook paper, starting at the left margin of the paper. You may copy the entire main idea sentence as it appears in the reading, shorten it, or put the idea in your own words. You can even jot down just a few key phrases from the printed text as long as they capture the main idea.

- Find the major details, following the suggestions in section **6b**. List them opposite or beneath your notes on the main ideas. Again you need not copy down whole sentences. Phrases or words will do. Your own wording of the printed text will do, as long as your notes capture the important facts or ideas.
- Use abbreviations, but make sure you will be able to understand their meanings when you return to the notes, weeks or months later.
- Add your own comments and thoughts in the margins or in a special section at the bottom of the page. These comments will help you think through the importance of the material or highlight its relation to other reading you have done.
- You can use a similar method for taking notes during course lectures. Make sure you keep up with the lecture. Don't get so caught up in taking notes that you stop listening. If you find the lecturer getting too far ahead of you, stop writing and start listening. If you skip a few lines, you can always complete your notes later from memory or from a friend's notes. During lectures, avoid fussing over the spelling and exact wording of your notes. You can always check the dictionary later.

EXERCISES

1. Taking Notes from Printed Material

1. Review Chapter 6 of this book by taking notes on a separate sheet of paper.
2. Select a newspaper article and take notes on it as you read. A few days later rewrite the article in your own words from your notes. Compare your story to the newspaper's printed version to see how accurate your notes are.

2. Taking Notes from Listening

1. Take notes during one of your course lectures. Compare your notes with those made by other students. Also, if possible, ask the professor to look over your notes and tell you how accurate your notes are. Did you write down the most important facts and ideas?
2. Watch the evening news on television, taking notes on one

of the major stories. Retell the news story to a friend or family member using your notes. How similar were the two versions?

3. Taking Notes on a Textbook Assignment

Return to the selection "Individual Creativity" on pages 323–324. Take study notes on the selection, using a separate sheet of paper.

13c Outlining

Outlining is an organized form of note taking. In an outline a system of numbering and indenting entries helps organize ideas by level of importance. The main ideas begin at the left margin, numbered with Roman numerals. Supporting ideas, indented under the main ideas, are marked with capital letters. Less important material is indented further and given Arabic numerals (and then lowercase letters at the next level).

An outline arrangement of your notes lets you see at a glance how the key ideas relate to one another and how the writer backs up the main points.

To Make Successful Outlines

- List only main ideas as main headings.
- Relate all subheadings to the main heading they follow.
- Make sure all the headings in a series fit together logically.
- Make sure the headings are clearly different, that they don't cover the same material. If there is too much overlap, you should reorganize the outline.
- Make sure that whenever you break down a heading you have at least two subheadings.
- Include everything important that appears in the selection you are outlining.
- Use whole sentences, phrases, or just single words, as long as the entries convey the information and are easy to understand. If you use sentences in one part, however, you should use sentences throughout the outline.
- Indent all items correctly.
- Put a period after each letter or number.

The following sample outline is based on the passage on the origin of coin money on pages 321–322.

I. First currency — cattle
   A. 9000 years ago
   B. Pecuniary — Latin for "cattle"
II. First metal money, in form of metal ingots
   A. Bronze used first
   B. Shaped like cattle
   C. 2000 B.C.
      1. Pretty and convenient
      2. Exchanged by weight
         a. Required honest scale
         b. Led to disputes
   D. Bronze replaced by rarer metals
      1. 1000 B.C.
      2. Gold, silver
      3. Shaped like cat heads
III. Coins with worth punched on
   A. First protocoins by Lydians
      1. About 800 B.C.
      2. Gold alloy
      3. Bean-shaped ingots
   B. First true coins by Lydians
      1. 640 B.C.
      2. Gold alloy
      3. Value in relief figure
   C. Coin value counted instead of weighed
      1. Convenience for commerce
      2. Allowed cheating
         a. Counterfeiting with cheaper metals
         b. Coin shaving
         c. Dust collected by friction
         d. Milled edge stopped shaving

Compare this outline to the notes on page 325 about the same passage. Notice how the outline gives a more complete picture of the organization of the ideas. On the other hand, making an outline is time consuming. When you really need to understand and remember the structure of particularly difficult material, outlining is the best study technique. Note taking is a more efficient study method for routine reading assignments.

EXERCISES

1. Outline Chapter 7 as a way of reviewing the sequence of ideas in paragraphs. Use a separate piece of paper.
2. Using a separate sheet of paper, outline the passage about the changing American male on pages 252–254.
3. Imagine that you have been assigned the textbook passage on pages 322–324 for a course on management. To prepare for a quiz on the material, make an outline of the selection.
4. Outline the following selection on the history, function, and value of the social custom of dating.

Does Dating Work?

The history of courtship in America begins with the Puritans (enough said), proceeds to the modest sexual revolution of the 18th century and the counter-revolution of the 19th, and then arrives, around the turn of the century, at the familiar practice called "dating." According to University of Michigan sociologist Martin King Whyte, however, all those centuries of romantic evolution may not have done much to improve one's chances of finding a good mate.

Dating was born among middle and upper-middle-class students, and by the 1920s, the earlier custom of "calling" — in which a young man, if invited, would call on a nubile maiden at her home, with her mother hovering protectively nearby — had largely disappeared. Not incidentally, Whyte says, more of the initiative in courtship shifted to the men.

America's prosperity had a great deal to do with the rise of dating. The expansion of secondary schooling and higher education provided "an arena in which females and males could get to know one another informally over many years," he notes. "Schools also organized athletic, social, and other activities in which adult supervision was minimal." Colleges provided an almost complete escape from parental supervision.

Increased affluence freed young people from the necessity of helping to put bread on the family table, and gave them the money and leisure to date. Whole industries sprang up to serve them. Youths could visit an ice cream parlor or an amusement park, dance to popular music recordings, or go to the movies. Automobiles not only got young people away from home but "provided a semi-private space with abundant romantic and sexual possibilities."

By contrast with "calling," Whyte points out, the main purpose of dating, at least in its initial stages, was not the selection of a spouse but the pursuit of pleasure, and perhaps romance. Eventually, of course, dating often led to "going steady," and from there to engagement and marriage.

In the popular mind, dating became the rough equivalent of shopping. Youths would make modest purchases in a variety of stores, have a good time doing so, and eventually find the best available "product" for them — a Mr. or Miss Right. A happy and enduring marriage would ensue.

The problem, Whyte says, is that things do not seem to work out so neatly. It's not that avid players of the dating game never find marital bliss, but that their playing the game doesn't seem to help. A survey of 459 women in the Detroit area Whyte conducted in 1984 revealed no clear connection between dating experience and a successful marriage. "Women who had married their first sweethearts were just as likely to have enduring and satisfying marriages as women who had married only after considering many alternatives." Nor was there any discernible difference between the marriages of women who were virgins when they wed and those of women who were not. One thing did seem to make a difference. Those women who recalled being "head over heels in love" when they wed had more successful marriages. Their memories were probably colored by subsequent experience, Whyte acknowledges, but nothing they said contradicted the familiar wisdom of poets and songwriters. Dating may not work, he concludes, but perhaps love really does conquer all.

— Wilson Quarterly

Critical Thinking in Writing

Write a one- or two-paragraph response to the question in the title: "Does dating work?" Draw on your own experiences and observations.

13d Summarizing Paragraphs

Summaries are brief statements about material you have read. Unlike notes or outlines, summaries fit together a selection's facts and ideas in readable sentences and paragraphs. Summaries are simply shorter versions of the original passages that are intended to convey the most important information in the most compact way. Write your summary by creating your own sentences to combine the most important ideas from the original.

How to Prepare a Summary

- Carefully read the entire passage to be summarized. Make sure you understand all the vocabulary and concepts. Check a dictionary when necessary.
- Underline or list separately the main ideas and major details of the reading.
- Select the main idea of the passage as the most important idea of the summary. This will usually be the first sentence of your summary.
- Rewrite facts and ideas into sentences that show the connections among them. If you combine several facts and ideas in one sentence, make their connections clear. Be careful not to combine information without any logical connection.
- Avoid repeating unnecessary words from the original material. Leave out all but the most important details.
- Present ideas and information in an organized way that reflects the meaning of the original version. Don't jump suddenly from one point to the next. Use connecting words like *first, second, on the other hand, because,* and *although* to show how your summary statements fit together.

A good way to build up your skills in summary writing is to write single-sentence summaries of whole paragraphs. Write one sentence that tells the most important meaning of a paragraph. If a paragraph has one concise main-idea sentence, you may decide just to rephrase it. You can eliminate unnecessary words in the sentence or rewrite it completely.

The best sentence summaries, however, usually require more work. Read a paragraph looking for all its important ideas and facts. Underline key words and phrases. Cross out any information that is not major. Then write a summary sentence that includes all the important material you have identified. One brief sentence can often show the relationships among several important parts of a paragraph.

Compare the next paragraph with the various single-sentence summaries that follow it.

> Although several early societies experimented with paper currency — most notably the Chinese during the 1st millennium B.C. — coins of silver and gold predominated as the major form of exchange. The reasons were understandable enough: coins were far more durable than paper and less likely to be destroyed by fire, and coins contained the very precious metals that made money worth its salt. It required a leap of both imagination and of courage to establish a form of currency that was only backed by a precious metal but of itself was intrinsically worthless.
>
> — *Charles Panati*

One approach would be to look at the opening sentence as a source for your own summary sentence:

1. Although several early societies experimented with paper currency — most notably the Chinese during the 1st millennium B.C. — coins of silver and gold predominated as the major form of exchange.

A few eliminations and some rewriting creates a compact summary based on the opening sentence:

2. Coins of silver and gold predominated as the major form of exchange over early experiments with paper currency.

You can produce an even more accurate summary than example 2 by taking key ideas from the *entire* paragraph, not just the opening topic sentence. Write them in your own words. In the original paragraph, the key information is not just that coins were the major form of exchange. We also learn *why* coins predominated (remained the leading elements). A good summary would include that information:

3. Because silver and gold coins were more durable, less flammable, and more intrinsically valuable, they predominated over early paper money.

EXERCISES

1. On a separate piece of paper write a one-sentence summary for each of the next two paragraphs in the spaces below. Use your own wording, not the author's.

The real origin of paper money in the Western world as medium of exchange that eclipsed the use of coins began in France in the early 18th century. Over a span of many decades most of the money in circulation gradually had come to consist not of actual gold or silver but of fiduciary notes — promises to pay up a debt in specified amounts of the precious metals. Both private citizens and banks issued such fiduciary money, either in the form of paper bank notes, or merely as transferable book entries that came to be called deposits. Over a period of time the state acquired control of this fiduciary system.

— *Charles Panati*

In the West, paper money was first used in 18th-century France, where banks and individuals issued fiduciary notes.

In addition to the French government, the American colonies under the Continental Congress printed their own paper money, called "fiats," which were really promises to pay. As can happen with any fiduciary money, fiats initially were overissued, diluting their worth. Soon their exchange could be redeemed only for a small fraction of the denoted value in metallic money. When the public refused to accept fiats, reins were tightened and paper money returned eventually to a vogue it has enjoyed — despite periodic overissuing and the departure from the gold standard — to the present day.

— *Charles Panati*

Although overissuing of "fiats" in the American colonies led people to distrust paper money, tightened controls restored its popularity.

2. On a separate piece of paper write a one-sentence summary for the paragraph about the first submarine escape (page 169).

Wilhelm Bauer and his crew made the first escape from a sunken submarine by using water pressure to help them.

3. On a separate piece of paper write a one-sentence summary for the paragraph on page 205 about people killed by lightning.

   Men are killed by lightning more often than women because they are outdoors more and are less likely to seek cover.

4. Select four long paragraphs from one of your textbooks in another course. On separate paper write a single-sentence summary for each of them. **Student responses will vary.**

13e Summarizing Long Passages

When you summarize a passage of several paragraphs or longer, you will need to write several sentences to summarize all the important information. In fact each sentence can summarize the information of each important paragraph. However, you may want to combine related information from several summary sentences into one sentence. You may also devote two or more sentences to summarize one long, important paragraph. Or you may choose not to summarize paragraphs that serve as transitions, repeat information you've already summarized, or provide lengthy illustrations.

In reading the following informative summary of the passage on the origin of coin money from pages 321–322, notice how important facts and ideas are combined and how less important information has been left out. Look at how the connections between ideas are brought out by combining sentences and using connecting words such as *because* and *then*. Also the clustering of sentences in separate paragraphs helps bring out the differences between ingots and coins.

> The use of cattle as currency, dating back 9000 years, was replaced in 2000 B.C. by bronze ingots in the shape of cattle. Because these pretty, convenient ingots were traded according to weight, disputes occurred over the honesty of the weighing. Gold and silver ingots in the shape of cat heads replaced the bronze ingots by 1000 B.C.
>
> The first protocoins, produced by the Lydians around 800 B.C. out of a gold alloy, had a punchmark showing their worth. The Lydians in 640 B.C. produced the first real coins

> with a figure on them signifying their value. The value of coins could be calculated then by counting instead of weighing — a process that made cheating possible (using cheap metals, shaving the coins, or wearing the coins down to obtain dust). The introduction of serrating coin edges in the late 17th century decreased the cheating.

An opening sentence giving the main idea of the passage is useful to tie a long summary together. This topic sentence reflects your reading of the entire passage. Be aware of how ideas in your different summary sentences fit together. Show the relations between sentences by having their ideas follow one another logically and by using connecting words and phrases to stress how the ideas fit together. For a summary that requires more than five or six sentences, cluster related summary sentences together in separate paragraphs. The paragraph breaks should show the main divisions of the author's original ideas.

Informative summaries are good study tools. They help you remember the most important information and how the ideas are put together by getting you to restate the information in your own way. Often study and exam questions can be answered successfully by summaries of appropriate parts of your reading. If you have already practiced putting the material together in a summary, you will be able to answer the questions more easily.

For study purposes a summary is usually about a quarter of the length of the original text. For example, the summary on page 325 of the coin passage on pages 321–322 is less than 150 words, compared with almost 500 words in the original. When you write an informative summary of a long textbook chapter, make your summary shorter in proportion to the original, perhaps as short as one-tenth the length.

In another kind of summary, the descriptive summary, you give a general overview of the selection in your own words and style. You do not try to adopt the style of the original writer. Descriptive summaries are sometimes useful for criticism and analysis. They are usually less useful as study tools than informative summaries because they are more cumbersome and present less complete and precise information.

A descriptive summary of the coin passage might begin this way:

The writer describes the history of coins from the earliest use of cattle as currency 9000 years ago up to the seventeenth century. In a series of steps, the writer discusses the various metals used in ingots and coins, the shapes of the metal, and the advantages and problems of each kind of currency. According to the writer, the use of bronze ingots in the shape of cattle around 2000 B.C. led to disputes over weighing the ingots to determine their worth. . . .

EXERCISES

1. Reread the selection "Americans Work Too Hard" (pages 281–282) and write a summary of that selection on a separate sheet of paper.
2. Reread the textbook selection "Individual Creativity" (pages 322–324) and write a summary of that selection on a separate sheet of paper.

14

Understanding Exam Questions

To find out how much you have learned during each semester through class lectures and assigned readings, teachers test you in examinations. You must pay close attention to the wording of the exam questions in order to give correct answers. No matter how much information you know, if you do not understand exam questions and provide what an instructor is asking for, your answers will be off target.

The two basic kinds of exam questions are *short-answer* (or objective questions) and *essay* questions. With short-answer questions, the teacher is testing whether you know specific pieces of information and can therefore solve straightforward problems that have a single answer. With essay questions, the teacher is testing not only whether you know specific information but also how well you understand and can apply that information to a subject.

Advice on how to read and answer both types of questions appears in section **14b** and **14c**, but you also must know how to prepare for exams. If you do not know the course material, you may not even be able to understand exam questions, let alone answer them correctly.

14a Preparing for Examinations

In the long run, the best way to prepare for examinations is to keep up with class lectures and assigned readings by underlining, taking notes, outlining, and summarizing (see Chapter **13**). But even if you have done the work throughout the semester and have a complete set of notes, your memory will probably be a bit fuzzy by exam time. The following steps will help you review course material and focus your studying for exams:

- *Get an overview of the entire course.* Looking over a syllabus, list of lectures, assignment sheet, or any material that the teacher handed out at the beginning of the course can help you see the shape of the entire course. Quickly skimming through your notes and the assigned books can also help you get an overview of the topics covered. Then, on a single sheet of paper, outline or list all the major topics covered in class and in the readings. See if you notice any pattern in what was studied and any major themes that the teacher kept emphasizing throughout the semester. For example, a psychology teacher might organize her course around different theories of psychology and emphasize how each theory explains abnormal behavior.
- *Think about the overview.* The overview should help you determine what a teacher considers important and what kinds of exam questions a teacher is likely to ask. The overview can also help you sort out which topics are fairly clear and fresh in your mind and which topics are unclear and fading fast. The fresh topics will require only a little study; the unclear ones may call for a long, thorough review of all your notes and study tools.
- *Schedule your study time.* Decide how much time you have available to study for the exam. Divide your time according to how important each topic appears to be and how well you know the topic. Don't waste time memorizing minor facts that you will probably not be tested on or studying material that probably was presented only to make the class more lively. Spend your study time on the most important material.
- *Study the material topic by topic, in an orderly way.* One good technique for studying each major topic is to combine in outline form the key concepts and facts from both class and reading assignments. Not only will you review the material, but you will also see how the parts fit together. The more you see the logical connections among the many facts and concepts, the more you will remember and the better you will understand the material.

EXERCISES

1. Make a list of all the major topics covered thus far in one of the courses you are taking this semester. Use your class notes, the textbook, and the course syllabus to help you.
   a. What pattern of organization can you find in the topics and in the order in which they were covered? Rewrite your list as an outline to reflect this organization. Now imagine that you will be examined on all this material in five days, and draw up a study schedule.
   b. For this same course, write down a list of three to five ideas or concepts that the teacher repeatedly stressed throughout the semester.
2. For a single topic, one that was covered in both class lectures and readings in a course you are now taking, write an outline of key concepts and facts to show how the information fits together.

14b Short-Answer Questions

The first and most important thing to do when taking any examination is to read the directions — all the directions for all the parts of the test. Then you will know right from the beginning what you have to do and how much time you have to complete each part. Reading the directions carefully will help you schedule your testing time and guide your decisions.

On a short-answer test, read the directions to learn the following pieces of vital information:

- *Discover how many questions you have to answer.* Knowing how much work you have ahead of you will help you plan your time.
- *Find out whether you have any choices.* If you have choices, make sure you understand and follow the directions exactly. If, in the first part of an exam, you are supposed to answer only ten out of twenty questions, but you answer all twenty anyway, you have wasted time. The last ten answers will not count on your test results. If in the second part you are supposed to answer twenty out of twenty-five questions, but you answer only fifteen, you will lose credit for five questions.

- *Pay attention to how much time you have.* You may have one block of time for the whole exam, or you may have smaller blocks for each part. In either case, you should estimate the time you have available for each question. In this way you will not waste too much time on a single question and then have to rush through all the remaining questions.
- *Determine how many points each question is worth.* If some questions are worth more points than others, you should spend more time on the more valuable questions. Also notice whether incorrect answers count against you. If there is no penalty, you should make your best guess, even if you are not sure of the answer. But if there is a penalty, you may be better off leaving some questions blank rather than making wild guesses.
- *Know beforehand what extra materials you are allowed.* You may be allowed to use the textbook, a calculator, your notes, or scrap paper. Usually the instructor will let you know ahead of time which materials are permitted so that you can bring them with you. If you do not bring the extra materials allowed, you are putting yourself at a serious disadvantage.
- *Find out where to record your answers.* Sometimes you may be allowed to fill in or circle the answer on the question itself, but more often special places are provided for the answers. If you have to fill in spaces on a machine-scored sheet, be sure to mark the spaces neatly and clearly. If you have to use a special pencil, be sure that you have one and that you use it. If your answer is in the wrong place or cannot be read, it will do you no good.
- *Notice what type or types of questions are included.* Different types of questions require different types of answers.

Fill-in questions ask you to write a missing word or phrase in a blank space within a statement. When filling in the blank, try to use the exact term used in class or in your textbook. If you cannot remember the exact term, describe your answer as carefully as you can. You may get credit for a partial or an approximate correct answer.

True-false questions require you to state whether or not a particular statement is true. In true-false questions, words such as *all, most, some, none, always, probably, never, more,* and *less* are very important. Pay close attention to them. In *modified true-false* questions, you may have a third or fourth choice, such as *uncertain* or *not enough data*. Make sure you know all the possible ways of answering before writing down an answer.

Matching questions provide you with two (or more) lists of information, such as a list of dates and a list of events. You must then indicate, next to each item on one list, the related item from the other list. Sometimes one column contains extra items, so that some will be left over. In answering matching questions, you should fill in the easiest answers first, crossing out items as you use them. This will make the unused choices easier for you to see.

Multiple-choice questions usually ask you to choose the best single answer out of four or five choices. But be careful: Sometimes the directions will tell you to choose the *worst* answer or the one item that does *not* apply. The directions may also give you the choice of *none of the above* or *all of the above*. In multiple-choice questions, make sure that you read all the possible answers before writing down your choice. The second choice may sound like a possible answer, but the fifth choice may turn out to be the most precise and therefore the correct answer. If you do not spot the correct answer the first time you read through the choices, you may be able to eliminate some clearly wrong answers. This approach makes it easier for you to choose among the remaining answers and at least improves your odds of being right if you must guess at the correct answer.

EXERCISES

1. This exercise tests how well you follow directions. Wrong answers will count against you. Do not begin answering any questions until you have read all the questions. You have one minute to complete all your answers. Write the answers in the spaces provided. Begin now.

   a. Write your name, last name first. ________________

   b. Count the letters in your name and write the number.

   ____

c. What year did Columbus discover America? **1492**

d. Divide answer *b* into answer *c*. ____________

e. What year did you begin high school? ____________

f. Multiply answer *d* by answer *e*. ____________

g. Write down the number of the one correct statement.

2

1. The Union army lost the battle of Gettysburg.
2. The Apollo Twelve landed on the moon in 1969.
3. Ronald Reagan was the fifty-first president of the United States.
4. There are fifteen planets in our solar system.

h. Square the number you answered in question *g*.

____

i. How many days are there in a leap year? **366**

j. Multiply answer *i* by answer *h*, and then multiply the product by answer *f*. ____________

k. If you understand this instruction write *yes*. Answer only every other question in this test beginning with *a*.

yes

l. Do not answer this question: Write the square root of the answer you gave in question *j*. ____________

2. The following questions test your ability *to guess* intelligently. Wrong answers will not be held against you. Answer the questions as directed and put your answers in the spaces provided. You have five minutes to complete the exercise. Begin now.

3 ________

a. Write down the number of the one *incorrect* statement.
   1. The photoelectric effect involves the release of electrons when metals are hit by photons of light.
   2. The photoelectric effect was discovered by R. A. Millikan.
   3. The photoelectric effect is the reason why you need to put batteries in your camera.
   4. The photoelectric effect is consistent with quantum theory, but it is contrary to the wave theory of light.

1,3,4 ________

b. Write down the numbers of the best answers.
   Controversial events in the administration of President Harry S Truman included
   1. dropping the atom bomb on Japan.
   2. calling for a decrease in unemployment.
   3. having his daughter sing at the White House.
   4. nationalizing the steel mills.
   5. starting the Vietnam war.

F ________

c. Write T if the following statement is true, F if it is false.
   Schizophrenia is always caused by a schizophrenic parent.

d. Fill in the blank.
   Gresham's law states that bad money tends to drive
   good money out of circulation.

3 ________

e. Write down the number of the one best answer.
   In legal terminology, *de jure* means
   1. de facto.
   2. according to a jury.
   3. according to law.
   4. a group of people who decide whether someone is guilty.
   5. handsome.

f. The first column lists names of famous people; the second column lists the occupations that made them famous. Match each name with its correct occupation by writing a letter from the occupation column next to a name.

f	1. Ludwig van Beethoven	a. cartoon character
d	2. Bruce Springsteen	b. astronaut
b	3. Sally Ride	c. scientist
e	4. Sylvester Stallone	d. rock musician
c	5. Marie Curie	e. actor
a	6. Bugs Bunny	f. composer
g	7. Jim Rice	g. baseball player

14c Essay Questions

You generally have greater freedom in answering essay questions than you do in answering short-answer questions because the teacher is testing how well you think as well as how thoroughly you know course material. You still must follow directions very carefully. If you do not answer an essay question the way the teacher wants it answered, the teacher may conclude that you do not understand the material. To get full credit, you need to answer a question the right way. Therefore, before you begin to write be sure to take the time to read each question carefully and to analyze exactly what the question asks.

In reading an essay question, look for two things in particular: the subject and the task.

The *subject* is the object, event, process, concept, or other piece of information that you are asked to discuss. It is frequently the name of something you have studied in the course. For example, look at this question from a history exam:

> Evaluate Winston Churchill's role as a leader during World War II.

The subject of the question is Winston Churchill and, more specifically, his leadership during World War II. You would be wrong if you discussed Franklin D. Roosevelt's leadership. You would also be wrong if you discussed Churchill's leadership after the war or during World War I. You must stay within the specific limits of an essay question.

Some questions have two or more subjects. For example, you may be asked to compare or relate two separate ideas. Look at the following question, also from a history exam:

> Compare Winston Churchill's power to inspire the British in the early days of World War II with Franklin D. Roosevelt's inability to alert Americans to the dangers of Hitler during the same period.

In this question you are asked to compare two subjects, which means that you must discuss each one in your answer. If you discuss only one, you are providing only half the information asked for. Your answer, therefore, would be incomplete.

The *task* is what you are asked to do with the information. The task is usually contained in a *key question word,* often the first word of the question. In the first example, the task was *to evaluate;* in the second, the task was *to compare.* These tasks require you to give different kinds of answers. If you are asked to give the causes of American isolationism between the two world wars, but you only list isolationist policies, you are not answering the question.

The following list of key question words defines and gives examples of the different tasks you may be asked to carry out on an essay examination. Make sure you know what to do to answer questions containing these different key question words.

agree, disagree, comment on, criticize, evaluate — Give your opinion about a book, quotation, or statement. If the question says *agree or disagree,* you must express either a positive or a negative opinion. If the question says *comment on, criticize,* or *evaluate,* your answer can include both positive and negative points.

"The first six weeks of life are the most important period in a child's emotional development. *Agree* or *disagree.*"

analyze — Break down a topic into all its parts. Be sure to include all the parts and to tell what makes each part different from the others.

	"*Analyze* the role that computers play in simplifying registration procedures at your college."
compare	Show how two subjects are both alike and different. Be sure to discuss each subject and give both likenesses and differences. "*Compare* the sculpture of Renaissance Italy with classical Greek sculpture."
contrast	Show only the differences between two subjects. Be sure to talk about each one. "*Contrast* the nervous system of a flatworm with the nervous system of a frog."
define	Give the exact meaning of a word, phrase, or concept. Show how what you are defining is different from everything else of its type. Cite examples. "*Define* the word *honor* using examples from your own life that show how you behaved in an honorable way."
explain why	Give the main reasons why an event mentioned happened or happens. "*Explain why* ocean tides are not high at the same time every night and *why* they are not always the same height."
describe, discuss	Tell what happened, what a subject looks like, or what a subject is. "*Describe* the conditions on the ships that brought slaves to America. Then *discuss* one rebellion that took place on a slave ship."
illustrate	Give one or more examples to support a general statement. Be sure to relate each example to the general statement.

"*Illustrate* the importance of freedom with examples of actions that you as a citizen of a free society can take that a citizen of a dictatorship cannot."

interpret — Explain the meaning of facts given. The question may specify a method of interpretation you must use. Be sure to go beyond just repeating the facts.

"In 1910 Farmtown, Kansas, had 502 farm workers, 37 other blue-collar workers, and 13 white-collar workers. In 1975 the same town had 153 farm workers, 289 other blue-collar workers, and 86 white-collar workers. *Interpret* these statistics in light of national labor trends during this period."

justify, prove — Give reasons to show why a statement is true.

"The Industrial Revolution allowed some people to accumulate great wealth. *Justify* this statement, using material you studied this semester."

list, state — Itemize important points. Be sure to list all the items asked for in the question. Do not give examples unless they are requested.

"*List* the conditions that trigger a response from the body's immune system."

outline, review, summarize — Give all the main points of a quotation, book, or theory. You do not have to include minor points.

"*Outline* the contribution that immigrants made to the quality of American life in the years between 1865 and 1925."

relate — Show how one object has an effect on another. Be sure to identify the connection between them.

"*Relate* the evolution of the horse to the changes in its environment."

trace, list the steps or stages List a series of important events, leading up to a final item or point. Be sure not to leave any item out or to include more than the question asks for. This type of exam question may refer to historical events, recall a process, or ask for detailed directions.

"*Trace* the development of the modern banking system from its origins in the Renaissance to the eighteenth century."

In answering essay questions, follow the principles of good writing that you have learned in your writing classes. Keep the following points in mind when you answer essay questions:

- Think about the question. Ask yourself:
  1. How does the question relate to the course material?
  2. Can I use any of the important ideas that the instructor emphasized?
  3. What, from the reading or lectures, would make good examples?
- Plan your essay. On scrap paper list the main points you want to make. Next to each main point note at least one supporting example.
- Make each point clearly.
  1. In the opening sentence of your answer, use words from the question. If the question says "Agree or disagree with the following quotation by Bertrand Russell," you should begin your answer with "I agree (or disagree) with the quotation by Bertrand Russell because . . ."
  2. Begin each of the middle paragraphs with a topic sentence that states one of your major points. Within each middle paragraph, support the major point with reasons and examples.
  3. In the conclusion of your essay, relate your answer to one important idea taught in the course.
- Read over the essay you have written. Be sure that all the sentences make sense. Make sure that your meaning is clear.

Check that your answer covers each part of the essay question. Make sure that your grammar, sentence structure, and spelling are correct.

EXERCISES

1. Explain why each of the following essay questions on the same topic requires a different answer. Use a separate sheet of paper.
   a. Describe the events leading to the collapse of communism in the Soviet Union.
   b. Compare the economic system in Russia today with the system ten years ago.
   c. List the major changes that have occurred in the former Soviet Union in the last ten years.
   d. Evaluate the current strengths and weaknesses of the Russian government and economy.
   e. Define the current political system being developed in Russia.
   f. Analyze the different interest groups that are trying to influence the shape of government in Russia.
   g. Explain how and why Russia's foreign policy will be substantially different from the Soviet Union's foreign policy over the last twenty years.
2. On a separate sheet of paper write essay questions for a course you are now taking using the following key question words:
   a. discuss
   b. illustrate
   c. relate
   d. review
   e. analyze

UNIT FOUR REVIEW

What are the risks over time for people who use tobacco? Read this selection from a health science textbook, using the basic study skills you explored in this unit. As you read, underline and mark the text to highlight important information. Then answer the questions that follow. **Unless otherwise indicated, student responses will vary.**

Tobacco's Long-Term Risks

The immediate effects of tobacco use worsen and multiply over time. These effects are dangerous to both smokers and nonsmokers. Several diseases and health risks have been linked to tobacco use.

Risks for Smokers

Hundreds of thousands of people in the United States die early because they smoke. Smokers have higher risks of getting certain diseases. They also need to receive hospital care more often than nonsmokers. Medical bills for diseases tied to smoking are estimated at $50 billion a year.

Heart disease Each year, about 125,000 Americans die from heart disease brought on by smoking cigarettes. Women in general have a lower risk of heart disease than men. But there has been a rise in the rate of heart disease among women. This is because more of them are smoking.

Nicotine and carbon monoxide are believed to be major factors in heart disease. Nicotine causes the heart to beat faster and raises blood pressure. Carbon monoxide decreases oxygen in blood. These factors place a great strain on the heart and increase the risk of heart disease. Heredity, stress, diet, and exercise habits all play a part in whether a person has a healthy heart. But the U.S. Surgeon General has called smoking the most controllable risk factor of heart disease.

Lung cancer Cigarette smoking is the leading cause of deaths due to cancer in this country. In fact, more than 80 percent of all lung cancer deaths are tied to cigarette smoking. Cancer of the lung is a major cause of death among men. Among women lung cancer has tripled in the last twenty years. This is a direct result of the added number of women who now smoke.

Cancer is an uncontrollable growth of cells that invade and destroy neighboring healthy cells. Some cancers spread to parts of the body far from where they begin. Substances that cause cancer are called **carcinogens. Benzopyrine** is a deadly carcinogen, found in cigarette smoke and coal tar. Researchers studying cancer cells use benzopyrine to cause cancer in laboratory rats. Tars and resins also contain promoters. **Promoters** are substances that do not start cancer, but help cancer cells grow faster.

Often the first sign of lung cancer comes after it has spread. Some people, however, will develop increased shortness of breath, and will cough up mucus and sometimes blood. These symptoms are so similar to the usual problems smokers have that most smokers ignore them. Eventually, the victim loses strength and body weight. Only 10 percent of the people found to have lung cancer are alive after five years. Lung cancer may be cured in the early stages. Treatment involves removing the diseased lung by surgery and using anticancer drugs.

Cigarettes multiply the effects of other carcinogens. Nonsmokers who work with asbestos, for example, are eight times more likely to get cancer than other nonsmokers. But asbestos workers who smoke are 92 times more likely to get lung cancer than nonsmokers who do not work with asbestos.

Other forms of cancer Smoking makes cancer of the voice box, esophagus, and bladder more likely. Smokers are twice as likely to die of bladder cancer as nonsmokers. The poisons from tobacco that collect in the bladder promote cancer.

Oral cancer is cancer of the mouth or throat area. People who smoke, chew tobacco, or take snuff are most likely to develop oral cancer. The cancers form where tobacco has touched the person's lips, mouth, and throat tissues and created leukoplakia. Smokers who also drink alcohol have an even higher risk of developing oral cancer.

Chronic lung diseases Cigarette smoking is the major cause of chronic lung disease in the United States. Chronic diseases are those that remain for a very long time. Smoking greatly adds to the chances of developing lung disease.

Asthma is a disease often caused by allergies that narrows the airways in the lungs. Sudden contraction of smooth muscles that encircle the air passages causes them to become so narrow that little air can reach the lungs.

Bronchitis is a redness and swelling of the linings of the air passages. When bronchitis occurs, the cilia are destroyed. Dust has gotten past the bronchi, invading the tiny air passages of the lungs. This dust often consists of matter from cigarette smoke. The air passages become irritated and then become clogged with mucus and dust. This can lead to infections.

Smoking can also cause emphysema. **Emphysema** is a disease in which the lungs lose their normal structure. Therefore the lungs do not exchange carbon dioxide for oxygen well. For a person with emphysema, the work of just breathing is immense, and the smallest effort causes shortness of breath. Quitting the smoking habit will keep the disease from getting worse, but the damage that has already been done is permanent.

Other health problems Smokers in general are in worse health than nonsmokers. This is because smoking damages the parts of the body that protect a person from disease. Smoking also triggers allergies and may lead to sinusitis. **Sinusitis** is the redness and swelling of the sinuses. Sinusitis causes nagging headaches, a constantly stuffy nose, and a sore throat. Smokers suffer more with the common cold because of irritated mouth and throat tissues. Smokers are also more likely to get infectious lung diseases, such as influenza and pneumonia.

Smokers have a 50 percent greater chance of developing peptic ulcers than nonsmokers. **Peptic ulcers** are open sores in the lining of the stomach or small intestine. Smoking makes ulcers difficult to treat. Habits that often go with smoking, such as drinking coffee, make ulcers worse and harder to heal.

Cigarette smoking promotes noncancerous oral diseases that affect the gums and bones of the mouth. Smoking contributes to loss of teeth and delays healing after dental surgery.

Risks to Nonsmokers

A nonsmoker sharing the same air with a smoker is called a **passive smoker.** Nonsmokers who are near heavy smokers can "smoke" the equivalent of one to ten cigarettes a day. The Environmental Protection Agency has estimated that 500 to 5000 deaths a year are caused by passive smoking. This makes cigarette smoke the most dangerous airborne carcinogen known.

Sidestream smoke There are two types of cigarette smoke. Smoke that has been inhaled and then exhaled by the smoker is called **mainstream smoke.** The smoker's lungs trap much of the matter and poisons in mainstream smoke. **Sidestream smoke** comes directly from the burning end of a cigarette. Sidestream smoke has not been inhaled or exhaled by a smoker or changed by a cigarette filter. So it is more harmful to the passive smoker than mainstream smoke. It contains twice the amount of tar and nicotine, three times the amount of benzopyrine, three times the carbon monoxide, and seventy times the ammonia of mainstream smoke.

Children of smoking parents especially suffer as passive smokers. The lungs of children whose parents smoke tend to grow at a slower rate. These children suffer more infections, miss more time from school, and need more days of hospital care than the children of nonsmokers.

Pregnancy and smoking The unborn baby of a pregnant woman who smokes is a passive smoker. Since carbon monoxide competes with oxygen, smoking reduces the oxygen supply to the baby. A woman who smokes two packs a day cuts her baby's oxygen supply by 40 percent. Nicotine increases the baby's heart rate and blood pressure. It also upsets chemical balances, interferes with vitamin use, and reduces nourishment to the baby's developing body.

Pregnant women who smoke double their chances of miscarriage. They have more stillbirths (the baby is born dead) and more premature births than nonsmokers. Babies born to mothers who smoke weigh less than those born to women who do not smoke. They also have a higher chance of having malformed organs and have a lower survival rate. Nicotine is excreted in breast milk, so a baby can receive nicotine by nursing.

Lesson Review

Heart disease and cancer are the two major causes of death in the United States today. The use of tobacco greatly increases the risk of developing these illnesses. Smokers suffer from these and other diseases on a much greater scale than nonsmokers. Nonsmokers who live and work around smokers also suffer the harmful effects of smoke. Pregnant women who smoke may harm their unborn children.

1. What is a carcinogen?
2. What is a promoter?
3. Name two deadly diseases that smokers are more likely to get than nonsmokers.
4. What is sidestream smoke?
5. What are the risks to an unborn child if the pregnant mother smokes?

— *Bud Getchell, Rusty Pippin, and Jill Varnes*

1. Review the selection "Tobacco's Long-Term Risks" by taking notes on a separate sheet of paper.
2. On a separate sheet of paper make an outline of the section "Risks to Nonsmokers" in the selection "Tobacco's Long-Term Risks."
3. Write a one-sentence summary of each paragraph under subheading "Heart Disease" (page 350).

___

___

___

4. Write a summary of the section "Pregnancy and Smoking" (page 353).

___

___

___

___

5. Write an essay question that you think a teacher might give to test your knowledge and understanding of the selection "Tobacco's Long-Term Risks." Then write an answer to that question. Use separate paper.

Reading Selections

Readings

Introduction

These selections will allow you to practice the reading skills you've learned so far. The questions that accompany each selection test your understanding of what you read. In some cases you will be able to answer the questions without returning to the selection. In other cases you will want to return quickly to specific passages before you choose an answer. Returning to the selection to check *every* response will slow you down and make your reading a chore. Therefore, try to retain as much information as you can when you read each piece for the first time. On the other hand, when you are not certain about something, it's best to check your response.

You'll notice that numbers in parentheses appear at the end of each question. These numbers refer to the chapter and section in the first part of the book where the skill required to answer the question is explained. Thus, if you are still stumped after you've checked the selection again, turn to the appropriate section of the handbook and review your skills.

Two approaches help you learn new words in each selection. The most difficult words appear with definitions in a section called "Word Highlights" right before the selection. When a difficult word appears in the selection, check the "Word Highlights" list for a definition. In addition, a vocabulary exercise appears at the end of the questions on each piece. The vocabulary exercises require that you answer questions about the uses and meanings of new words. You will want to add the new words to your reading, writing, and speaking vocabularies as soon as possible. The best way to learn the words is to write them down, use them in sentences, and follow the other guidelines given in Chapter 1. You also should keep a list of other words you don't know in each selection. Check their meanings and learn them too.

The writing assignments provided for each selection will help you think critically about what you have read. Use a separate sheet of paper for these assignments.

The works chosen for this anthology will teach you, amuse you, and make you think. You'll find articles, essays, and sections of books, newspapers, and magazines. You'll find selections from textbooks in psychology, history, and chemistry. You'll find short stories and a poem. In short, the anthology provides a varied program of study similar to that required of today's college student.

1

Six Keys to Quicker Learning

Patricia Skalka

Do you forget things easily? This essay shows how to improve learning in six easy steps. Read to find out what you can do to learn faster and to improve your memory.

Prereading

Before you read the selection, make a word map on the topic *learning more quickly*. **[3a(2)]** Use separate paper.

Word Highlights

absorbent (¶2) able to soak something up
retention (¶5) ability to remember
enhancing (¶9) helping; increasing in value
gimmick (¶14) tricky device
cognitive (¶14) relating to how we acquire knowledge
distractions (¶21) things that draw attention away from a focus or direction

A friend of mine was at a dinner party where two men she knew were discussing *The Right Stuff*, a book about the Mercury space program. While Ted went on and on about the technical details he had picked up from the book, Dan offered only a few tentative comments. "Ted got so much more out of the reading than I did," Dan later said to my friend. "Is he much smarter than I am?"

2 My friend, an educator, was curious. She knew the two men had similar educational backgrounds and intelligence levels. She talked with each and discovered the answer: Ted just knew how to learn better than Dan did. Ted had made his brain more absorbent by using a few simple skills.

3 For years, experts had believed that an individual's ability to learn was a fixed capacity. During the last two decades, however, leading psychologists and educators have come to think otherwise. "We have increasing proof that human intelligence is expandable," says Jack Lochhead, director of the Cognitive Development Project at the University of Massachusetts in Amherst. "We know that with proper skills people can actually improve their learning ability."

4 Moreover, these skills are basic enough so that almost anyone can master them with practice. Here, gathered from the ideas of experts across the country, are six proven ways to boost your learning ability.

5 1. *Look at the big picture first.* When reading new, unfamiliar material, do not plunge directly into it. You can increase your comprehension and retention if you scan the material first. Skim subheads, photo captions, and any available summaries. With reports or articles, read the first sentence of each paragraph; with books, glance at the table of contents and introduction.

6 All this previewing will help anchor in your mind what you then read.

7 2. *Slow down and talk to yourself.* While speed-reading may be fine for easy material, slower reading can be much more effective for absorbing complex, challenging works. Arthur Whimbey and Jack Lochhead, co-authors of the high-school and college handbook *Problem Solving and Comprehension,* have isolated three basic differences in how good and bad learners study:

- Good learners vocalize, or voice, the material, either silently or aloud. They slow down, listening to each word as they read.
- Good learners, when stymied, automatically reread until they understand the material. Poor readers, by contrast, just keep going if they don't get it the first time.
- Good learners become "actively involved" with new information. They think about what they read, challenge it, make it their own.

8 In 1979, Whimbey introduced a slow, vocalized reading method into a five-week, pre-freshman program at Xavier University in New Orleans. Many of the 175 students using this technique jumped two grade levels in comprehension, and their college-aptitude test scores rose by as much as 14 percent.

9 3. *Practice memory-enhancing techniques.* When I was eight and couldn't spell *arithmetic,* a teacher taught me a sentence that has remained locked in my mind for decades: "A rat in Tom's house may eat Tom's ice cream." The first letters of each word spell *arithmetic.*

10 All such memory-enhancing techniques, called mnemonics, transform new information into more easily remembered formulations.

11 Other first-letter mnemonics include "Homes" (the names of the Great Lakes — Huron, Ontario, Michigan, Erie, and Superior); "George Eaton's old granny rode a pig home yesterday" (for spelling *geography*); and "My very educated mother just served us nine pickles" (the planet system in order — Mercury, Venus, Earth, Mars, Jupiter, Saturn, Uranus, Neptune, Pluto).

12 Mnemonics can also work with images. The trick is to invent visual clues that will make unfamiliar material mean something to you.

13 In studying Spanish, for example, you might learn that the word for "duck" is *pato. Pato* sounds like the English word *pot.* To link the two, imagine a duck waddling about with a large pot over its head. You will have a clear image that reminds you pot = *pato* = duck.

14 Once dismissed by researchers as a mere gimmick, mnemonics are now considered an effective means of boosting memory — doubling or even tripling the amount of new material that test subjects can retain. "A good memory is the key to all cognitive processes," according to William G. Chase, professor of psychology at Carnegie-Mellon University in Pittsburgh. "And it is something we can all have with practice."

15 Cognitive research shows that we have two kinds of memory: short-term and long-term. Short-term memory (STM) lasts for about 30 to 60 seconds. We call directory assistance for a phone number, dial the number, and then forget it. Long-term memory (LTM), however, can last a lifetime. The secret to developing a good memory, says

Francis S. Bellezza, author of *Improve Your Memory Skills,* is learning how to transfer useful information from STM to LTM and how to retrieve that information when needed.

16 Mnemonics can be the key that puts data into LTM and gets the information back out again. Remember, the mind and memory are like muscles — the more you use them, the stronger they get.

17 4. *Organize facts into categories.* In studies at Stanford University, students were asked to memorize 112 words. These included names of animals, items of clothing, types of transportation, and occupations. For one group, the words were divided into these four categories. For a second group, the words were listed at random. Those who studied the material in organized categories consistently outperformed the others, recalling two to three times more words.

18 "Trying to digest new information in one lump is difficult," says Thomas R. Trabasso, professor of education and behavioral science at the University of Chicago. "By analyzing new material and dividing it into meaningful chunks, you make learning easier."

19 For example, to remember the names of all former U.S. Presidents in proper order, cluster the leaders into groups — those before the War of 1812, those from 1812 until the Civil War, those from the Civil War to World War I, and those after World War I. By thus organizing complex material into logical categories you create a permanent storage technique.

20 5. *Focus your attention.* The next time you are faced with new material you need to master, ask yourself, What do I want to learn from reading this, and how will I benefit from the knowledge gained? "By telling ourselves what the learning will do for us, we reduce our resistance to studying and become better learners," says Russell W. Scalpone, a psychologist and manager at A. T. Kearney, Inc., an international management-consulting firm.

21 Scalpone recommends four other techniques for improving concentration and focus:

- Establish a time and a place for learning. Take the phone off the hook; close the door. By regulating your environment, you create the expectation that learning will occur.
- Guard against distractions. Don't be shy about hanging

a "Do Not Disturb" sign on your door. You have a right to your time.

- Try a variety of learning methods. Diagramming, note taking, outlining, even talking into a tape recorder are study techniques that can increase concentration. Use whatever study skills you are most comfortable with. Be creative.
- Monitor your progress. Being busy is not always the same as being productive. Stop occasionally and ask yourself, Am I contributing right now to my learning goal? If the answer is yes, keep working. If no, ask yourself why. If you're not making progress because of tension or fatigue, take a break — without feeling guilty. Regular breaks can improve the learning process.

22 6. *Discover your own learning style.* Educators Rita and Ken Dunn tell the story of three children who each received a bicycle for Christmas. The bikes, purchased unassembled, had to be put together by parents. Tim's father read the directions carefully before he set to work. Mary's father laid out the pieces on the floor and handed the directions to Mary's mother. "Read this to me," he said, as he surveyed the components. George's mother instinctively began fitting pieces together, glancing at the directions only when stymied. By day's end, all three bikes were assembled, each from a different approach.

23 "Although they didn't realize it," says Rita Dunn, professor of education at St. John's University in New York City, "the parents had worked according to their own learning styles."

24 "Our approaches to unfamiliar material are as unique and specialized as we are, and a key to learning is recognizing — and accommodating — the style that suits us best," says Ken Dunn, professor of education at Queens College in New York City.

25 Learning styles can vary dramatically. The Dunns have developed a Productivity Environment Preference Survey, which identifies 21 elements that affect the way we learn. These factors include noise level, lighting, amount of supervision required, even the time of day.

26 What's *your* style? Try some self-analysis. What, for example, is your approach to putting together an unassem-

bled item? Do you concentrate better in the morning or in the evening? In a noisy environment or a quiet one? Make a list of all the pluses and minuses you can identify. Then use this list to create the learning environment best for you.

27 Whichever style works for you, the good news is that you *can* expand your learning capacity. And this can make your life fuller and more productive. ❑

EXERCISES

Understanding What You Have Read

c ______ 1. The main idea of this selection is that **(5)**
   a. either you're born with a good memory or you aren't.
   b. people who don't study don't succeed in life.
   c. people can learn to improve their study habits.
   d. learning to study isn't easy for most people.

b ______ 2. According to the selection, the key to all cognitive processes is **(6a)**
   a. intelligence.
   b. a good memory.
   c. reading.
   d. studying.

a ______ 3. "A rat in Tom's house may eat Tom's ice cream" is a sentence intended to help people remember **(6a)**
   a. how to spell *arithmetic*.
   b. the names of the Great Lakes.
   c. the Spanish word for "duck."
   d. not to leave food out for rats.

b ______ 4. Which learning technique is *not* recommended by the author? **(6a)**
   a. Talking to yourself
   b. Speed reading
   c. Looking at the big picture
   d. Organizing information into categories

c ______ 5. The article says that human intelligence **(6a)**
   a. is fixed at birth.
   b. is generally the same for people in the same family.

c. can be expanded.
d. varies according to social or economic group.

a 6. Which of the following does the psychologist Russell W. Scalpone recommend for effective studying? **(6a)**
a. No distractions
b. Group study
c. Tape-recorded background music
d. Any setting

c 7. The technique suggested for learning the names of all former U.S. presidents is **(6a)**
a. organizing them into alphabetical order.
b. making one sentence using all their names.
c. grouping them according to historical periods.
d. repeating their names over and over again.

d 8. The writer recommends speed-reading **(6a)**
a. for scientific subjects.
b. for all kinds of reading.
c. only for really bright people.
d. only for easy reading.

d 9. The example of the three parents who assemble bicycles for their children shows that **(6a)**
a. mechanical skills are easy to learn.
b. every child needs a bicycle.
c. if at first you don't succeed, try, try again.
d. people learn things in different ways.

b 10. STM and LTM are **(6a)**
a. practice memory exercises.
b. abbreviations for *short-term memory* and *long-term memory*.
c. abbreviations for *strong-terminal mnemonics* and *loose-terminal mnemonics*.
d. mnemonics to remember how to spell *SiTuation coMedy* and *Laser TrauMa*.

a 11. According to this article, you can monitor your learning progress by **(6a)**
a. asking yourself questions.
b. taking a break.

c. taking a test.
d. making progress.

12. Below, write *maj* next to major details from the selection and *min* next to minor details. **(6b)**

maj ____ a. Learning skills are easy to master.

min ____ b. Ted had read *The Right Stuff.*

maj ____ c. Mnemonics are not gimmicks.

min ____ d. The word for "duck" in Spanish is *pato.*

min ____ e. Mercury is the planet closest to the sun.

min ____ f. There is a cognitive development project at the University of Massachusetts in Amherst.

maj ____ g. Memory is improved by transferring information from short-term memory to long-term memory.

Interpreting and Evaluating

a ____ 1. We can infer from this article that **(8)**
a. everybody has the potential to be a good learner.
b. only some people can improve their ability to learn.
c. some people will never learn, no matter what they do.
d. most people don't need to improve their learning habits.

b ____ 2. We can infer that the reason many people haven't used the techniques recommended in the selection is that **(8)**
a. they are too stubborn.
b. they are not aware of cognitive research.
c. they don't believe these techniques work.
d. no one has published anything about learning theory.

a ____ 3. We can infer that looking closely for important factual details as you read a selection **(8)**
a. is an excellent way to boost your learning ability.
b. won't help you improve your learning ability.
c. will help you talk to yourself.
d. is a study method preferred by cognitive psychologists.

c ______ 4. We can conclude from this selection that research into how people learn **(10)**
a. no longer interests scholars.
b. is supported by government funding.
c. interests scholars and researchers in many different places.
d. won't produce any more information than we already have.

a ______ 5. We can predict that the author might recommend using the sentence "Yes, I eat limes daily" as a means to remember **(10)**
a. how to spell *yield.*
b. how to spell *limes.*
c. to eat certain foods every day.
d. how important a regular diet of fruits is.

6. Put a checkmark next to any generalizations you can draw from the selection. **(11)**

√ ______ a. By collecting and examining new data, experts can change their views on important issues.

√ ______ b. Talking aloud is a learning tool.

______ c. Mental pictures do not help us retain information for very long.

√ ______ d. Our physical surroundings influence how we learn.

______ e. Very educated mothers sometimes serve pickles to their children.

c ______ 7. Which of the following kind of evidence does the writer *not* present in this selection? **(12b)**
a. Quotations from books
b. Excerpts from interviews with friends
c. Data collected from her own laboratory research
d. Information based on interviews with experts

d ______ 8. This selection is intended especially for **(12)**
a. educational psychologists and other researchers.
b. elementary school children.

c. college students.
d. anyone who wants to improve learning.

9. Next to each of the following statements write F if the statement is fact and O if the statement is opinion. **(12a)**

F ____ a. We have proof that intelligence can be expanded.

O ____ b. Good learners involve themselves actively with new information.

O ____ c. We reduce our resistance to study by telling ourselves how the learning will benefit us.

F ____ d. Some students in a vocalized reading program at Xavier University raised their aptitude test scores by as much as 14 percent.

F ____ e. Researchers describe two kinds of memory: short-term memory and long-term memory.

a ____ 10. The author's basic purpose in this selection is to **(12d)**
a. teach.
b. narrate events.
c. argue a controversial point.
d. describe a vivid scene.

Vocabulary

Using sentence clues and word part clues, choose the best meaning for each word in italics and write the letter in the space below. Return to the selection for help as required. Use a dictionary only if necessary. Put a checkmark beside any question for which you had to use a dictionary. **(1)**

b ____ 1. only a few *tentative* comments
a. definite
b. uncertain
c. ridiculous
d. intelligent

c ____ 2. intelligence is *expandable*
a. well developed
b. hard to define

c. able to increase in size or amount
d. able to exist without further support

b ______ 3. do not *plunge* directly into it
a. pull
b. dive
c. ask
d. speak

a ______ 4. *vocalize,* or voice the material
a. say aloud
b. sing
c. read
d. violate

c ______ 5. when *stymied,* automatically reread
a. interested
b. pleased
c. blocked
d. helped

a ______ 6. memory-enhancing techniques, called *mnemonics*
a. tricks for improving memory
b. techniques for naming new objects
c. ways to avoid unpleasant memories
d. stereophonics

c ______ 7. once *dismissed* by researchers
a. ordered
b. supported
c. rejected
d. discovered

d ______ 8. effective means of *boosting* memory
a. reducing
b. cheering
c. comparing
d. increasing

d ______ 9. reduce our *resistance to* studying
a. desire for
b. hatred of

c. boredom with
d. opposition to

a ______ 10. create the *expectation* that learning will occur
a. state of looking ahead to something
b. memory
c. mnemonic
d. state of reading carefully

WRITING PRACTICE

1. Write a paragraph or two in which you summarize the major learning techniques presented in this selection.
2. Describe your study habits. Explain some of the ways you study and some of the learning techniques you use. Based on reading this article, how might these change?

of answers: We get born again, we grow new skin, we still talk to each other, we'll still see each other, right? Right?

2 "No one really knows," I repeat. He says he wants to live forever. I say part of us does live forever — our spirit. He wants to know what that is. It's what people remember about us. He hates this. He swats away my answers; rejects them like bad milk.

3 Four, the experts tell me, is the age of phobias, when children bounce off the opposite feelings of power and powerlessness as recklessly as a hard-hit squash ball. "I wish I were He-Man," my son announces on the way home from a movie he found scary, "because then I wouldn't be afraid." I assure him that everyone feels fear. I try to hug him. But four has also seen the dawn of some new feelings about me. No longer does he return my every hug, no longer does he automatically melt into my arms during a snuggle. Now he pushes me away, scowling, his little body hard and muscular. "Not here, Ma."

4 So, I am thinking of loss too, and not for the first time do I feel as if my son and I are navigating the same developmental waters together.

5 "Trees die in winter," my son announces during his bath, thinking I don't know what he's up to, "and are born again in spring, right?" I assure him that he is. "And people die when they are very old, and are born again, right?" I tell him that I really don't know for sure. "But you have to be really old," he says, and I wonder whom he is thinking of — his great-grandmother?

6 Her son, my father, was recently diagnosed as having cancer. My grandmother calls me every week about it. "Don't worry," I tell her, "he's in good hands."

7 "Don't worry?" she cries, this matriarch who has survived 87 rough years, with whom I feel a painful stab of empathy. "How can I not worry? He's my son."

8 Last week, at a street fair, my son and I lost each other. He had wanted to go on a trolley ride. I saw him get on the car, and when it returned from its two-minute trip, didn't see him get off. I waited until the car had emptied and a few moments more, uncomprehendingly. I grabbed one of the men steering the ride. "What is he wearing?" he asked.

9 That's when I began my mad rushing through the sunny crowd of parents and children as if it were a cave I had to claw my way out of. The panic was unlike any I had previously

experienced. Breathing not air but lethal panic, I screamed inwardly, "No, it can't happen," knowing with dead certainty that it could. When I finally stumbled into the clown, the only person I could find with a megaphone, she said, "Calm down, it won't help to be hysterical; he's only the fifth one today who's been lost and we found them all." She started calling his name. Trailing behind her, imagining calling my husband, calling my parents, my in-laws, I pictured my son's empty room, his closet full of clothes; I felt the enormity of the city and the tininess of my son, dressed in nothing more remarkable than jeans and a T-shirt.

10 Suddenly amid a swell of voices I heard a man calling, "Yes, over here, we have him."

11 There he was, standing impassively on the steps of the school, and when I ran and hugged him and sobbed uncontrollably he jammed both his hands over my mouth.

12 "I thought you didn't keep your word," he said. I assured him that I had been waiting for him, that we just missed each other, that it was no one's fault. He worried that he had done something wrong, but, in fact, he had done everything exactly right: When he didn't see me, he went to a man in a blue shirt and said, "I can't find my Mommy."

13 He only referred to the experience once more, a day later, when he sat up in bed during our good-nights and said, "We were *separated*," as if the words finally were joined to an experience that we had talked about, rehearsed many times before.

14 But I think of it more often than I'd like: doing the laundry, teaching a class, I am inexplicably back in the impossible darkness of his absence. How could I have survived losing him?

15 I take a cab home from the hospital the evening after my father's most recent operation, and the driver turns into Central Park. Weaving from the snow-covered, silent, remote interior to the perimeter where buildings are ablaze with lights, with families busy living and dying, I think of what I will try to tell my son about spirit. Shamelessly borrowing from a conglomerate of religious beliefs, I thought I had concocted a spiritualism I felt comfortable with, yet now it seems indistinguishable from a heartfelt injunction to remember. I wish I had an orthodoxy to fall back on as my father found in his middle years — a messianic vision to comfort my son with. But he doesn't need mine; he seems to have been born believing in the doctrine of reincarnation. Whatever its origin, he draws from it effortlessly.

d. both mother and child were terrified when they lost each other.

d ______ 8. Overall the various incidents and thoughts of the entire essay are arranged in **(7a)**
a. place order.
b. time order.
c. order of importance.
d. order of building emotions.

d ______ 9. Throughout the selection there are many comparisons **(7d)**
a. between the writer and her son.
b. between the writer and her grandmother.
c. between the writer and her father.
d. among all four.

c ______ 10. The main point of these comparisons is that **(7d)**
a. parents cannot always live up to their children's expectations.
b. children grow up to become parents.
c. we are all children who feel lost without our parents.
d. parents worry about their children.

Interpreting and Evaluating

c ______ 1. We can infer from the fact that the son has so many answers about what happens when we die that the boy **(8)**
a. understands much about death.
b. has studied many theories about death.
c. does not fully understand the meaning of death.
d. is trying to cheer his mother up.

b ______ 2. We can infer that the boy is not satisfied with his mother's answers about death because he **(8)**
a. knows his mother is wrong.
b. wants simple reassuring answers.
c. wants his mother to feel better.
d. is not worried about death.

c ______ 3. The comparison of the four-year-old to a squash ball is an example of **(9)**
a. a major detail.

b. evidence.
c. figurative language.
d. twisting the truth.

a ______ 4. Overall the tone of this essay is **(12d)**
a. desperately uncertain.
b. quietly confident.
c. sad.
d. strong in the face of adversity.

c ______ 5. The essay ends with the words "right? Right?" The author uses the repetition **(12d)**
a. for strong emphasis.
b. to make the reader ask the question.
c. to underscore her desperate need for reassurance.
d. to be unusual.

a ______ 6. We can conclude that the writer **(10)**
a. is on the edge of panic at the thought of her father's death.
b. will be able to answer all her son's questions eventually.
c. always plays the part of a responsible adult.
d. has come to terms with her father's death.

7. Put a checkmark in the blank space next to each generalization that you think the writer would agree with. **(11)**

√ ______ a. Young children have many questions about death.

______ b. Parents should avoid discussing death with their young children.

√ ______ c. It's hard for a very young child to understand the finality of death.

√ ______ d. Losing one's child, even for a few minutes, is one of the most horrible moments of panic in a parent's life.

√ ______ e. Everyone must learn to deal with loss.

______ f. Religious background offers no help for people facing the death of a loved one.

Vocabulary

Using word-part clues and sentence clues, write a definition for each of the italicized words from the selection. **(1c, 1d)**

1. navigating the same *developmental* waters together

   slowly unfolding or growing

2. recently *diagnosed* as having cancer

   identified

3. this *matriarch* who has survived 87 rough years

   woman who is the head of a family

4. with whom I felt a painful stab of *empathy*

   understanding someone's feelings

5. I waited until the car had emptied and a few moments more, *uncomprehendingly*

   not understanding

6. it won't help to be *hysterical*

   uncontrollably upset

7. I felt the *enormity* of the city

   great size

8. standing *impassively* on the steps of the school

   expressionless; motionless

9. His voice *quivers*

   shakes

10. Daddy, Mommy — these *primitive syllables*

    basic sounds

WRITING PRACTICE

1. Write a paragraph summarizing the feelings the writer expresses in this essay.
2. Write a few paragraphs describing an incident in which you had the feeling of being lost, separated, or alone.

4

My Husband's Nine Wives

Elizabeth Joseph

Many of us have set ideas about what marriage is like. But how would you feel if you were part of a plural marriage like the one described by Elizabeth Joseph, a Utah lawyer?

Getting Started

Make a list of everything that comes to your mind when you think of marriage. **[3a(1)]**

Word Highlights

paradox (¶4) a riddle; a seeming contradiction
at first blush (¶4) in the beginning
commiserate (¶10) to talk sympathetically with another person
spontaneity (¶13) unplanned action

I married a married man.

2 In fact, he had six wives when I married him 17 years ago. Today, he has nine.

3 In March, the Utah Supreme Court struck down a trial court's ruling that a polygamist couple could not adopt a child because of their marital style. Last month, the national board of the American Civil Liberties Union, in response to a request from its Utah chapter, adopted a new policy calling for the legalization of polygamy.

4 Polygamy, or plural marriage, as practiced by my family is a paradox. At first blush, it sounds like the ideal situation for

the man and an oppressive one for the women. For me, the opposite is true. While polygamists believe that the Old Testament mandates the practice of plural marriage, compelling social reasons make the life style attractive to the modern career woman.

5 Pick up any women's magazine and you will find article after article about the problems of successfully juggling career, motherhood and marriage. It is a complex act that many women struggle to manage daily; their frustrations fill up the pages of those magazines and consume the hours of afternoon talk shows.

6 In a monogamous context, the only solutions are compromises. The kids need to learn to fix their own breakfast, your husband needs to get used to occasional microwave dinners, you need to divert more of your income to insure that your pre-schooler is in a good day care environment.

7 I am sure that in the challenge of working through these compromises, satisfaction and success can be realized. But why must women only embrace a marital arrangement that requires so many trade-offs?

8 When I leave for the 60-mile commute to court at 7 A.M., my 2-year-old daughter, London, is happily asleep in the bed of my husband's wife, Diane. London adores Diane. When London awakes, about the time I'm arriving at the courthouse, she is surrounded by family members who are as familiar to her as the toys in her nursery.

9 My husband Alex, who writes at night, gets up much later. While most of his wives are already at work, pursuing their careers, he can almost always find one who's willing to chat over coffee.

10 I share a home with Delinda, another wife, who works in town government. Most nights, we agree we'll just have a simple dinner with our three kids. We'd rather relax and commiserate over the pressures of our work day than chew up our energy cooking and doing a ton of dishes.

11 Mondays, however, are different. That's the night Alex eats with us. The kids, excited that their father is coming to dinner, are on their best behavior. We often invite another wife or one of his children. It's a special event because it only happens once a week.

12 Tuesday night, it's back to simplicity for us. But for Alex and the household he's dining with that night, it's their special time.

13 The same system with some variation governs our private time with him. While spontaneity is by no means ruled out, we basically use an appointment system. If I want to spend Friday evening at his house, I make an appointment. If he's already "booked," I either request another night or if my schedule is inflexible, I talk to the other wife and we work out an arrangement. One thing we've all learned is that there's always another night.

14 Most evenings, with the demands of career and the literal chasing after the needs of a toddler, all I want to do is collapse into bed and sleep. But there is also the longing for intimacy and comfort that only he can provide, and when those feelings surface, I ask to be with him.

15 Plural marriage is not for everyone. But it is the life style for me. It offers men the chance to escape from the traditional, confining roles that often isolate them from the surrounding world. More important, it enables women, who live in a society full of obstacles, to fully meet their career, mothering and marriage obligations. Polygamy provides a whole solution. I believe American women would have invented it if it didn't already exist. ❑

EXERCISES

Understanding What You Have Read

1. Write the main idea of this selection in your own words. **(5b)**

   Being a wife of a husband who has many wives is an advantage to a modern woman.

d 2. According to the essay, what careers do Elizabeth and Alex have? **(6a)**
   a. They are both writers.
   b. Elizabeth is a writer and Alex is a lawyer.
   c. They are both lawyers.
   d. Elizabeth is a lawyer and Alex is a writer.

c 3. Delinda and Diane are **(6a)**
   a. Elizabeth's children.
   b. Alex's children.

c. Alex's other wives.
d. London's cousins.

b
______ 4. When Elizabeth goes to work early in the morning, her daughter **(6a)**
a. goes along with her.
b. stays in bed with Diane.
c. goes to work with Delinda.
d. stays alone on her best behavior.

c
______ 5. On Monday nights **(6a)**
a. the family eats a simple dinner.
b. Alex eats with another household.
c. the kids are excited because their father is coming to dinner.
d. Alex chats over coffee with one of his wives.

d
______ 6. Which of the following paragraph patterns does paragraph 6 draw on? **(7)**
a. Description
b. Narration
c. Comparison and contrast
d. Cause and effect

a
______ 7. If Elizabeth wants to be with her husband on a night that he is not scheduled to be with her, she **(6a)**
a. makes an appointment.
b. visits him spontaneously.
c. has to wait until her time with him comes.
d. works late to take her mind off him.

Interpreting and Evaluating

c
______ 1. Which of the following inferences definitely *cannot* be made about Diane, one of Alex's other wives? **(8)**
a. She has her own children living at home with her.
b. Her house is not far from Elizabeth's.
c. She lives near the courthouse.
d. She enjoys having London stay with her.

a
______ 2. Joseph believes that polygamy is a paradox because it only seems **(8)**
a. bad for the woman but really is not.

b. good for the man but really is not.
c. good for both but really is not.
d. bad for both but really is not.

b ______ 3. Since Elizabeth married Alex, he has married **(10)**
a. nine women.
b. two women.
c. six women.
d. no other women.

c ______ 4. From Joseph's essay, we can safely conclude that Alex **(10)**
a. likes having dinner with Diane and London more than with his other wives and children.
b. eats with each wife and her child alone at least once a week.
c. may not be able to have dinner weekly with each of his wives.
d. does not enjoy eating with more than one wife at a time.

c ______ 5. We can predict that if Alex married another woman now, Elizabeth would **(10)**
a. be very angry.
b. ask her to take care of London.
c. welcome her.
d. encourage her to find a career.

a ______ 6. About the rights of polygamous couples, the state of Utah generally **(11)**
a. supports them.
b. opposes them.
c. takes no position on them.
d. refers them to the American Civil Liberties Union.

a ______ 7. With which of the following generalizations would Joseph *not* agree? **(11)**
a. Women should enter polygamous marriages.
b. Polygamy is an option that some modern women may find attractive.
c. People should not have to compromise their lives in order to solve problems.
d. Women should not have to sacrifice any of their obligations — having a career, being a wife, being a mother.

d ______ 8. To support the points in this essay, Joseph essentially **(12)**
   a. relies on data and statistics.
   b. avoids personal experience.
   c. quotes extensively from reliable sources.
   d. ignores unfavorable or opposing arguments.

Vocabulary

Use sentence clues from the selection to define, in your own words, the words in italics. Write your definitions on the blank lines. **(1c)**

1. *Polygamy,* or plural marriage, . . . is a paradox

   Polygamy means **marriage to more than one person at the same time**.

2. the Old Testament *mandates* the practice of plural marriage

   Mandates means **orders, commands**.

3. In a monogamous context, the only solutions are *compromises*

   Compromises means **agreement reached through negotiation**.

4. why must women only embrace a *marital* arrangement that requires so many trade-offs

   Marital means **related to being married**.

5. if my schedule is *inflexible,* I talk to the other wife and we work out an arrangement

   Inflexible means **not easy to change**.

6. to fully meet their career, mothering and marriage *obligations*

Obligations means duties ______________________________

____.

WRITING PRACTICE

1. Write several paragraphs in which you argue in favor of or against polygamy.
2. Write a narrative from the point of view of a child in a polygamous marriage. Tell about how you would relate to your mother, to your father's other wives, to your father, and to your brothers and sisters.

5

The Beauty of Quantitative Thinking Begins with Counting Things

John W. Harrington

Numbers are the basic language of much of science, social science, economics, and business. Read the following section from an introductory science textbook to find out why numbers are so useful.

Prereading

Before reading this selection, make a list of whatever comes to your mind about the word *numbers.* **[3a(1)]**

Word Highlights

fundamental (¶3) basic
parasite (¶3) an organism that feeds off another organism
commitment (¶5) assignment
uncompromising (¶7) rigid; not giving way to objections

The beauty of numbers is in their precision. They express exactly how much, neither more nor less. Numbers reveal relationships more clearly and more accurately than any other language. That is a strong statement, but it is true. Once numbers are correctly established, they eliminate all differences of opinion. Eight fingers are more than seven fingers. No amount of eloquence will change the established fact that eight is greater than seven. Counting things adds rigor to scientific reasoning by reducing the potential error in deciding what is and what is not least astonishing.

2 Suppose that we are interested in contrasting employment practices in economically developed countries with those in undeveloped countries. The United States of America and the People's Republic of China are good examples. A study of these two countries reveals a startling set of numbers. We may wonder about the source of the figures given in Table 1 and about the exact boundaries between categories, but we cannot ignore their impact.

3 Distribution of farm employment is by far the most surprising. Seventy-five percent of all the people gainfully employed in China work on farms; only 4 percent work on farms in the United States. This is a fundamental distinction, for it tells us something of the effort necessary to stay alive in these two countries. All animals, including humans, are parasites that

TABLE 1 Percentages of Gainfully Employed Work Force, People's Republic of China vs. United States

OCCUPATION	PEOPLE'S REPUBLIC OF CHINA	UNITED STATES OF AMERICA
Agriculture	75%	4%
Manufacturing	8	23
Handicrafts	3	0
Mining	3	1
Construction	2	4
Trade and commerce	3	38
Transportation and communication	2	6
Other special services	4	24
Total	100%	100%
Total population	859,480,000	215,625,800
Gainfully employed	270,000,000	84,783,000
Percent of total population gainfully employed	31%	39%

These figures indicate that a well-developed economy depends on an efficient food source. (Adapted from Table 1.4, pages 26, 27, 230, Goode, John Paul, *Goode's World Atlas*, 15th ed., copyright © 1978, by Rand McNally Company. Reprinted by permission.)

live directly or indirectly on energy that plants absorb from sunlight. Obviously, the Chinese have not been able to reap the plant harvest as efficiently as we do in the United States.

4 Farm employment in China is so high that only 15 percent of the workers are available to carry on trade, commerce, manufacturing, and other special services. The same group of occupations in the United States is carried on by 85 percent of the work force. The significance of these two figures is shown best by listing the occupations considered in the category "other special services."

5 These figures indicate that a well-developed economy places great emphasis on manufacturing, trade, commerce, and services. Raw materials on which these functions are based are obtained efficiently with a small manpower commitment. Underdeveloped countries exhaust their manpower resources in the effort to obtain enough food. The people who make life comfortable for the rest of us are the doctors, lawyers, preachers, teachers, artists, hair dressers, repairmen, cobblers, entertainers, civil servants, and military personnel. Imagine the price paid by the Chinese with only 4 percent of their gainfully employed population working in service jobs! The same category makes up 24 percent of the gainfully employed population of the United States.

6 Much of the wealth of the United States is drawn from manufacturing, trade, and commerce. These fields employ 61 percent of the workers in the United States and only 11 percent of the Chinese workers. That is quite a difference. Without manufacturing, trade, and commerce there can be little in the way of consumer goods available to the people. The United States was in this position in the eighteenth and early nineteenth centuries. At that time, our population was centered on the farms and forced to make things for themselves. This is exactly what we saw in China as the decade of the 1970s came to a close. Science, aided by a new technology, especially the availability of abundant farm machinery, will put an end to the China we once knew.

7 The lesson here is not really one in economics. It rests with an understanding of numbers. Counting things gives reliable information and permits us to draw reliable conclusions. There is a formal beauty and uncompromising power in measurement. ❑

EXERCISES

Understanding What You Have Read

a ______ 1. The main idea of this selection is that **(5)**
   a. numbers show precise relationships.
   b. economics is based on numbers.
   c. more people are farmers in China than in the United States.
   d. the United States is economically more developed than China.

2. Write *maj* before major details and *min* before minor details from the selection. **(6b)**

min ______ a. Eight fingers are more than seven.

maj ______ b. Seventy-five percent of Chinese laborers work in agriculture.

maj ______ c. Well-developed economies place greater emphasis on manufacturing, trade, commerce, and services.

min ______ d. Lawyers, preachers, and hairdressers make life more comfortable.

min ______ e. All animals are parasites.

maj ______ f. Twenty-four percent of American laborers work in service jobs.

c ______ 3. According to the passage, which of the following statements is *not* true? **(6a)**
   a. In the eighteenth century, most Americans lived on farms.
   b. A greater percentage of Chinese workers are employed in mining than are American workers.
   c. In total numbers, more Americans work than Chinese.
   d. Accurate numbers eliminate all differences of opinion.

c 4. Which of the following paragraphs use the comparison-and-contrast pattern? **(7d)**
a. Paragraph 6
b. Paragraphs 3, 4, and 5
c. All the paragraphs except the first and the last
d. All the paragraphs

Interpreting and Evaluating

a 1. From Table 1 we can infer all of the following *except* that **(4d, 8)**
a. China produces about one-third the manufactured goods that the United States produces.
b. an American is more likely to be gainfully employed than a Chinese.
c. an American worker has almost one chance in four of working in the category of other special services.
d. there are more total Chinese workers than American workers.

c 2. From paragraph 3 of the selection we can infer that **(8)**
a. China produces more agricultural goods than the United States.
b. American farmers work harder than Chinese farmers.
c. more effort is necessary to produce food in China than in the United States.
d. all animals eat only plants.

b 3. We can safely conclude that the author believes that **(10)**
a. the United States is more powerful than China.
b. numbers usually give more powerful and more exact answers to questions than do words.
c. numbers are never misleading.
d. counting things is very useful in the fields of economics and science, but not so useful in the field of psychology.

b 4. We can predict on the basis of this selection that **(10)**
a. in a few years China will produce more farm products than the United States.
b. technology will change the job patterns in China.
c. American farmers will continue to decrease in number.

d. consumer goods will continue to be scarce in China for many decades.

c ______ 5. The purpose of this selection is to **(12d)**
   a. prove that the United States has a more modern economy than China.
   b. compare written and numerical language.
   c. give evidence of the power of numbers.
   d. theorize about the significance of numbers.

a ______ 6. The tone and mood of this selection can be described as **(12d)**
   a. admiring but serious.
   b. exciting and lively.
   c. uncertain and confused.
   d. moralistic and dull.

d ______ 7. How would you evaluate the use of facts, opinions, and evidence in this passage? **(12a, 12b)**
   a. The author expresses no opinions, just facts.
   b. The author presents many opinions with no evidence.
   c. The author's evidence does not fit the idea he is presenting.
   d. The author uses appropriate evidence to back up his main opinion.

Vocabulary

In the blanks in the paragraph below, fill in the words from the following list that best fit the meaning of the sentences. Look back to the selection for context clues. You may need to use certain words more than once, and some words may not be used at all. Use a dictionary only if you need one. **(1c)**

economically	precision
eloquence	reliable
gainfully	rigor
manpower	significance
population	technology

The very large ___population___ of the country could not be measured with ___precision___ because people did not trust the census takers. When asked questions, the people would not give **reliable** answers. As a result, the census takers could not interpret the **significance** of their results. The country was **economically** at a disadvantage because it was impossible to make accurate estimates of the **manpower** available for various jobs. Officials then decided to use the latest **technology** to obtain results that would have greater **rigor**.

WRITING PRACTICE

1. Write a paragraph to illustrate the importance of numbers in your daily life. Give examples.
2. Study Table 1, which concerns employment statistics in the United States and China. Make some comparisons not discussed in the article and present your conclusions in a paragraph.

6

What's Your Best Time of Day?

Susan Perry
Jim Dawson

At different times of the day, we are better at doing different kinds of things, according to the scientific findings summarized in this magazine article. As you read, think about how the ideas apply to your own body clock.

Prereading

On a separate sheet of paper make a list of questions about the words *body clock.* Write down as many questions as you can raise about the topic. **[3a(4)]**

Word Highlights

cravings (¶1) desires
accommodating (¶2) agreeable
mollusks (¶3) shellfish and related water animals
menstrual (¶3) relating to the monthly discharge of unused eggs by women
flux (¶4) change
manual dexterity (¶13) ability to do things with your hands

Every fall, Jane, a young mother and part-time librarian, begins to eat more and often feels sleepy. Her mood is also darker, especially when she awakens in the morning; it takes all her energy just to drag herself out of bed.

These symptoms persist until April, when warmer weather and longer days seem to lighten her mood and alleviate her cravings for food and sleep.

2 Joseph, a 48-year-old engineer for a Midwestern computer company, feels cranky early in the morning. But as the day progresses, he becomes friendlier and more accommodating.

3 All living organisms, from mollusks to men and women, exhibit biological rhythms. Some are short and can be measured in minutes or hours. Others last days or months. The peaking of body temperature, which occurs in most people every evening, is a daily rhythm. The menstrual cycle is a monthly rhythm. The increase in sexual drive in the autumn — not in the spring, as poets would have us believe — is a seasonal, or yearly, rhythm.

4 The idea that our bodies are in constant flux is fairly new — and goes against traditional medical training. In the past, many doctors were taught to believe the body has a relatively stable, or homeostatic, internal environment. Any fluctuations were considered random and not meaningful enough to be studied.

5 As early as the 1940s, however, some scientists questioned the homeostatic view of the body. Franz Halberg, a young European scientist working in the United States, noticed that the number of white blood cells in laboratory mice was dramatically higher and lower at different times of day. Gradually, such research spread to the study of other rhythms in other life forms, and the findings were sometimes startling. For example, the time of day when a person receives X-ray or drug treatment for cancer can affect treatment benefits and ultimately mean the difference between life and death.

6 This new science is called chronobiology, and the evidence supporting it has become increasingly persuasive. Along the way, the scientific and medical communities are beginning to rethink their ideas about how the human body works, and gradually what had been considered a minor science just a few years ago is being studied in major universities and medical centers around the world. There are even chronobiologists working for the National Aeronautics and Space Administration, as well as for the National Institutes of Health and other government laboratories.

7 With their new findings, they are teaching us things that can literally change our lives — by helping us organize ourselves so we can work *with* our natural rhythms rather than

against them. This can enhance our outlook on life as well as our performance at work and play.

8 Because they are easy to detect and measure, more is known of daily — or circadian (Latin for "about a day") — rhythms than other types. The most obvious daily rhythm is the sleep/wake cycle. But there are other daily cycles as well: temperature, blood pressure, hormone levels. Amid these and the body's other changing rhythms, you are simply a different person at 9 A.M. than you are at 3 P.M. How you feel, how well you work, your level of alertness, your sensitivity to taste and smell, the degree with which you enjoy food or take pleasure in music — all are changing throughout the day.

9 Most of us seem to reach our peak of alertness around noon. Soon after that, alertness declines, and sleepiness may set in by midafternoon.

10 Your short-term memory is best during the morning — in fact, about 15 percent more efficient than at any other time of day. So, students, take heed: when faced with a morning exam, it really does pay to review your notes right before the test is given.

11 Long-term memory is different. Afternoon is the best time for learning material that you want to recall days, weeks or months later. Politicians, business executives or others who must learn speeches would be smart to do their memorizing during that time of day. If you are a student, you would be wise to schedule your more difficult classes in the afternoon, rather than in the morning. You should also try to do most of your studying in the afternoon, rather than late at night. Many students believe they memorize better while burning the midnight oil because their short-term recall is better during the wee hours of the morning than in the afternoon. But short-term memory won't help them much several days later, when they face the exam.

12 By contrast, we tend to do best on cognitive tasks — things that require the juggling of words and figures in one's head — during the morning hours. This might be a good time, say, to balance a checkbook.

13 Your manual dexterity — the speed and coordination with which you perform complicated tasks with your hands — peaks during the afternoon hours. Such work as carpentry, typing or sewing will be a little easier at this time of day.

14 What about sports? During afternoon and early evening, your coordination is at its peak, and you're able to react the

quickest to an outside stimulus — like a baseball speeding toward you at home plate. Studies have also shown that late in the day, when your body temperature is peaking, you will *perceive* a physical workout to be easier and less fatiguing — whether it actually is or not. That means you are more likely to work harder during a late-afternoon or early-evening workout, and therefore benefit more from it. Studies involving swimmers, runners, shot-putters and rowing crews have shown consistently that performance is better in the evening than in the morning.

15 In fact, all of your senses — taste, sight, hearing, touch and smell — may be at their keenest during late afternoon and early evening. That could be why dinner usually tastes better to us than breakfast and why bright lights irritate us at night.

16 Even our perception of time changes from hour to hour. Not only does time seem to fly when you're having fun, but it also seems to fly even faster if you are having that fun in the late afternoon or early evening, when your body temperature is also peaking.

17 While all of us follow the same general pattern of ups and downs, the exact timing varies from person to person. It all depends on how your "biological" day is structured — how much of a morning or night person you are. The earlier your biological day gets going, the earlier you are likely to enter — and exit — the peak times for performing various tasks. An extreme morning person and an extreme night person may have circadian cycles that are a few hours apart.

18 Each of us can increase our knowledge about our individual rhythms. Learn how to listen to the inner beats of your body; let them set the pace of your day. You will live a healthier — and happier — life. As no less an authority than the Bible tells us, "To every thing there is a season, and a time to every purpose under heaven." ❑

EXERCISES

Understanding What You Have Read

1. Write in your own words the main idea of this selection. **(5)**

   Listening to your individual rhythms and adjusting your lifestyle will improve the way you live.

b ______ 2. This main idea of the selection is stated most directly in the **(5b)**
a. final sentence of the first paragraph.
b. opening sentence of paragraph 3.
c. opening sentence of paragraph 5.
d. final sentence of paragraph 17.

d ______ 3. The main idea of the opening paragraph about Jane is **(5b)**
a. stated in the first sentence.
b. stated in the second sentence.
c. stated in the third sentence.
d. implied only.

4. Write in your own words the main idea of the opening paragraph (see question 3). **(5b)**

Jane's body follows some rhythm that leads her to be more sleepy and hungry in autumn than in spring.

c ______ 5. Sexual drive is at a peak **(6a)**
a. in the morning.
b. monthly.
c. in the fall.
d. when the mood strikes you.

c ______ 6. The main idea of paragraph 8 is **(5b)**
a. in the first sentence of that paragraph.
b. in the third sentence.
c. in the last sentence.
d. only implied.

d ______ 7. The most important detail about Franz Halberg is that he **(6b)**
a. was young.
b. was European, even though he worked in the United States.
c. worked with the white blood cells of laboratory mice.
d. noticed changes in white blood cell count depending on the time of day.

b ______ 8. Most of us are alert **(6a)**
a. in the morning.
b. around noon.
c. late in the afternoon.
d. in the winter.

c ______ 9. Which of the following is *not* at a peak during the late afternoon and early evening? **(6a)**
a. Senses of sight and smell
b. Athletic performance
c. Cognitive ability
d. Sense of time passing rapidly

a ______ 10. Paragraph 11 follows a pattern of **(7)**
a. listing of details.
b. cause and effect.
c. classification.
d. comparison and contrast.

d ______ 11. Paragraphs 11 and 12 are related by **(7)**
a. cause and effect.
b. time order.
c. order of importance.
d. contrast.

Interpreting and Evaluating

1. Put a checkmark before each statement we can properly conclude from this selection. **(10)**

√ ______ a. We all follow a daily pattern of changing skills.

______ b. We all are best at the same things at the same times.

√ ______ c. People tend to be mentally quicker in the morning but more thoughtful in the afternoon.

______ d. Jane suffers a serious disorder of her circadian cycle.

√ ______ e. Cognitive tasks and studying use different types of skills.

√ f. Daily patterns of mood change are to be expected.

___ g. Scientists fully understand the effects of biological rhythms.

√ h. Body temperature seems to be related to keenness of the senses and perception of time.

√ i. Traditional medical beliefs about the body being a homeostatic system are incorrect.

√ j. What scientists have learned about circadian rhythms is useful knowledge.

√ k. The timing of body rhythms varies from person to person.

2. Based on the information in this article, predict the time of day that you would most likely perform the activity best. Write your answer on the blank line. **(10)**

a. Doing a crossword puzzle **morning**

b. Knitting **afternoon**

c. Enjoying a party **evening**

d. Taking a nap **midafternoon**

e. Memorizing a speech **afternoon**

f. Preparing for a morning quiz **morning**

g. Preparing for an afternoon quiz **afternoon**

h. Archery **afternoon**

i. Playing Jeopardy **morning**

j. Playing basketball **afternoon/early evening**

k. Enjoying watching basketball **late afternoon**

l. Tasting wine **late afternoon/early evening**

m. Working with dangerous tools **afternoon**

n. Running a marathon **late afternoon/early evening**

d 3. Based on the information in this selection you can generalize that you would do best if you **(11)**
   a. follow the same strict schedule every day.
   b. don't plan your activities, but do what you feel like doing.
   c. do all your thinking in the morning.
   d. pay attention to your body rhythms.

a 4. The purpose of this selection is to **(12d)**
   a. help the reader live more healthfully, happily, and successfully.
   b. amuse the reader.
   c. persuade the reader to support chronobiological research.
   d. make the reader distrust doctors who have a homeostatic view of biology.

b 5. The tone of the selection is **(12d)**
   a. ironic and bitter.
   b. matter-of-fact and helpful.
   c. pompous and overly serious.
   d. technical and cool.

d 6. The authors write from the point of view of **(12d)**
   a. chronobiologists arguing for their work.
   b. people who have suffered from not understanding their biological rhythms properly.
   c. ordinary people who are unfamiliar with scientific research.
   d. ordinary people who have studied the scientific research on chronobiology.

Vocabulary

In the selection, both sentence clues and word-part clues help you with the meaning of many words. In the space next to each of the following words, write down the sentence clues and word part clues that you can find. Then write down the best meaning you can come up with for the word. **(1c, 1d)**

1. *symptoms* ______

   ______

   Meaning **indications of a condition**

2. *alleviate* ______

   ______

   Meaning **relieve**

3. *homeostatic* ______

   ______

   Meaning **staying the same**

4. *fluctuations* ______

   ______

   Meaning **irregular variations**

5. *chronobiology* ______

   ______

   Meaning **study of the relation of different times to the body and its functions**

6. *circadian* ______

   ______

Meaning **recurring approximately every twenty-four hours (a cycle)**

7. *cognitive* ______________________

Meaning **learning; thinking**

8. *stimulus* ______________________

Meaning **something that causes a response**

WRITING PRACTICE

1. In a paragraph summarize the main points made by this selection.
2. Write several paragraphs describing your own body clock.

7

Looking for Work

Gary Soto

When Gary Soto was a child, he got many ideas about life from watching television. These ideas didn't always match the reality of life with his family. As you read about his childhood plans and experiences, think about the differences between real life and life portrayed on the television screen.

Prereading

Before you read the selection, freewrite about plans you had to make money when you were a child. **[3a(3)]**

Word Highlights

mimicked (¶2) copied in a humorously critical way
egg candler (¶4) someone who examines chicken eggs to determine whether they have been fertilized
muu-muu (¶5) a loose-fitting housedress
contorted (¶8) twisted
contagious (¶10) easily transmitted, such as a disease
feigned (¶12) pretended
stern (¶12) serious
posture (¶12) body position
chavalo (¶25) an informal Spanish word meaning "boy"

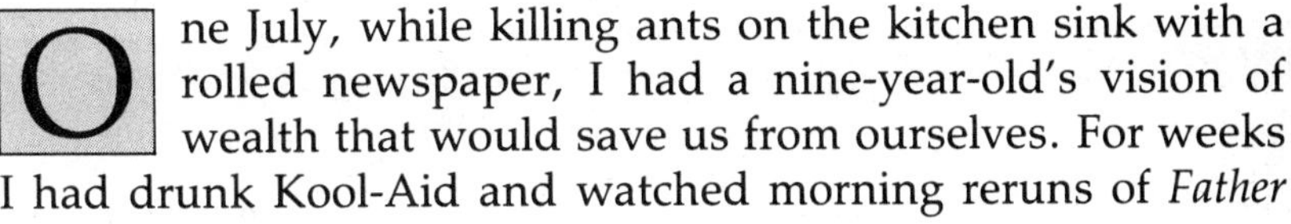

One July, while killing ants on the kitchen sink with a rolled newspaper, I had a nine-year-old's vision of wealth that would save us from ourselves. For weeks I had drunk Kool-Aid and watched morning reruns of *Father*

Knows Best, whose family was so uncomplicated in its routine that I very much wanted to imitate it. The first step was to get my brother and sister to wear shoes at dinner.

2 "Come on, Rick — come on, Deb," I whined. But Rick mimicked me and the same day that I asked him to wear shoes he came to the dinner table in only his swim trunks. My mother didn't notice, nor did my sister, as we sat to eat our beans and tortillas in the stifling heat of our kitchen. We all gleamed like cellophane, wiping the sweat from our brows with the backs of our hands as we talked about the day: Frankie our neighbor was beat up by Faustino; the swimming pool at the playground would be closed for a day because the pump was broken.

3 Such was our life. So that morning, while doing-in the train of ants which arrived each day, I decided to become wealthy, and right away! After downing a bowl of cereal, I took a rake from the garage and started up the block to look for work.

4 We lived on an ordinary block of mostly working class people: warehousemen, egg candlers, welders, mechanics, and a union plumber. And there were many retired people who kept their lawns green and the gutters uncluttered of the chewing gum wrappers we dropped as we rode by on our bikes. They bent down to gather our litter, muttering at our evilness.

5 At the corner house I rapped the screen door and a very large woman in a muu-muu answered. She sized me up and then asked what I could do.

6 "Rake leaves," I answered, smiling.

7 "It's summer, and there ain't no leaves," she countered. Her face was pinched with lines; fat jiggled under her chin. She pointed to the lawn, then the flower bed, and said: "You see any leaves there — or there?" I followed her pointing arm, stupidly. But she had a job for me and that was to get her a Coke at the liquor store. She gave me twenty cents, and after ditching my rake in a bush, off I ran. I returned with an unbagged Pepsi, for which she thanked me and gave me a nickel from her apron.

8 I skipped off her porch, fetched my rake, and crossed the street to the next block where Mrs. Moore, mother of Earl the retarded man, let me weed a flower bed. She handed me a trowel and for a good part of the morning my fingers dipped into the moist dirt, ripping up runners of Bermuda grass. Worms surfaced in my search for deep roots, and I cut them

in halves, tossing them to Mrs. Moore's cat who pawed them playfully as they dried in the sun. I made out Earl whose face was pressed to the back window of the house, and although he was calling to me I couldn't understand what he was trying to say. Embarrassed, I worked without looking up, but I imagined his contorted mouth and the ring of keys attached to his belt — keys that jingled with each palsied step. He scared me and I worked quickly to finish the flower bed. When I did finish Mrs. Moore gave me a quarter and two peaches from her tree, which I washed there but ate in the alley behind my house.

9 I was sucking on the second one, a bit of juice staining the front of my T-shirt, when Little John, my best friend, came walking down the alley with a baseball bat over his shoulder, knocking over trash cans as he made his way toward me.

10 Little John and I went to St. John's Catholic School, where we sat among the "stupids." Miss Marino, our teacher, alternated the rows of good students with the bad, hoping that by sitting side-by-side with the bright students the stupids might become more intelligent, as though intelligence were contagious. But we didn't progress as she had hoped. She grew frustrated when one day, while dismissing class for recess, Little John couldn't get up because his arms were stuck in the slats of the chair's backrest. She scolded us with a shaking finger when we knocked over the globe, denting the already troubled Africa. She muttered curses when Leroy White, a real stupid but a great softball player with the gift to hit to all fields, openly chewed his host when he made his First Communion; his hands swung at his sides as he returned to the pew looking around with a big smile.

11 Little John asked what I was doing, and I told him that I was taking a break from work, as I sat comfortably among high weeds. He wanted to join me, but I reminded him that the last time he'd gone door-to-door asking for work his mother had whipped him. I was with him when his mother, a New Jersey Italian who could rise up in anger one moment and love the next, told me in a polite but matter-of-fact voice that I had to leave because she was going to beat her son. She gave me a homemade popsicle, ushered me to the door, and said that I could see Little John the next day. But it was sooner than that. I went around to his bedroom window to suck my popsicle

and watch Little John dodge his mother's blows, a few hitting their mark but many whirring air.

12 It was midday when Little John and I converged in the alley, the sun blazing in the high nineties, and he suggested that we go to Roosevelt High School to swim. He needed five cents to make fifteen, the cost of admission, and I lent him a nickel. We ran home for my bike and when my sister found out that we were going swimming she started to cry because she didn't have the fifteen cents but only an empty Coke bottle. I waved for her to come and three of us mounted the bike — Debra on the cross bar, Little John on the handle bars and holding the Coke bottle which we would cash for a nickel and make up the difference that would allow all of us to get in, and me pumping up the crooked streets, dodging cars and pot holes. We spent the day swimming under the afternoon sun, so that when we got home our mom asked us what was darker, the floor or us? She feigned a stern posture, her hands on her hips and her mouth puckered. We played along. Looking down, Debbie and I said in unison, "Us."

13 That evening at dinner we all sat down in our bathing suits to eat our beans, laughing and chewing loudly. Our mom was in a good mood, so I took a risk and asked her if sometime we could have turtle soup. A few days before I had watched a television program in which a Polynesian tribe killed a large turtle, gutted it, and then stewed it over an open fire. The turtle, basted in a sugary sauce, looked delicious as I ate an afternoon bowl of cereal, but my sister, who was watching the program with a glass of Kool-Aid between her knees, said, "Caca."

14 My mother looked at me in bewilderment. "Boy, are you a crazy Mexican. Where did you get the idea that people eat turtles?"

15 "On television," I said, explaining the program. Then I took it a step further. "Mom, do you think we could get dressed up for dinner one of these days? David King does."

16 "*Ay, Dios,*" my mother laughed. She started collecting the dinner plates, but my brother wouldn't let go of his. He was still drawing a picture in the bean sauce. Giggling, he said it was me, but I didn't want to listen because I wanted an answer from Mom. This was the summer when I spent the mornings in front of the television that showed the comfortable lives of

white kids. There were no beatings, no rifts in the family. They wore bright clothes; toys tumbled from their closets. They hopped into bed with kisses and woke to glasses of fresh orange juice, and to a father sitting before his morning coffee while the mother buttered his toast. They hurried through the day making friends and gobs of money, returning home to a warmly lit living room, and then dinner. *Leave It to Beaver* was the program I replayed in my mind:

17 "May I have the mashed potatoes?" asks Beaver with a smile.

18 "Sure, Beav," replies Wally as he taps the corners of his mouth with a starched napkin.

19 The father looks on in his suit. The mother, decked out in earrings and a pearl necklace, cuts into her steak and blushes. Their conversation is politely clipped.

20 "Swell," says Beaver, his cheeks puffed with food.

21 Our own talk at dinner was loud with belly laughs and marked by our pointing forks at one another. The subjects were commonplace.

22 "Gary, let's go to the ditch tomorrow," my brother suggests. He explains that he has made a life preserver out of four empty detergent bottles strung together with twine and that he will make me one if I can find more bottles. "No way are we going to drown."

23 "Yeah, then we could have a dirt clod fight," I reply, so happy to be alive.

24 Whereas the Beaver's family enjoyed dessert in dishes at the table, our mom sent us outside, and more often than not I went into the alley to peek over the neighbor's fences and spy out fruit, apricots or peaches.

25 I had asked my mom and again she laughed that I was a crazy *chavalo* as she stood in front of the sink, her arms rising and falling with suds, face glistening from the heat. She sent me outside where my brother and sister were sitting in the shade that the fence threw out like a blanket. They were talking about me when I plopped down next to them. They looked at one another and then Debbie, my eight-year-old sister, started in.

26 "What's this crap about getting dressed up?"

27 She had entered her profanity stage. A year later she would give up such words and slip into her Catholic uniform, and

into squealing on my brother and me when we "cussed this" and "cussed that."

28 I tried to convince them that if we improved the way we looked we might get along better in life. White people would like us more. They might invite us to places, like their homes or front yards. They might not hate us so much.

29 My sister called me a "craphead," and got up to leave with a stalk of grass dangling from her mouth. "They'll never like us."

30 My brother's mood lightened as he talked about the ditch — the white water, the broken pieces of glass, and the rusted car fenders that awaited our knees. There would be toads, and rocks to smash them.

31 David King, the only person we knew who resembled the middle class, called from over the fence. David was Catholic, of Armenian and French descent, and his closet was filled with toys. A bear-shaped cookie jar, like the ones on television, sat on the kitchen counter. His mother was remarkably kind while she put up with the racket we made on the street. Evenings, she often watered the front yard and it must have upset her to see us — my brother and I and others — jump from trees laughing, the unkillable kids of the very poor, who got up unshaken, brushed off, and climbed into another one to try again.

32 David called again. Rick got up and slapped grass from his pants. When I asked if I could come along he said no. David said no. They were two years older so their affairs were different from mine. They greeted one another with foul names and took off down the alley to look for trouble.

33 I went inside the house, turned on the television, and was about to sit down with a glass of Kool-Aid when Mom shooed me outside.

34 "It's still light," she said. "Later you'll bug me to let you stay out longer. So go on."

35 I downed my Kool-Aid and went outside to the front yard. No one was around. The day had cooled and a breeze rustled the trees. Mr. Jackson, the plumber, was watering his lawn and when he saw me he turned away to wash off his front steps. There was more than an hour of light left, so I took advantage of it and decided to look for work. I felt suddenly alive as I skipped down the block in search of an overgrown flower bed and the dime that would end the day right. ❑

EXERCISES

Understanding What You Have Read

c ______ 1. The topic of this selection is **(5b)**
   a. how to find a job in a Mexican-American neighborhood.
   b. watching television with a Mexican-American family.
   c. part of a day in the life of a young Mexican-American boy.
   d. getting along with family members.

c ______ 2. The main idea of this selection is that **(5b)**
   a. television is harmful for young children.
   b. looking for work is tough for a nine-year-old.
   c. for a poor Mexican-American child, dreams based on television do not match real life.
   d. ambition and hard work as a child pay off in adulthood.

b ______ 3. Paragraph 2 is organized in a pattern of **(7)**
   a. classification.
   b. listing of details.
   c. comparison and contrast.
   d. cause and effect.

d ______ 4. The main idea of the second paragraph is **(5b)**
   a. the importance of dressing for dinner.
   b. the oppressive summer heat.
   c. that Soto's family led a good life.
   d. that Soto found his family's life unpleasant.

5. Arrange the events listed below in the order in which they took place in the selection by writing a 1 in front of the first event, a 2 in front of the second, and so on. **(7a)**

4 ______ a. Gary Soto earns a nickel for getting a Pepsi.

1 ______ b. Little John got stuck in a chair.

9 ______ c. Gary asks his mother for turtle soup.

12 ______ d. Gary looks for work another time in the evening.

5 ______ e. Mrs. Moore has him weed a flower bed.

10 ______ f. Gary argues with his sister and brother about dressing up for dinner.

3 ______ g. The family eats a dinner of beans and tortillas.

7 ______ h. Gary Soto met Little John in an alley.

6 ______ i. Gary Soto ate two peaches.

8 ______ j. Debbie, John, and Gary went swimming.

11 ______ k. Mr. Jackson was watering his lawn.

2 ______ l. Frankie was beaten by Faustino.

Interpreting and Evaluating

b ______ 1. From the first few paragraphs we can infer that the "us" in the opening sentence phrase "would save us from ourselves" refers to **(8)**
a. Gary Soto and his friends.
b. Gary Soto's family.
c. all the people in the neighborhood.
d. all the children who watched too much television.

d ______ 2. We can infer from the opening sentence that the author thought his family **(8)**
a. was living a happy life.
b. had some small problems.
c. was as good as any family on television.
d. did not live life the way the boy wanted them to.

c ______ 3. We can infer from Rick's way of dressing at dinner that he **(8)**
a. thought Gary made a lot of sense.
b. was planning on going swimming after dinner.
c. rejected Gary's plans and ambitions.
d. was trying to get his mother upset.

a ______ 4. From her actions and attitudes we can predict that Miss Marino **(10)**
a. would be surprised to discover that Soto is a writer.

b. would view Soto's success as proof of the value of her teaching methods.
c. still has some things to scold Soto about.
d. would be pleased by Soto's description of her class.

b 5. From the information in the story we can conclude that Little John's mother **(10, 11)**
a. thought the author was a bad influence on her son.
b. had strong moods and emotions.
c. was always harsh and cruel.
d. was successful in controlling her son's behavior.

d 6. We can conclude that on the day of the episode described here the author **(10, 11)**
a. made a lot of money.
b. learned that he would never get rich.
c. became depressed about spending the little money he had earned.
d. remained optimistic about the future.

b 7. When Soto was a child, he believed that television **(12a)**
a. would get you into trouble.
b. gave a realistic picture of life's possibilities.
c. was totally unrealistic.
d. gave him the hope that helped him be optimistic about the future.

d 8. Today, as an adult, Soto believes that television **(12a)**
a. gets children into trouble.
b. gives a realistic picture of life's possibilities.
c. is totally unrealistic and leads to frustrated hopes.
d. gave him hope and encouraged his plans for the future.

b 9. Overall, the events of the day are told in a mood of **(12d)**
a. bitter disappointment.
b. youthful optimism.
c. regret.
d. intellectual evaluation.

Vocabulary

The writer creates many vivid images in this selection. In your own words, restate the meanings of the following images. **(9)**
Student responses will vary.

1. gleamed like cellophane

____

2. the train of ants

____

3. her face was pinched with lines

____

4. runners of Bermuda grass

____

5. palsied step

____

6. blows, a few hitting their mark but many whirring air

____

7. toys tumbled from their closets

____

8. a breeze rustled the trees

____

WRITING PRACTICE

1. Describe in a few paragraphs how Soto's attitudes and plans differed from those of his family and the other people around him.
2. Write a page discussing how television gave you views of life that were different from your actual surroundings and how that knowledge affected your goals and attitudes.

8

Career Planning

Bruce Shertzer

How do you decide which career to choose? Once you have decided, how do you go about preparing for it? In this selection from a college textbook on career planning, Bruce Shertzer points out some basic problems for students who are thinking about future occupations.

Prereading

Before you read this selection, on a separate sheet of paper make a list of questions you might like to ask an adviser about choosing the right career for yourself. **[3a(4)]**

Word Highlights

alternative (¶1) one of several choices or options
feasible (¶1) possible
flaws (¶3) imperfections; defects; weaknesses
dominant (¶3) having the most influence
confronted (¶4) faced up to
resorting (¶4) turning to for relief
implications (¶4) logical results or consequences
contrived (¶5) planned; devised
vigilance (¶6) careful watchfulness
contingency (¶6) occurrence that depends on chance or uncertain conditions
stigma (¶20) mark of disgrace or blame
routine (¶20) something ordinary

areer planning does not necessarily follow routine or logical steps. Each of us places weight on different factors and may consider certain phases of career

planning at different times. Career planning includes gathering information about ourselves and about occupations, estimating the probable outcomes of various courses of action, and finally, choosing alternatives that we find attractive and feasible.

2 Many observers have pointed out that students are not very efficient career planners. They cite evidence that (1) most students choose from among a very narrow group of occupations; (2) as many as 40 to 60 percent choose professional occupations, when in reality only 15 to 18 percent of the work force is engaged in professional work; (3) young men show a striking lack of interest in clerical, sales, and service occupations, although these fields offer many job opportunities; and (4) as many as a third of the students are unable to express any choice of occupation.

3 In their book *Decision Making* (Free Press, 1977), Irving Janis and Leon Mann identify serious flaws in the ways many people make decisions. These flaws seem to be associated with the patterns people use to cope with problems. The first flaw is *complacency*. People who ignore challenging information about the choices they make demonstrate complacency. People who take the attitude that "It won't affect me" or "It will never happen" use complacency as a dominant pattern of behaving. Of course, complacency is appropriate for any decision in which nothing much is at stake, but that does not describe career decisions.

4 A second flaw in the way people cope with decisions is *defensive avoidance*. When confronted with a decision and unable to believe they can find an acceptable solution, some people remain calm by resorting to wishful thinking or daydreaming. Students who fail to think about the implications of their career choices often engage in rationalization (deceiving oneself with self-satisfying but incorrect explanations for one's behavior) or procrastination (putting off or delaying). Facing the situation may produce anxiety, but examining alternatives could also bring relief.

5 A third flaw is *hypervigilance*. This occurs in career decision making when people believe there is not enough time to find a solution and they panic. They search frantically for career possibilities and seize on hastily contrived solutions, overlooking the consequences of their choice as well as other alternatives. People who are in a panic sometimes do not think clearly or logically.

6 The best coping behavior is *vigilance.* Vigilant decision making occurs when people believe that (1) a choice should be made, (2) they can find a solution, and (3) there is enough time. Under these conditions, students can conduct an effective search for alternative careers, carefully evaluate each alternative, and work out contingency plans in case one or another risk appears.

Keys to Career Planning

7 1. *Study yourself.* This is the key to career planning. It has been suggested several times before, but its importance cannot be emphasized too much. Understanding what you are like, what you value, and what you want to become is the foundation for all career planning. In studying yourself, you examine your strengths and weaknesses, your goals, and the trends in your personal development. The self-understanding that you gain enables you to imagine how certain occupations may best fit your personality, interests, abilities, and goals. All career decisions require us to learn both about ourselves and about work, and to integrate these two kinds of knowledge.

8 2. *Write your career goals down.* A technique useful for organizing ideas about your career development is actually to write them down by time blocks in your life, for example, ages nineteen to twenty-two, twenty-three to thirty, thirty-one to forty-five, forty-six to sixty-five. Writing something down forces you to crystallize your thinking and to recognize fuzzy and half-formed ideas. It may lead to new insights about your possibilities and may help you to see new relationships, patterns, and trends, or to identify gaps in your thinking about your career development. For example, during the age period fourteen to eighteen, did you take courses that would best prepare you for ages nineteen to twenty-two or twenty-three to thirty?

9 3. *Set up some hypotheses or predictions about yourself in a career.* Consider the kind of person you are, what you are likely to be like, what changes are likely to take place in an occupation, what basic problems you might meet, and what you need to solve your problems. These hypotheses, or educated guesses, should represent your understanding of yourself at present, how you got that way, what you can do, and what you will do.

10 For example, you hypothesize that you are a person with considerable mechanical interest and ability and predict that you would be "at home" in a plumbing shop between the ages of twenty-three to thirty. Further, you project that between the ages of nineteen and twenty-three, you enter apprenticeship training to be a plumber or pipe fitter. But you guess that being accepted as an apprentice plumber might be one problem, while parental disapproval might be another. You need to estimate ways of maximizing your chances of being accepted for such a training program and ways of explaining to your parents why you have chosen that field. Hypotheses could also be set up about being married and having children and what this would mean to your career plans.

11 For each of these time periods, you can set up several statements as to what you might do, under what conditions you would choose such an alternative, and which ones you are most likely to choose. In our example of the plumbing shop, you state whether you would be likely to stay in the apprenticeship program or the conditions under which you would drop out of it. Alternative hypotheses and predictions can help you think in terms of the different actions open to you and prepare you for different possibilities.

12 4. *Become familiar with the pathways for entering occupations that interest you.* There are several ways of entering most occupations. A pathway to many skilled trades is through apprenticeship programs. Each year some 270,000 persons are in apprentice programs in this country, and some 60,000 complete the two- to five-year programs. Another way to enter many occupations is to enter trade or technical schools. Many communities have such schools, and they offer both short-term (less than two weeks) and long-term (two years or longer) programs.

13 Another pathway to some occupations is the training provided by industry or government. Some companies select young people for training who they believe will stay with the company for a long time. Automobile companies, airlines, and public utilities, such as gas and electric companies, are examples. In government programs young people can learn skills needed for employment. The military services also provide training opportunities that help some individuals when they come to enter the civilian work force.

14 Other pathways to occupations are the junior or community colleges and four-year colleges and universities. Completion of a college degree and graduate study is the route for entering most professional occupations.

15 Finally, an important way to enter some occupations is by holding a succession of jobs during early years in the labor force. Many large companies hire workers at the lowest level and advance them as they gain seniority (years of service) and skill. People work their way up in such companies by being on the job and educating themselves (mostly through part-time schooling).

16 More pathways into an occupation are available to high school graduates than to dropouts, more are available to those who have some type of further training beyond high school than to high school graduates, and more are available to college graduates than to others. When you engage in career planning, you must figure out ways to enter those occupations in which you are interested. Early in your planning, you should concentrate on deciding which pathways appeal to and are possible for you. It is important to decide whether to get more schooling and, if so, how to finance it.

17 5. *Review your plans and progress periodically with another person.* Every so often, take stock of your situation and consider what steps have to be taken next. Taking inventory of progress and planning further steps can help you cope with the changes that you undergo and the changes that take place in the labor market. Talking over your plans with a college counselor, your parents, and your friends helps you define your goals and improve your career plans to make them work.

18 6. *If you choose a career that does not fit you, you can start over.* Today, growing numbers of men and women are changing careers or getting second starts in careers that have greater appeal to them. Many of those who find that their line of work is unsatisfactory retrain themselves for a different occupation. Often their new occupation is one that they overlooked when they were young or that they did not have an opportunity to pursue at that time for financial or other reasons.

19 We have mentioned several times in this text that decisions, once made, affect subsequent decisions. Certainly, time spent in one occupation is likely to narrow the range

of later occupational choices. Very few people have the motivation and financial resources to start a completely new career in mid-life. Albert Schweitzer, famous medical missionary, turned from music to medicine when he was over forty, but that is quite unusual. Most people move to a related field that involves a minimum of new training.

20 Sociologists say that there are few changes in careers that involve "downward" movement; most involve the traditional business of "getting ahead." Society no longer attaches the stigma of "instability" to the idea of career hopping, as it once did. Motives or reasons for changing careers vary widely, but many people move because they feel stale or fed up with a grinding or dull routine. For some, a second start grows out of the realization that what they want out of life is not what they are doing, and they decide to do those things they enjoy and believe to be important. Most go back to school to get the training they need to make the shifts.

21 Job changes and career shifts occur at all ages. It has been estimated that as many as one out of four male workers between the ages of twenty and twenty-five change their lines of work. About half that number do so between the ages of twenty-five and forty-four. Seymour Wolfbein, a Department of Labor specialist, has said that on the average a man of forty can expect to make two or more job changes during his years of work. Some married women combine child-rearing responsibilities with new career lines.

Summary

22 Career planning does not guarantee that all the problems, difficulties, or decision-making situations that face you in the future will be solved or made any easier. No formula can be given to do that. But career planning should help you to approach and cope better with new problems, such as deciding whether or not to enter educational or training programs, deciding whether or not to change jobs, and analyzing the difficulties you are having with a situation or a person.

23 Career planning involves problem-solving skills and adjustment skills. Quite often it helps people see the kinds of assistance they need to do what they want and helps direct them to available resources.

24 Nobody can foresee what the future holds for any of us. There are social, emotional, and moral considerations in our

future that cannot be foreseen. But the most important lesson of this often-unhappy modern world is that progress comes from planning. Ignorance about one's career is not bliss; reason is better than chance and fate. Although there is no sure way to make career plans work out, there are things that you can do now to shape your career possibilities. ❑

EXERCISES

Understanding What You Have Read

a ______ 1. The main idea of this selection is that **(5)**
   a. we can avoid flaws in choosing careers by planning career decisions carefully.
   b. most people do not make appropriate career choices.
   c. changing careers is not a good idea.
   d. defensive avoidance is a serious problem for people deciding on future careers.

d ______ 2. The main idea of paragraph 2 is that **(5b)**
   a. one-third of all students cannot express career choices.
   b. men should show more interest in clerical, sales, and service occupations.
   c. women should have more job opportunities in a wider range of careers.
   d. most students do not plan their careers very effectively.

c ______ 3. Which of the following does the selection *not* name as a flaw in the way people make career decisions? **(6a)**
   a. Hypervigilance
   b. Defensive avoidance
   c. Progress inventory development
   d. Complacency

b ______ 4. If you are *hypervigilant,* you **(2, 6a)**
   a. look carefully for the right job opportunity at the right time.
   b. choose a career quickly because you panic about not having enough time.
   c. are almost certainly a student.
   d. should probably not choose clerical work as a career.

c ______ 5. The flaw of *complacency* refers to **(6a)**
a. gathering incorrect information about your career.
b. being unable to express a career preference.
c. not worrying about career decisions because you believe that problems won't affect you.
d. aggressive behavior in choosing a job.

a ______ 6. Rationalization and procrastination are **(6a)**
a. parts of defensive avoidance
b. parts of all careful job decisions.
c. reserved only for entry-level decision makers.
d. traits that students should use when looking for jobs.

a ______ 7. In choosing a career, you should study yourself and your needs because **(6a)**
a. knowing your needs and personality will help you identify jobs that suit you.
b. employers want to know that you are in good mental health.
c. job applications generally ask personal questions.
d. study skills are important for most jobs that interest college graduates.

b ______ 8. Which of the following is *not* a career path identified in the selection? **(6a)**
a. Government or industrial training programs
b. Home study programs like correspondence courses
c. Apprenticeship programs
d. Programs in trade schools, community colleges, and four-year colleges and universities

c ______ 9. Job changes and career shifts are **(6a)**
a. impossible for most people.
b. not a good idea because they show that you are not responsible.
c. more possible today because society no longer views a career change as a sign of instability.
d. goals that we all should try to achieve.

10. Write *maj* next to major details in the selection and *min* next to minor details in the selection. **(6b)**

maj ______ a. Many students choose from a narrow group of jobs.

min ______ b. Albert Schweitzer was a missionary.

min ______ c. The Free Press published *Decision Making*.

maj ______ d. It is good to write down career goals.

maj ______ e. Making guesses about your future career is useful.

Interpreting and Evaluating

b ______ 1. The writer believes that flaws in decision making are **(8)**
   a. present in only a small part of the general population.
   b. possible to overcome.
   c. impossible to overcome.
   d. useful for choosing the right career.

c ______ 2. From the example that the writer gives of the person who chooses to be a plumber, we can infer that **(8)**
   a. not enough men and women enter mechanical careers.
   b. being married and having children are important parts of every person's career choice.
   c. thinking in advance about possible problems related to career choices helps you address those problems.
   d. the ages between nineteen and twenty-three are the best time to enter most apprenticeship programs.

a ______ 3. About the relation between the number of people each year who enter apprenticeship programs (270,000) and those who complete the programs (60,000), we can conclude that **(10)**
   a. the programs are difficult to complete successfully.
   b. not enough programs are available.
   c. the government should provide more support for these programs.
   d. jobs for which apprenticeship programs prepare you do not pay enough money.

d ______ 4. In regard to professional occupations, we can conclude from the selection that more **(10)**
   a. people should consider them as career options.
   b. community college students should choose them.

c. men are choosing them than are women.
d. people are choosing them than the work force can bear.

c ____ 5. Suppose the person who chose to be a plumber discovers when he or she is thirty that the job no longer is enjoyable. What can you predict that the writer of this selection would recommend? **(10)**
a. Choose a completely different career.
b. Work harder and try to find pleasure that you may not have noticed on the job before.
c. Consider choosing a different but related career.
d. Get married and raise a family.

6. Which of the following generalizations can you draw safely from the selection? Put a checkmark next to your choices. **(11)**

√ ____ a. People have to learn to make important decisions consciously and with careful planning.

√ ____ b. Not everyone is suited for all careers.

____ c. Careful advance planning guarantees job success.

√ ____ d. Try to make important decisions on your own.

____ e. We cannot overcome the effects of chance and fate on our lives.

7. Put an F next to each item that is a fact in the selection. Put an O next to each item that is an opinion. **(12a)**

F ____ a. Albert Schweitzer turned from music to medicine when he was over forty.

O ____ b. It is unusual for a person to start a completely new career in midlife.

O ____ c. The best coping behavior is vigilance.

F ____ d. Military service provides job-training opportunities.

o ______ e. Writing something down helps you think about it more clearly.

Vocabulary

Each sentence below gives good clues to the meaning of words from the selection that you may not have known. Use the sentence clues to write definitions in your own words for the words in italics. Write your definitions on the blank lines. **(1c)**

1. Students who fail to think about the implications of their career choices often engage in *rationalization* (deceiving oneself with self-satisfying but incorrect explanations for one's behavior) or *procrastination* (putting off or delaying). Facing the situation may produce *anxiety*, but examining alternatives could also bring relief.

   Rationalization means **deceiving oneself with incorrect explanations for one's behavior**.

   Procrastination means **to postpone; to delay needlessly**.

   Anxiety means **worry; concern**.

2. Writing something down forces you to *crystallize* your thinking and to recognize fuzzy and half-formed ideas. It may lead to new *insights* about your possibilities.

   Crystallize means **to structure; to give definite form to**.

   Insights means **penetrating glimpses within; inward views**.

3. These *hypotheses*, or educated guesses, should represent your understanding of yourself at present.

Hypotheses means **thoughtful projections of what might happen or be true**.

4. . . . you enter *apprenticeship* training to be a plumber or pipe fitter. But you guess that being accepted as an apprentice plumber might be one problem.

   Apprenticeship means **learning a trade or occupation**.

5. Many large companies hire workers at the lowest level and advance them as they gain *seniority* (years of service) and skill.

   Seniority means **older or higher in rank**.

6. . . . decisions, once made, affect *subsequent* decisions.

   Subsequent means **following in time or order**.

7. Nobody can *foresee* what the future holds for any of us.

   Foresee means **to see or know beforehand**.

WRITING PRACTICE

1. Write a one-paragraph summary of the six keys to career planning presented in this selection.
2. Using what you learned from this selection, think about your own career possibilities. Write a paragraph or two in which you name some careers that interest you and explain why they interest you.

9

My Father's Song

Simon J. Ortiz

In this poem a Native American of the Acoma Pueblo of New Mexico remembers his father and a special moment they shared. What are the poet's feelings for his father?

Prereading

Before you read, freewrite on a special moment you shared with your father, your uncle or grandfather, or some other adult male when you were a child. **[3a(3)]**

Wanting to say things,
I miss my father tonight.
His voice, the slight catch,
the depth from his thin chest,
the tremble of emotion
in something he has just said
to his son, his song:

We planted corn one Spring at Acu —
we planted several times
but this one particular time
I remember the soft damp sand
in my hand.

My father had stopped at one point
to show me an overturned furrow;
the plowshare had unearthed
the burrow nest of a mouse
in the soft moist sand.

Very gently, he scooped tiny pink animals
into the palm of his hand

and told me to touch them.
We took them to the edge
of the field and put them in the shade
of a sand moist clod.

I remember the very softness
of cool and warm sand and tiny alive mice
and my father saying things. ❑

EXERCISES

Understanding What You Have Read

b 1. The main idea of this poem is that the **(5)**
   a. father showed his son some animals.
   b. son misses his father.
   c. father had a memorable voice.
   d. son helped the father plant crops.

d 2. The incident in the poem was the time that the father and son **(6a)**
   a. talked together.
   b. planted corn together.
   c. looked at animals together.
   d. discovered a mouse burrow together.

a 3. The poem begins **(7a)**
   a. in the present.
   b. when the poet was a child.
   c. during planting season.
   d. at the earliest part of the story.

b 4. The poet **(6a)**
   a. hears his father's voice next to him.
   b. misses his father's voice.
   c. does not remember his father's voice.
   d. never paid attention to his father's words.

a 5. The memory of the father's voice **(6a)**
   a. brings back the memory of a particular incident.
   b. makes the poet sad.

c. is the only thing the poet can remember about his father.
d. quickly becomes lost to the poet.

b ______ 6. The middle of the poem takes place **(7a)**
a. in the present.
b. when the poet was a child.
c. before the poet could remember.
d. during the last planting season.

b ______ 7. The father found a mouse burrow **(6a)**
a. in the grass where he was walking.
b. in the ground where he was plowing.
c. in the shade where he was resting.
d. by the warmth of the ground.

d ______ 8. The father **(6a)**
a. left the mice alone.
b. disturbed the mice unnecessarily.
c. kept the mice.
d. showed the mice to his son and then protected them.

a ______ 9. The poem ends **(7a)**
a. in the present as the poet remembers.
b. when the poet was a child.
c. at the earliest part of the story.
d. with the poet standing in the fields.

d ______ 10. The details of sand, furrow, burrow, mouse, father's hand, and voice are arranged in **(7a)**
a. time order.
b. space order.
c. order of importance.
d. All of the above

d ______ 11. The effect of the ordering of details discussed in question 10 is to **(12d)**
a. show the reader what happened.
b. increase the sense of life gradually.
c. move the reader into the father's spirit.
d. All of the above

Interpreting and Evaluating

c

1. We can infer from the details about the father's voice that his voice was **(8)**
   a. hard to remember.
   b. frightening and powerful.
   c. gentle and filled with emotion.
   d. joyful and energetic.

d

2. We can infer from the fact that the father stopped plowing when he reached the burrow that he **(8)**
   a. was irritated to find an animal nest blocking his way.
   b. was tired and wanted a break.
   c. needed to warn his son about destroying wildlife.
   d. wanted to protect the animals.

a

3. We can infer from the fact that the father showed the mice to his son and had his son touch them that the **(8)**
   a. father wanted his son to appreciate life.
   b. son was asking many questions about what the father was doing.
   c. mice needed to be calmed.
   d. mice were old enough to know what was happening to them.

a

4. We can infer from the details of the poem that the mice they found were **(8)**
   a. babies.
   b. sick.
   c. full grown.
   d. frightened.

5. What details did you use to infer the answer to question 4?

   "burrow nest"; "tiny pink animals";

   "tiny alive mice"

d

6. We can infer from the fact that the poet does not tell us the exact words his father said that **(8)**

a. he does not remember the point of what his father said.
b. he never paid much attention to what his father said.
c. the father said strange and secret things that should not be repeated.
d. the feeling of the father's voice, not his words, are more important to this memory.

b ______ 7. We can conclude that the son feels his father **(10)**
a. did not tell him much that he can remember.
b. taught him important things about life.
c. was not with him often enough.
d. was an excellent farmer.

8. How does the way the father treats the mice compare to how the son feels about his father? **(9)**

The father is gentle with him; he is compassionate and kind.

a ______ 9. The poem's style is **(12d)**
a. simple and descriptive.
b. filled with complex symbols.
c. like the style of a newspaper story.
d. filled with unusual ethnic words and thoughts.

c ______ 10. The poem's mood can be described as **(12d)**
a. sad and depressed.
b. respectful and proper.
c. gently emotional.
d. dramatically emotional.

Vocabulary (1, 2)

d ______ 1. From context clues you can tell that *Acu* is
a. the name of a holiday.
b. a kind of corn.
c. a time of day.
d. the name of a place.

2. Put the letter of the definition in the right-hand column next to the appropriate word in the left-hand column.

d 1. furrow

a 2. plowshare

e 3. unearthed

c 4. burrow

b 5. clod

a. a tool for preparing the ground for planting
b. a ball of earth
c. an underground animal nest
d. a plowed trench for planting
e. exposed from the ground

3. In this poem each of the following words has a special meaning in relation to the father's voice. Explain in your own words the meaning of these words as used in the poem. **Student responses will vary.**

a. catch **slight sob**

b. depth **full; with much meaning**

c. tremble **shaking**

WRITING PRACTICE

1. Write a paragraph discussing what you think the father's song (line 7) is in the poem and what it means to the poet.
2. Write approximately a page describing a memory of a special moment you shared with a parent or another adult when you were young.

10

Organizing Labor

Thomas V. DiBacco
Lorna C. Mason
Christian G. Appy

As America's industries developed in the nineteenth century, America's labor unions grew strong. This selection from a history text traces the expansion of the labor movement. What attraction did unions have for workers after the Civil War?

Skimming

Before reading the selection, skim it to answer the following questions. **(3b)**

1. What two major questions does the selection intend to answer?

   1. How did American unions change after the Civil War? 2. What were some important unions in the late 1800s?

2. What are the four stages of the business cycle?

   expansion; recession; depression; recovery

3. What were the major unions formed in the late 1800s?

   National Labor Union (1866); Knights of Labor (1869);

American Federation of Labor (1886)

4. What led indirectly to the Haymarket Riot?

a strike by the Knights of Labor at Chicago's McCormick-Harvester plant

Word Highlights

monotonous (¶2) boring
recruited (¶2) supplied with new members
incentive (¶3) motivation; reason to act
fatigue (¶5) tiredness
laissez-faire (¶6) the idea that government should not interfere with business
baron (¶14) here, someone with great power in an area of business
atheistic (¶18) not believing in God
fatal (¶20) leading to death
sweeping (¶21) wide ranging; extensive
tactic (¶24) plan; strategy
devote (¶25) give one's energy and time entirely to a single activity

The growth of industry in the post–Civil War era produced evolutionary changes in the American economy and thus in American society. Government, at first, could not keep pace with these changes. As a result, workers and farmers formed organizations to defend their interests. At the same time, they pressured government to play a more active role in the economic life of the country. While their efforts never fully succeeded, they paved the way for new government policies in the early 1900s.

Growth of Unions

2 Unions had been on the American scene since the late 1700s. The early unions were small, local organizations made up of skilled workers — tailors, carpenters, weavers, and so on. The building of factories brought into the work force many unskilled workers, who performed simple, monotonous chores that required little or no training. But few early unions recruited unskilled workers. In fact, the skilled workers regarded unskilled workers as rivals because they worked for lower wages. Partly because of this lack of worker unity, the early unions were not strong enough to survive the Panic of 1837.

3 Not until after the Civil War did the labor movement again gather strength. A number of factors led to this revival. Most important was the need to bargain effectively with employers. The growth of industry produced a tremendous expansion in the labor force. Millions of new workers — immigrants, farmers, women — entered the factories. Skilled workers forced out of business by machine-made goods also took factory jobs. Factory owners, meanwhile, knew that they could easily replace any workers who quit. Thus they had no incentive to raise wages or improve working conditions. As one cap maker explained:

> 4 We were helpless; no one girl dared stand up for anything alone. Matters kept getting worse. The bosses kept making reductions in our pay. . . . One girl would say that she didn't think she could make caps for the new price, but another would say that she thought she could make up for the reduction by working a little harder, and then the first would tell herself: "If she can do it, why can't I?"

5 Even those who worked long and hard without complaint had no guarantees of long-term economic security. Laboring day after day at breakneck speed, factory workers suffered from fatigue and accidents. Between 1880 and 1900, accidents killed an average of five people each day.

6 Economic slumps also threatened the well-being of workers. In the 1800s, as today, the national economy operated according to the business cycle. A period of prosperity would be followed by hard times, a pattern sometimes called "boom and bust." In 1873 and 1893 the economy fell into a depression — a time of high unemployment, low consumer spending,

This early photograph of a factory shows workers painting mowing-machine frames by hand.

THE BUSINESS CYCLE

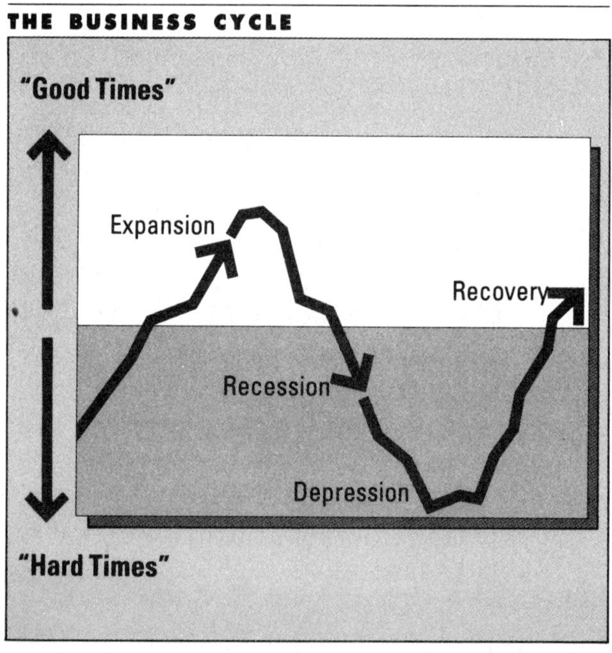

This diagram outlines the phases of the business cycle. Economic changes, however, are not as regular as the diagram suggests.

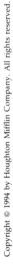

and many business failures. There were also recessions, milder economic downturns. Today government is expected to take action to lessen the swings of the cycle — pumping up a sluggish economy or slowing an overheated one. But in the 1800s, the government's laissez-faire approach rejected these kinds of policies. Companies reacted to the economic slumps by cutting wages and firing workers, and government provided little help.

7 Unions offered workers a chance to join forces against the threats to their security. Some unions, eager to increase membership, began admitting the many new unskilled workers. They also tried to combine local unions into large national organizations. Only by gaining size and strength, union leaders realized, could they hope to compete with the growing size and strength of industry. For unions, as for industry, this was an era of "bigness."

The National Labor Union

8 The first American union to unite skilled and unskilled workers was the National Labor Union (NLU). It was founded in 1866 by William Sylvis, a former head of the iron-molders union in Philadelphia. Sylvis was a dedicated leader. "I love this union cause," he once remarked. "I hold it more dear than I do my family or my life. I am willing to devote to it all that I am or have or hope for in this world." Within five years the NLU boasted a membership of 600,000. It included people who were not industrial laborers, such as farmers.

9 Sylvis saw the NLU as a broad-based popular movement. He believed that it should work to improve the lives of average Americans. Rather than confront employers with strikes, the NLU urged workers to become more self-sufficient by forming cooperatives — businesses owned and run by the workers themselves. Because these businesses would aim at breaking even, not making a profit, they would be able to charge workers lower prices.

10 The NLU also looked to government for help. Arguing that Chinese immigrants were taking jobs from native-born American workers, the NLU pushed Congress for a ban on Chinese immigration. (One was passed in 1882.) The union urged Congress to pass legislation setting an eight-hour limit to the work day. Finally, the NLU entered politics as an independent party. In 1872 it became the National Labor Reform Party and nomi-

nated a candidate for President. But the party received only two electoral votes in the election won easily by Ulysses S. Grant. Its membership and influence quickly faded.

The Knights of Labor

11 Already, however, there was a competing union. This was the Noble and Holy Order of the Knights of Labor, founded in 1869 by Uriah S. Stephens. The Knights of Labor began as a secret society. It had a special initiation ceremony and a secret password and handshake. The aims of the Knights were high-sounding:

12 > To secure to the toilers [workers] a proper share of the wealth that they create; more of the leisure that rightfully belongs to them; more societary advantages; more of the benefits, privileges, and emoluments [profits] of the world; in a word, all those rights and privileges necessary to make them capable of enjoying, appreciating, defending, and perpetuating the blessings of good government.

13 Like the NLU, the Knights pinned their hopes on political action rather than strikes. Their political platform called for an end to child labor and for public ownership of railroads and telegraph lines. The Knights shared the NLU's goals of eight-hour work days and worker cooperatives. In fact, the union set up some 100 cooperatives, including a coal mine and a shoe-making plant. Most failed because of a lack of money or poor business decisions.

14 Membership in the Knights of Labor remained small until 1879, when Terence V. Powderly took over. Powderly reversed the union's emphasis on secrecy and recruited thousands of new members. These included many blacks — one-tenth of the total members by 1886. Thousands of women also joined the union, some rising to leadership positions. For example, Elizabeth Flynn Rogers, a housewife and mother of twelve children, headed the Chicago branch of the union. The Knights attracted even more workers when some of its members struck against railroad baron Jay Gould in 1885 and won. Soon after the 1885 strike, the Knights were 700,000 strong.

The Haymarket Riot

15 At first the Knights of Labor profited from strikes. But the union was losing control of its members. Union leaders did

WASON MANUFACTURING COMPANY OF SPRINGFIELD, MASS.
RAILWAY CAR BUILDERS.
CAR WHEELS AND GENERAL RAILWAY WORK.

Throughout the 1800s, factories became increasingly frequent sights in the Northeast. Rivers provided their power. This print from 1872 shows a railroad car factory on the Connecticut River near Springfield, Massachusetts.

not dare criticize the strikers publicly for fear of splintering the union. They worried, however, that if their members became too radical, public opinion would swing against the union. That is exactly what happened.

16 On May 1, 1886, some Knights and other workers in Chicago went on strike in support of the eight-hour work day. Anarchists — people who oppose all forms of government — supported the strikers, hoping to take advantage of the rising tension. On May 3, police clashed with strikers at the McCormick-Harvester works. One striker was killed. The next day a demonstration was held in Haymarket Square to protest the violence.

17 The demonstration began as a typical rally: pamphlets were handed out and speeches were made. As a cold rain began to fall, 200 police officers arrived on the scene, sent there to break up the group. Suddenly a bomb exploded in the police ranks. The police fired into the crowd. Seven police officers and four workers died, and more than a hundred people were injured. Eight of the demonstrators were immediately arrested and charged with murder.

18 The public outcry was swift. *The Washington Post* argued that the defendants were a "horde of foreigners, representing

Terence Powderly (1849–1924), who worked as a machinist, joined the Knights of Labor in 1874. Five years later he became its Grand Master Workman. Powderly dreamed of a labor force in which "each man is his own employer." While many unions focused on such immediate demands as better wages and shorter hours, Powderly tried to promote more fundamental social changes. Powderly appears at right surrounded by other leaders of the Knights of Labor, including Uriah Stephens (top) and Samuel Gompers (left side, third from bottom).

almost the lowest stratum [level] found in humanity." *The Albany Law Journal* went even further, calling them "long-haired, wild-eyed, bad-smelling, atheistic, reckless foreign wretches who never did an honest hour's work in their lives."

19 Public opinion sealed the fate of the defendants. The prosecutor could not prove that any of them had actually thrown the bomb. Six of them, in fact, had not even been in Haymarket Square on May 4. No matter. All eight were convicted of conspiracy to kill a police officer. Four were hanged, another com-

This engraving of the 1886 Haymarket Riot appeared in *Harper's* magazine. A strike by the Knights of Labor at Chicago's McCormick-Harvester plant led indirectly to the riot. Most Americans blamed the violence on the labor movement.

mitted suicide, and the remaining three received long prison sentences. The governor of Illinois pardoned the surviving prisoners several years later, claiming they had not received a fair trial.

20 The Haymarket Riot dealt a fatal blow to the Knights of Labor. Powderly tried to distance the union from the violence. He declared that "Honest labor is not to be found in the ranks of those who march under the red flag of anarchy, which is the emblem of blood and destruction." Yet the public now linked the union with anarchists. Membership dropped sharply, and by the 1890s the union had all but disappeared.

The American Federation of Labor

21 The NLU and the Knights of Labor had followed the same basic strategy. This was to unite skilled and unskilled workers into one giant union, then to demand broad reforms from government. The failure of the NLU and the radicalism of the Knights led many in the union movement to abandon this strategy. Unskilled workers, many felt, weakened a union be-

cause an employer could easily replace them in the event of a strike. Unions should therefore include only skilled workers. Some union leaders also decided that unions should not try to push for sweeping social change. Instead, unions should bargain directly with employers and limit their demands to concrete issues such as wages. An organization that followed this new approach was the American Federation of Labor (AFL).

22 The AFL was founded in 1886. Samuel Gompers, a cigarmaker, was elected president; Peter J. McGuire, a carpenter, became secretary. Both men had colorful backgrounds. In 1863 Gompers had come to New York City from England at age 13. He got a job rolling cigars, and listened as other workers discussed ways to improve conditions. Some called on workers to take over industries from the owners. Others wanted government to take over industries. Gompers rejected these ideas as unrealistic. Unions, in his view, should work within the existing system, gaining improved conditions by bargaining with their employers.

23 McGuire had grown up in the East in the years after the Civil War. The son of Irish immigrants, he was forced to start working at age 11. He held almost every kind of job during his early years — except, he later joked, that of a sword swallower. "And sometimes," he said, "I was so hungry, a sword — with mustard, of course — would have tasted fine." McGuire finally found his trade as a carpenter and helped to set up the United Brotherhood of Carpenters in 1881.

24 Both Gompers and McGuire believed that only skilled unions joined together in a national federation could deal with employers. These unions would push for the establishment of a closed shop, meaning that the employer would agree to hire only union workers. The union's tactic would be collective bargaining — direct talks between organized workers and their employer. If the unions failed to gain their goals through collective bargaining, then they would use the strike. When Gompers was asked to summarize the philosophy of the AFL, he said, "More."

25 The AFL set up rules for its member unions. Each union was expected to admit only those workers who had gone through training to learn their skills. Unskilled workers, blacks, women, and recent immigrants were not allowed to join. Workers paid regular dues to their union so that the union would have money on hand to aid workers on strike. Unions

were always reminded to devote their energy to reasonable, concrete goals.

26 The AFL grew steadily, becoming the nation's largest union. Its membership jumped from fewer than 200,000 in 1886 to 1,750,000 eighteen years later. However, that figure accounted for only a small fraction of the total number of industrial workers in the United States. The majority of industrial workers were unskilled and did not belong to any union. The American labor movement still had a long way to go. ❑

EXERCISES

Understanding What You Have Read

c ______ 1. What is the topic of this selection? **(5b)**
   a. The Haymarket Riot
   b. Labor unions in America
   c. How American labor unions grew
   d. How the AFL attracted skilled workers as members

2. In your own words write the main idea of the selection. **(5b) Student responses will vary.**

   In the late 1800s the labor movement gathered strength as workers unhappy with job conditions began to organize and join new unions.

3. In your own words write the key idea of the first sentence of paragraph 1. **(5a) Student responses will vary.**

   Industrial growth produced dramatic changes in this country's economy and society.

b ______ 4. Unions have been on the American scene since the **(6a)**
   a. end of the Civil War.
   b. late 1700s.
   c. Panic of 1837.
   d. American Revolution.

d ______ 5. Which of the following reasons best explains the growth in labor unions after the Civil War? **(6a)**
   a. Skilled workers forced out of jobs by machine-made goods
   b. The entry into the job market of former slaves
   c. A tremendous expansion of the labor force
   d. The need for workers to bargain with their employers

a ______ 6. The graph on the business cycle (page 444) shows that **(4e)**
   a. expansion is followed by recession, depression, and then recovery.
   b. after economic recovery, recression usually leads to depression.
   c. expansion and recovery ultimately lead to hard times.
   d. in good times, a recession is followed quickly by recovery.

d ______ 7. Union leaders wanted to gain size and strength for their organizations so that the unions could **(6a)**
   a. earn more money for the leaders.
   b. admit unskilled workers.
   c. combine local groups into national organizations.
   d. compete with industry's growing size and strength.

c ______ 8. In the United States, skilled and unskilled workers first united under the **(6a)**
   a. Knights of Labor.
   b. American Federation of Labor.
   c. National Labor Union.
   d. National Labor Reform party.

b ______ 9. By the 1890s, the Knights of Labor had just about vanished because **(6a)**
   a. members now preferred the skilled workers' union established by Gompers, the American Federation of Labor.
   b. the public's association of the union with anarchists sharply reduced membership.
   c. Terence Powderly supported the violence that led to the Haymarket Riot.
   d. All of the above

10. Write *maj* next to major details in the selection and *min* next to minor details. **(6b)**

maj ______ a. Samuel Gompers founded the AFL in 1886.

maj ______ b. The AFL became the nation's largest union.

min ______ c. Gompers worked as a cigar roller at the age of thirteen.

maj ______ d. The NLU urged members to become more self-sufficient by forming cooperatives.

min ______ e. Elizabeth Flynn Rogers of the Knights of Labor had twelve children.

maj ______ f. The defendants in the Haymarket Riot case were convicted of conspiracy to kill a police officer.

maj ______ g. Gompers and McGuire believed that if unions could not achieve their goals, they should strike.

min ______ h. Union members handed out pamphlets before the Haymarket Riot began.

Interpreting and Evaluating

a ______ 1. We can infer from the engraving on page 449 that the artist had **(4, 8)**
   a. more sympathy for the police than for the rioters.
   b. more sympathy for the rioters than for the police.
   c. most sympathy for the owners of the McCormick-Harvester plant.
   d. no particular sympathy for one group over another.

c ______ 2. If we assume a six-day work week between 1880 and 1900, how many workers were killed in factory accidents each week? **(8)**
   a. 5
   b. 1,900
   c. 30
   d. 60

b ______ 3. We can infer that after the Civil War, carpenters and tailors **(8)**

a. were in great demand.
b. could not earn a living at their trades.
c. went on strike against factory workers.
d. refused to join small, local unions.

c ______ 4. We may conclude that the authors provided a quote from a cap maker (paragraph 4) to show **(10)**
a. that cap makers were more important to the labor movement than most other factory workers.
b. that many unskilled workers resisted joining unions in the early days of the labor movement.
c. the pressures needing a job imposed on the workers themselves.
d. that cap makers hated their bosses.

d ______ 5. From the print of the 1872 railroad car factory and the caption (page 447), we can safely conclude that the town of Springfield **(10)**
a. opposed having a manufacturing plant so close to town.
b. developed procedures for purifying polluted waters.
c. produced all of America's railroad cars for the great expansion of the railroads in the nineteenth century.
d. was able to supply many workers to the factory because the town was close by.

b ______ 6. From the Haymarket Riot we can generalize that **(11)**
a. union organizers were often anarchists.
b. public sentiment sometimes cannot be changed even in light of facts.
c. police often stimulate the very riots they are sent to control.
d. union demonstrations invariably turn violent.

a ______ 7. The statements from the *Washington Post* and the *Albany Law Journal* are examples of **(12)**
a. opinions.
b. facts.
c. evidence.
d. propaganda.

c ______ 8. We can safely conclude that the success of the AFL, which is still powerful today, is mainly a result of **(10)**
a. the American workers' basic need to form and join unions.
b. the greed of factory owners.
c. its focus on skilled workers and on bargaining directly with employers on work issues.
d. its devotion to politics and to sweeping social change.

b ______ 9. We can conclude that a Chinese worker who wanted to join the National Labor Union would **(10)**
a. be offered a position of leadership in the union.
b. not be welcomed into the union.
c. be forced to work less than an eight-hour day.
d. be asked to work for the National Labor Reform party.

10. Before each of the following statements from the selection, write F if the statement is a fact and O if the statement is an opinion. **(12a)**

O ______ a. The growth of industry produced revolutionary changes in the American economy.

F ______ b. In 1873 and again in 1893 the economy fell into a depression.

F ______ c. The NLU was founded by William Sylvis in 1866.

F ______ d. A ban on Chinese immigration was passed in 1882.

O ______ e. The aims of the Knights of Labor were high-sounding.

O ______ f. The public outcry about the Haymarket Riot was swift.

O ______ g. The Haymarket Riot dealt a fatal blow to the Knights of Labor.

F ______ h. Unions, in Gompers' view, should work within the existing system.

F ______ i. Unskilled workers, blacks, women, and recent immigrants were not allowed to join the newly formed AFL.

Vocabulary

Context clues in the selection help define all the words below. Check back in the selection to determine the meaning of each term and write a definition in your own words in the space provided. Do not use a dictionary. **(1, 2) Student responses will vary.**

1. business cycle **a period of prosperity followed by hard times**
2. boom and bust **the business cycle pattern of prosperity followed by hard times**
3. depression **a period of high unemployment, low consumer spending, and business failures**
4. recessions **mild economic downturns**
5. sluggish **inactive; lazy**
6. cooperatives **businesses owned and run by workers themselves**
7. anarchists **people who oppose all forms of government**
8. stratum **level**
9. closed shop **work environment in which only union members are hired**
10. collective bargaining **direct talks between workers and employers**

WRITING PRACTICE

1. Imagine yourself at the Haymarket Riot as either a police officer or a union demonstrator. Now write a journal entry about your experience during the riot. What did you see? How did you feel? What did you do?
2. Many people argue that unions are vital to protect America's work force; others argue that workers have won so many benefits that unions are no longer necessary. With which position do you agree? Write several paragraphs expressing your views.

11

The Struggle to Be an All American Girl

Elizabeth Wong

A woman looks back on her childhood and on the way the culture into which she was born seemed to disturb her efforts to be an American. Read to discover the complexity of her feelings then and now.

Prereading

Before you read, freewrite on what you think it would be like to live with your family in a culture different from your own. **[3a(3)]**

Word Highlights

stoically (¶1) in a manner unaffected by joy, grief, pleasure, or pain
stern (¶3) severe in appearance; inflexible
repressed (¶3) held back; secret
kowtow (¶6) a Chinese greeting in which one touches the forehead to the ground to express respect
phonetic (¶6) representing speech sounds with symbols, each of which stands for a separate sound
fragile (¶8) frail
raunchy (¶8) slang for "indecent"or "obscene"
pidgin (¶10) a mixture of two or more languages
smatterings (¶10) fragmented, superficial knowledge; bits of information
Cinco de Mayo (¶13) Mexican Independence Day

It's still there, the Chinese school on Yale Street where my brother and I used to go. Despite the new coat of paint and the high wire fence, the school I knew 10 years ago remains remarkably, stoically the same.

2 Every day at 5 P.M., instead of playing with our fourth- and fifth-grade friends or sneaking out to the empty lot to hunt ghosts and animal bones, my brother and I had to go to Chinese School. No amount of kicking, screaming, or pleading could dissuade my mother, who was solidly determined to have us learn the language of our heritage.

3 Forcibly, she walked us the seven long, hilly blocks from our home to school, depositing our defiant tearful faces before the stern principal. My only memory of him is that he swayed on his heels like a palm tree, and he always clasped his impatient twitching hands behind his back. I recognized him as a repressed maniacal child killer, and knew that if we ever saw his hands we'd be in big trouble.

4 We all sat in little chairs in an empty auditorium. The room smelled like Chinese medicine, an imported faraway mustiness. Like ancient mothballs or dirty closets. I hated that smell. I favored crisp new scents. Like the soft French perfume that my American teacher wore in public school.

5 There was a stage far to the right, flanked by an American flag and the flag of the Nationalist Republic of China, which was also red, white and blue but not as pretty.

6 Although the emphasis at the school was mainly language — speaking, reading, writing — the lessons always began with an exercise in politeness. With the entrance of the teacher, the best student would tap a bell and everyone would get up, kowtow, and chant, "Sing san ho," the phonetic for "How are you, teacher?"

7 Being ten years old, I had better things to learn than ideographs copied painstakingly in lines that ran right to left from the tip of a *moc but,* a real ink pen that had to be held in an awkward way if blotches were to be avoided. After all, I could do the multiplication tables, name the satellites of Mars, and write reports on "Little Women" and "Black Beauty." Nancy Drew, my favorite book heroine, never spoke Chinese.

8 The language was a source of embarrassment. More times than not, I had tried to disassociate myself from the nagging loud voice that followed me wherever I wandered in the nearby

American supermarket outside Chinatown. The voice belonged to my grandmother, a fragile woman in her seventies who could outshout the best of the street vendors. Her humor was raunchy, her Chinese rhythmless, patternless. It was quick, it was loud, it was unbeautiful. It was not like the quiet, lilting romance of French or the gentle refinement of the American South. Chinese sounded pedestrian. Public.

9 In Chinatown, the comings and goings of hundreds of Chinese on their daily tasks sounded chaotic and frenzied. I did not want to be thought of as mad, as talking gibberish. When I spoke English, people nodded at me, smiled sweetly, said encouraging words. Even the people in my culture would cluck and say that I'd do well in life. "My, doesn't she move her lips fast," they would say, meaning that I'd be able to keep up with the world outside Chinatown.

10 My brother was even more fanatical than I about speaking English. He was especially hard on my mother, criticizing her, often cruelly, for her pidgin speech — smatterings of Chinese scattered like chop suey in her conversation. "It's not 'What it is,' Mom," he'd say in exasperation. "It's 'What *is* it, what *is* it, what *is* it'!" Sometimes Mom might leave out an occasional "the" or "a," or perhaps a verb of being. He would stop her in midsentence: "Say it again, Mom. Say it right." When he tripped over his own tongue, he'd blame it on her: "See, Mom, it's all your fault. You set a bad example."

11 What infuriated my mother most was when my brother cornered her on her consonants, especially "r." My father had played a cruel joke on Mom by assigning her an American name that her tongue wouldn't allow her to say. No matter how hard she tried, "Ruth" always ended up "Luth" or "Roof."

12 After two years of writing with a *moc but* and reciting words with multiples of meanings, I finally was granted a cultural divorce. I was permitted to stop Chinese school.

13 I thought of myself as multicultural. I preferred tacos to egg rolls; I enjoyed Cinco de Mayo more than Chinese New Year.

14 At last, I was one of you; I wasn't one of them.

15 Sadly, I still am. ❑

EXERCISES

Understanding What You Have Read

d _____ 1. The main idea of this selection is to show **(5b)**
a. the course of study at a Chinese school in America.
b. how Chinese families fight about the correct pronunciation of words.
c. the pressures on Nationalist Chinese who emigrate to America.
d. how a Chinese girl's desire to be an American won out over her family's interest in her studying her Chinese heritage.

a _____ 2. The children kicked and screamed because they **(6a)**
a. did not want to go to Chinese school at all.
b. did not like going to Chinese school so late in the day.
c. didn't like the long walk to the schoolhouse.
d. were scared of the ghosts in the empty lot.

c _____ 3. A *moc but* is a(n) **(1c)**
a. phonetic sentence for "How are you, teacher?"
b. ideograph.
c. pen that blotches easily.
d. copy pad.

d _____ 4. In Chinese school the children learned **(6a)**
a. reading and speaking skills.
b. how to use a special pen to draw ideographs.
c. lessons in politeness.
d. all of the above.

b _____ 5. The school the author attended ten years ago **(6a)**
a. is exactly the same now as it was then.
b. is pretty much the same now as it was then.
c. is no longer standing.
d. was moved to Yale Street.

d _____ 6. By *cultural divorce* the author means that she **(1, 9)**
a. separated from her American husband.
b. left her Chinese family.

c. no longer visited Chinatown.
d. stopped taking instruction in Chinese culture.

d
______ 7. The author did not like the sound of the Chinese language because it **(6a)**
a. was spoken too softly.
b. sounded too much like French.
c. was too rhythmical.
d. was not slow, soft, or beautiful.

Interpreting and Evaluating

d
______ 1. An example of a figurative expression is **(9)**
a. "he swayed on his heels like a palm tree."
b. "the room smelled like Chinese medicine, an imported faraway mustiness."
c. "smatterings of Chinese scattered like chop suey in her conversation."
d. All of the above

d
______ 2. We can safely infer that the empty lot **(8)**
a. had been a Chinese graveyard.
b. was just outside the high wire fence beyond the school.
c. was a fenced-in area that the writer's parents encouraged the children to visit.
d. was a place where the children liked to play after school.

c
______ 3. We can conclude that the writer believed the American flag was more attractive than the flag of the Nationalist Republic of China because **(10)**
a. the Chinese flag needed more color.
b. the American flag stood taller on the stage.
c. she preferred American things to Chinese things.
d. the principal preferred the Chinese flag.

b
______ 4. We can infer that the child who tapped the bell at the teacher's arrival received the job **(8)**
a. as a punishment.
b. as a reward for excellence.
c. because she or he was the principal's pet.
d. because she or he drew the best ideographs.

c 5. In all probability, the writer's grandmother was an embarrassment because she **(8)**
   a. spoke no French.
   b. did not know how to deal with street vendors.
   c. spoke Chinese.
   d. had no sense of humor.

b 6. We can safely infer that the writer's mother **(8)**
   a. preferred her daughter's name to her own.
   b. had no say in the choice of her American name.
   c. joked about her American name.
   d. was pleased that her husband chose the name Ruth for her.

c 7. From the last two lines, we can conclude that the writer **(10)**
   a. now hates American ways.
   b. wishes she were really "one of you."
   c. regrets becoming so Americanized.
   d. now prefers the Chinese New Year to Cinco de Mayo.

d 8. If she had a child of her own, we can safely assume that the writer **(10)**
   a. would not send the child to Chinese school.
   b. would not send the child to American school.
   c. might not send the child to American school.
   d. might send the child to Chinese school.

d 9. A generalization with which the writer would probably agree is that **(11)**
   a. to become completely a part of another person's culture is an important goal.
   b. a person should not try to become part of another culture.
   c. intermarriage between Chinese Americans and Americans who are not Chinese is not a good idea.
   d. becoming part of another culture should not mean giving up one's own culture completely.

b 10. A generalization with which the writer would probably *not* agree is that **(11)**

a. children's wishes should not be observed fully in regard to educational choices.
b. a wrong choice made in childhood is easy to correct in adulthood.
c. children often put pressure on their parents to make choices that are not always in the children's best interests.
d. children of Chinese parents like to play the way other children play.

Vocabulary

Using sentence clues from the selection, determine the meanings of the words in italics in the following groups. Then select the most appropriate choice given below the words and write your answer in the space provided. Do not use a dictionary. **(1c)**

c ______ 1. the language of our *heritage*
a. parents
b. friends and neighbors
c. tradition and legacy
d. old folks

a ______ 2. could *dissuade* my mother
a. discourage
b. encourage
c. anger
d. help

b ______ 3. our *defiant* tearful faces
a. dirty
b. resistant to authority
c. pleading
d. silly

a ______ 4. ideographs copied *painstakingly*
a. with extreme care
b. with great suffering
c. full of complaints
d. weakly

b ______ 5. the quiet, *lilting* romance of French

a. loving
b. full of gentle melody
c. loud
d. adventurous

d 6. Chinese sounded *pedestrian*
a. a person traveling on foot
b. boring
c. terrible
d. ordinary

b 7. chaotic and *frenzied*
a. lazy
b. frantic
c. friendly
d. fearful

d 8. as talking *gibberish*
a. too loud
b. insanely
c. childishly
d. nonsense

c 9. more *fanatical* than I about speaking English
a. interested
b. uninterested
c. overly enthusiastic
d. unsure

b 10. what *infuriated* my mother
a. interested
b. angered
c. impressed
d. amused

Use word-part clues to determine the meanings of the following words. Write your definitions in the space provided. **(1d)**

11. forcibly **effected through force**

12. maniacal **overly enthusiastic; insane; like a maniac**

13. mustiness **moldy odor**

14. ideograph **form of writing that uses symbols that are representations of whole words; idea pictures**

15. chaotic **without order; in a state of chaos**

WRITING PRACTICE

1. Write a paragraph describing how the writer felt as a child about being Chinese.
2. Write a paragraph describing how you felt about your family background as you grew up.

12

An Introduction to Sociology

Richard T. Schaefer

This is an excerpt from a college textbook in sociology, the study of how people behave in society. Read to find out how sociologists think about the behavior of individuals and groups.

Previewing

Before reading the selection, preview it. Then answer these questions: **(3c)**

1. According to the title, what is the selection about?

   an introduction to the study of sociology

2. What would you expect to find in the paragraphs under the first subheading? **a definition of sociology**

   the second subheading? **how sociology fits into social sciences**

Richard T. Schaefer, "An Introduction to Sociology," from *Sociology*. Copyright © 1983 by McGraw-Hill, reprinted by permission.

the last subheading? **how common sense relates to sociology**

3. What do the two captions and the pictures tell you about the content of the selection?

First caption **how filmmaking relates to sociology**

Second caption **sociologists' interests in different groups**

Word Highlights

authenticity (¶2) quality of being real or genuine
spectators (¶3) observers of an event
perspective (¶3) outlook; point of view
dynamics (¶3) forces that create motion and change in any system
alienation (¶5) withdrawal of feelings; emotional isolation
recurring (¶7) happening over and over
remote (¶9) distant; far off
priorities (¶14) orders or ranks by importance
adulation (¶16) adoring attention; almost worship
disintegrates (¶18) falls apart

On a narrow avenue in New York City's "Little Italy" section in the early 1970s, hundreds of men, women, and children stood in long lines, wearing traditional Italian parade costumes. Many carried musical instruments and banners. On the sidewalks, crowds were stuffed behind ropes, with an occasional police officer present to keep them from running into the street. Yet this was no ordinary New York ethnic festival. Instead, director Francis Ford Coppola was filming a scene for *The Godfather: Part Two.*

2 Typically, when movies are shot during the day in the midst of a large city, huge crowds gather to watch. Onlookers often hope to catch a glimpse of a star in "real life." Of course, if a film student viewed the scene, he or she would have very different concerns as an observer. The student would pay special attention to camera angles, to the authenticity of the setting, and to the work of the sound crew.

3 What if a sociologist joined these spectators? He or she would bring a perspective quite unlike that of the average movie fan or film student. The sociologist would see the people working on the film — the director, the stars, the extras, and the crew — as part of a group. As an observer, the sociologist would carefully examine the structure and dynamics of the group — both the apparent work relationships and the social relationships among group members.

4 The sociologist would wonder: "What role does the director (here, Coppola) play in the group? How are responsibilities divided among the director's assistants? How does the crew decide where a camera should be placed? Do stars like Al Pacino and Robert DeNiro interact with other actors and with the crew? How does the group deal with 'outsiders' (the audience on the sidewalks)?" All these questions would be asked by the sociologist while observing the shooting of this movie scene.

What Is Sociology?

5 As we have seen, the sociologist has a distinctive way of examining human interactions. *Sociology* is the systematic study of social behavior and human groups. It focuses primarily on the influence of social relationships and on how societies are established and change. As a field of study, sociology has an extremely broad scope. Therefore, this textbook deals with families, gangs, business firms, political parties, schools, religions, and labor unions. It is concerned with love, poverty, conformity, discrimination, alienation, overpopulation, and community.

6 In American society, newspapers, television, and radio are the usual sources of information about such groups and problems. However, while the basic function of journalists is to report the news, sociologists bring a different type of understanding to such issues. The perspective of sociology involves

Observing the filming of a motion picture, such as *Hanky Panky* with Gene Wilder and Gilda Radner, allows a sociologist to analyze the roles of various members of the production crew as well as the relationship between the stars of the movie and passersby.

seeing through the outside appearances of people's actions and organizations.

7 One major goal of this perspective is to identify underlying, recurring patterns of and influences on social behavior. Thus, sociologists study the passionate desire of movie fans to see in person, to talk with, even to grab the clothing of a star. Why do people feel this need so powerfully? To what extent does participation in a crowd allow individuals to act more boldly than they otherwise might? Will people gain greater respect from family members and friends if they have shaken hands with Al Pacino and exchanged three sentences of conversation?

8 Importantly, the sociological perspective goes beyond identifying patterns of social behavior; it also attempts to provide explanations for such patterns. Here the focus of sociology on the group becomes a central consideration. Sociologists are not content to look at the individual fan's personality or "unique" reasons for wanting to meet Al Pacino, Jane Fonda, or Richard Pryor. Rather, they recognize that millions of Americans wish to meet movie stars, and they examine the *shared* feelings and behavior of fans within the larger social context of American culture.

9 In attempting to understand social behavior, sociologists rely on an unusual type of creative thinking. C. Wright Mills (1959) described such thinking as the *sociological imagination* — an awareness of the relationship between an individual and the wider society. This awareness allows people (not simply sociologists) to comprehend the links between their immediate, personal social settings and the remote, impersonal social world that surrounds them and helps to shape them.

10 A key element in the sociological imagination is the ability to view one's own society as an outsider, rather than from the limited perspective of personal experiences and cultural biases. Thus, instead of simply accepting the fact that movie stars are the "royalty" of American society, we could ask, in a more critical sense, why this is the case. Conceivably, an outsider unfamiliar with the United States might wonder why we are not as interested in meeting outstanding scientists, or elementary school teachers, or architects. . . .

Sociology and the Social Sciences

11 In a general sense, sociology can be considered a science. Like other scientific disciplines, it engages in organized, systematic study of phenomena (in this case, human behavior) in order to enhance understanding. All scientists, whether studying mushrooms or murderers, attempt to collect precise information through methods of study which are as objective as possible. They rely on careful recording of observations and accumulation of data.

12 Of course, there is a great difference between sociology and physics, between psychology and astronomy. For this reason, the sciences are commonly divided into natural and social sciences. *Natural science* is the study of the physical features of nature and the ways in which they interact and change. Astronomy, biology, chemistry, geology, and physics are all categorized as natural sciences. *Social science* is the study of various aspects of human society. The social sciences include sociology, anthropology, economics, history, psychology, and political science.

13 These academic disciplines share a common focus on the social behavior of individuals, yet each has a particular orientation in studying such behavior. Anthropologists usually study cultures of the past and preindustrial societies that remain in existence today. They use this knowledge to examine contem-

Sociologists use the scientific method to investigate social behavior, whether between parent and child, in a dance performance, or within a crowd.

porary and even industrial societies. Economists explore the ways in which people produce and exchange goods and services, along with money and other resources. Historians are concerned with the peoples and events of the past and their significance for us today. Political scientists study international relations, the workings of government, and the exercise of power and authority. Psychologists investigate personality and individual behavior. In contrast to other social sciences, sociology emphasizes the influence that groups can have on people's behavior and attitudes. Humans are social animals; therefore, sociologists scientifically examine our social relationships with other people.

14 Although social scientists have slightly different priorities, their efforts can overlap in a positive way. Suppose that a city is attempting to provide new housing for the elderly. The city council recognizes the growing need to establish a senior citizens' housing project and decides to consult social scientists for expert assistance. Sociologists, using techniques such as survey and observation research, could provide guidelines as to the types of services and leisure time facilities needed by residents.

15 Psychologists might explore ways of reducing the anxiety and alienation that senior citizens experience when moving to this type of housing. Economists could estimate the short-range and long-term costs of the project for the occupants and for the city. Other useful contributions might be offered by historians, anthropologists, and political scientists. In short, each discipline of social science has expertise that is valuable in developing humane, safe, and reasonably priced housing for the elderly.

Sociology and Common Sense

16 As we have seen, sociology and other social sciences focus on the study of certain aspects of human behavior. Yet human behavior is something about which we all have experience and at least a bit of knowledge. Many of us, even without Ph.D. degrees in the social sciences, could make suggestions about how to best construct a positive environment for a senior citizens' community. All of us might well have theories about why movie stars are the subject of so much attention and adulation. Our theories and suggestions come from our experiences and from a cherished source of wisdom — common sense.

17 In our daily lives, we rely on common sense to get us through many unfamiliar situations. Unfortunately, this source of knowledge is not always reliable. It was once considered "common sense" to accept that the earth was flat — a view rightly questioned by the scientist Galileo. Incorrect common-sense notions are not just a part of the distant past; they remain with us today.

18 In American society, it is common sense to know that, given the unprecedented level of divorces, virtually no first marriages reach their twentieth anniversaries. It is common sense to realize that when a racial minority group moves into a previously all-white neighborhood, property values decline. And it is common sense to know that people panic when faced

with natural disasters, such as floods and earthquakes, with the result that all social organization disintegrates.

19 Interestingly, like the view that the earth is flat, all these commonsense notions are untrue; each has been disproved by sociological research. Three out of four first marriages in the United States celebrate their twentieth wedding anniversaries, while one out of five reach their fiftieth! Race has been found to have no relationship to property values; such factors as zoning changes, overcrowding, and age of housing are more significant. Finally, disasters do not generally produce panic. In the aftermath of natural disasters, *greater* social organization and structure emerge to deal with a community's problems.

20 Like other social scientists, sociologists do not accept something as a fact because "everyone knows it." Instead, each piece of information must be tested and recorded, then analyzed in relationship to other data. Sociology relies on scientific studies in order to describe and understand a social environment. At times, the findings of sociologists may seem like common sense because they deal with facets of everyday life. Yet it is important to stress that such findings have been *tested* by researchers. It is now common sense to know that the earth is round. But this particular commonsense notion is based on centuries of scientific work upholding the breakthrough made by Galileo. ❑

EXERCISES

Understanding What You Have Read

c ______ 1. The main point of this selection is to explain **(5)**
- a. why people enjoy watching famous performers filming a scene for a movie.
- b. the importance of common sense in understanding human behavior.
- c. the meaning of *sociology* and how it compares with other disciplines.
- d. the role of sociologists on film sets like that of *The Godfather*.

b ______ 2. In paragraph 3 the main idea is that sociologists **(5b)**
- a. are like filmmakers.
- b. study the structure and dynamics of a group.

c. enjoy watching films as much as movie fans do.
d. are the major students of filmmaking.

a ______ 3. Which of the following ideas best states the sociologist's perspective? **(6a)**
a. Looking at people's actions in organizations
b. Changing the behavior of people and organizations
c. Explaining why people like movie stars
d. Using mathematics to explain people and groups

a ______ 4. What is the *sociological imagination?* **(6a)**
a. An awareness of the relation between individuals and society
b. The ability to describe social behavior in interesting ways
c. The ability to invent new types of social behavior
d. An awareness of how sociologists think

d ______ 5. Into which large category of study would you place sociology? **(6a)**
a. History
b. Natural science
c. Physical science
d. Social science

c ______ 6. Sociology is similar to other scientific disciplines because of its **(6a)**
a. emphasis on common sense.
b. use of laboratory equipment.
c. reliance on carefully gathered data.
d. interest in group dynamics.

b ______ 7. A sociologist would accept as fact **(6a)**
a. information that everyone knows.
b. only information that has been tested, recorded, and analyzed.
c. anything not related to common sense.
d. anything that C. Wright Mills said.

d ______ 8. The photographs in the selection all show examples of **(4a)**
a. human behavior.
b. parent–child relations.

c. antisocial relations.
d. social behavior.

9. Put a T next to each statement that is true according to the selection and an F next to each statement that is false. **(6a)**

F a. Sociologists are primarily Americans.

T b. Human beings are social animals.

F c. Sociologists try hard to view society from the inside.

F d. Personal experience is the most important part of a sociologist's perspective.

T e. Sociology has practical applications.

F f. Sociologists believe movie stars are the royalty of American society.

10. Put a checkmark next to each statement that has been proved by sociological research. **(6)**

√ a. Three out of four married couples celebrate their twentieth anniversary.

___ b. When minority group members move into an area, property values fall.

___ c. People panic when faced with natural disasters.

___ d. Robert DeNiro is a better actor than Gene Wilder.

√ e. Overcrowding and zoning laws have a significant effect on property values.

___ f. Common sense is never reliable.

11. Write *maj* next to major details from the selection and *min* next to minor details. **(6b)**

min a. Gilda Radner starred in *Hanky Panky*.

maj ______ b. Sociological imagination is an unusual type of creative thinking.

maj ______ c. Common sense once told us that the earth was flat.

maj ______ d. Sociologists use techniques like surveys and observation.

min ______ e. *The Godfather* was filmed in the early 1970s.

Interpreting and Evaluating

a ______ 1. We can infer from the selection that filming a movie scene would **(8)**
   a. be a good subject for sociologists to study.
   b. not be an appropriate subject for sociological study.
   c. be boring for most sociologists, who are busy with their research.
   d. be easier if a sociologist was on the staff to work with the director.

c ______ 2. We can safely assume that sociologists do most of their work **(8)**
   a. in a laboratory.
   b. with computers.
   c. by studying groups close up.
   d. by studying groups through books and other library resources.

c ______ 3. We can infer that the writer thinks that sociologists should choose as their object of study the social behavior of **(8)**
   a. only a small and limited type of group.
   b. families, gangs, business firms, political parties, schools, religions, and labor unions but nothing else.
   c. any human interactions.
   d. whatever group other social scientists are not interested in studying.

4. Which of the following situations do you think would interest a sociologist who was observing a third-grade classroom? Put a checkmark next to your choices. **(10)**

_______ a. The inner thoughts of the children

_______ b. The salary of the teacher

√______ c. How the children relate to one another

√______ d. How the teacher relates to the children

√______ e. The shared feelings of the children toward the teacher

c______ 5. We can conclude from this selection that the author believes sociologists **(10)**
a. are exactly like other researchers.
b. are completely different from other researchers.
c. share some goals and procedures with other researchers but have their own unique perspective.
d. think that the idea that the earth is round needs further testing.

a______ 6. We can conclude that the writer discusses senior citizens' housing because he **(10)**
a. wants to show how social scientists can work together to address different aspects of a problem.
b. wants to show that a sociologist's solution to this problem is the best solution.
c. has deep feelings for the aged in America.
d. believes that city councils should stay out of issues relating to the welfare of urban citizens.

7. What generalizations can we draw from this selection? Put a checkmark next to your choices. **(11)**

√______ a. To understand a group, judge it objectively.

√______ b. Sociologists can help identify the services that special groups require.

_______ c. Some social sciences are inferior to others.

_______ d. Few differences exist among the social sciences.

√______ e. Careful investigation may disprove long-held beliefs.

Vocabulary

1. The words in italics below all have word-part clues that may help you identify meaning. Examine the word in the phrase or sentence in which it appears in the selection. Using sentence clues and word-part clues, try to figure out what the word means. Write the meaning on the lines. Do not use a dictionary. **(1c, 1d)**

   a. huge crowds gather to watch. *Onlookers* often hope to catch a glimpse of a star **people who look on**

   b. distinctive way of examining human *interactions* **actions between**

   c. sociology has an *extremely* broad scope **very**

   d. remote, *impersonal* social world **cold; distant; not having personal reference or connection**

   e. *preindustrial* societies that remain in existence today **before industry**

f. *overlap* in a positive way **cover and extend over**

g. *unprecedented* level of divorces **without former reference to similar events; no preceding instance or case**

h. property values *decline* **go down**

i. such factors as zoning changes, *overcrowding* **exces-sive gathering of people together**

j. *upholding* the breakthrough made by Galileo **sustain-ing; keeping from sinking; supporting**

2. The words in the following list come from the selection. Try to figure out their meanings, using a dictionary when necessary. Then do the crossword puzzle on the next page, filling in the words that best suit the meanings in the clues. **(1, 2)** Finally, copy the circled letters. Rearrange them to spell a word used in sociology.

accumulation
biases
comprehend
contemporary
distinctive
expertise
glimpse
precise
royalty
systematic

[1]ACCUMULATION
[2]CONTEMPORARY
[3]GLIMPSE
[4]BIASES
[5]ROYALTY
[6]PRECISE
[7]SYSTEMATIC
[8]EXPERTISE
[9]COMPREHEND
[10]DISTINCTIVE

Across

1. Collection; gathering together
7. Orderly; regularly; according to a plan
9. Understand
10. Serving to set apart from others

Down

2. Current; at the present time
3. Brief look at something
4. Prejudices; unquestioned beliefs
5. Kings, queens, and their relatives
6. Exact
8. Skill

WRITING PRACTICE

1. Write a summary of the section titled "Sociology and Common Sense."
2. Write a paragraph in which you explain to a group of junior high school students what sociologists do. Take your information from the selection but use your own words. Remember, your readers are a group of young teenagers. Make your paragraph particularly clear and understandable.

13

What Is News?

Alan R. Gitelson
Robert L. Dudley
Melvin J. Dubnick

This selection from a textbook on American government discusses why we receive the news that we do. As you read, decide whether the authors' statements agree with your impression of newspapers and television news.

Skimming

Before reading the selection, skim it to answer the following questions: **(3b)**

1. What is the motto of the *New York Times*?

   "All the News That's Fit to Print"

2. What is the best explanation of what news is?

   "News is what reporters, editors, and producers decide is news."

3. What are the five criteria used most often for selecting news?

   high impact; existence of violence, conflict, disaster, or scandal; familiarity; location; timeliness and novelty

Word Highlights

unarticulated (¶3) not clearly and directly stated
criteria (¶3) rules for making a judgment (singular, *criterion*)
penny press (¶5) sensationalist newspapers in the early part of this century
document analysis (¶9) close dicussion of a published statement
intrinsic (¶10) within itself; on its own merits

Prominently displayed on the front page of the *New York Times* is the company motto: "All the News That's Fit to Print." Admirable as this sentiment may be, it is not, nor can it be, true. Indeed, a more accurate rephrasing of the motto might be "all the news that fits." No form of mass media can carry every newsworthy event; all are constrained by costs and availability of space and time. For instance, the average daily newspaper fills approximately 62 percent of its space with advertising, leaving a mere 38 percent for news accounts, along with human interest stories, and pure entertainment features.

2 Network television news is even more limited. Each half-hour program contains only twenty-two and a half to twenty-three minutes of news and human interest stories. Contrary to the mirror-to-society myth, news is not simply out there; it must be picked from a multitude of happenings, only a few of which will ever be covered. What then is news? Perhaps the best explanation is "that news is what reporters, editors, and producers decide is news."[10]

3 Although the basis of news judgment often seems vague and unarticulated, Doris Graber has identified five criteria most often used in selecting stories.[11]

4 ■ To qualify as news the story must have a *high impact* on the audience, that is, the events covered must be relevant to

[10]Kathleen Hall Jamieson and Karlyn Kohrs Campbell, *The Interplay of Influence* (Belmont, Calif.: Wadsworth, 1983), p. 16.
[11]Doris A. Graber, *Mass Media and American Politics* (Washington, D.C.: Congressional Quarterly Press, 1984), pp. 77–79.

people's lives. Events in the Middle East, for example, are news when they have a measurable effect on American hostages there or on the supply of oil at home.

5 ■ Newsworthiness is heightened by the presence of *violence, conflict, disaster, or scandal.* Violent crime, for example, was a staple of the penny press and continues to dominate contemporary news. Even nonviolent conflict makes news. Larry Speakes, who served as deputy press secretary to former President Ronald Reagan, once noted that no one pays attention when one hundred members of Congress come out of a White House meeting and say that the president's program is great. "But if one says it stinks, that's news."

6 ■ *Familiarity* is also an element of newsworthiness. Events are more likely to be covered as news if they involve individuals that the public already knows. Approximately 85 percent of the domestic news stories covered by television and news magazines involve well-known people — mostly those holding official positions.[12] Unknown people are most newsworthy as victims of crime or natural disasters.

7 ■ *Local events* are more newsworthy than those far away. In a nation linked by instant communications, however, close to home may also include such familiar locations as Washington, D.C., and Wall Street.

8 ■ Stories must be *timely and novel* to capture the attention of the media. They must be what reporters call breaking stories, and they must also be unusual. The routine is considered unworthy of coverage even though it may have a significant impact on people's lives. As a former editor of the old *New York Sun* put it, "When a dog bites a man, that is not news, because it happens so often. But if a man bites a dog, that is news."

9 To this list might be added the availability of individuals for interviews. Reporters rely almost exclusively on interviewing and only occasionally on the reading of documents. The dependence on the interview results partly from the need to personalize the news — especially in television journalism, with its demand for visuals. Interviews with adversaries also increase the sense of conflict, adding a dramatic element to the

[12] Herbert J. Gans, *Deciding What's News: A Study of CBS Evening News, NBC Nightly News, Newsweek and Time* (New York: Vintage, 1980), p. 9.

story. The fact that most reporters find document analysis dull and boring also increases their dependence on interviews.[13] Whatever the cause, the result is a bias in favor of those willing and able to talk.

10 These criteria have little to do with the intrinsic importance of news stories and stress mainly ways of keeping the audience interested. Because media outlets make their profit from the sale of advertising, they must keep their ratings or circulations high. . . . This concern for audience appeal has an impact on the way politics is conducted in the United States. ❑

EXERCISES

Understanding What You Have Read

a ______ 1. The main idea of this selection is that **(5)**

a. reporters, editors, and producers decide what is news largely to keep audiences interested.
b. newspapers print only the news that fits.
c. news stories are selected for their high impact.
d. audience interest is important because media outlets depend on the sale of advertising.

b ______ 2. The main idea of the first paragraph of the selection is that **(5b)**

a. the motto of the *New York Times* is not true.
b. media can present only a limited amount of news.
c. newspapers devote 62 percent of their space to advertising.
d. newspapers share the space for news with entertainment and human interest stories.

b ______ 3. In the first paragraph, the main idea is **(5b)**

a. stated in the opening sentence.
b. stated in the middle of the paragraph.
c. stated at the end of the paragraph.
d. only implied.

---

[13] Stephen Hess, *The Washington Reporters* (Washington, D.C.: The Brookings Institution, 1981), pp. 16–19.

4. Place a checkmark before each detail that you consider major. **(6b)**

_____ a. The *New York Times* prints its motto on the front page.

_____ b. Doris Graber has identified five criteria for news selection.

√_____ c. One criterion of newsworthiness is high impact.

√_____ d. Conflict heightens newsworthiness.

_____ e. Larry Speakes was deputy press secretary to Ronald Reagan.

_____ f. Larry Speakes said, "But if one says it stinks, that's news."

√_____ g. Network news shows have only about twenty-three minutes available for news and human interest stories.

_____ h. Reporters find document analysis dull.

√_____ i. The availability of individuals for interviews affects the selection of the news.

5. List two details that support the idea that only limited news is presented in the media. **(6, 12b)**

Sixty-two percent of newspaper space is for ads;

half-hour news programs have only about

twenty-three minutes of news and human

interest stories.

c_____ 6. This selection is largely organized **(7)**
a. in order of importance.
b. as a comparison of different news media.
c. as a list of criteria.
d. in time order.

Interpreting and Evaluating

b ______ 1. We can infer from the selection that to understand issues, news reporters **(8)**
a. cannot trust the people they interview.
b. do not rely much on written sources.
c. rely too much on written sources.
d. must take an active role.

a ______ 2. We can conclude that the authors of this selection believe that Americans get all the news **(10)**
a. that they are interested in.
b. they need.
c. that is important for understanding the world.
d. there is.

c ______ 3. In general, news media are **(11)**
a. most interested in presenting a balanced, complete picture of the news.
b. concerned with educating their audiences.
c. very concerned with appealing to their audiences.
d. interested in increasing the space devoted to news.

a ______ 4. If a famous Hollywood actor was involved in a fistfight with another movie star, most newspapers would probably **(10)**
a. print the story.
b. not print the story.
c. print the story only if they could squeeze it in on the back page.
d. get permission to print the story from the two celebrities.

c ______ 5. Regarding the information found in this selection, we can conclude that the authors **(10)**
a. based their assertions only on their own personal opinions.
b. drew on years of experience as media executives.
c. did a good deal of research on the topic.
d. consulted with Larry Speakes and Ronald Reagan.

6. Before each of the following statements from the selection,

write F if it is a statement of fact or O if it is a statement of opinion. **(12a)**

F a. The *New York Times* prints its motto on the front page.

O b. The motto is not true.

F c. No form of mass media can carry every newsworthy event.

O d. News is what reporters, editors, and producers say it is.

F e. Thirty-eight percent of the average daily newspaper is available for stories.

F f. Eighty-five percent of domestic news stories involve well-known people.

O g. Local events are more newsworthy than distant ones.

O h. News needs to be personalized.

7. Who holds each of the following opinions? After each statement, identify the person or people who first made it. **(12)**

   a. There are five criteria most often used in selecting news stories. **Doris Graber**

   b. A sixth criterion can be added. **authors**

   c. "But if one says it stinks, that's news." **Larry Speakes**

   d. "But if a man bites a dog, that is news." **former *New York Sun* editor**

   e. News media are constrained by costs. **authors**

Vocabulary

In your own words define each of the italicized words. **(1, 2)**

1. *prominently* displayed on the front page

   openly

2. admirable as this *sentiment* may be

   feeling

3. a more *accurate* rephrasing

   exact

4. *constrained* by costs

   held back

5. stories must be *timely* and *novel*

   on time; unusual

6. interviews with *adversaries*

   opponents

7. keep their *ratings* or *circulations* high

   score of quality, compared with others; number of copies sold

WRITING PRACTICE

1. Define each of the six criteria of newsworthiness in one or two sentences.
2. Discuss the selection of stories you read on the front page of today's newspaper or see on tonight's network news in relation to the criteria of newsworthiness presented in this selection.

14

Looking Forward, Looking Back

Robert DeBlois

A careless accident turns a young man into a quadriplegic — a person who has lost the use of both arms and legs. Read this selection to find out how the writer, now a college teacher, views his past and future life.

Prereading

Before you read, make a list of everything that comes to mind when you think of the word *quadriplegic*. Use a separate sheet of paper. **[3a(1)]**

Word Highlights

repertoire (¶2) selection of songs, plays, poems, or other pieces that a person or group is prepared to perform
irony (¶2) an intended meaning opposite to what is actually said or done
ordeal (¶2) painful experience
prognosis (¶5) prediction of the course and outcome of an illness
claustrophobia (¶8) fear of small enclosed places
compromise (¶9) settling of differences
ambivalence (¶14) conflicting feelings
pathetic (¶15) arousing pity or sorrow
stagnation (¶15) staying inactive; failing to change or develop
stasis (¶15) a stable, balanced state
hokey (¶16) worthless

Eleven years.

2 When I was in the spinal-cord injury, intensive-care unit of a Boston VA hospital, some union musicians would come in once a month, set up amid the beds of men who would not be walking again, and go through their repertoire. They always started with "The Way We Were" and seemed not to notice the irony of it. I hope they never came to a realization of its significance and stopped playing it out of fear of offending someone. It was an appropriate song. Time looms large at the beginning of the ordeal, and looking back at the past is more pleasant than pondering the future.

3 May 19, 1975, was a warm day in New Hampshire. I was 21 years old and had just finished my junior year at the University of New Hampshire. I went swimming in a nearby river, where I broke my neck when I dove onto a rock. Although not the most intelligent thing I had ever done, it was certainly the most dramatic. A few days later, when the neurosurgeon solemnly told me that, in effect, he wouldn't bet the ranch on my walking again and that my arms would not be of much use either, I took the news right in stride. The doctor was surprised and, I have always suspected, just a little disappointed. I think he was ready for a Hollywood performance in which I would rant and rave and swear through my tears that he was wrong and that, by God, I would walk again and, in fact, would start training for the next Olympics right then and there. "Bring me some barbells, please, Doctor."

4 Shortly after the doctor gave me the news, I was awakened one morning by my new nurse, Lollie Ball. As a symbol of snuffed-out youth, I had been getting the royal treatment by the staff, and Lollie was determined to put some discipline into my life. If the Pillsbury Doughboy had a middle-aged daughter, she would look like Lollie — a powdery white complexion, plump, and jolly behind her no-nonsense manner. "Time to wake up, Robert. Today we are going to brush our teeth."

5 Lollie was one of my first real annoyances after I got hurt, and in this respect she served an important purpose. Annoyances were something I was going to have to get used to. The doctor knew this when he gave me his prognosis. He was solemn because he understood the significance of my injury. Quadriplegic, to me, was just a word.

6 The most immediate annoyance I encountered was hospitals. One of the first thoughts I had after I came to on a grassy

slope next to the river was that I would have to endure a couple of weeks in a hospital. It turned out to be six months, and all but the first was spent in a VA hospital, where I was given special permission to occupy an empty bed.

7 Another annoyance I couldn't anticipate when the doctor told me of my future was the lack of privacy I would have. This didn't mean I wouldn't be alone at times (although these times are infrequent). It did mean, though, that I could never really do anything while I was alone. Privacy is being able to do something with your aloneness.

8 The personal-care attendant entered my life. One spends a lot of energy when he has to spend 40 hours a week with someone who is paid to be a companion. Things can get annoying. Like the premed student who didn't know how to make a peanut-butter-and-jelly sandwich. Or the woman who insisted I was discriminating against her when I (my wife, really) wouldn't let her go topless when she worked around the yard, as had been the case with male attendants. Or the woman who had claustrophobia and could not ride elevators, sometimes leaving me to travel through a building at the whim of those who pushed the elevator call buttons.

9 Don't get the feeling it's all fun and games, though. Life became considerably more complex and required more compromise. I began to realize this when I moved to a VA hospital that specialized in spinal-cord injuries. Here the compromised future forced itself upon me in the form of bent-over old men in wheelchairs and men of all ages bedridden with urinary tract infections, made noticeable by the blood-red urine in the bags attached to their beds.

10 If someone were to ask me what I feel I missed out on most, it would not be sex, athletic ability or even the ability to walk. These are things that TV movies concentrate upon because they are easy for physically sound people to understand.

11 What I feel I missed most was the opportunity to experiment with my ideals and ideas as I moved into adulthood, that "real world" which floats nebulously outside the gates of colleges where American adult-children prepare to answer the question "What now?"

12 The question intrigued me. I was anxious to get to the real world, but in an instant the future was transformed into "the long haul." I found myself unable to test my ideals of simplicity, unable to learn that these ideals might have been naive,

unable to learn through trial and error that life is, after all, complicated, that it is the rare person who gets to have his life on his own terms and call his own shots. The fact that I have come to these conclusions through another route is no consolation. The pain is in opportunity lost, experience missed.

13 When I was graduated from college, I began teaching, which is what I had planned to do before I got hurt. Before the accident though, teaching was just one of many possibilities. Afterward, it was one of the few realistic choices. And then marriage to the woman who was my girlfriend at the university, whose sense of loyalty is equal to our golden retriever's. Still, the romance was difficult, as was the decision to get married.

14 None of this is to imply that I regret what has happened since the accident. But I cannot keep from wondering. As I understand it, Franklin Roosevelt once mused over whether he became president in spite of his paralysis or because of it. He was referring, I think, not to the public's sympathetic view of him but, rather, to his own ambivalence about his motives to take on challenges and, in effect, to prove himself.

15 For persons who wish to assign qualities of heroism to those of us who have to live with readily discernible disabilities, I would suggest caution. That "normal" people are fascinated by different handicaps is evidenced by the way the media latched onto the disabled a few years ago. For a while there, being crippled almost became chic. The poorer films depicted characters who heroically salvaged happiness from pathetic despair. The better movies, such as "Coming Home" and "The Other Side of the Mountain," showed that courage does not really enter into the picture. The lack of alternatives takes the heroism out of it. Growth may be painful, but stagnation is more so. Being disabled, like being normal, is a process, not a stasis for which one easy approach or formula can be developed. This is an optimistic idea, not a pessimistic one. It means an anticipation and enthusiasm for the future can still be present. Time will not be denied, but it need not only be faced and endured.

16 This may be a little hokey, but then, being crippled is also a little hokey, a little absurd, a little tragic, a little funny, a little fascinating, plenty weird and plenty frustrating. Eleven years later, this is the way things are. Not exactly the way things were, but at least, looking forward is now about as easy as looking back. ❑

EXERCISES

Understanding What You Have Read

b 1. The main point of this selection is that **(5b)**
   a. it is difficult to be handicapped.
   b. life for a person with handicaps is filled with problems and opportunities just like everyone else's life is.
   c. life in a VA hospital can be amusing even for those with serious injuries.
   d. it is possible for someone to overcome even the most serious handicaps with hard work if he or she is determined and heroic.

c 2. The main idea of paragraph 8 is that **(5b)**
   a. people who are handicapped have to spend forty hours a week with home caregivers.
   b. it can be annoying to travel up and down in elevators at the whim of the person pushing the buttons.
   c. spending many hours a week with a personal-care attendant can be bothersome.
   d. people who work around the yard should be allowed to go topless if they want to.

b 3. The writer's injury was a result of **(6a)**
   a. preparing for the Olympics.
   b. a swimming accident.
   c. a gunshot wound during a robbery.
   d. a disease that attacks the spinal column.

c 4. The author states that the most difficult aspect of being handicapped for him is **(6a)**
   a. being unable to walk or participate in sports.
   b. losing privacy.
   c. losing the opportunity to experiment with ideas and ideals.
   d. getting along with personal-care attendants.

b 5. According to the article, people who are handicapped are most different from other people in that they **(6a)**
   a. do not live life on their own terms.
   b. lose opportunities and experiences.
   c. are likely to become stagnant and depressed.
   d. are unable to plan for the future.

d ______ 6. The most important thing that the writer learned from Lollie Ball, the nurse, was **(6a)**
a. how to brush his teeth.
b. to be disciplined.
c. that he had to wake up on time.
d. that he would have to learn to get used to annoyances.

a ______ 7. How long had DeBlois been handicapped when he wrote this article? **(6a)**
a. Eleven years
b. Just a few months
c. From birth
d. Eight years

b ______ 8. The author believes that we should not call people with handicaps heroic because these people **(6a)**
a. are very sad and should be pitied.
b. have no choice but to live their lives the best they can.
c. lack opportunities to perform heroic acts.
d. cannot make important decisions in the same way as people without disabilities.

d ______ 9. About living life according to your own terms and conditions, DeBlois believes that **(6a)**
a. most people can have such a life.
b. mostly everyone but those with handicaps can live such a life.
c. only veterans know how to live such a life.
d. only very few people are able to live such a life.

a ______ 10. Deciding to get married was **(6a)**
a. a difficult choice for the writer to make.
b. the only choice the writer could make.
c. related to the writer's love of golden retrievers.
d. not supported by the writer's doctors.

Interpreting and Evaluating

c ______ 1. The writer probably believes that it is ironic to sing "The Way We Were" to a group of people who will never walk again because **(8)**
a. they're not in the mood for music.

b. they prefer more sentimental songs, from the 1950s.
c. they themselves can never again be the way they were.
d. after being seriously injured, people should look to the past, not the future.

b ______ 2. The writer probably believes that the way he reacted to the news of his permanently crippling injury was **(8)**
a. typical of how most people would react.
b. highly unusual.
c. like a Hollywood performance.
d. very immature.

b ______ 3. We can infer from his reference to President Franklin Roosevelt that the writer **(8)**
a. wants to be president of the United States.
b. is not sure how his handicap influences his choices.
c. does not want the public's sympathy.
d. regrets what has happened to him since his accident.

a ______ 4. We can infer that the writer felt the nurse, Lollie Ball, was **(8)**
a. amusing but irritating.
b. boring but helpful.
c. hostile.
d. unfair.

d ______ 5. From the selection we can conclude that being alone is **(10)**
a. not as important as being with friends.
b. scary for a person who is handicapped.
c. essential for emotional well-being.
d. of value only if you are able to do something while you're alone.

c ______ 6. We can predict that in the future the writer will **(10)**
a. be cured of his serious handicap.
b. never be happy.
c. live the same kind of life he's been living all along.
d. go to medical school in order to help others with spinal cord injuries.

7. Put a checkmark next to the generalizations we can draw from the selection. **(11)**

√ ______ a. Failing to grow as a human being is more painful than being physically handicapped.

______ b. People who believe in modern science can learn to live with even the worst illness and pain.

√ ______ c. What some people call heroism is what others call surviving with limited choices.

√ ______ d. People have to learn to make the most of the lives they have.

______ e. Putting some discipline into daily life is an important goal for everyone.

c ______ 8. The tone of this selection is very **(12d)**
a. negative.
b. violent.
c. realistic.
d. humorous.

Vocabulary

Using sentence clues, determine the meanings of the words in italics. Then select the best definition from the choices given and write the letter of your answer on the blank line. **(1c)**

c ______ 1. time *looms* large
a. weaves
b. booms
c. appears as a threat
d. ticks softly

b ______ 2. a symbol of *snuffed-out* youth
a. wild
b. ended suddenly
c. sneezing
d. irresponsible

a ______ 3. floats *nebulously* outside the gates
a. vaguely
b. strongly
c. heartlessly
d. sadly

c ______ 4. the question *intrigued* me
a. worried
b. amused
c. fascinated
d. helped

d ______ 5. the future was *transformed*
a. changed very slightly
b. denied
c. evil
d. changed greatly

c ______ 6. ideals might have been *naive*
a. necessary
b. silly
c. immature
d. religious

a ______ 7. is no *consolation*
a. comfort
b. importance
c. assistance
d. weakness

c ______ 8. readily *discernible* disabilities
a. painful
b. annoying
c. noticeable
d. curable

c ______ 9. heroically *salvaged* happiness
a. danced for
b. bought
c. rescued
d. fought

d 10. an *optimistic* idea
a. sad
b. thoughtful
c. useless
d. positive

WRITING PRACTICE

1. Write a paragraph or two in which you describe what you think are the worst problems that a person with a serious handicap faces. Conclude with your recommendations for those who are disabled.
2. How much of the advice DeBlois offers to people who are disabled also applies to those who are not? Choose one or more pieces of advice from the selection and, in about a page, explain how a person who is physically sound might profit from the suggestions.

15

How They Get You to Do That

Janny Scott

In this newspaper feature Janny Scott reports on the techniques people use to persuade us to do things. As you read the article, think about how someone may have used these techniques on you.

Prereading

Make a list of all the techniques you can think of that advertisers use to make you buy a product or vote for a candidate. **[3a(1)]**

Word Highlights

wielding (¶3) using a tool effectively
compliance (¶4) giving in to a request, wish, or demand
telemarketing (¶7) selling through television and telephone
exponentially (¶9) extremely rapidly at an increasing pace
bunco (¶26) swindling
tout (¶38) to push a product; to sell

The woman in the supermarket in a white coat tenders a free sample of "lite" cheese. A car salesman suggests that prices won't stay low for long. Even a penny will help, pleads the door-to-door solicitor. Sale ends Sunday! Will work for food.

2 The average American exists amid a perpetual torrent of

propaganda. Everyone, it sometimes seems, is trying to make up someone else's mind. If it isn't an athletic shoe company, it's a politician, a panhandler, a pitchman, a boss, a billboard company, a spouse.

3 The weapons of influence they are wielding are more sophisticated than ever, researchers say. And they are aimed at a vulnerable target — people with less and less time to consider increasingly complex issues.

4 As a result, some experts in the field have begun warning the public, tipping people off to precisely how "the art of compliance" works. Some critics have taken to arguing for new government controls on one pervasive form of persuasion — political advertising.

5 The persuasion problem is "the essential dilemma of modern democracy," argue social psychologists Anthony Pratkanis and Elliot Aronson, the authors of "Age of Propaganda: The Everyday Use and Abuse of Persuasion," published last year.

6 As the two psychologists see it, American society values free speech and public discussion, but people no longer have the time or inclination to pay attention. Mindless propaganda flourishes, they say; thoughtful persuasion fades away.

7 The problem stems from what Pratkanis and Aronson call our "message-dense environment." The average television viewer sees nearly 38,000 commercials a year, they say. The average home receives 216 pieces of junk mail annually and a call a week from telemarketing firms.

8 Bumper stickers, billboards and posters litter the public consciousness. Athletic events and jazz festivals carry corporate labels. As direct selling proliferates, workers patrol their offices during lunch breaks, peddling chocolate and Tupperware to friends.

9 Meanwhile, information of other sorts multiplies exponentially. Technology serves up ever-increasing quantities of data on every imaginable subject, from home security to health. With more and more information available, people have less and less time to digest it.

10 "It's becoming harder and harder to think in a considered way about anything," said Robert Cialdini, a persuasion researcher at Arizona State University in Tempe. ". . . More and more, we are going to be deciding on the basis of less and less information."

11 Persuasion is a democratic society's chosen method for

decision-making and dispute-resolution. But the flood of persuasive messages in recent years has changed the nature of persuasion. Lengthy arguments have been supplanted by slogans and logos. In a world teeming with propaganda, those in the business of influencing others put a premium on effective shortcuts.

12 Most people, psychologists say, are easily seduced by such shortcuts. Humans are "cognitive misers," always looking to conserve attention and mental energy — which leaves them at the mercy of anyone who has figured out which shortcuts work.

13 The task of figuring out shortcuts has been embraced by advertising agencies, market researchers and millions of salespeople. The public, meanwhile, remains in the dark, ignorant of even the simplest principles of social influence.

14 As a result, lay people underestimate their susceptibility to persuasion, psychologists say. They imagine their actions are dictated simply by personal preferences. Unaware of the techniques being used against them, they are often unwittingly outgunned.

15 As Cialdini tells it, the most powerful tactics work like jujitsu: They draw their strength from deep-seated, unconscious psychological rules. The clever "compliance professional" deliberately triggers these "hidden stores of influence" to elicit a predictable response.

16 One such rule, for example, is that people are more likely to comply with a request if a reason — no matter how silly — is given. To prove that point, one researcher tested different ways of asking people in line at a copying machine to let her cut the line.

17 When the researcher asked simply, "Excuse me, I have five pages. May I use the Xerox machine?" only 60% of those asked complied. But when she added nothing more than, "because I have to make some copies," nearly everyone agreed.

18 The simple addition of "because" unleashed an automatic response, even though "because" was followed by an irrelevant reason, Cialdini said. By asking the favor in that way, the researcher dramatically increased the likelihood of getting what she wanted.

19 Cialdini and others say much of human behavior is mechanical. Automatic responses are efficient when time and at-

tention are short. For that reason, many techniques of persuasion are designed and tested for their ability to trigger those automatic responses.

20 "These appeals persuade not through the give and take of argument and debate," Pratkanis and Aronson have written. ". . . They often appeal to our deepest fears and most irrational hopes, while they make use of our most simplistic beliefs."

21 Life insurance agents use fear to sell policies, Pratkanis and Aronson say. Parents use fear to convince their children to come home on time. Political leaders use fear to build support for going to war — for example, comparing a foreign leader to Adolf Hitler.

22 As many researchers see it, people respond to persuasion in one of two ways: If an issue they care about is involved, they may pay close attention to the arguments; if they don't care, they pay less attention and are more likely to be influenced by simple cues.

23 Their level of attention depends on motivation and the time available. As David Boninger, a UCLA psychologist puts it, "If you don't have the [time] or motivation, or both, you will pay attention to more peripheral cues, like how nice somebody looks."

24 Cialdini, a dapper man with a flat, Midwestern accent, describes himself as an inveterate sucker. From an early age, he said recently, he had wondered what made him say yes in many cases when the answer, had he thought about it, should have been no.

25 So in the early 1980s, he became "a spy in the wars of influence." He took a sabbatical and, over a three-year period, enrolled in dozens of sales training programs, learning firsthand the tricks of selling insurance, cars, vacuum cleaners, encyclopedias and more.

26 He learned how to sell portrait photography over the telephone. He took a job as a busboy in a restaurant, observing the waiters. He worked in fund raising, advertising and public relations. And he interviewed cult recruiters and members of bunco squads.

27 By the time it was over, Cialdini had witnessed hundreds of tactics. But he found that the most effective ones were rooted in six principles. Most are not new; but they are being used today with greater sophistication on people whose fast-paced lifestyle has lowered their defenses.

28 ■ *Reciprocity:* People have been trained to believe that a favor must be repaid in kind, even if the original favor was not requested. The cultural pressure to return a favor is so intense that people go along rather than suffer the feeling of being indebted.

29 Politicians have learned that favors are repaid with votes. Stores offer free samples — not just to show off a product. Charity organizations ship personalized address labels to potential contributors. Others accost pedestrians, planting paper flowers in their lapels.

30 ■ *Commitment and consistency:* People tend to feel they should be consistent — even when it no longer makes sense. While consistency is easy, comfortable and generally advantageous, Cialdini says, "mindless consistency" can be exploited.

31 Take the "foot in the door technique." One person gets another to agree to a small commitment, like a down payment or signing a petition. Having done so, studies show that it becomes much easier to get the person to comply with a much larger request.

32 Another example Cialdini cites is the "low-ball tactic" in car sales. Offered a low price for a car, the potential customer agrees. Then at the last minute, the sales manager finds a supposed error. The price is increased. But customers tend to go along nevertheless.

33 ■ *Social validation:* People often decide what is correct based on what other people think. Studies show that is true for behavior. Hence, sitcom laugh tracks, tip jars "salted" with a bartender's cash, long lines outside nightclubs, testimonials and man on the street ads.

34 Tapping the power of social validation is especially effective under certain conditions: When people are in doubt, they will look to others as a guide; and when they view those others as similar to themselves, they are more likely to follow their lead.

35 ■ *Liking:* People prefer to comply with requests from people they know and like. Charities recruit people to canvass their friends and neighbors. Colleges get alumni to raise money from classmates. Sales training programs include grooming tips.

36 According to Cialdini, liking can be based on any of a number of factors. Good-looking people tend to be credited with traits like talent and intelligence. People also tend to like

people who are similar to themselves in personality, background and lifestyle.

37 ■ *Authority:* People defer to authority. Society trains them to do so; and in many situations, it is beneficial. Unfortunately, obedience is often automatic, leaving people vulnerable to exploitation by compliance professionals, Cialdini says.

38 As an example, he cites the famous ad campaign that capitalized on actor Robert Young's role as Dr. Marcus Welby Jr. to tout the alleged health benefits of Sanka decaffeinated coffee.

39 An authority, according to Cialdini, need not be a true authority. The trappings of authority may suffice. Con artists have long recognized the persuasive power of titles like doctor or judge, fancy business suits and expensive cars.

40 ■ *Scarcity:* Products and opportunities seem more valuable when the supply is limited.

41 As a result, professional persuaders emphasize that "supplies are limited." Sales end Sunday and movies have limited engagements — diverting attention from whether the item is desirable to the threat of losing the chance to experience it at all.

42 The use of influence, Cialdini says, is ubiquitous.

43 Take the classic appeal by a child to a parent's sense of consistency: "But you said. . . ." And the parent's resort to authority: "Because I said so." In addition, nearly everyone invokes the opinions of like-minded others — for social validation — in vying to win a point.

44 One area in which persuasive tactics are especially controversial is political advertising — particularly negative advertising. Alarmed that attack ads might be alienating voters, some critics have begun calling for stricter limits on political ads.

45 In Washington, legislation pending in Congress would, among other things, force candidates to identify themselves at the end of their commercials. In that way, they might be forced to take responsibility for the ads' contents and be unable to hide behind campaign committees.

46 "In general, people accept the notion that for the sale of products at least, there are socially accepted norms of advertising," said Lloyd Morrisett, president of the Markle Foundation, which supports research in communications and information technology.

47 "But when those same techniques are applied to the political process — where we are not judging a product but a person, and where there is ample room for distortion of the record or falsification in some cases — there begins to be more concern," he said.

48 On an individual level, some psychologists offer tips for self-protection.

49 ■ Pay attention to your emotions, says Pratkanis, an associate professor of psychology at UC Santa Cruz: "If you start to feel guilty or patriotic, try to figure out why." In consumer transactions, beware of feelings of inferiority and the sense that you don't measure up unless you have a certain product.

50 ■ Be on the lookout for automatic responses, Cialdini says. Beware foolish consistency. Check other people's responses against objective facts. Be skeptical of authority, and look out for unwarranted liking for any "compliance professionals."

51 Since the publication of his most recent book, "Influence: The New Psychology of Modern Persuasion," Cialdini has begun researching a new book on ethical uses of influence in business — addressing, among other things, how to instruct salespeople and other "influence agents" to use persuasion in ways that help, rather than hurt society.

52 "If influence agents don't police themselves, society will have to step in to regulate . . . the way information is presented in commercial and political settings," Cialdini said. "And that's a can of worms that I don't think anybody wants to get into." ❑

EXERCISES

Understanding What You Have Read

b____ 1. The sentence from the selection that best conveys the main idea is **(5)**

a. "The average American exists amid a perpetual torrent of propaganda."

b. "The weapons of influence they are wielding are more sophisticated than ever, researchers say."

c. "Some critics have taken to arguing for new government controls on one pervasive form of persuasion — political advertising."

d. "Persuasion is a democratic society's chosen method for decision-making and dispute-resolution."

d ______ 2. A researcher reports that when she asked people in line if she could use the photocopying machine, she **(6a)**
   a. always got permission to cut in.
   b. never got permission to cut in.
   c. got permission to cut in more frequently when she gave a good reason.
   d. got permission to cut in more frequently when she gave any reason, no matter how silly.

b ______ 3. In recent years, reasoned persuasion and lengthy argumentation have **(6a)**
   a. filled up our time.
   b. been replaced with slogans and logos.
   c. become more subtle and complex.
   d. become too difficult for undereducated Americans.

a ______ 4. In order to conserve mental energy, people **(6a)**
   a. look for mental shortcuts.
   b. avoid decision-making situations.
   c. rely on professional opinions for mental benefit.
   d. turn off their minds when they hear propaganda.

b ______ 5. Compliance professionals **(6a)**
   a. frequently tell lies.
   b. use people's mental shortcuts to gain agreement.
   c. are experts at argument and reason.
   d. have used the same tricks for many years.

d ______ 6. People pay close attention **(6a)**
   a. whenever they need to make a choice.
   b. whenever their emotions are involved.
   c. whenever they have time.
   d. only when they care and have time.

c ______ 7. The major fact about Robert Cialdini is that he **(6b)**
   a. works at Arizona State University.
   b. is a hopeless sucker.
   c. has found that six principles guide the most effective persuasion tactics.
   d. has worked in many kinds of jobs that use persuasion.

a ______ 8. Which of the following paragraphs uses the pattern of listing details? **(7b)**
a. Paragraph 1
b. Paragraph 12
c. Paragraph 49
d. Paragraph 51

b ______ 9. Which of the following paragraphs lists details in the order of importance? **(7a)**
a. Paragraph 1
b. Paragraph 12
c. Paragraph 21
d. Paragraph 49

b ______ 10. Which of the following paragraphs uses the pattern of cause and effect? **(7e)**
a. Paragraph 1
b. Paragraph 12
c. Paragraph 21
d. Paragraph 49

a ______ 11. Paragraphs 28 through 41 are organized in a pattern of **(7)**
a. classification.
b. time order.
c. cause and effect.
d. comparison and contrast.

12. List the six principles used in effective persuasion and explain each in your own words. **(7, 14)**

Reciprocity — people feel favors must be returned.

Commitment and consistency — people feel they shouldn't change their mind.

Social validation — people are concerned with what others think.

Liking — people listen to people they like.

Authority — people follow powerful leaders.

Scarcity — people think something scarce is valuable.

13. State in your own words some of the advice offered by Pratkanis and Cialdini. **(7, 14)**

    Student responses will vary.

Interpreting and Evaluating

a 1. Based on this selection we can infer that cognitive shortcuts **(8)**
   a. are behind many of the behaviors described in the selection.
   b. make us obey authority without questioning it.
   c. keep us committed even when we know we are being manipulated by a salesperson.
   d. are why we are vulnerable to slogans.

b 2. Based on this selection we can predict that cognitive shortcuts will **(10)**
   a. be avoided by all careful people.
   b. cause you not to pay careful attention to television ads.
   c. get you into trouble the next time you buy a car.
   d. be a subject for research in the next decade.

a 3. Based on this selection we can conclude about cognitive shortcuts that **(10)**
   a. they result from the great number of demands on our attention.
   b. they make us vulnerable to fear.
   c. we never have enough motivation to avoid them.
   d. psychologists fully understand them.

c 4. Based on this selection we can generalize that cognitive shortcuts **(11)**

a. have no positive function.
b. are so natural that we can never overcome them.
c. allow shrewd people to take advantage of us.
d. are a good way to escape getting too involved in situations.

5. Place a P in front of every prediction you can make based on this selection, a C in front of every conclusion, and a G in front of every generalization. If a statement cannot be made based on this selection, or if it is not a valid prediction, conclusion, or generalization, place an N in front of it. **(10, 11)**

P a. If a fellow student asks for a piece of paper in a class and gives you a reason, you will probably hand him or her the paper.

P b. Panhandlers who give reasons will usually do better than those who just ask for money.

N c. If a panhandler asks you for $5, you will probably give it if you like the reason.

N d. Robert Cialdini will never be tricked again.

C e. Robert Cialdini has learned a great deal about how sales pitches affect people.

G f. Compliance professionals have developed many tricks of the trade.

G g. People like to appear friendly and moral.

C h. Fear can convince people to do things.

N i. People obey authority, even if it makes them appear inconsistent and unsocial.

G j. You need to watch out to avoid being tricked by compliance professionals.

d 6. Concerning the influence of compliance professionals on politics, we can conclude that **(10)**

a. in an age of television, voters no longer can make rational choices.
b. political advertising must be banned if Americans are going to vote wisely.
c. compliance professionals are now more important than the candidates or the issues.
d. voters need more information and must pay closer attention to overcome the harmful effects of manipulative political advertising.

b ______ 7. Which of the following facts are used to support the opinion that we live in a "message-dense environment"? **(12d)**
a. Stores offer free samples, and charities send gifts to potential contributors.
b. People receive an average of 216 pieces of junk mail and watch 38,000 television commercials each year.
c. Robert Cialdini worked in fundraising, advertising, public relations, and sales.
d. None of the above

a ______ 8. Which of the following facts are used to support the opinion that people believe a favor must be returned? **(12d)**
a. Stores offer free samples, and charities send gifts to potential contributors.
b. People receive an average of 216 pieces of junk mail and watch 38,000 television commercials each year.
c. Robert Cialdini worked in fundraising, advertising, public relations, and sales.
d. None of the above

d ______ 9. Which of the following facts are used to support the opinion that much of human behavior is mechanical? **(12d)**
a. Stores offer free samples, and charities send gifts to potential contributors.
b. People receive an average of 216 pieces of junk mail and watch 38,000 television commercials each year.
c. Robert Cialdini worked in fundraising, advertising, public relations, and sales.
d. None of the above

10. Match each principle in List A with an example of that principle at work in List B. Put the number of the example

from List B in front of the appropriate principle in List A. **(10, 12e)**

	List A	*List B*
3	a. Reciprocity	1. Wanting to go to a crowded restaurant and not wanting to go to an empty one
6	b. Commitment and consistency	2. Teachers dressing differently from their students
1	c. Social validation	3. Taking a client out to lunch
5	d. Liking	4. An automobile ad that states that only five more cars are left at the sale price
2	e. Authority	5. Trying to fit in in dress and manners with the people at work
4	f. Scarcity	6. A charity asking whether you agree that children ought to be taken care of before asking you for a donation

Vocabulary

In the selection, combinations of words take on special meaning in phrases. Define each of the following phrases in your own words. **(1, 9) Student responses will vary.**

1. message-dense environment

   Being flooded with lots of information, ideas, and requests

2. decision-making and dispute-resolution

   choosing alternatives and coming to agreement despite differences

3. cognitive misers

   people who don't like to think more than they have to

4. art of compliance

getting people to agree with you

5. compliance professional

an expert at getting people to agree

Select the best definition for each italicized word in the phrases below. **(1, 2)**

c 6. a *perpetual* torrent of propaganda
   a. large
   b. on and off
   c. continuous
   d. rapid

b 7. a perpetual *torrent* of propaganda
   a. cases
   b. rapid flow
   c. hot liquid
   d. confusion

a 8. a perpetual torrent of *propaganda*
   a. beliefs spread by tricks
   b. lies
   c. advertisements
   d. political instructions

d 9. more *sophisticated* than ever
   a. spontaneous
   b. untruthful
   c. unhappy
   d. refined

b 10. one *pervasive* form of persuasion
   a. persuasive
   b. spread everywhere

c. chosen
d. deceptive

c ______ 11. the essential *dilemma*
a. truth
b. tragedy created by untruthfulness
c. choice of unsatisfactory alternatives
d. limitations of the problem

c ______ 12. the time or *inclination* to pay attention
a. space
b. belief
c. desire
d. money

a ______ 13. direct selling *proliferates*
a. grows and spreads
b. takes advantage
c. presents a deceptive appearance
d. is profitable

d ______ 14. more *peripheral* cues
a. uncertain
b. important
c. in the center
d. at the side

b ______ 15. the power of social *validation*
a. pressure
b. approval
c. disapproval
d. values

b ______ 16. leaving people *vulnerable* to exploitation
a. capable of being convinced
b. weak and unprotected
c. capable of reacting
d. strong in battle

d ______ 17. leaving people vulnerable to *exploitation*
a. convincing
b. travel and discovery

c. decision making
d. being taken advantage of

__a__ 18. use of influence . . . is *ubiquitous*
a. everywhere
b. questionable
c. in hiding
d. dangerous

WRITING PRACTICE

1. Describe in a page or so recent examples you have seen of the kinds of techniques reported in this selection. If you were influenced in any of these cases, describe how and why you were influenced and what you felt about it later.
2. Using whatever persuasive techniques you think appropriate or effective, write an advertisement or promotion for a product or political candidate of your choice.

16

The Most Influential Investment

Lawrence Summers

The chief economist at the World Bank reminds us of the relation between how well we educate young women and the state of the world's economy.

Prereading

Before you read, freewrite on what you think women in America contribute to our economy. To what degree do you think that this contribution is affected by a woman's education? **[3a(3)]**

Word Highlights

enhancing (¶1) increasing; making greater
mortality (¶5) death rate
interventions (¶5) treatments
econometric (¶6) applying statistics to economics
caveats (¶9) warnings

Educating girls quite possibly yields a higher rate of return than any other investment available in the developing world. Women's education may be unusual territory for economists, but enhancing women's contribution to development is actually as much an economic as a social issue. And economics, with its emphasis on incentives, provides guideposts that point to an explanation for why so many young girls are deprived of an education.

2 Parents in low-income countries fail to invest in their daughters because they do not expect them to make an economic contribution to the family: girls grow up only to marry into somebody else's family and bear children. Girls are thus less valuable than boys and are kept at home to do chores while their brothers are sent to school — the prophecy becomes self-fulfilling, trapping women in a vicious cycle of neglect.

3 An educated mother, on the other hand, has greater earning abilities outside the home and faces an entirely different set of choices. She is likely to have fewer, healthier children and can insist on the development of all her children, ensuring that her daughters are given a fair chance. The education of her daughters then makes it much more likely that the next generation of girls, as well as boys, will be educated and healthy. The vicious cycle is thus transformed into a virtuous circle.

4 Few will dispute that educating women has great social benefits. But it has enormous economic advantages as well. Most obviously, there is the direct effect of education on the wages of female workers. Wages rise by 10 to 20 percent for each additional year of schooling. Returns of this magnitude are impressive by the standard of other available investments, but they are just the beginning. Educating women also has an impressive impact on health practices, including family planning.

5 Let us look at some numbers in one country as an illustration of the savings from improved hygiene and birth control. In Pakistan, educating an extra 1,000 girls an additional year would have cost approximately $40,000 in 1990. Each year of schooling is estimated to reduce mortality of children younger than five years by up to 10 percent. Since an average woman in Pakistan has 6.6 children, it follows that providing 1,000 women with an extra year of schooling would prevent roughly 60 infant deaths. Saving 60 lives with health care interventions would cost an estimated $48,000.

6 Educated women also choose to have fewer children. Econometric studies find that an extra year of schooling reduces female fertility by approximately 10 percent. Thus, a $40,000 investment in educating 1,000 women in Pakistan would avert 660 births. A typical family-planning evaluation concludes that costs run approximately $65 for each birth averted, or $43,000 for 660 births.

7 Even beyond those savings, one can calculate that an additional year of schooling for 1,000 women will prevent the deaths of four women during childbirth. Achieving similar gains through medical interventions would cost close to $10,000.

8 These estimates are of course crude. On one hand, I have failed to discount benefits to reflect the fact that female education operates with a lag. On the other, I have neglected the add-on gains as healthier, better educated mothers have not only healthier, better educated children but healthier, better educated grandchildren. (When the average mother in Pakistan has nearly 40 grandchildren, this is no small thing.)

9 Even with these caveats, the social improvements brought about by educating women are more than sufficient to cover its costs. Given that education also yields higher wages, it seems reasonable to conclude that the return on getting more girls into school is in excess of 20 percent, and probably much greater. In fact, it may well be the single most influential investment that can be made in the developing world.

10 So what can we do to promote investment in the education of girls? Scholarship funds should be established and more free books and other supplies given to girls. Providing schooling that responds to cultural and practical concerns is also essential: female enrollment depends heavily on schools' being nearby, on the provision of appropriate sanitation facilities and on the hiring of female teachers. Flexible hours and care for younger siblings can also be helpful.

11 Raising the primary school enrollment of girls to equal that of boys in the world's low-income countries would involve educating an extra 25 million girls every year at a total cost of approximately $938 million. Equalizing secondary school enrollment would mean educating an additional 21 million girls at a total cost of $1.4 billion. Eliminating educational discrimination in the low-income countries would thus cost a total of $2.4 billion. This sum represents less than one quarter of 1 percent of the gross domestic product of the low-income countries, less than 1 percent of their investment in new capital goods and less than 10 percent of their defense spending.

12 When compared with investments outside the social sector, education looks even more attractive. Take power generation as an example. Projections suggest that developing countries will spend approximately $1 trillion on power plants over the

next 10 years. Because of poor maintenance and pricing problems, many of these nations use less than 50 percent of the capability of existing power plants. In a sample of 57 developing countries, the overall return on power-plant physical assets averaged less than 4 percent over the past three years and less than 6 percent over the past decade — returns that cannot even compare with those of 20 percent or more from providing education for females.

13 No doubt developing countries will improve their efficiency in generating power. And I have probably understated somewhat the difficulty of raising enrollment rates by neglecting capital costs and not taking explicit account of the special costs incurred in targeting girls. Nevertheless, it is hard to believe that building 19 out of every 20 planned power plants and using the savings to finance equal educational opportunity for girls would not be desirable.

14 There are those who say educating girls is a strategy that pays off only in the long run. This argument reminds me of a story, which John F. Kennedy used to tell, of a man asking his gardener how long it would take for a certain seed to grow into a tree. The gardener said it would take 100 years, to which the man replied, "Then plant the seed this morning. There is no time to lose." ❑

EXERCISES

Understanding What You Have Read

c ______ 1. What is the topic of this essay? **(5)**
   a. Financial investments and banking
   b. Young females
   c. Educating girls
   d. Planting seeds

d ______ 2. Which sentence from the selection best indicates the main idea? **(5a)**
   a. "There are those who say educating girls is a strategy that pays off only in the long run."
   b. "Educated women also choose to have fewer children."
   c. "Scholarship funds should be established and more free books and other supplies given to girls."

d. "Educating girls quite possibly yields a higher rate of return than any other investment available in the developing world."

3. In your own words state the main idea of paragraph 2. **(5b) Student responses will vary.**

Daughters are not educated in poor countries because they are not expected to contribute to the family economy.

4. In your own words state the key idea of this sentence from paragraph 5: "Each year of schooling is estimated to reduce mortality of children younger than five years by up to 10 percent." **(5a) Student responses will vary.**

Schooling reduces mortality.

a 5. The selection says that every year of schooling for a woman **(6a)**
   a. increases her wages by 10 to 20 percent.
   b. decreases her wages by 10 to 20 percent.
   c. decreases her contact with her family by 10 to 20 percent.
   d. increases her chances for promotion on the job.

b 6. What is the relation between education and family size? **(6a)**
   a. Educated women have more and healthier children.
   b. Educated women have fewer and healthier children.
   c. Uneducated women tend to come from large families.
   d. Uneducated women choose not to stay in school so that they can raise large families to increase family earnings.

c ______ 7. The writer recommends all of the following ways to promote girls' education *except* **(6a)**
   a. providing child care for younger brothers and sisters.
   b. hiring women teachers.
   c. decreasing the number of boys in elementary school classes.
   d. making schools available nearby.

a ______ 8. What is the estimated total cost of providing equal educational opportunities for women in low-income countries? **(6a)**
   a. $2.4 billion
   b. $938 million
   c. $1.4 billion
   d. $1 trillion

d ______ 9. According to the writer, how could we raise the money to finance equal educational opportunity? **(6a)**
   a. Raise taxes on the wealthy
   b. Solve maintenance and pricing problems in industry
   c. Increase the gross domestic product of low-income countries
   d. Cut one of every twenty planned power plants

10. Write *maj* next to major details from the selection and *min* next to minor details. **(6b)**

maj ______ a. Educating 1,000 women could prevent the death of 4 women in childbirth.

maj ______ b. Educated women have healthier grandchildren.

min ______ c. John F. Kennedy told a story about a gardener.

maj ______ d. The financial return on educating girls is more than 20 percent.

min ______ e. The average mother in Pakistan has about forty grandchildren.

Interpreting and Evaluating

a ______ 1. We can infer that the writer uses examples from Pakistan because **(8)**
   a. Pakistan is a poor country.
   b. he has lived in Pakistan for many years.
   c. Pakistan is attempting to improve the education it offers women.
   d. he understands how the country's power plants operate.

b ______ 2. We can infer that economists **(8)**
   a. regularly study women's education.
   b. rarely study women's education.
   c. cannot understand the effects of women's education on the economy.
   d. see a high rate of return on all investments in the developing world.

a ______ 3. To save sixty children's lives in Pakistan, education — as opposed to health care — would cost how much less money each year per 1,000 women? **(10)**
   a. $8,000
   b. $40,000
   c. $60,000
   d. $48,000

d ______ 4. How much money would be saved per 1,000 women in Pakistan if we educated them instead of providing family-planning services? **(8)**
   a. $40,000
   b. $65
   c. $43,000
   d. $3,000

5. Put an F beside each statement that is a fact and an O beside each statement that is an opinion. **(12a)**

O ______ a. "The vicious cycle is thus transformed into a virtuous cycle."

O ______ b. "The social improvements brought about by educating women are more than sufficient to cover its costs."

F ______ c. "Each year of schooling is estimated to reduce mortality of children younger than five years by up to 10 percent."

F ______ d. "I have failed to discount benefits to reflect the fact that female education operates with a lag."

F ______ e. "There are those who say educating girls is a strategy that pays off only in the long run."

c ______ 6. At the end of the selection, the writer recounts a story told by John F. Kennedy. That story is a figurative example of which of the following ideas? **(9)**
   a. Plant before the weather changes, and you will be rewarded.
   b. Gardeners and politicians can learn from each other.
   c. If something takes lots of time, better start doing it immediately.
   d. Big things grow from small ideas.

a ______ 7. We can conclude that compared with educated women, uneducated women earn wages at a rate of **(8, 10)**
   a. 10–20 percent less.
   b. 10 percent less.
   c. 10–20 percent more.
   d. 10 percent more.

c ______ 8. In regard to power plants, we can conclude that developing countries **(10)**
   a. do not build enough of them.
   b. build double the number they need.
   c. do not know how to run them well.
   d. over time will solve their pollution problems.

b ______ 9. We can predict that a girl born to an educated mother will **(10)**
   a. choose not to have any children.
   b. have healthier, better educated children of her own.
   c. encourage her daughters to marry rich men.
   d. better understand the workings of power plants and how to improve them.

10. Mark with a checkmark the generalizations with which the writer would agree. **(11)**

√ ______ a. Developing countries can improve their educational systems.

______ b. Spending money on improving technology is important to improve the economy of poor countries.

√ ______ c. The long-term economic gains from educating young women are more significant than the short-term gains.

√ ______ d. Developing countries are neglecting an important resource in their own populations.

______ e. Education guarantees long life and high wages.

√ ______ f. Developing countries are investing more than necessary in technological improvements that are poorly managed.

Vocabulary

Using the list of words below, write in the blanks provided the word that best suits the definition. Then, use the letters in boxes to form a two-word phrase that states an important idea in the selection. Write the phrase on the blank line. **(1, 2)**

assets	incurred
deprived	magnitude
dispute	prophecy
explicit	transformed
impact	vicious
incentives	virtuous

1. reasons for doing things i n c [e] n t i v e s
2. brought on by one's actions i n c u r r e [d]
3. argue against d i s p [u] t e
4. prediction of the future p r o p h e [c] y

5. strong effect i m p [a] c t
6. valuable items a s s e [t] s
7. took something away from d [e] p r i v e d
8. great size m a [g] n i t u d e
9. evil; foul; flawed v [i] c i o u s
10. pure; righteous v i [r] t u o u s
11. spelled out; clear e x p [l] i c i t
12. changed markedly t r a n [s] f o r m e d

educate girls

WRITING PRACTICE

1. Write a letter to the ambassador or other high-level government agent in a developing country, explaining how he or she can improve education for girls.
2. What other problems can countries of the world solve by following the advice of the man in the story told by John F. Kennedy: "Then plant the seed this morning. There is no time to lose." Write several paragraphs in which you address one particular problem and explain the steps to take immediately to help solve the problem, even though the full solution may be years away.

17

Crime and Violence

David Sue
Derald Sue
Stanley Sue

This selection from an abnormal psychology textbook discusses the causes of criminal and violent behavior. Is it possible to understand the criminal mind? As you read, think about how the information adds to what you know about the subject.

Prereading

Before reading this selection, on a separate sheet of paper draw a word map presenting what you currently think about the causes of criminal and violent behavior. **[3a(2)]**

Previewing

Preview the selection before you read it and answer the following questions: **(3c) Student responses will vary.**

1. From the title and subtitles, what do you think this selection is about?

 crime and the factors responsible for it

 ____

 ____

 ____

2. What does the list of ten items include?

 various categories of prisoners

 ____

3. What kinds of theories of crime are examined, according to the subtitles?

   genetic and physiological; family; sociocultural

Word Highlights

demographic (¶2) relating to characteristics of human populations
demarcation (¶3) boundary
delinquent (¶3) criminal
composition (¶3) makeup
socioeconomic (¶4) both social and economic
perpetrator (¶4) person who commits a crime
heterogeneous (¶5) mixed
recidivism (¶7) repeated criminal behavior
psychotherapy (¶12) psychological treatment
propensity (¶16) strong tendency
clinical (¶16) technical
EEG (¶17) electroencephalogram; a test to determine brain damage
MZ (¶18) monozygotic — from the same egg; identical
DZ (¶18) dizygotic — from two eggs; fraternal
detrimental (¶20) harmful
correlates (¶21) factors that vary together

Americans are much concerned about crime and violence — and with good reason: Our crime rate is higher than those of most other countries. In 1982 over 12 million serious crimes were reported in the United States; the serious crimes, as categorized by the FBI, include homicide, forcible rape, aggravated assault, robbery, burglary, larceny, and auto theft (*Uniform Crime Reports* 1983).

2 Crime statistics tend to vary from year to year, and the variation may represent real changes in crime rates. However,

it may also result from changes in record-keeping systems or in the willingness of victims to report crimes. In any event, the statistics do indicate that demographic factors such as age, sex, race, and social class are highly related to the commission of crime.

3 At least half of all reported murders, violent street crimes, and thefts are committed by persons under twenty-six years of age. One of every ten children will probably appear in juvenile court before the age of eighteen. [We should note, however, no sharp line of demarcation separates delinquent individuals, on the one hand, from nondelinquent individuals on the other (Van Erva 1983). Among all juveniles, one may find almost every degree of delinquent behavior, as measured by frequency and seriousness.] Because age is related to the commission of certain crimes, a change in the age composition of a population may alter the frequency of these crimes. The United States population is now growing older (that is, we have a higher proportion of older persons than ever before). Individuals born during the post-World-War II baby boom are now nearing 40 years of age. This demographic shift may signal lower rates for those crimes that are associated with youth.

4 The vast majority of crimes among both adults and juveniles are committed by males, although females are committing a greater proportion of total crimes each year. In terms of race and socioeconomic status, statistics indicate that blacks and individuals from the lower socioeconomic classes are overrepresented among those arrested for and convicted of crimes — especially violent crimes. Victims tend to be of the same race or socioeconomic class as the perpetrator of the crime. A word of caution: There is often a tendency to use such statistics in a way that exaggerates the amount of crime among members of certain ethnic or socioeconomic groups, or even to attribute most crime to those groups. But a variety of factors combine to result in the published crime figures, and the figures alone cannot indicate what those factors are.

Theories of Crime

5 What type of individual commits crimes? According to Megargee and Bohn (1977, 1979), criminals are a heterogeneous group. On the basis of psychological tests, personal histories, and observations of inmates in prison, they were able to categorize prisoners into no fewer than ten classes.

6 1. *Items* are friendly and nonaggressive individuals who have been convicted of such crimes as drug dealing. Comprising a large subgroup of prisoners, they come from stable family backgrounds and are good candidates for probation.

7 2. *Easy* inmates come from good family backgrounds and are underachievers. They have low recidivism rates and are good candidates for probation.

8 3. *Bakers* are anxious, socially isolated, and frequently alcoholic. They appear to be neurotic delinquents who would benefit from treatment.

9 4. *Ables* are somewhat psychopathic, immature, and amoral. They would function well in a controlled living situation in the community.

10 5. *Georges* are criminals whose crimes are economically motivated. They are loners and are somewhat psychopathic. Treatment should initially be targeted toward their motives for committing crime.

11 6. *Deltas* are psychopathic and bright. They are impulsive, show little anxiety, and are easily provoked to violence. Their antisocial nature should be addressed in any treatment program.

12 7. *Jupiters* come from severely deprived family backgrounds. They are motivated to adjust, but they lack the necessary skills, abilities, and education. Educational and academic training, along with supportive group psychotherapy, may be beneficial.

13 8. *Foxtrots* are emotionally disturbed and antisocial. They rebel against authority, and treatment is often ineffective.

14 9. *Charlies* are probably the most disturbed of any subgroup. They are violent, bitter, and paranoid. Treatment is difficult because of their strong paranoid tendencies.

15 10. *Hows* come from deprived backgrounds. They are anxious and are isolated because their social behaviors result in rejection from others. They need almost all forms of treatment.

16 Megargee and Bohn thus found that prison inmates vary considerably with regard to a number of characteristics: emotional disturbance, family background, skills and abilities, propensity for violence, motivation for crime, type of treatment needed, and response to treatment. Given the diversity of indi-

viduals who exhibit delinquent or criminal behavior, it is not surprising that there are a number of theories about the causes of crime and aggression. Many of these theories are variations of the explanations for antisocial personality. However, it is important to realize that, even in prison populations, fewer than 30 percent of the inmates are considered psychopathic (Hare 1981). Indeed, most criminals are not disturbed in the clinical sense, and criminality cannot be attributed to a single specific personality type.

17 **Genetic and Physiological Research** Early investigators were interested in determining whether there are physiological differences between criminals and noncriminals. Some researchers felt that criminals were more likely to show EEG or genetic abnormalities. As in the case of antisocial personality, however, there is little evidence that such abnormalities can explain criminal behavior.

18 More recently, researchers have sought to establish whether criminal behavior patterns can be influenced by heredity. The research strategies used and the results obtained are very similar to those discussed with respect to antisocial personality. For example, MZ twins show a higher concordance rate than DZ twins for criminality; and, among criminals adopted early in life, their biological parents show a higher rate of criminality than their adoptive parents (Hutchings and Mednick 1977; Mednick and Christiansen 1977). Such findings show at most a hereditary *tendency* toward criminality, thus suggesting that environmental factors are also important. In fact, in the "adopted criminal" study, the highest rate of crime among offspring occurred when both the biological *and* the adoptive fathers had committed crimes.

19 These heredity studies suffer from two major limitations: First, they do not include individuals who commit crimes but have escaped detection or conviction. Second, they do not indicate *how* hereditary factors might predispose one toward criminality — how one's genetic makeup leads to criminality or interacts with environmental factors to produce criminality.

20 **Family Factors** Megargee and Bohn (1977, 1979) also noted that many criminals are reared in unstable or detrimental family environments. Criminals often come from families where parents are separated or divorced. Some are subjected to incon-

sistent or harsh forms of punishment as children. Others have parents who were themselves antisocial or criminal. Presumably, children may learn delinquency and criminal behavior through the modeling of parents who use physical punishment or engage in antisocial behavior.

21 Criminals frequently described their home environments as frustrating and as lacking affectionate relationships. Such conditions may not allow youngsters the opportunity to learn to internalize the values associated with prosocial or appropriate behaviors (Hetherington and Martin 1979). In a study of correlates of serious and repeated crime among adolescents, Hanson et al. (1984) found that low levels of mother–son affection and cold and conflicting father–son relations were predictors of criminal activity in the sons. There is general agreement that family environment plays a role in delinquency and criminality (Van Evra 1983).

22 **Sociocultural Factors** Merton (1968) has suggested that certain conditions in American society combine to encourage crime. These are the common goals of wealth, power, and status; the existence of "haves" and "have-nots"; and the limited availability of legitimate means for achieving goals. The "American dream" is that these goals are attainable by all in this, the land of opportunity. Yet inequities exist and the have-nots are unable to succeed. For example, the children of wealthy and well-educated parents find it easier to obtain good educations and pursue professional careers than the children of poor families or members of ethnic minority groups. The have-nots may resort to illegitimate means (that is, crime) as a strategy for surviving or getting ahead.

23 Whereas Merton stresses motivation and opportunities as factors in crime, Sutherland and Cressey (1966) have argued that individuals may be *socialized* into a life of professional crime through exposure to the value systems of criminals. A powerful predictor of serious and repeated crime among male adolescents is their loyalty to and strong participation in *delinquent peer groups*. These peer groups provide adolescents with a sense of belongingness, support, and the behavioral norms of delinquency (Hanson et al. 1984). Sutherland and Cressey's hypothesis and that of Merton may also explain white-collar crime (such as illegal financial dealings, price fixing, and bribery) and organized crime, in which "families" or hierarchies

of criminals engage in extortion, gambling, prostitution, drug dealing, and loan-sharking.

24 The role of television and other mass media in American society has come under increasing scrutiny. Although it can be argued that television programming merely reflects the preferences and practices of society, television programs can also be a powerful force in socialization. Many investigators believe that the frequent displays of criminal behavior and violence on television shows can increase the tendency of viewers to engage in such behaviors. . . . Because the content of media presentations is both influenced by the preferences of society and capable of influencing vast numbers of people, it is viewed as a sociocultural force.

Treatment and Punishment

25 In our society, the treatment of crime and criminals has generated divergent opinions and emotional arguments. One segment of society is primarily concerned with the treatment and rehabilitation of criminals. From its perspective, society is best served by efforts to find a means of reforming criminals and preventing recidivism. Rather than punish criminals, society should work to change the lifestyles, personality patterns, and behaviors of criminals.

26 In opposition to this view, another segment of society believes that criminals should be punished. Its members advocate certain, immediate, and severe punishment for crime, with fixed rather than indeterminate sentences. Punishment is viewed as a form of retribution through which criminals pay for their crimes. It may also serve to deter others from crime or to isolate criminals in prison, away from law-abiding citizens and the opportunity to commit more crimes.

27 Still another segment of society is primarily concerned with the conditions that give rise to crime. Its emphasis is on the prevention of crime through modification of the social and economic conditions that breed crime. The elimination of poverty, racial inequities, and motives for committing crime is its objective.

28 Obviously, it is possible to hold all three views. One may advocate treatment for those who commit first-time, minor offenses; swift and severe punishment for "hardened" criminals who engage in heinous crimes; and the alteration of social conditions that encourage criminal behavior. However, we should

note that attempts to find a way to reduce crime and prevent recidivism among criminals have been largely unsuccessful (Rappaport 1977). What is needed is a continuing effort to test alternative programs, including reform within the criminal justice system. ❑

EXERCISES

Understanding What You Have Read

d
_____ 1. The main idea of the selection is that **(5)**
   a. criminals are often young males.
   b. prison is the best punishment for criminals.
   c. television is the main cause of violence.
   d. people become criminal or violent for many different reasons.

a
_____ 2. The main idea of paragraph 3 is that **(5b)**
   a. certain crimes are committed mostly by young people.
   b. young people are likely to be delinquent.
   c. crime will decrease because the population is getting older.
   d. older people do not commit murder and violent street crimes.

c
_____ 3. According to the selection, crime statistics **(6a)**
   a. bear no relation to reality.
   b. are always reliable.
   c. can vary depending on record keeping and victim reports.
   d. give us no useful information.

b
_____ 4. Victims are most often **(6a)**
   a. totally unlike the perpetrator of the crime.
   b. members of the same race or socioeconomic group as the perpetrator.
   c. friends or family members of the perpetrator.
   d. females.

c
_____ 5. The numbered list that begins with paragraph 6 follows an overall pattern of **(7)**

a. cause and effect.
b. comparison and contrast.
c. classification.
d. all of the above.

c _____ 6. The ten items in the list mentioned in question 5 are arranged in **(7)**
a. space order.
b. alphabetical order.
c. order of seriousness of disturbance.
d. reverse order of seriousness of disturbance.

a _____ 7. Paragraph 22 follows a pattern of **(7)**
a. cause and effect.
b. comparison and contrast.
c. classification.
d. listing of details.

8. The writer suggests several likely causes of criminality and violence. Put a checkmark in front of each likely cause. **(6a)**

_____ a. Genetic abnormalities

√ _____ b. Heredity

√ _____ c. Unstable families

_____ d. Overly protective families

√ _____ e. Unaffectionate families

√ _____ f. Criminal families

√ _____ g. Child abuse

√ _____ h. Cultural goals of wealth

√ _____ i. Poverty

√ _____ j. Bad friends

_____ k. Overactive imagination

_______ l. Lack of strict upbringing

√ m. Television

Interpreting and Evaluating

1. In which category would you predict that Megargee and Bohn would likely place each of the following prisoners? Write the category in the space following each description. **(10)**

   a. Sam does not trust anyone. He attacked the social worker who tried to talk with him. When alone in his cell he mutters to himself about how he was cheated by his partners. **Charlie**

   b. Terry is an eighteen-year-old school dropout. His two brothers are college graduates and are beginning successful careers, but Terry says he does not like school and would rather hang out. While hanging out with a motorcycle gang he became involved in an armed bank robbery. **Easy**

   c. Rita always did very well in school, although her fierce temper often got her into fights with her classmates and conflicts with her teachers. Despite her success in school she decided that straight life was too dull and she got caught up in high-society drug sales. She seemed to enjoy watching her clients destroy themselves while she got rich off them. After being caught she showed no remorse for what she had done. All she said was, "Fun while it lasted." **Delta**

   d. Mike is an easygoing college student who financed his college education by selling marijuana and hashish to his friends until he got caught. His family was surprised when he got into trouble, but they have been supportive and have visited him regularly in prison. **Item**

   e. As a child, Nell moved around from foster home to foster home and never was able to settle into a single school. She fell further and further behind in school and finally dropped out. To support herself she tried various unskilled jobs, but she could never hold on to them. She moved from boyfriend to boyfriend looking for one to support her. Finally, with no place to turn, she became a prostitute. **Jupiter**

2. Based on Megargee and Bohn's discussion, which one of the five prisoners in the previous question would you predict would benefit most from academic training? **(10)**

   Nell (the Jupiter)

   Which would resist treatment?

   Sam (the Charlie)

   Which might benefit from individual psychotherapy?

   Rita (the Delta)

3. Put a checkmark before each generalization you can reasonably make on the basis of this selection. **(11)**

______ a. Criminals can all be successfully treated.

√ b. People become criminals for many different reasons.

______ c. By examining a person's heredity you can reliably predict whether he or she will become a criminal.

√ d. Family disorders are a major cause of people's becoming criminals.

______ e. All poor people will do anything to become rich and successful.

√ f. People often learn to become criminals from their friends.

√ g. Because people become criminals for so many different reasons, one must look at each case individually.

______ h. We understand well how to decrease crime.

4. Put an E before statements from the selection that are strongly supported by evidence. Put a U before the statements about which the evidence is uncertain. **(12b)**

E ______ a. "Americans are much concerned about crime and violence."

E ______ b. "Demographic factors such as age, sex, race, and social class are highly related to the commission of crime."

U ______ c. "Criminal behavior patterns can be influenced by heredity."

E ______ d. "Family environment plays a role in delinquency and criminality."

E ______ e. "Certain conditions in American society combine to encourage crime."

E ______ f. "Individuals may be socialized into a life of professional crime."

d ______ 5. The authors of this selection refer to many researchers in parentheses to show **(12)**
a. that they have read a lot.
b. that students have a lot to learn.
c. who is to blame for mistakes.
d. the sources of their ideas and information.

Vocabulary

For each word in the left-hand column, write the letter of the best definition from the right-hand column. Use word-part clues and context clues from the selection. **(1c, 1d)**

d ______ 1. juvenile

f ______ 2. proportion

i ______ 3. statistics

h ______ 4. heredity

a. person of equal status
b. conditions that are unequal or unfair
c. brought into a group of people
d. a young person
e. make insensitive and violent

b 5. inequities
c 6. socialized
a 7. peer
j 8. behavioral
e 9. brutalize
g 10. commission

f. part
g. the carrying out of an act
h. characteristics transmitted from parents to offspring
i. numerical data
j. referring to actions

WRITING PRACTICE

1. Imagine this selection is assigned reading for a course you are taking in psychology. Write a set of study notes for the assignment.
2. Based on your own experiences and observations, write a few paragraphs discussing whether violence in the movies and on television increases violent behavior.

18

The Disappearing Black Teacher

Charles Whitaker

Teaching was once an attractive career for black men and women. So why are fewer and fewer young black people today choosing teaching for their life's work? Charles Whitaker offers some disturbing answers in this article from Ebony *magazine.*

Prereading

On a separate sheet of paper, freewrite about why you think black people are not choosing to become teachers. **[3a(3)]** Read the selection after you do your freewriting.

Word Highlights

precociously (¶1) in an unexpectedly mature way
cherubs (¶1) angels
chronically (¶2) constantly; lasting for a long time
aspiring (¶4) trying to reach a goal
attrition (¶6) gradual reduction in numbers
quizzical (¶12) in a puzzled or surprised way
wracked (¶13) caused severe damage
crux (¶17) main point; essential feature

Well before most parents begin to suspect such things, Nora Brooks Blakely's parents knew that she was destined to become a teacher. A precociously bright child, Nora began preparing for her future at age three by marshaling the children of her South Side Chicago neighborhood into her make-believe schoolhouse for daily lessons. By age 20, when she earned a bachelor's degree in education from the University of Illinois, there was little doubt in anyone's mind — least of all Nora's — that she would spend the rest of her life surrounded by chalkboards and cherubs. "I assumed that I was going to be teaching until they rolled me out of the classroom in a wheelchair," she says.

2 But the reality of life in an urban school system proved to be unsettling. Discipline problems, chronically underachieving students, and an indifferent administration dimmed Ms. Blakely's enthusiasm for a long career in education. After eight years of teaching upper level elementary school pupils in a Chicago public school, she called it quits, and now directs her own children's theater company, Chocolate Chips.

3 "It just got to be an overwhelming drain," she says of her years in the classroom. "Teachers were expected to be prison guards, secretaries and social workers. You got no respect or support from either parents or the administration. And when you're working with eighth graders whose reading scores ranged from the fifth-grade level down to first grade, you don't get those blinding success stories that make you forget about all the negatives."

4 Unfortunately, Ms. Blakely's is not an isolated case. More and more of the nation's talented Black teachers are abandoning careers in education. At the same time, increasing numbers of Black college students — daunted by the low pay and poor working conditions — are also turning their backs on teaching as a career option. To make matters worse, many states have instituted standardized licensing exams that have all but driven out many young, Black aspiring teachers.

5 As a result, Black classroom teachers are becoming a scarce educational resource. It is a frightening trend, and recent studies suggest that should it go unchecked, its effect on American education could be devastating.

6 Statistics bring this pending crisis into dramatic focus. Presently, Black children constitute more than 16 percent of the population of the nation's elementary and secondary public schools, according to a 1987 survey by the National Education Association. Yet, only 6.9 percent of the country's public school teachers are Black. The survey also suggested that at the current rate of population growth and minority teacher attrition, Blacks may make up more than 40 percent of the children in

public schools by the year 2000, while constituting less than five percent of the teaching force.

7 Adding to the problem is the rising rate of mass defections by Black teachers already in the field. A national survey conducted by the Metropolitan Life Insurance Co. in 1988 noted that 41 percent of the Black and Hispanic teachers polled stated that they would leave teaching in the next five years, compared with only 25 percent of the White teachers who said they planned to leave the field.

8 Why is it that teaching — once the mainstay of the Black middle class — has lost its appeal as a career choice? The reasons are varied, and not entirely negative, many say.

9 One of the greatest drains on the minority teaching pool has been the windows of opportunity that have opened for Blacks in other, higher-paying fields. "When I came into teaching in the '60s, education was the province of women and minorities," says Mary Hatwood Futrell, president of the National Education Association. "But as these opportunities have opened up in business and private industry, many of the talented people who may have gone into teaching were directed elsewhere."

10 It is the steering of academically talented students away from careers in education that continues to make many in the field bristle. "There often is this feeling in the Black community that if a student is bright, he or she is somehow too good to be a teacher," says Dr. Elaine P. Witty, dean of the school of education at Norfolk State University in Virginia. "The community will rain praise on students who say they are in engineering or pre-med programs, but the student who is in education doesn't get that kind of encouragement."

11 Joyce Nelson, 21, a senior at Grambling State University in Louisiana, says that when she told her high school teachers that she was interested in a career in education they were dumbfounded. "They all wanted to know why such a good student would want to be a teacher," she says. "Even now, people give me a puzzled look when I tell them I'm in education."

12 Part of the reason for the quizzical looks is the tarnished reputation teaching has developed. While it was never considered an occupation in which one could make a fortune, teaching paid livable wages and, in most corners of the country, was considered a highly respectable profession.

13 But the poverty and overcrowding that have wracked the nation's inner-cities, have helped turn many urban schools into battlegrounds. Teaching began to resemble police work as instructors grappled with their charges for control of the classroom. With more disciplining than instruction going on, test scores plummeted, and teachers took the lion's share of the blame. Salaries remained low as the public groused about declining scores on standardized tests.

14 While there was much governmental tinkering done to improve urban schools, teachers were seldom included in the planning. This fact, too, was not lost on many potential educators. "When we ask young people why they don't want to go into teaching, they not only cite the low pay and the poor conditions, they say that teachers aren't treated like professionals," says Mrs. Futrell. "Teachers are treated like very tall children and are given very little input."

15 Another critical barrier to Blacks in education has been the institution of standardized exams. In 44 states, would-be teachers must pass a competency exam to be certified. Unfortunately, Black college students fail these exams at a disproportionately high rate.

16 To many educators, the tests simply serve as a means of weeding Blacks out of teaching and are not a true indicator of teacher competency. "There is no evidence that suggests a relationship between the instructional skills that Black teachers have and their ability to pass these tests," says Dr. Charles V. Willie, a sociologist and professor of education and urban studies at Harvard University. "In fact Black teachers have cultivated Black students to the point where the majority of Black bachelor's degree holders in the United States continue to come from predominantly Black institutions."

17 And therein lies the crux of the educational crisis posed by the dwindling number of Black teachers. Many experts say that the academic performance of students is closely related to their role models. "If a Black child during the course of his school years has only one or two Black teachers out of say 40, you can imagine the message that child gets about academic achievement," says Dr. Witty of Norfolk State.

18 Despite the grim outlook painted for minorities in teaching, students continue to seek careers in education.

19 Take Debbie E. Locke, 33, who is pursuing teacher certification at Norfolk State after leaving a successful career as a

recruiter for the Bell & Howell Educational Group. "I feel I have a lot to share with students," she says. "Students today need a lot. They need direction and discipline. It excites me to get in there and try to motivate them."

20 Kenneth Coutee, 21, a senior at Grambling State, says he wants to help guide and groom future Black leaders much in the way that he was guided by his eighth grade guidance counselor in his hometown of Alexandria, La. "We need dedicated Black teachers right now," he says. "The monetary reward in it may not be great, but it's worth it to be able to inspire the next generation of leaders."

21 And there are the dedicated professionals like Beverly Porter, 35, who after nearly 13 years in the Chicago Public School System remains enthusiastic about her job as a head start teacher. There are problems, she states. "But I see myself as a contributing agent for change in the community and in the field," she says. "And when you have those days when your lessons have gone well, and the children are actually getting your message, you can see it, and it keeps you going." ❑

EXERCISES

Understanding What You Have Read

b ____ 1. The main idea of this selection is that **(5)**

a. the teacher shortage is a serious national problem.
b. black teachers are becoming a scarce educational resource.
c. we must expand opportunities for minorities in education.
d. discipline problems in Chicago's schools keep many blacks from teaching there.

a ____ 2. The main idea in the first paragraph is that **(5b)**

a. Nora Blakely wanted to be a teacher.
b. University of Illinois degree programs help students overcome career doubts.
c. support from parents is essential for a child planning a career.
d. teachers in wheelchairs face many problems in the classroom.

c ______ 3. Compared with white teachers, how many more black and Hispanic teachers already in the field say that they will leave teaching? **(6a)**
a. Twenty-five percent more than white teachers
b. Forty-one percent more than white teachers
c. Sixteen percent more than white teachers
d. The rate is about the same.

d ______ 4. According to the selection, by the year 2000, black children in public schools will **(6a)**
a. make up the majority.
b. be under 5 percent.
c. constitute about 16 percent of the population.
d. make up more than 40 percent of the population.

a ______ 5. A major problem for blacks who want to enter education is **(6a)**
a. standardized exams.
b. poor college preparation.
c. biased surveys.
d. low rates of membership in the National Education Association.

6. Put *maj* beside facts that you think are major; put *min* beside facts that you think are minor. **(6b)**

min ______ a. Nora Brooks Blakely got her bachelor's degree when she was twenty.

maj ______ b. Only 6.9 percent of America's teachers are black.

maj ______ c. Talented black students often are steered away from education.

maj ______ d. Standardized tests can serve to weed blacks out of education.

min ______ e. Nora Brooks Blakely directs a children's theater company called Chocolate Chips.

min ______ f. The president of the National Education Association is Mary Hatwood Futrell.

maj g. Poor classroom conditions turn many blacks away from careers in education.

min h. Kenneth Coutee comes from Alexandria, Louisiana.

maj i. Young black children could benefit from having black teachers as role models.

min j. Dr. Charles Willie is a sociologist at Harvard University.

Interpreting and Evaluating

b 1. This article appeared with a photograph of a classroom full of students. Instead of a teacher at the front of the class, there was a question mark on the chalkboard. We are to infer that the question mark **(4a, 8)**

a. was made by the black children in the class.
b. stands for the question of who will teach in the classroom.
c. reflects the writer's confusion about why blacks are not choosing teaching as a career.
d. was made by the teacher to stimulate children to raise their hands and answer questions.

d 2. From Nora Brooks Blakely's new profession as director of Chocolate Chips, we can infer that **(8)**

a. she is very unhappy.
b. she will change careers many more times in her life.
c. her interests in baking and in children have finally brought her to the right career.
d. her love for children still guides her career choice.

a 3. From the data on teachers leaving the profession, we can infer that black teachers **(8)**

a. are less happy with their jobs than are white teachers.
b. are more happy about their jobs than are white teachers.
c. are about equally happy with their jobs as are white teachers.
d. cannot be compared with white teachers.

d 4. We can infer from the comments by Kenneth Coutee that for him **(8)**

a. money is a very important consideration in making a career choice.
b. black students should take courses in leadership to become high-paid teachers in the future.
c. leadership is impossible to teach in the classroom.
d. money is not as important as being able to influence future leaders.

c ______ 5. We can safely predict from this article that if more black adults do not become teachers, **(10)**
a. our entire educational system will fall apart.
b. fewer black children will get the education they need to become doctors, lawyers, and other professionals.
c. few black schoolchildren will themselves choose teaching as a career.
d. many states will end their competency exams for teaching.

a ______ 6. From this selection we can safely draw all of the following conclusions *except* that **(10)**
a. no talented black students today are seeking careers in education.
b. classroom conditions must change if young black people are going to choose teaching careers.
c. our society must convince young blacks that teaching is a valued career.
d. by the next century, we will see a sharp difference between the number of black children in our schools and the number of black teachers teaching them.

7. Put a checkmark next to the generalizations that we can safely make from this selection. **(11)**

______ a. All standardized tests should be eliminated.

√ ______ b. We should develop ways other than standardized tests to judge people's abilities.

√ ______ c. People do not always choose careers to fill society's greatest needs.

______ d. Hard work and study make it possible for someone to succeed at just about any career he or she chooses.

_______ e. More white people should give up their jobs to make room for needed black people.

_______ f. Blacks and whites have much to gain by working together.

Vocabulary

1. The following words come from the selection. Try to figure out their definitions by using word-part clues. **(1d)** Write the definitions on the lines provided. Then do the crossword puzzle, filling in the words that best suit the meanings in the clues.

disproportionately **Student responses will vary.**

____

dumbfounded _______________

____

mainstay _______________

____

respectable _______________

____

underachieving _______________

____

									1M								
				2U	N	D	E	R	A	C	H	I	E	V	I	N	G
			3R						I								
			E						N								
			S						S								
4D	I	S	P	R	O	P	O	R	T	I	O	N	A	T	E	L	Y
			E						A								
			C						Y								
			T														
			A														
5D	U	M	B	F	O	U	N	D	E	D							
			L														
			E														

Across

2. Accomplishing below expected standards
4. In a manner that is not in a correct relation or ratio with a related issue or quantity
5. Made speechless

Down

1. Major support
3. Worthy; deserving esteem

Using sentence clues from the selection, determine the meanings of the words in italics. Then select the best definition from the choices given and write the letter of your answer on the blank line. **(1c)**

a _____ 2. *destined* to become a teacher
   a. influenced by fate
   b. designed
   c. taught
   d. tried

d _____ 3. *marshaling* the children
   a. commanding
   b. pushing
   c. helping
   d. organizing

c 4. *indifferent* administration
a. strange
b. highly unusual
c. unconcerned
d. highly typical

b 5. not an *isolated* case
a. extremely cold
b. separated from a group
c. related
d. open-and-shut

b 6. *abandoning* careers in education
a. choosing
b. giving up
c. enjoying greatly
d. hating

a 7. *daunted* by the low pay
a. discouraged
b. made poor
c. followed
d. angered

c 8. *pending* crisis
a. serious
b. minor
c. awaiting
d. unexpected

d 9. *grappled* with their charges
a. laughed
b. punished
c. helped
d. struggled

c 10. test scores *plummeted*
a. rose dramatically
b. went unreported
c. fell sharply
d. vanished

a 11. *grousad* about
a. complained
b. raised questions
c. heard
d. asked permission

WRITING PRACTICE

1. Write a one-paragraph summary of the reasons that blacks are turning away from careers in education.
2. Develop a plan for increasing the number of black teachers in the United States. Write a paragraph or two to explain what steps you would take to end the problem of the disappearing black teacher.

19

To Make a DNA Print

Cassandra Franklin-Barbajosa

Through a sequence of illustrations, the author helps us understand a new way to identify people. As you read the text and study the pictures, try to understand how each step grows from the previous one.

Prereading

Before looking at this selection, form groups of students and answer these questions: What qualities did you inherit from your mother, father, or other blood relatives? How do people inherit physical or emotional traits? What do you know about heredity, genes, or DNA? **[3a(4)]**

Skimming

Before reading this selection, skim it to answer these questions. **(3b)**

1. What is the overall process presented in the illustration?

   how a DNA print is made

2. How many steps are there in this process?

   seven

3. What is the main material worked with in this process?

   DNA

4. Where does this material come from?

   human cells (for example, from blood, semen, or saliva)

Word Highlights

chromosome long molecular strand containing genetic information
nucleated containing cell nuclei
centrifuge device for separating chemicals by rapid spinning
alkaline caustic reactive chemical

Deep in the animated network of the cell nucleus lies the molecule of heredity — DNA. Its twin spirals are built from four interlocking chemical bases — adenine paired with thymine and cytosine paired with guanine. Code messages, genes, are stored along a chromosome in sequences of these chemical bases. Genes define the unique characteristics of each living thing. It is here, for example, that butterflies are given their wing patterns and people are assigned eye color.

Scientists have been challenged by the inner workings of DNA since 1944, when American researcher Oswald Avery defined its role in transferring hereditary characteristics. James D. Watson and Francis Crick described the spiral structure of DNA in 1953. In 1984 Alec Jeffreys, a geneticist in Leicester, England, devised a way to visually identify DNA found between the genes. In certain regions the DNA patterns vary distinctively from person to person except in cases of identical twins. Jeffreys's method of identification, known as DNA fingerprinting (simplified in the figure), has become a valuable technique for investigating crimes in which biological clues are left behind. Now, in some jurisdictions, suspects can be linked to a crime by evidence that incriminates them to their very molecules.

EXERCISES

Understanding What You Have Read

b 1. The main purpose of this selection is to **(5)**
   a. give the history of DNA.
   b. explain how DNA can be used to identify people.

3 Cut DNA into Fragments

Enzymes that recognize certain sequences in the chemical base patterns are added to the DNA. These enzymes, proteins that cause a chemical reaction, act like molecular scissors and cut the DNA molecule at specific points, leaving fragments of various lengths.

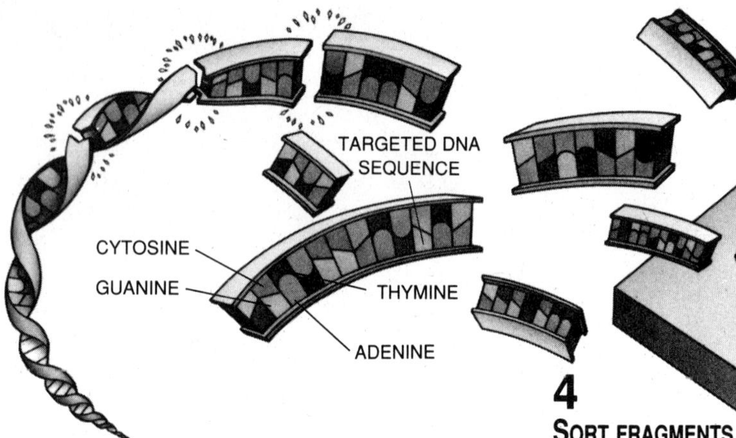

4 Sort Fragments by Length

The DNA fragments are placed on a bed of gel, and an electric current is applied. The DNA, which is negatively charged, moves toward the positive end. Several hours later the fragments have become arranged by length.

CHROMOSOME

WHITE BLOOD CELL

NUCLEUS

2 Extract and Purify DNA

The sample is treated with chemicals to break open the white blood cells. In a centrifuge, DNA is separated from the cells and later purified.

1 Collect the Sample

The bloodied shirt of a murder victim contains enough of the wounded killer's white blood cells to draw a sample. DNA can also be extracted from traces of semen, saliva, hair roots, or bone—wherever nucleated cells are found.

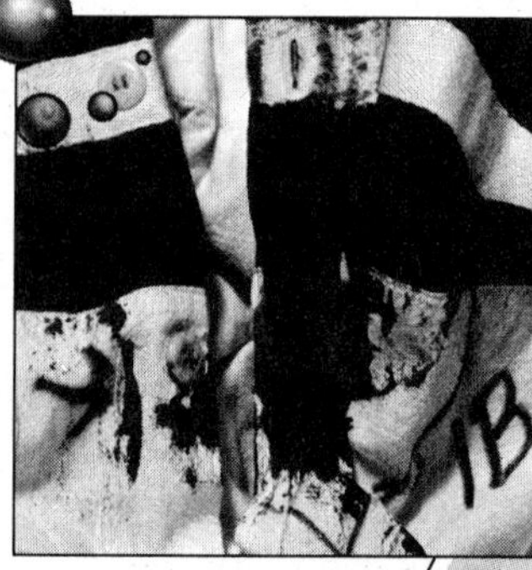

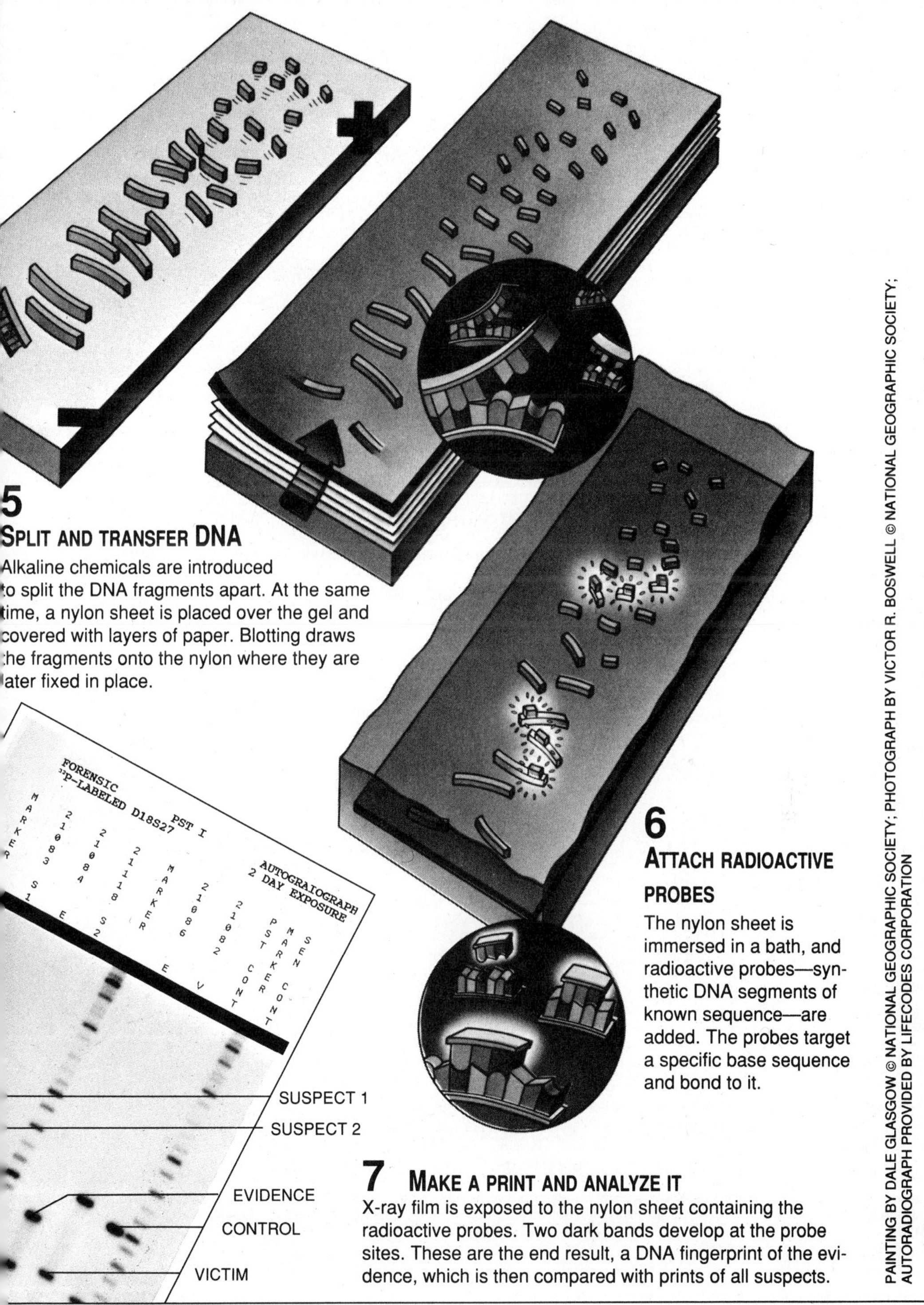

5

SPLIT AND TRANSFER DNA

Alkaline chemicals are introduced to split the DNA fragments apart. At the same time, a nylon sheet is placed over the gel and covered with layers of paper. Blotting draws the fragments onto the nylon where they are later fixed in place.

6

ATTACH RADIOACTIVE PROBES

The nylon sheet is immersed in a bath, and radioactive probes—synthetic DNA segments of known sequence—are added. The probes target a specific base sequence and bond to it.

7 MAKE A PRINT AND ANALYZE IT

X-ray film is exposed to the nylon sheet containing the radioactive probes. Two dark bands develop at the probe sites. These are the end result, a DNA fingerprint of the evidence, which is then compared with prints of all suspects.

PAINTING BY DALE GLASGOW © NATIONAL GEOGRAPHIC SOCIETY; PHOTOGRAPH BY VICTOR R. BOSWELL © NATIONAL GEOGRAPHIC SOCIETY; AUTORADIOGRAPH PROVIDED BY LIFECODES CORPORATION

c. explain how DNA carries genetic information.
d. describe how criminals are caught using DNA fingerprints.

c ______ 2. The main idea of the first paragraph is that **(5b)**
a. DNA is located in the cell nucleus.
b. the spirals of adenine, thymine, cytosine, and guanine carry coded genetic information.
c. genes define the unique characteristics of each living thing.
d. genes give butterflies their wing patterns.

c ______ 3. The main idea of the second paragraph is that **(5b)**
a. Oswald Avery defined the role of DNA.
b. Watson and Crick described DNA's spiral structure.
c. scientists have discovered how to identify people through DNA fingerprinting.
d. some courts allow genetic fingerprints to be used as evidence.

a ______ 4. The second paragraph is arranged in **(7)**
a. time order.
b. space order.
c. order of importance.
d. the cause-and-effect pattern.

d ______ 5. The DNA of different humans is **(6a)**
a. exactly the same, which distinguishes them from other animals.
b. always different in all ways.
c. different in some regions for all people.
d. different in some regions except for identical twins.

a ______ 6. DNA fingerprinting is **(6a)**
a. a method of identifying individuals from biological evidence.
b. a method for identifying fingerprints.
c. less accurate than traditional fingerprinting.
d. foolproof.

b ______ 7. DNA fingerprinting can be used as evidence **(6a)**
a. in all courts.

b. in courts in some jurisdictions.
c. in murder cases only.
d. whenever physical evidence is found.

8. Put the following steps in creating a DNA print in order by placing a 1 before the first step, a 2 before the second, and so on. **(7a)**

6 a. Attach radioactive probes.

2 b. Extract and purify the DNA.

1 c. Collect the sample.

5 d. Split and transfer the DNA.

3 e. Cut the DNA into fragments.

7 f. Make a print and analyze it.

4 g. Sort the fragments by length.

9. a. Explain how step 1 makes step 2 and the following steps possible. **(4, 6)**

You need a sample to extract and analyze the DNA from.

b. Explain how step 2 makes step 3 and the following steps possible. **(4, 6)**

Extracting and purifying the DNA gives you material to manipulate and analyze.

c. Explain how step 3 makes step 4 and the following steps possible. **(4, 6)**

Cutting the DNA into fragments produces small pieces that can be sorted, split, and identified.

d. In step four, what function does electricity serve? **(4, 6)**

The positive charge attracts the negatively charged fragments. Over a period of several hours, the fragments become arranged by length.

e. In step 5, how are the DNA fragments separated? **(4, 6)**

Alkaline chemicals split the DNA apart.

f. In step 6, what is the purpose of radioactive probes? **(4, 6)**

The probes identify the segments by targeting a specific sequence and attaching to it.

g. What kind of information results from step 7? **(4, 6)**

An X ray that shows the pattern of probe sites. This "fingerprint" can then be compared with prints made from the evidence.

a 10. Overall, the illustrations in the section **(4)**
a. show the DNA as it is being collected, cut apart, and analyzed.
b. are photographs of DNA fragments.
c. show scientists at work on a difficult process.
d. are samples of DNA evidence that has been used in court.

b 11. How does the time order of the second paragraph compare to the time order of the sequence of illustrations? **(7a)**
a. The second paragraph follows exact time order, while the pictures jump backward and forward.
b. The second paragraph follows a single sequence of ac-

tual historical events, while the pictures follow a sequence that can be carried out at any time.
c. The second paragraph is historically accurate, while the pictures reflect a plan that has been thought about but never actually implemented.
d. They both present the same kind of time sequence.

Interpreting and Evaluating

c ______ 1. We can infer from the selection that James Watson and Francis Crick's description of DNA's spiral structure **(8)**
a. completed our knowledge of genetics.
b. contradicted the work of Oswald Avery.
c. made possible the later work on DNA fingerprinting.
d. was not based on the work of any other scientists.

d ______ 2. If a suspect's DNA fingerprint is found in blood stains on the carpet at a stabbing murder site, the strongest inference we can make is that the suspect **(8)**
a. cut himself while stabbing the victim.
b. stabbed the victim in self-defense.
c. was at the scene of the crime.
d. was at the scene of the crime and injured.

b ______ 3. DNA identification is called *DNA fingerprinting* because it **(9)**
a. uses actual fingerprints to get the biological sample.
b. can be used instead of traditional fingerprinting.
c. is used with traditional fingerprinting techniques.
d. creates patterns that resemble fingerprint patterns.

a ______ 4. In step 3, enzymes are compared to scissors because the enzymes **(9)**
a. cut the DNA into smaller pieces.
b. work in pairs, coming together.
c. create sharp blades that cut mechanically.
d. can be controlled manually by the scientist.

d ______ 5. From the selection we can conclude that **(10)**
a. DNA fingerprinting has replaced traditional fingerprinting in most courts.
b. the police use DNA fingerprinting in most cases.

c. DNA fingerprinting is inexpensive and foolproof.
d. DNA fingerprinting is starting to be used more widely.

a ______ 6. Based on information in the selection, we can predict that DNA fingerprinting would be especially useful in cases of **(10)**
a. rape.
b. embezzlement.
c. drug sales.
d. murder by poison.

c ______ 7. Which of the following might provide samples for DNA fingerprinting? **(10)**
a. A shirt ripped from the back of the assailant
b. Fingerprints left on a glass
c. The assailant's still-moist cigarette butt
d. Hair strands cut from the assailant's head

c ______ 8. We can conclude that DNA fingerprinting is useful for proving **(10)**
a. guilt.
b. intentions.
c. presence at the scene of a crime.
d. the victim's knowledge of the suspect.

b ______ 9. In general, DNA fingerprinting seems to offer a(n) **(11)**
a. cheap, efficient method of identification in all situations.
b. reliable method where biological samples are available.
c. identification method only for criminal cases.
d. way to catch most criminals.

b ______ 10. Which of the following statements does the selection support with specific evidence? **(12b)**
a. Genes assign people their eye colors.
b. Scientists have been challenged by the workings of DNA.
c. DNA fingerprinting is a valuable tool for criminal investigation.
d. DNA fingerprinting can be used as evidence in some legal jurisdictions.

a ______ 11. The overall style of writing in this piece is **(12d)**
a. straightforward and informative.
b. enthusiastic and filled with praise.
c. critical and analytic.
d. poetic and imaginative.

d ______ 12. This piece appears to be written for **(12d)**
a. biologists and other scientists only.
b. lawyers, judges, and police officers.
c. high school science students.
d. general readers interested in scientific advances.

b ______ 13. The illustrations in this selection **(4, 12d)**
a. relate closely to the two paragraphs on page 553.
b. make the steps described in the numbered paragraphs more vivid.
c. convey the entire story without the need for words.
d. are not closely related to the words.

Vocabulary

Define each of the words in List A by placing in front of it the number of the appropriate definition from List B. **(1)**

List A

i ______ 1. animated

l ______ 2. heredity

e ______ 3. adenine

f ______ 4. thymine

g ______ 5. cytosine

h ______ 6. guanine

k ______ 7. molecule

n ______ 8. geneticist

a ______ 9. jurisdiction

d ______ 10. incriminates

c ______ 11. enzymes

j ______ 12. semen

b ______ 13. saliva

m ______ 14. radioactive

List B

a. region covered by a court
b. a digestive liquid
c. proteins that cause chemical reactions
d. identifies as a criminal
e. chemical paired with thymine to code genetic information
f. chemical paired with adenine to code genetic information
g. chemical paired with guanine to code genetic information
h. chemical paired with cytosine to code genetic information
i. living
j. male reproductive fluid
k. a stable structure of atoms
l. transmission of characteristics from parents to offspring
m. giving off radiation
n. a biologist who works with genes

WRITING PRACTICE

1. In a few paragraphs, describe the steps in making a DNA print.
2. Using diagrams as illustrations, give instructions for baking a pie, tying a knot, or completing some other simple task.

20

Classroom Focus Shifting to the Art of Thinking

Joseph Berger

This selection presents ways teachers are helping students learn to think. How do the teaching methods described here compare with those you experienced in your own education?

Prereading

Before reading this article, freewrite for ten minutes about how much and in what ways your elementary school teachers encouraged thinking in the classroom. **[3a(3)]**

Word Highlights

mission (¶7) assignment; goal
curriculums (¶8) planned programs for school; courses
advocates (¶9) supporters
dispositions (¶12) tendencies; inclinations
quiverfull (¶16) enough arrows to fill a container that holds arrows
recitation (¶18) repeating aloud

Children in kindergarten here are learning how to think. Not just to read and write and spell, but to think.

2 "What's inside the box?" asks the teacher, Robin Mosley Keffer, holding up a foot-long blue box sealed with tape. The 5-year-olds make some wild guesses: an egg, a fake animal, a big book, a balloon, high-heeled shoes, a cookie, spaghetti.

Kindergartners examining a closed box to try to determine its contents in a thinking exercise at the North Mianus School in Greenwich, Connecticut.

3 Ms. Keffer passes the box around and lets the children shake it, listen to it, smell it. She prods them to use their "powers of analysis" to eliminate some possibilities. The children decide the object is not a cookie because they could have smelled it. It is not an egg because an egg would have broken. A furry toy animal would not have made the rustling noise heard when the box was shaken.

4 The children never do guess that the box contains snapshots of them. But the wave of giggles when they peek inside suggests they have savored the thrill of deduction with the zest of Sherlock Holmes. They have practiced making inferences and learned how to support their hunches with a well-reasoned argument.

New Classroom Emphasis

5 An increasing number of teachers, from kindergarten through college, have altered lesson plans to include the art of thinking. Many others are being trained so they can shift the classroom emphasis away from just giving pupils information and more

toward making them think about the issues raised by that information.

6 These educators say that American students have become obsessed with getting the right answers on tests and are weak at analyzing what they are learning and at grasping implications. These weaknesses, the educators say, will affect the students' ability to make future decisions about career and marriage, what candidates to vote for and what products to buy.

7 While schools have always assumed that thinking was part of their mission, educators are making the teaching of thinking skills a more formal part of their programs.

8 Articles on teaching the concept of "critical thinking" have flourished since the late 1970's, and there has been a dramatic push in the last few years by at least 28 states and hundreds of school districts to re-train teachers and revise curriculums.

Rephrasing Questions to Make Pupils Think

These examples show how teachers can phrase the same questions traditionally to elicit one correct answer, or rephrase it to provoke thought and discussion using the critical-thinking method.

TRADITIONAL	REPHRASED
"Give me liberty or give me death," were the . . . words of: Thomas Jefferson, Patrick Henry or Benjamin Franklin.	Analyze a modern-day counterpart to the Sons of Liberty. What are the similarities, what are the differences?
Draw a scale model of a local shopping mall.	Draw a scale model projecting your local shopping mall into the year 2025, based on predictable changes in population and consumer needs.
Identify the manager of the New York Mets.	What qualities did Casey Stengel and Davey Johnson share that produced winning performances?

9 Advocates say their movement has gained new strength as a response to an exaggerated stress on memorized information created by the pressure to raise student performance on standardized tests. That stress, they say, is one of the unseen and harmful consequences of the "back to basics" calls of the 1970's.

Ability to Solve Problems

10 "It's not just the ability to remember things and feed them back on tests that determines how well you're going to do in life," said Dr. Heidi Jacobs, a professor at Teachers College at Columbia University. "It's the ability to solve problems and reflect and to, in fact, think critically." Dr. Jacobs is a consultant on thinking skills to the school systems of Greenwich, Conn., Mount Pleasant, N.Y., and several others in the New York metropolitan area.

11 About 80 percent of class questions, she said, are designed simply to have students recall information.

12 Robert H. Ennis, a professor of educational philosophy at the University of Illinois who is a leader of the critical-thinking movement, says the aim is to instill "dispositions and habits of mind, like trying to be well-informed, looking at things from another person's point of view, withholding a decision when the evidence is insufficient, being open-minded."

13 In the early 1980's reports by several influential commissions warned of the need to improve reasoning abilities for a population that would have to adjust to sweeping changes in technology in a more competitive world.

14 Since 1985 the California State University system has required its one million students to take a course in critical thinking before they can graduate. New York City's Board of Education created a Reasoning Skills Unit to promote analytical questions in various subjects.

15 Still, even proponents are aware that, like many educational trends, this one could be short-lived. "Maybe it's the fad of the 80s," said Ira Ewen, head of New York's Reasoning Skills Unit. "But not every fad is wrong. The question is will this have lasting impact."

Range of New Skills

16 In the meantime, students across the country are being taught a quiverfull of analytical skills: inferring explanations, supporting an argument, judging the credibility of a source, validating an observation, identifying underlying assumptions, designing experiments so a variable can be controlled.

17 Such skills are not always taught in distinct lessons, as Ms. Keffer did in her kindergarten class, but are often integrated into normal subjects.

18 An elementary lesson on the Boston Tea Party is usually a

recitation of facts about the colonists who protested a tea tax by disguising themselves as Indians and throwing tea from three ships into Boston harbor.

19 David N. Perkins, co-director of a cognitive skills project at the Harvard Graduate School of Education, says that when critical-thinking apostles teach about the Tea Party, they ask students to imagine themselves as colonists. Then they have to consider alternatives of protest like boycotting tea or sinking the boat.

20 "Kids will say: 'When people were in that situation they had to think about what to do. I never thought of people thinking back then,'" Mr. Perkins says.

21 He supports the value of lessons like this, even though they may take time from presentation of information, because, he argues, "people don't retain what they learn in school."

22 "A great deal of research in cognitive psychology," he says, "shows that the more actively you process information, the more you retain it."

23 Some educators caution that there is a danger if the teaching of how to think is divorced from regular course content.

24 "It's like teaching typing as an end in itself," said Dr. Diane Ravitch, coauthor of "What Do Our 17-Year-Olds Know?" which argues that American children have glaring gaps in essential knowledge. "It becomes an empty basket of skills. You have to have subject matter to think about."

25 The critical-thinking movement is so hardy that it has already sprouted six journals, three professional associations and three factions: those who say thinking should be taught separately, those who argue that it should be only integrated into the normal curriculum, and those who believe in both approaches.

26 Even in teaching mathematics, some proponents suggest instructors can move away from the assumption that there is always one correct answer. Instead, they say, students should be encouraged to explain how they arrived at a different answer.

27 Mr. Ewen said he could accept 6 as a plausible answer to "What is 27 divided by 5?" if the student provided a reasonable explanation.

28 A student, he said, might calculate that 27 chips divided into piles of 5 each will yield 6 piles, even though one of the piles is shorter than the other.

29 "The greatest discoveries," he said, "have come from peo-

ple who have looked at a standard situation and seen it differently." ❑

EXERCISES

Understanding What You Have Read

d 1. The main idea of this article is that **(5)**
   a. children in kindergarten are learning how to think.
   b. thinking has always been part of education.
   c. research on thinking has increased.
   d. schools teach thinking more than they previously did.

2. Write *maj* before each major detail from the article and write *min* before each minor detail. **(6b)**

min a. Kindergarten children try to guess what is in a box.

min b. The blue box is sealed with tape.

min c. The box contains snapshots.

maj d. The children say learning to think is fun.

maj e. The children have practiced making inferences.

maj f. Teachers have altered lessons to include more thinking skills.

maj g. Twenty-eight states have retrained teachers and revised curriculums.

min h. High school biology students are asked to identify unfamiliar plants and animals.

maj i. Eighty percent of class questions test recall only.

min j. Robert H. Ennis teaches at the University of Illinois.

min k. Students imagine the alternatives the colonists had.

min l. Typing is taught as an end in itself.

maj m. The more actively you process information, the more you retain it.

min n. The critical-thinking movement has six journals.

a 3. Choose the answer that states the key idea of this sentence: "Advocates say their movement has gained new strength as a response to an exaggerated stress on memorized information created by the pressure to raise student performance on standardized tests." **(5a)**
a. People support the teaching of thinking as a reaction to the emphasis on memorizing facts.
b. Standardized test scores have gone up.
c. Supporters of thinking skills believe students need to learn information to do well on tests.
d. Supporters of memorization stress the need for students to respond to information.

d 4. All of the following thinking or reading skills are mentioned in the selection *except* **(6a)**
a. inference.
b. deductive logic.
c. identifying underlying assumptions.
d. extrasensory perception.

d 5. Diane Ravitch **(6a)**
a. is totally opposed to teaching critical thinking.
b. is totally in support of teaching critical thinking.
c. belives that information is more important than thinking.
d. believes that students need subject information to think about.

b 6. The discussion of the lesson on the Boston Tea Party is an example of **(6a)**
a. the difference between classes that use critical thinking and those that don't.
b. teaching children to learn facts through imagination.
c. the weaknesses of critical thinking in helping students learn history.
d. the difference between mathematics and history.

c ______ 7. The story of the child dividing 27 by 5 at the end of the selection is an example **(6a)**
a. of wrong thinking.
b. of inferring explanations.
c. showing that there is not always one correct answer.
d. showing that students need to improve their mathematical skills.

c ______ 8. The table on page 565 **(4c)**
a. repeats examples from the selection.
b. shows how critical thinking helps improve learning.
c. compares questions that use critical thinking to ones that don't.
d. shows that traditional questions are less wordy than are nontraditional questions.

b ______ 9. The photograph **(4a)**
a. shows that students can be confused when they don't know the answer to a problem.
b. illustrates an incident described in the article.
c. shows how an older child can teach a younger one how to think.
d. shows students examining an animal and discussing what it eats.

Interpreting and Evaluating

c ______ 1. From the reaction of the kindergarten children to the guessing game about the box, we can infer that the children **(8)**
a. are frustrated by not guessing the right answer.
b. find the game silly.
c. are mentally excited by the game.
d. are interested in becoming detectives.

c ______ 2. From the quotation by Heidi Jacobs, we can predict that she would support having students **(10)**
a. study the facts of history.
b. write long essays.
c. solve thinking problems.
d. practice taking standardized exams.

d _______ 3. From Ira Ewen's comments about critical thinking being "the fad of the 80s," we can infer that he thinks critical thinking **(8)**
a. will soon vanish.
b. is not a correct approach to education.
c. has built a strong, firm foundation.
d. is useful but is unsure that it will last as an educational priority.

a _______ 4. The phrase "a quiverfull of analytic skills" uses figurative language to compare **(9)**
a. ways of thinking to arrows.
b. thinking to use a bow and arrow.
c. skills to a container for arrows.
d. analyzing to fighting a battle.

b _______ 5. Diane Ravitch uses the figurative phrase "an empty basket of skills" to **(9)**
a. compare thinking to emptiness.
b. suggest that you have to put something in the thinking for it to be useful.
c. show that you can hold ways of thinking together in one place.
d. suggest that students have to put skills in their baskets.

c _______ 6. From the differences among the three groups in the critical-thinking movement, we can infer that **(8)**
a. not all teachers support the critical-thinking movement.
b. whenever you get teachers together, they disagree.
c. teachers believe in different ways of teaching critical thinking.
d. thinking is not part of learning other subjects.

a _______ 7. From the entire selection you can conclude that **(10)**
a. educators are concerned about teaching thinking.
b. teachers have discovered totally new methods for teaching thinking.
c. students learn to think in all classrooms.
d. students are thinking better than they did in the past.

c
8. Generally the authorities quoted in this selection would support the belief that **(11)**
   a. to each question there is only one right answer.
   b. getting the right answer is of no special value.
   c. thinking through problems is as valuable as getting a right answer.
   d. students who get wrong answers have learned nothing.

b
9. The selection quotes many education experts to show that **(12)**
   a. they all say the same thing.
   b. there is wide interest in critical thinking.
   c. the critical-thinking movement is correct.
   d. the writer has done his homework.

d
10. We can conclude that the writer thinks that the critical-thinking movement **(10)**
   a. is well intentioned but misguided.
   b. is totally correct in its approach.
   c. will be the major force in teaching for many years.
   d. is currently influencing many schools.

Vocabulary

Using sentence clues and word-part clues, determine the meaning of the words in italics. Then write the letter of the best definition in the space provided. **(1c, 1d)**

b
1. *savored* the thrill of deduction
   a. eliminated
   b. tasted with pleasure
   c. tasted with disgust
   d. decided on

a
2. shift the classroom *emphasis* away from
   a. main attention
   b. discussion
   c. work
   d. desk

d
3. an *exaggerated* stress
   a. well-placed
   b. large
   c. needless
   d. overly large

d
4. performance on *standardized* tests
   a. educational
   b. hard
   c. quality control
   d. made similar for comparison

b
5. when the evidence is *insufficient*
   a. conflicting
   b. not enough
   c. misleading
   d. overwhelming

a
6. judging the *credibility* of a source
   a. believability
   b. loan-worthiness
   c. amazement
   d. origin

c
7. *validating* an observation
   a. discussing
   b. eliminating
   c. checking
   d. correcting

d
8. identifying underlying *assumptions*
   a. criticisms to be evaluated
   b. facts to be questioned
   c. questions for discussion
   d. ideas taken for granted

a
9. often *integrated* into normal subjects
   a. brought together
   b. kept separate
   c. compared with
   d. helped by

b 10. some *proponents* suggest
a. experts
b. supporters
c. critics
d. teachers

WRITING PRACTICE

1. List, describe, and give an example of each of the critical-thinking skills mentioned in this selection.
2. Write a paragraph evaluating which you think is more important — knowing information or knowing how to think.

21

Conflict and Cooperation

Robert A. Dahl

In this selection from a political science textbook, a professor of government discusses some interesting theories about what makes human beings political animals. Read carefully to understand how the structure of governments helps people cooperate.

Prereading

Before you read the selection, make a word map for *conflict*. Use a separate sheet of paper. **[3a(2)]**

Word Highlights

capacity (¶1) ability to do something
theologians (¶3) people who study religion
animosity (¶4) bitter hatred; hostility
mercantile (¶4) pertaining to merchants or trade
actuated (¶4) put into action
dismal (¶6) dreary; gloomy; depressed
communion (¶6) a possessing or a sharing in common
tendencies (¶7) leanings; inclinations to behave in certain ways

Like other forms of life on this planet, human beings confront a basic task: to deal satisfactorily with their conflicts and thereby secure the advantages of community and cooperation. Unlike other forms of life, human beings are endowed with a capacity to reflect on this task and to search for better solutions by conscious thought and deliberate choices.

2 The task of overcoming conflicts and achieving community and cooperation arises because human beings are unable and unwilling to live in complete isolation. The advantages of cooperation and community life are so numerous and so obvious that they must have been evident to man from earliest times. By now, our ancestors have closed off the choice; for most of us the option of total isolation from a community is, realistically speaking, no longer open.

3 Nonetheless, however strongly human beings are driven to seek the company of one another, and despite thousands of years' practice, they have never discovered a way in which they can live together without conflict. Conflict exists when one individual wishes to follow a line of action that would make it difficult or impossible for someone else to pursue his own desires. Conflict seems to be an inescapable aspect of the community and consequently of being human. Why conflict seems inescapable is a question that has troubled many people: philosophers, theologians, historians, social scientists, and doubtless a great many ordinary people. James Madison held that conflict was built into the very nature of men and women. Human beings have diverse abilities, he wrote in *The Federalist*, and these in turn produce diverse interests.

4 "As long as the reason of man continues fallible, and he is at liberty to exercise it," Madison wrote, "different opinions will be formed." Different opinions about religion, government, and other matters together with attachments to different leaders have "divided mankind into parties, inflamed them with mutual animosity, and rendered them much more disposed to vex and oppress each other than to cooperate for their common good." Thus, he concluded, "a landed interest, a manufacturing interest, a mercantile interest, a moneyed interest, with many lesser interests, grow up of necessity in civilized nations, and divide them into different classes, actuated by different sentiments and views."[1]

5 Whatever the explanation for conflict may be, and Madison's is but one of many, its existence is one of the prime facts of all community life. Yet if this were the only fact, then human

[1] Alexander Hamilton, John Jay, and James Madison, *The Federalist* (New York: Modern Library, n.d.), pp. 55–56. Madison's famous passages in *The Federalist*, too long to include here, are worth reading in full.

life would fit the description by the English political philosopher, Thomas Hobbes, in his *Leviathan* (1651). Hobbes describes mankind in a state of nature — a condition without government — having little in the way of agriculture, industry, trade, knowledge, arts, letters or society. "And which is worst of all," he concluded in a famous sentence, to exist without government would mean "continual fear, and danger of violent death and the life of man, solitary, poor, nasty, brutish, and short."[2]

6 But life is not so dismal. A condition of totally unregulated conflict is, as Hobbes himself argued, obviously incompatible with community life. Along with the human need for living in communion with fellow human beings and the inevitable conflicts that are generated whenever people try to live together, as far back into the past as one can pry, there have been traces of a search for ways in which human beings can cooperate. Means have been sought for settling conflicts within a community without extensive violence and bloodshed, according to standards of justice held, at the very least, among those who enforce the rules. We cannot pause to probe the mystery; but the evidence is so great that we can safely accept it as a fact.

7 Thus our existence as social beings — social animals, if you prefer — is conditioned by a set of contradictory tendencies that, taken altogether, makes us members of some political system:

8 1. Our need for human fellowship and the advantages of cooperation create communities.
9 2. But we are unable to live with others without conflict.
10 3. Consequently, communities search for ways of adjusting conflicts so that cooperation and community life will be possible and tolerable.

11 The third stage is the turning point — from men and women as social animals to men and women as political animals. If conflicts are to be settled, somewhere in the community there must be individuals or groups with enough authority or power to secure — or compel — a settlement. Someone must make sure that the parties to a conflict abide by the judgment of

[2]Thomas Hobbes, *Leviathan* (New York: Macmillan, 1947), p. 82.

the ruler, existing rules, their own agreement, or law. At any rate, human communities do not seem ever to have existed without some such powers — without, that is, political institutions. ❑

EXERCISES

Understanding What You Have Read

d

1. The main point of this selection is that **(5)**
   a. human beings by their nature will always be in conflict with one another.
   b. human communities do not seem ever to have existed without political institutions.
   c. James Madison and Thomas Hobbes made many thoughtful comments about human beings as political animals.
   d. human beings try to seek solutions for our conflicts and that those efforts make us political animals.

a

2. A person who wants to live completely isolated from a community would **(6a)**
   a. not be able to achieve this goal.
   b. be following in the footsteps of Thomas Hobbes.
   c. be in conflict with wild animals.
   d. make the best kind of leader.

c

3. *The Federalist* was **(6a)**
   a. a novel by the author of this selection.
   b. an essay about Hobbes's *Leviathan*.
   c. a book that expressed the ideas of James Madison.
   d. the name given to an early American political system.

a

4. This essay says that conflict exists **(6a)**
   a. when one person's actions would prevent other people from doing what they wanted.
   b. as an outgrowth of humanity's instincts for war.
   c. when someone tries to steal something that belongs to someone else.
   d. All of the above

b

5. Just why human beings cannot avoid conflict is an issue that has concerned **(6a)**

a. political scientists mostly.
b. people of many different interests and backgrounds.
c. only religious leaders and theologians.
d. just a few major philosophers like Madison and Hobbes.

d ______ 6. According to James Madison, people are more inclined to **(6a)**
a. cooperate than to oppress each other.
b. live in isolation than to live in a community.
c. read Hobbes's *Leviathan* than his own *The Federalist*.
d. oppress each other than to cooperate.

a ______ 7. Robert A. Dahl, the author of this selection, believes that conflict is **(6a)**
a. a basic fact of community life.
b. a condition without government.
c. part of the basic need for human fellowship.
d. avoidable by means of a strong educational system throughout the world.

d ______ 8. Among the conditions that make human beings social animals, the one that turns us into political animals is the fact that **(6a)**
a. we have different interests and needs.
b. we cannot live in a community without conflict.
c. communities arise from our need for human fellowship and from the apparent advantages of cooperation.
d. communities try to find ways to resolve conflicts.

b ______ 9. The major pattern of organization in this selection is **(7)**
a. chronological order.
b. comparison and contrast.
c. order of importance.
d. listing of details.

c ______ 10. A key element in a community's ability to settle conflicts is **(6a)**
a. its weaponry and its armies.
b. the benevolent feelings of its citizens.
c. leaders who can secure or force a settlement.
d. all of the above.

Interpreting and Evaluating

a ______ 1. We can infer that the reason why humans cannot avoid conflict **(8)**
   a. is still not fully understood.
   b. is best explained by Madison's belief that conflict is built into the very nature of men and women.
   c. is that wide-ranging differences exist in religious backgrounds.
   d. has to do with economic differences in society.

c ______ 2. We can infer that for Thomas Hobbes, a basic element in community life was **(8)**
   a. agriculture.
   b. violent death.
   c. government.
   d. industry.

c ______ 3. It is safe to conclude from this selection that faced with conflict, wild animals are not able to **(10)**
   a. resolve them through tests of power.
   b. live as a community.
   c. think about the conflict and make conscious, deliberate choices.
   d. cooperate.

d ______ 4. The writer concludes that in light of the principle of human conflict, our condition on earth is **(10)**
   a. dismal because we are like animals.
   b. advancing nonetheless because of humanity's skills in science and technology.
   c. solitary because we can ensure our survival only by living in isolation.
   d. not hopeless because we have made efforts to cooperate.

c ______ 5. From the selection we can conclude about our ancestors that if an argument or some other serious conflict arose, they **(10)**
   a. had little interest in resolving it.
   b. usually settled it with violence and bloodshed.
   c. might have tried to settle it according to some rules of justice.
   d. None of the above

a ______ 6. Hobbes believed that a society without government would **(10)**
a. create terrible living conditions for humankind.
b. put human beings in an isolated state of nature.
c. stimulate agriculture, industry, trade, knowledge, the arts, and society.
d. fit the description offered by most political philosophers.

c ______ 7. Based on the quotations provided in this selection, if Hobbes and Madison could discuss conflict together they would **(10)**
a. completely disagree with each other.
b. completely agree with each other.
c. find some common ground for agreement.
d. probably want to write a book together.

b ______ 8. In general we can assume from the selection that successful community living anywhere depends on **(11)**
a. similar economic goals.
b. successful governmental structures.
c. shelter and the absence of hunger.
d. democratic political systems.

9. The following statements are based on information in the selection. Put an F next to each statement of fact; put an O next to each statement that is the author's opinion. **(12a)**

F ______ a. James Madison said that the varied interests in civilized nations divide people into different classes with different views.

O ______ b. The basic task for humans and other forms of life on this planet is to deal with their conflicts successfully.

O ______ c. Our need for human fellowship and the advantages of cooperation create communities.

F ______ d. Humans have not yet been able to achieve complete harmony and to live without conflict.

F ______ e. Thomas Hobbes wrote *Leviathan* in 1651.

F ______ f. Hobbes said that to exist without government would mean fear and danger of death.

O ______ g. We become political animals when we try to resolve conflicts.

b ______ 10. The author uses quotations from Madison and Hobbes **(12)**
   a. in an effort to convince us to agree with him because two famous people agree with him.
   b. to provide evidence about conflict and cooperation drawn from important political philosophers in the past.
   c. to demonstrate his own intelligence and scholarship.
   d. to convince us of the excellent writing skills of these two political philosophers.

Vocabulary

Prefixes, suffixes, and roots contribute to the meanings of the following words from the selection. In column 1 copy out the word parts in italics; in column 2 write definitions for those parts; and in column 3 write a definition of the word. If you need one, use a dictionary to help you determine the definition for column 3. **(1d, 2)**

	1	2	3
Example:			
*im*possible	im	not	not possible
1. *con*front	con	against	face with hostility
2. *re*flect	re	again; back	to think seriously
3. isolat*ion*	ion	state; quality	state of being alone

4. *in*escap*able*	in	not	not capable of
	able	capable of	getting away
		being	
5. econom*ic*	ic	relating to	relating
			to economy
6. *un*regulated	un	not	not regulated;
			not controlled
7. *in*compat*ible*	in	not	not able to be
	ible	capable of	in harmony
		being	
8. *in*evit*able*	in	not	not able to
	able	capable of	be prevented
		being	
9. *contradictory*	contra	against;	characterized by
		opposite	expressing the
			opposite
(*contra* +	dict	state; say	
dict + *ory*)	ory	characterized	
		by	
10. toler*able*	able	capable of	able to
		being	be tolerated

For each word in the left-hand column of the following list, write the letter of the best definition from the right-hand column. Use context clues from the selection. Refer to a dictionary only if necessary. **(1c, 2)**

j 11. compel
h 12. conflict
b 13. disposed
g 14. diverse
a 15. endowed
c 16. fallible
i 17. oppress
f 18. probe
e 19. solitary
d 20. vex

a. equipped with talent or quality
b. inclined toward
c. capable of error
d. irritate; bother; annoy
e. alone
f. investigate
g. varied
h. disagreement; struggle
i. conquer; rule by unjust use of force or authority
j. force

WRITING PRACTICE

1. Write a one-page summary of this selection.
2. In this selection Dahl writes, "Our need for human fellowship and the advantages of cooperation create communities." Discuss in a paragraph some of the ways in which the people in your hometown cooperate with one another.

22

The Computer

George J. Brabb
Gerald W. McKean

How well do you understand computers? This definition of the computer appears at the beginning of a textbook that explains how to use computers in business. The technical precision of the definition will help you understand what a computer is.

Prereading

Before you read, make a list of ideas that enter your mind when you think of the word *computer*. Use a separate sheet of paper. **[3a(1)]**

Word Highlights

inanimate (¶2) not living
impulses (¶5) sudden pushes of energy
magnetized (¶6) having a magnetic charge
Boolean algebra (¶7) kind of mathematical reasoning
$a = b$ (¶7) *a* equals *b*
$a < b$ (¶7) *a* is less than *b*
$a > b$ (¶7) *a* is greater than *b*
allowable (¶8) permitted according to the rules, instructions, or program
finite (¶8) limited in number
modify (¶9) change
versatile (¶9) able to be used in many different ways
cognitive (¶9) related to learning and thinking

The *automatic electronic digital* **computer** is a *machine* that utilizes *electronic circuits to manipulate data* expressed in a *symbolic form* according to *specific rules* in a *predetermined* but *self-directed* way. This complete definition is somewhat hard to absorb as a whole. Let's look at its individual parts.

2 First of all, the computer is a *machine.* This means that it is inanimate and requires an outside power source. This also means it can perform only those activities for which the basic capabilities have been specifically designed into the machine. In other words, it is limited to its designed capabilities and such outside direction as can be given it. If separated from its outside power source, it ceases to function.

3 Second, it is *automatic.* This means that once started, it continues to run without outside interference.

4 Third, it is *electronic;* that is, it is made up of electronic circuits and runs on electrical energy.

5 Fourth, the computer is a *symbol manipulator.* It manipulates data, not physical entities. These data are represented as electronic impulses within the machine. The electronic impulses are combined to form number (*digital*) representations of data. Electronic circuits are used to manipulate these symbols.

6 Electronic devices are largely two-state devices. For example, a switch is either on or off, a spot on the surface of a magnetic tape is either magnetized or not magnetized, a particular location on a punched card or punched paper tape is either a hole or it is not, and a particular point on a wire at a particular instant either contains an electrical impulse or it does not. It therefore seems natural and reasonable to use the base 2 or **binary number system** as the basic data-representation method in the computer. Only two digits exist in the binary number system, 0 (zero) and 1 (one). They can easily be matched to the two states of the electronic devices. Combinations of 0s and 1s can be used to represent nonnumeric data as well as numeric data.

7 Fifth, the computer must follow *specific rules* in manipulating data. These rules are, in the main, the rules of Boolean algebra. That is, the computer can perform *only* the processes of *addition, subtraction, multiplication, division,* and *comparison* ($a = b$, $a < b$, $a > b$), in addition to data transfer between components.

8 Sixth, the computer must follow a *predetermined* sequence of its allowable processes. That is, someone (the programmer) must prepare a finite sequence of the allowable individual operations, a **program,** for the computer to follow.

9 Finally, the computer can follow the predetermined sequence in a *self-directed* way. It can store the program within its own memory and then follow it through under its own direction, without further outside guidance. This **stored-program** characteristic is what differentiates the computer from other data processing machines. That is, the computer can be made, in effect, to *learn* a process, *store* the instructions in its memory, and *follow* them through *unaided* by further supervision and direction. Since the instructions are stored in the memory and the memory is accessible to a user, the instructions can be changed. The computer can thus be given the ability to handle many different jobs. It is much more flexible than the "programmable" accounting machines because its programs are a sequence of logic and arithmetic operations. The availability of logic (decision-making) powers allows the machine to modify its operations while working on a job, making it more versatile and giving it great power to duplicate human cognitive mental processes.

10 In summary, then, we find that *the electronic digital computer is a symbol-manipulating machine that can be "instructed" to perform any sequence of logical or arithmetical operations on data.* Further, these instructions are easily modified, either by being totally replaced or by being modified by the machine in accordance with results it obtains during an operation. ❑

EXERCISES

Understanding What You Have Read

c 1. Which of the following sentences contains the main idea of the passage? **(5b)**
   a. "Electronic devices are largely two-state devices."
   b. "The computer can be made, in effect, to *learn* a process, *store* the instructions in its memory, and *follow* them through *unaided* by further supervision and direction."
   c. "The *automatic electronic digital computer* is a *machine* that utilizes *electronic circuits to manipulate data* expressed in

a *symbolic form* according to *specific rules* in a *predetermined* but *self-directed* way."

d. "The availability of logic (decision-making) powers allows the machine to modify its operations while working on a job, making it more versatile and giving it great power to duplicate human cognitive mental processes."

2. Put a T next to the statements that are true according to the passage and an F next to the ones that are false. **(6a)**

F ______ a. Computers can start and run by themselves.

F ______ b. Computers can direct their own activities.

T ______ c. The binary number system uses only two digits.

T ______ d. Computers use electronic circuits to manipulate data.

F ______ e. The computer can follow an infinitely variable sequence of operations.

F ______ f. Once started, computers do not need an outside power source.

b ______ 3. This passage is organized **(7)**
   a. in time order.
   b. by listing the detailed terms of the definition.
   c. in order of importance.
   d. by looking at the subject from many different viewpoints.

Interpreting and Evaluating

c ______ 1. On the basis of the selection we can safely conclude that computers **(10)**
   a. do not need human beings.
   b. need human beings to check on how a program is running.
   c. need human beings both to set instructions and to modify them.
   d. need human beings only to set instructions.

b ____ 2. Under which of the following conditions can we safely predict a computer will work? **(10)**
a. The computer is given no program.
b. The instructions are too complicated for most people to follow.
c. The computer is not supplied with an energy source.
d. The computer is cut off from its memory.

3. Put a checkmark next to those operations that could be considered binary. **(11)**

____ a. A person who answers yes, nor, or maybe

____ b. A basketball shot that scores 3, 2, 1, or 0 points

√ ____ c. A basketball that either goes into the basket or does not

____ d. A dimmer light switch with an infinite number of levels of brightness

√ ____ e. A buzzer that either makes a noise or does not

√ ____ f. A baseball player who either scores a run or does not

d ____ 4. Basically the same sentence is repeated at the beginning and near the end of this selection. Why? **(12d)**
a. At the beginning the sentence introduces the concepts to be discussed.
b. At the end the sentence summarizes the concepts.
c. At the end the reader should understand the sentence better than at the beginning.
d. All of the above

b ____ 5. The main purpose of this passage is to **(12d)**
a. entertain.
b. present basic concepts.
c. give concrete examples.
d. distinguish computers from accounting machines.

a ____ 6. Which of the following statements describes the use of evidence in this passage? **(12b)**

a. The authors define terms without proof.
b. The authors use mathematical proofs.
c. The authors offer many facts as evidence.
d. The authors offer only their personal opinions.

Vocabulary

Examine the following list of words and determine their meanings based on the context clues in the selection. Then complete the puzzle by filling in the numbered blanks with the words that best fit the definitions in the numbered list that follows the word list. When you are finished, a word should be formed as you read down the letters in the boxes. Find a one-sentence definition of that word in the selection and write it on the blank lines below the puzzle. **(1c)**

1. L O G I [C]
2. P R [O] G R A M
3. S Y [M] B O L
4. [P] R E D E T E R M I N E D
5. A [U] T O M A T I C
6. [T] W O - S T A T E
7. E L [E] C T R O N I C
8. S T O [R] E

automatic	program
electronic	store
logic	symbol
predetermined	two-state

1. System of making conclusions or decisions based on starting information
2. The set of instructions of allowable operations
3. A sign for something else
4. Set ahead of time
5. Running without outside interference

6. Existing in only one of two possible conditions; binary
7. Using electrons within electrical devices
8. Place information or a program into a computer's memory

a machine that utilizes electronic circuits to manipulate data expressed in a symbolic form according to specific rules in a predetermined but self-directed way; or a symbol-manipulating machine that can be "instructed" to perform any sequence of logical or arithmetical operations on data

WRITING PRACTICE

1. Describe in one paragraph the chief characteristics of a computer.
2. Even if you are not very familiar with computers, you have probably had some contact with them, perhaps with computerized checkouts in a store, with computerized records in your college registration process, or with video games. Describe in approximately one page your experiences with computers. Have they been interesting or confusing? Helpful or troublesome?

23

Minority Student

Richard Rodriguez

During his college years the writer found that his family background meant he would receive special treatment. Read this selection to see how that special treatment came about and how the writer felt about it.

Prereading

Before you read this selection, freewrite on what it's like or you think it would be like to be a minority student in college. Use separate paper. **[3a(3)]**

Skimming

Before reading the selection, skim it to answer the following questions: **(3b)**

1. Where did Richard Rodriguez go to college and graduate school?

   college — Stanford; graduate schools — Columbia and Berkeley

2. When was he first identified as a minority student?

   in 1967, in an English class in college

3. When was he invited to teach at a community college?

   1968

4. What was the subject of the articles he published in 1973?

his being educated away from the culture of his parents

Word Highlights

affirmative action (¶2) the government policy of giving members of minority groups preference for jobs and education
tally (¶2) count
HEW (¶2) the U.S. Department of Health, Education, and Welfare, which was in charge of affirmative action programs during the 1960s and 1970s
surname (¶2) last name; family name
juxtaposition (¶3) side-by-side placement
alienation (¶4) a feeling of being separate or different
radically (¶5) extremely
de facto (¶6) in fact, as opposed to by law
prompted (¶9) caused
contingents (¶9) groups
rhetorically (¶9) for effect only
los gringos (¶13) Mexican term for people from the United States; white people
los pobres (¶13) Spanish term for poor people
unfounded (¶15) without basis; wrong
fawning (¶17) flattering; seeking favor

Minority student — that was the label I bore in college at Stanford, then in graduate school at Columbia and Berkeley: a nonwhite reader of Spenser and Milton and Austen.

2 In the late 1960s nonwhite Americans clamored for access to higher education, and I became a principal beneficiary of the academy's response, its programs of affirmative action. My presence was noted each fall by the campus press office in its proud tally of Hispanic-American students enrolled; my progress was followed by HEW statisticians. One of the lucky ones.

Rewarded. Advanced for belonging to a racial group "under-represented" in American institutional life. When I sought admission to graduate schools, when I applied for fellowships and summer study grants, when I needed a teaching assistantship, my Spanish surname or the dark mark in the space indicating my race — "check one" — nearly always got me whatever I asked for. When the time came for me to look for a college teaching job (the end of my years as a scholarship boy), potential employers came looking for me — a minority student.

3 Fittingly, it falls to me, as someone who so awkwardly carried the label, to question it now, its juxtaposition of terms — minority, student. For me there is no way to say it with grace. I say it rather with irony sharpened by self-pity. I say it with anger. It is a term that should never have been foisted on me. One I was wrong to accept.

4 In college one day a professor of English returned my term paper with this comment penciled just under the grade: "Maybe the reason you feel Dickens's sense of alienation so acutely is because you are a minority student." *Minority student.* It was the first time I had seen the expression; I remember sensing that it somehow referred to my race. Never before had a teacher suggested that my academic performance was linked to my racial identity. After class I reread the remark several times. Around me other students were talking and leaving. The professor remained in front of the room, collecting his papers and books. I was about to go up and question his note. But I didn't. I let the comment pass; thus became implicated in the strange reform movement that followed.

5 The year was 1967. And what I did not realize was that my life would be radically changed by deceptively distant events. In 1967, their campaign against southern segregation laws successful at last, black civil rights leaders were turning their attention to the North, a North they no longer saw in contrast to the South. What they realized was that although no official restrictions denied blacks access to northern institutions of advancement and power, for most blacks this freedom was only theoretical. (The obstacle was "institutional racism.") Activists made their case against institutions of higher education. Schools like Wisconsin and Princeton long had been open to blacks. But the tiny number of nonwhite students and faculty members at such schools suggested that there was more than

the issue of access to consider. Most blacks simply couldn't afford tuition for higher education. And, because the primary and secondary schooling blacks received was usually poor, few qualified for admission. Many were so culturally alienated that they never thought to apply; they couldn't imagine themselves going to college.

6 I think — as I thought in 1967 — that the black civil rights leaders were correct: Higher education was not, nor is it yet, accessible to many black Americans. I think now, however, that the activists tragically limited the impact of their movement with the reforms they proposed. Seeing the problem solely in racial terms (as a case of *de facto* segregation), they pressured universities and colleges to admit more black students and hire more black faculty members. There were demands for financial aid programs. And tutoring help. And more aggressive student recruitment. But this was all. The aim was to integrate higher education in the North. So no one seemed troubled by the fact that those who were in the best position to benefit from such reforms were those blacks least victimized by racism or any other social oppression — those culturally, if not always economically, of the middle class.

7 The lead established, other civil rights groups followed. Soon Hispanic-American activitists began to complain that there were too few Hispanics in colleges. They concluded that this was the result of racism. They offered racial solutions. They demanded that Hispanic-American professors be hired. And that students with Spanish surnames be admitted in greater numbers to colleges. Shortly after, I was "recognized" on campus: an Hispanic-American, a "Latino," a Mexican-American, a "Chicano." No longer would people ask me, as I had been asked before, if I were a foreign student. (From India? Peru?) All of a sudden everyone seemed to know — as the professor of English had known — that I was a minority student.

8 I became a highly rewarded minority student. For campus officials came first to students like me with their numerous offers of aid. And why not? Administrators met their angriest critics' demands by promoting any plausible Hispanic on hand. They were able, moreover, to use the presence of conventionally qualified nonwhite students like me to prove that they were meeting the goals of their critics.

9 In 1968, the assassination of Dr. Martin Luther King, Jr.,

prompted many academic officials to commit themselves publicly to the goal of integrating their institutions. One day I watched the nationally televised funeral; a week later I received invitations to teach at community colleges. There were opportunities to travel to foreign countries with contingents of "minority group scholars." And I went to the financial aid office on campus and was handed special forms for minority student applicants. I was a minority student, wasn't I? the lady behind the counter asked me rhetorically. Yes, I said. Carelessly said. I completed the application. Was later awarded.

10 In a way, it was true. I was a minority. The word, as popularly used, did describe me. In the sixties, *minority* became a synonym for socially disadvantaged Americans — but it was primarily a numerical designation. The word referred to entire races and nationalities of Americans, those numerically underrepresented in institutional life. (Thus, without contradiction, one could speak of "minority groups.") And who were they exactly? Blacks — all blacks — most obviously were minorities. And Hispanic-Americans. And American Indians. And some others. (It was left to federal statisticians, using elaborate surveys and charts, to determine which others precisely.)

11 I was a minority.

12 I believed it. For the first several years, I accepted the label. I certainly supported the racial civil rights movement; supported the goal of broadening access to higher education. But there was a problem: One day I listened approvingly to a government official defend affirmative action; the next day *I* realized the benefits of the program. I was the minority student the political activists shouted about at noon-time rallies. Against their rhetoric, I stood out in relief, unrelieved. *Knowing:* I was not really more socially disadvantaged than the white graduate students in my classes. *Knowing:* I was not disadvantaged like many of the new nonwhite students who were entering college, lacking good early schooling.

13 Nineteen sixty-nine. 1970. 1971. Slowly, slowly, the term *minority* became a source of unease. It would remind me of those boyhood years when I had felt myself alienated from public (majority) society — *los gringos. Minority. Minorities. Minority groups.* The terms sounded in public to remind me in private of the truth: I was not — in a *cultural* sense — a minority, an alien from public life. (Not like *los pobres* I had encountered during my recent laboring summer.) The truth was sum-

marized in the sense of irony I'd feel at hearing myself called a minority student: The reason I was no longer a minority was because I had become a student.

14 *Minority student!*

15 In conversations with faculty members I began to worry the issue, only to be told that my unease was unfounded. A dean said he was certain that after I graduated I would be able to work among "my people." A senior faculty member expressed in confidence that, though I was unrepresentative of lower-class Hispanics, I would serve as a role model for others of my race. Another faculty member was sure that I would be a valued counselor to incoming minority students. (He assumed that, because of my race, I retained a special capacity for communicating with nonwhite students.) I also heard academic officials say that minority students would someday form a leadership class in America. (From our probable positions of power, we would be able to lobby for reforms to benefit others of our race.)

16 In 1973 I wrote and had published two essays in which I said that I had been educated away from the culture of my mother and father. In 1974 I published an essay admitting unease over becoming the beneficiary of affirmative action. There was another article against affirmative action in 1977. One more soon after. At times, I proposed contrary ideas; consistent always was the admission that I was no longer like socially disadvantaged Hispanic-Americans. But this admission, made in national magazines, only brought me a greater degree of success. A published minority student, I won a kind of celebrity. In my mail were admiring letters from right-wing politicians. There were also invitations to address conferences of college administrators or government officials.

17 My essays served as my "authority" to speak at the Marriott Something or the Sheraton Somewhere. To stand at a ballroom podium and hear my surprised echo sound from a microphone. I spoke. I started getting angry letters from activists. One wrote to say that I was becoming the *gringos'* fawning pet. What "they" want all Hispanics to be. I remembered the remark when I was introduced to an all-white audience and heard their applause so loud. I remembered the remark when I stood in a university auditorium and saw an audience of brown and black faces watching me. I publicly wondered whether a person like me should really be termed a minority.

But some members of the audience thought I was denying racial pride, trying somehow to deny my racial identity. They rose to protest. One Mexican-American said I was a minority whether I wanted to be or not. And he said that the reason I was a beneficiary of affirmative action was simple: I was a Chicano. (Wasn't I?) It was only an issue of race. ❑

EXERCISES

Understanding What You Have Read

c ____ 1. The main idea of this passage is that the author **(5)**
   a. benefited greatly from the label *minority student.*
   b. feels alienated from most Hispanic Americans.
   c. is unhappy with the label *minority student.*
   d. has had a successful life.

c ____ 2. This main idea is stated directly **(5b)**
   a. in the opening paragraph.
   b. in paragraph 2.
   c. in paragraph 3.
   d. nowhere but is implied throughout.

c ____ 3. The label *minority student* helped Rodriguez get **(6a)**
   a. into college.
   b. a good early education.
   c. into graduate school.
   d. a job counseling Hispanic Americans.

4. Place the following events in time order by placing a 1 next to the earliest event, a 2 next to the event that happened second, and so on. **(7a)**

5 ____ a. Richard Rodriguez was given scholarship and travel offers.

8 ____ b. The writer gave speeches and gained some celebrity.

4 ____ c. Dr. Martin Luther King, Jr., was assassinated.

1 ____ d. Black civil rights leaders won legal battles in the South.

6 ______ e. Rodriguez became uneasy with the term *minority student.*

3 ______ f. Hispanic-American activists complained about the lack of Hispanics in college.

7 ______ g. Rodriguez wrote several articles attacking affirmative action.

2 ______ h. Civil rights leaders looked at *de facto* segregation in the North.

9 ______ i. Rodriguez was attacked by activists.

d ______ 5. The author first became implicated in the reform movement of affirmative action when he **(6a)**
a. accepted a scholarship.
b. spoke out against the policy.
c. entered college.
d. quietly accepted a comment on an English paper.

6. Put a checkmark next to the causes the author gives for the low black enrollment at legally integrated northern colleges. **(7e)**

√ ______ a. Black students did not qualify because of poor education.

______ b. Black students left after meeting prejudice.

______ c. Black students preferred all-black colleges.

√ ______ d. Black students could not afford college.

√ ______ e. Black students never thought to apply.

______ f. White admissions officers quietly discarded the applications of black students.

d ______ 7. Rodriguez was highly rewarded because **(6a)**
a. administrators needed to answer critics.

b. government statisticians had established minority quotas.
c. he was a conventionally qualified student but had a Spanish surname.
d. All of the above

b ______ 8. As a result of questioning whether he should have been labeled *minority,* Rodriguez was attacked by Hispanic activists for all of the following reasons *except* **(6a)**
a. denying racial pride.
b. being ungrateful for the benefits he received.
c. becoming white people's ideal Hispanic.
d. lying to himself.

Interpreting and Evaluating

d ______ 1. From various clues scattered throughout the selection we can infer that the writer grew up **(8)**
a. poor and disadvantaged.
b. in a wealthy part of Mexico.
c. in a poor Mexican village.
d. in a middle-class Mexican-American home.

b ______ 2. We can infer that the English professor who wrote the comment on the author's term paper **(8)**
a. considered Rodriguez the same as the other students.
b. placed Rodriguez in a special category.
c. did not like Rodriguez.
d. was consciously trying to discriminate against the author by telling him he did not think like white people.

b ______ 3. We can infer that the author did not say anything to that English professor because he **(8)**
a. knew he would benefit from the label.
b. was uncertain of the label's meaning.
c. was frightened of the professor.
d. took a privately ironic attitude.

a ______ 4. "The reason I was no longer a minority was because I had become a student." We can infer that Rodriguez wrote this statement because he **(8)**
a. thought minority culture and student culture were two separate groups.

b. looked down on his roots.
c. thought he could get a better job by hiding his minority background.
d. wanted to avoid responsibilities to his people.

c ______ 5. We can infer from the tone of his presentation of the conversations he had with faculty members in paragraph 15 that the author **(8, 12d)**
a. looked forward to becoming a role model for other Hispanics.
b. was finally satisfied with his identity.
c. believed the faculty members did not understand his unease.
d. thought the faculty members were deliberately trying to mislead him.

a ______ 6. It is Rodriguez's opinion that black leaders were correct in believing that **(12a)**
a. blacks did not have equal access to higher education.
b. the segregation problem was racial.
c. they needed to apply pressure for more black students and faculty.
d. minorities must stick together to fight the white establishment.

d ______ 7. We can conclude from this selection that Rodriguez feels that affirmative action programs **(10)**
a. have helped all Hispanics.
b. have achieved the government's goals.
c. create role models for other minority students.
d. have primarily benefited middle-class students.

b ______ 8. We can conclude that Rodriguez would now most like to be identified as a **(10)**
a. minority student.
b. student and teacher.
c. Mexican American.
d. political activist.

c ______ 9. On the basis of information presented in this selection, we can predict that the author would support **(10)**

a. the continuation of affirmative action programs.
b. all attempts to end segregation.
c. special programs only for disadvantaged students.
d. hiring and admissions quotas.

c 10. From this selection we can generalize that **(11)**
a. affirmative action programs have only hurt people.
b. well-meaning faculty members usually confuse their students.
c. labeling people can create unfortunate social pressures.
d. government programs always do exactly what they were designed to do.

a 11. We can further generalize that **(11)**
a. people sometimes feel more in common with those outside their own ethnic group.
b. education never changes people's identities.
c. people do not always appreciate all the good that life brings.
d. only by identifying with ethnic causes can people improve their lives.

a 12. The tone of this selection is **(12d)**
a. angry and ironic.
b. resigned and straightforward.
c. hateful and destructive.
d. hopeful and positive.

d 13. The purpose of this selection is to **(12d)**
a. make us feel sympathy for the author.
b. argue for the end of all programs to help black and Hispanic students.
c. deny that some minority people are disadvantaged.
d. make us think about what happens when we label people *minority*.

Vocabulary

Next to each phrase from the selection in Column A write the letter of the meaning from Column B that best matches the word in italics. You may want to refer back to the selection for context clues. **(1c)**

Column A

e 1. became *implicated* in the strange reform movement

o 2. *deceptively* distant events

b 3. no official *restrictions*

h 4. denied blacks *access*

k 5. activists *tragically* limited the impact

i 6. principal *beneficiary* of the academy's response

j 7. principal beneficiary of the *academy's* response

m 8. more *aggressive* student recruitment

g 9. least *victimized* by racism

p 10. any *plausible* Hispanic on hand

c 11. *conventionally* qualified nonwhite students

d 12. *unrepresentative* of lower-class Hispanics

l 13. followed by HEW *statisticians*

f 14. proposed *contrary* ideas

a 15. won a kind of *celebrity*

n 16. essays served as my "*authority*"

Column B

a. fame
b. rules against; limitations
c. in the ordinary way
d. not typical; different from
e. involved
f. opposite
g. hurt
h. ability or right to enter
i. person who receives benefits
j. all colleges and universities
k. unfortunately
l. people who keep track of numbers
m. bold; active
n. proof of expertise
o. misleadingly
p. seemingly acceptable; likely

WRITING PRACTICE

1. Summarize in a paragraph Rodriguez's reasons for feeling uncomfortable with the label *minority* and for not identifying strongly with most other Hispanic Americans.
2. In a paragraph describe a time during which you felt uncomfortable with a label other people gave you.

24

Perception

James D. Laird
Nicholas S. Thompson

This selection from a psychology textbook discusses how our mind helps us figure out what we see. As you read try to understand how the theory of perception explains the kind of "mind trick" described at the beginning of the selection.

Prereading

Before reading the selection draw a word map or a picture representing your ideas about how your mind helps you interpret what your eyes see. **(3a)**

Previewing

Preview the selection before you read it and answer the following questions: **(3c)**

1. From the title and subtitles, what ideas about perception do you think this chapter discusses?

   the processes of perception; different theories of perception including the constructionist theory; cues, assumptions, and inferences; percepts

2. Examine the four illustrations. What processes do they illustrate?

   cues, assumptions, and principles of inferences; tricks of perception; how expectancies influence perception; assumptions and perception

3. What words are defined in the margin?

perception; constructionist theory; perceptual cue; expectancy; illusion; principles of inference; nativists; empiricists; percept

4. Look at the recap at the end of the selection. How many points are reviewed **eight**

Restate those points in your own words. **Student responses will vary.**

Word Highlights

arbor (¶1) a garden structure to support vines
irritably (¶2) nervously
rickety (¶3) weak; unstable
aligned (¶4) lined up evenly
nanometer (¶20) one-billionth of a meter

I've been a bird watcher all my life. I don't get up early or travel great distances to make my observations. Instead I do my bird watching from the breakfast table, looking out over the redwood deck on the west side of my house to the grape arbor beyond. Like all bird watchers, I always hope to see a rare species; but given the informal nature of my bird-watching program, I don't expect to see one very often.

2 So you can imagine my surprise when I saw a 500-pound robin in my garden one warm spring day. I looked up from my bowl of oatmeal and there it was, perched on the grape arbor just 100 feet away, glaring out across the pasture and flicking its tail feathers irritably. It had to weigh at least 500 pounds because it was fully 6 feet long and 4 feet high.

3 I had less than a second to wonder why this huge bird wasn't crushing the rickety arbor with its weight, when suddenly it was gone. In its place was a normal-sized robin, perched on the deck railing about 12 feet away. The bird chirped twice and flew off to the garden, where it disappeared among the lettuce.

4 Suddenly I realized the trick my eyes had played on me. From where I sat at the kitchen table, the railing of the deck and the top of the arbor aligned. As I looked up quickly from my breakfast, my brain had assumed that the bird was perched, not on the railing nearby, but on the arbor 100 feet away. Given that assumption, the only reasonable interpretation of the image was that the bird was very large. My 500-pound robin was a perceptual illusion.

The Perceptual Processes

5 Why do we see things that aren't there? To answer this question, we have to ask another.

How does the brain translate sensory information into a coherent picture of the world?

Perception The process of organizing, interpreting, and integrating sensory information.

6 **Perception** is the process of organizing, interpreting, and integrating sensory information. The perceptual processes take that information and turn it into experience. These processes are not exactly the same as the sensory processes, but they are closely related.

7 The sensory processes transform stimuli from the environment and the body into nerve impulses. Simultaneously, they organize information so that by the time it reaches the cortex of the brain, it has already been interpreted to a certain extent. But sensory processes are usually tied to a single sense, and they involve little learning. Perceptual processes — the processes that turn sensory information into the world we actually experience — often integrate information from more than one sense and clearly are shaped by learning.

8 Nineteenth-century psychologists believed that sensations are bits of raw information collected from the environment and that perceptions are interpretations of that information. But the more we learn about sensation and perception, the more we find that the processes of gathering and interpreting information are connected, that they differ mainly in degree and timing.

The Study of Perception: Traditional Theory

9 Within psychology, there are two schools of thought on how perception should be defined and research on perception undertaken. The first, the traditional perspective, traces its roots to the earliest days of psychology. It claims that the nervous system constructs our perceptions from the bits of information it acquires through the sense organs.

10 Later in this chapter we talk about a newer theory, a theory that emphasizes the ways in

which perception puts us directly in touch with the world around us. That theory initiated a research dialogue that continues today.

The Constructionist Approach

Constructionist theory The theory that the nervous system assembles fragments of sensory information into human experience.

11 The traditional theory originated from the work of Hermann von Helmholtz, a nineteenth-century physiologist. . . . Helmholtz and his followers developed **constructionist theory.** They believed that perceptions are constructed from information gathered by our senses — that our nervous system assembles these fragments of sensory information into experience, much as a child assembles pieces into a model plane. But unlike the process of putting together a model plane, perception, according to Helmholtz, is largely unconscious.

12 According to constructionist theory, perception is an incredibly fast reasoning process, the product of *unconscious inference* (Helmholtz, 1866/1968). When you leap out of bed each morning, you're behaving as though you know for sure that the floor is going to be there. But that knowledge is actually an inference. You know the floor has always been there before, and you have lots of reasons to suppose it's still there, but you don't *know* it's there. In fact, sometimes when you're away from home, sleeping in a strange bed, you leap out only to find that the floor isn't quite where you "knew" it to be. Your inference was that the floor is the same distance below the bed as it is at home, and you hit the floor with a thump.

13 Now you may be asking, "What inference? I never inferred anything from my getting out of bed." To that question Helmholtz would have answered, "That's why we say perceptual inferences are unconscious." The inferences you make when you perceive the world are just like the inference you make

when you jump out of bed without looking to see if the floor is still there. They are reasonable inferences, and they are usually correct. But you're totally unaware that you're making them.

14 Today, psychologists often speak about *information processing* rather than unconscious inference, and they believe that perception is closely related to the cognitive processes we discuss in Chapter 8. But the basic idea — that raw sensory data are processed and elaborated to construct perceptions — has not changed over time (Gregory, 1981).

Constructionist Methods

15 Constructionist theory focuses on identifying the cues, assumptions, and principles of inference that generate our perceptions. Figure 4.1 shows how these elements interact to produce perception.

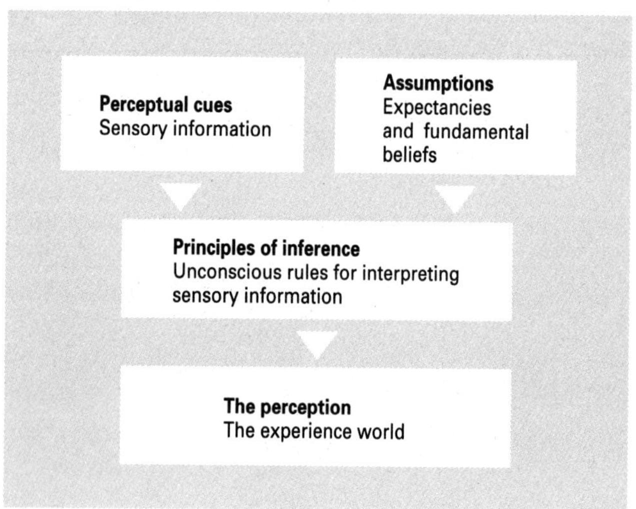

FIGURE 4.1 Cues, Assumptions, and Principles of Inference In perception, perceptual rules of inference are used to combine cues from the world with assumptions about that world to make the *percept,* the product of the perceptual process.

Perceptual cue An element of sensory information from which perceptions are constructed.

16 ***Cues*** According to constructionist theory, our perceptions are constructed from **perceptual cues,** bits of information that our senses deliver to the central nervous system. In the case of the 500-pound robin, two important perceptual cues were at work: the size of the robin image on the retina and the alignment of the nearby robin with the distant arbor (see Figure 4.2).

17 ***Assumptions*** Every perception also relies on assumptions about the world. What was the assumption in the case of the giant robin? That because the robin's body and the top of the arbor were aligned, the robin must be perched on the arbor. Remember, I didn't make this assumption consciously. At no

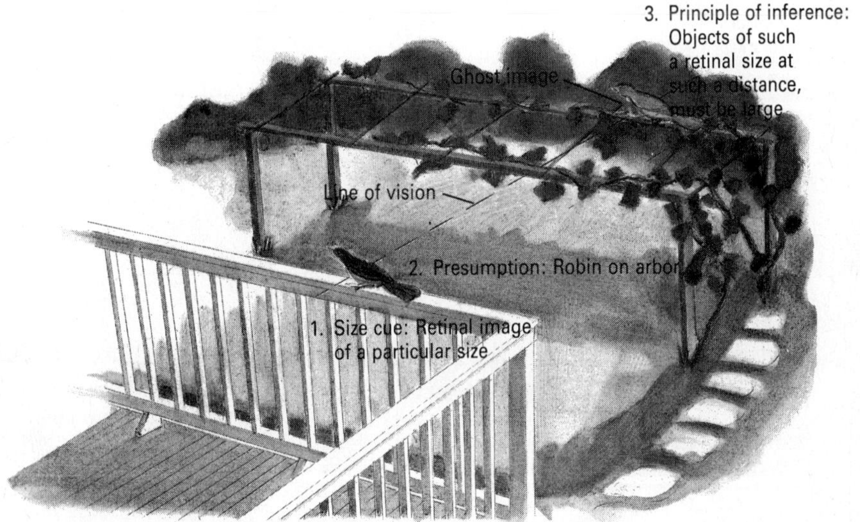
4. Conclusion (percept): Robin is very large
3. Principle of inference: Objects of such a retinal size at such a distance, must be large
Ghost image
Line of vision
2. Presumption: Robin on arbor
1. Size cue: Retinal image of a particular size

FIGURE 4.2 The 500-Pound Robin The interaction among cues, assumptions, and principles of inference often becomes clear when we misperceive a situation. The illusion of the giant robin was produced when the retinal image of a particular object combined with a faulty distance cue that placed the robin not on the nearby rail but on the distant arbor. The observer's perception combined the distance cue and the faulty assumption about the robin's location with the perceptual rule that for a given size a distant retinal image indicates a larger object than a near one to yield what in this case turned out to be a monstrous avian apparition.

point did I say to myself, "Hey, look at that bird. I assume it's on the grape arbor. It must be a giant bird."

Expectancy An assumption that is based on experience.

18 Some of the important assumptions we make about the world are based on our experience. These assumptions are called **expectancies.** Expectancy contributed to my perception of the 500-pound robin because I'd often seen robins perched on the grape arbor but had never seen one on the railing. The expectation that the robin would be on the arbor influenced my perception of the robin's size.

19 Expectations are so powerful that we sometimes overlook something we don't expect to see — even though it's there. Irving Biederman and his colleagues asked their subjects to look for certain objects in pictures (see Figure 4.3). The subjects often had difficulty seeing things in places where they didn't expect to see them (Biederman et al., 1981).

20 Other assumptions are so fundamental to perception that they seem to be built into our sensory systems. For example, our visual system "assumes" that only those wavelengths

FIGURE 4.3 Expectancies and Perception Expectations can make such a powerful contribution to perception that we may fail to see things because we don't expect to see them. Irving Biederman and his colleagues asked subjects to detect elements in drawings such as these. These subjects were much more likely to overlook elements in unexpected locations such as the fire hydrant on the mailbox or the automobile parked in the motel room.

of light between 380 and 760 nanometers are significant, so it doesn't respond to any other wavelengths.

Illusion A distorted perception of reality.

21 Psychologists can demonstrate that our nervous system makes assumptions about the world by violating those assumptions in experiments. **Illusions** — distorted perceptions — are one product of that violation. They help us understand the cues, assumptions, and principles of inference that underlie our perceptions.

Principles of inference Guidelines that tell the perceptual system how to interpret sensory information.

22 ***Principles of Inference*** Our perceptual system seems to use **principles of inference** to turn cues into perceptions. These guidelines tell the perceptual system how to interpret sensory information. In the robin example, the principle was "the farther away an object is, the bigger it must be to cast a retinal image of a particular size." Combined with the assumption that the robin was on the arbor, this principle led to the conclusion that the robin was very large.

Nativists Those who believe that perceptual principles are present at birth.

Empiricists Those who believe that perceptual principles are learned through experience with the environment.

23 Where do principles of inference come from? Psychologists have been debating this question since the nineteenth century. **Nativists** believe that perceptual principles are part of our biological makeup, that they are present at birth. **Empiricists** believe that we learn those principles through long experience with the environment.

24 As you will find repeatedly within the field of psychology, the question has no easy answer. Some perceptual principles seem to be innate; others seem to be learned. Still others seem to be partially innate and partially learned. . . .

Percepts

Percept The product of perception — the thing we see, feel, or hear.

25 Psychologists call the product of the perceptual processes, the thing we think we see or feel or hear, the **percept.** Because we are not

aware of the inferences our nervous system has been making, we experience percepts as facts. I didn't say to myself, "I have a hunch that might be a giant robin sitting on my grape arbor"; I simply saw a giant robin. Even when a percept was ridiculous, I experienced it as real.

26 In the next few sections, we'll take a closer look at the perceptual processes by examining three forms of perception: the localization of sound, the perception of brightness, and the

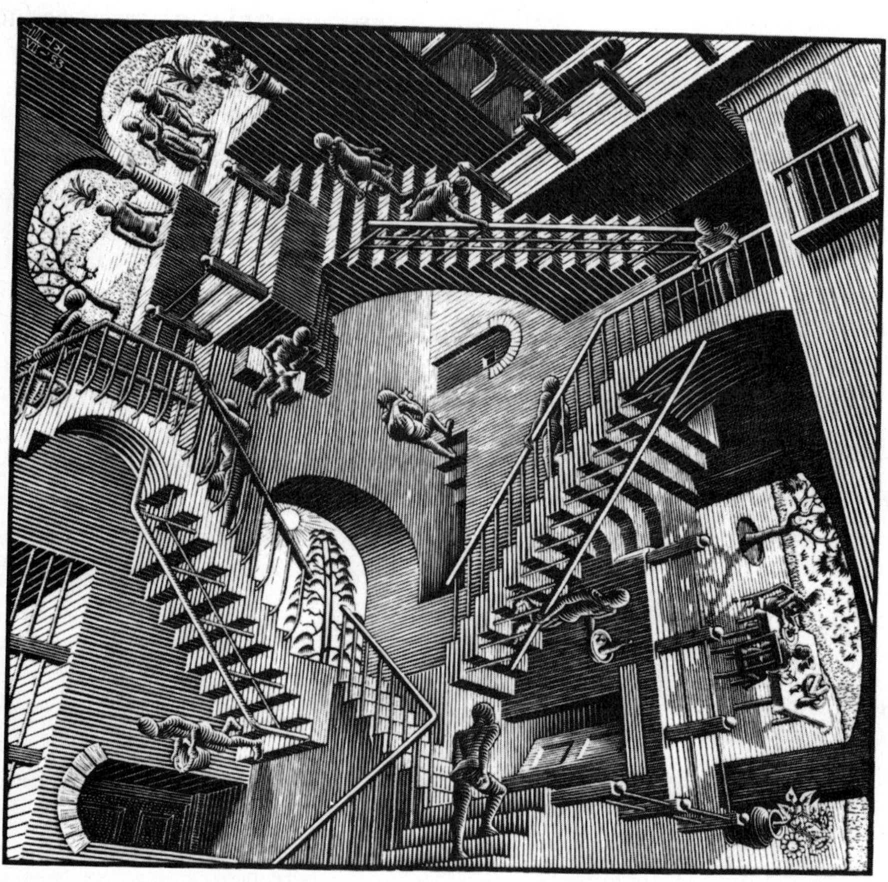

We have a powerful tendency to assume that straight lines in pictures are the edges of rooms and objects that they meet in corners. In his woodcut, *Relativity,* M. C. Escher has taken advantage of our assumptions to create an impossible world.

perception of depth. Although these three forms are just a small part of the large and complex subject of perception, they allow us to see how cues, assumptions, and principles of inference interact to create our percepts of the world.

Recap

- Perception is the process of organizing, interpreting, and integrating sensory information.
- According to constructionist theory, the nervous system assembles our experience — what we perceive — from the information gathered by our senses.
- Constructionists believe that perception is a very fast reasoning process, the product of unconscious inference.
- Constructionist theory focuses on identifying the cues, assumptions, and principles of inference that generate our perceptions.
- Assumptions that are based on experience are called expectancies.
- Perceptual illusions often reveal the principles of perception.
- Nativists believe that perceptual principles are innate; empiricists believe that they are learned.
- We experience percepts — the things we think we see or feel or hear — as reality. ❑

EXERCISES

Understanding What You Have Read

a ______ 1. The topic of this selection is **(5)**
   a. organizing and interpreting what we learn from our senses.
   b. bird watching from the breakfast table.
   c. percepts and facts.
   d. the constructionist approach.

2. Write the main idea of the selection in your own words. **(5) Student responses will vary.**

   A variety of theories help explain how the brain translates sensory information into a coherent picture of the world.

d ______ 3. The main point of the first four paragraphs of the selection is that the **(5b)**
   a. writer is a bird watcher.
   b. writer spotted a 500-pound robin in his garden.
   c. robin turned out to be normal size.
   d. writer's eyes played a trick on him.

b ______ 4. The first four paragraphs are told in the order of **(7a)**
   a. space, time, and importance.
   b. space and time.
   c. importance and time.
   d. time only.

5. In your own words write the main idea of this sentence in paragraph 8: "But the more we learn about sensation and perception, the more we find that the processes of gathering and interpreting information are connected, that they differ mainly in degree and timing." **(5a) Student responses will vary.**

   Gathering and interpretive processes are connected.

6. Place a checkmark before each of the following statements about perception that is true according to the selection. **(6a)**

______ a. Perceptual processes are the same as sensory processes.

✓ ______ b. Perceptual processes may integrate information from several senses.

______ c. Sensations are bits of raw information.

√ ______ d. Nineteenth-century psychologists believed that sensations are bits of raw information.

√ ______ e. Raw sensory data are processed and elaborated to construct perceptions.

______ f. Perceptions are influenced by imagination.

√ ______ g. Perception relies on assumptions.

______ h. We never miss something right in front of our eyes.

√ ______ i. Principles of inference influence perception.

______ j. We experience illusions as unreal.

______ k. We are always aware of the inferences we make.

√ ______ l. We at times overlook things we don't expect to see.

√ ______ m. We treat our perceptions as real and factual.

b ______ 7. Unconscious inference is an explanation of **(6a)**
a. why your feet land on the floor.
b. why you behave as though your feet are going to land on the floor.
c. conscious logical processes.
d. how we correct perceptual mistakes.

a ______ 8. Which of the following paragraphs is organized according to a pattern of cause and effect? **(7e)**
a. Paragraph 4
b. Paragraph 7
c. Paragraph 12
d. Paragraph 26

d ______ 9. Which of the following paragraphs is organized according to a listing-of-details pattern? **(7b)**
a. Paragraph 4
b. Paragraph 7
c. Paragraph 12
d. Paragraph 26

b ______ 10. Which of the following paragraphs is organized according to a pattern of comparison and contrast **(7d)**
a. Paragraph 4
b. Paragraph 7
c. Paragraph 12
d. Paragraph 26

Interpreting and Evaluating

b ______ 1. In the story about the 500-pound robin, the writer first inferred that **(8)**
a. the robin was sitting on top of the grape arbor.
b. the robin was sitting on a nearby railing.
c. the robin was in the garden to eat grapes.
d. he would be a world-famous bird watcher.

b ______ 2. From the story about the 500-pound robin we can infer that the **(8)**
a. robin's appearance was a true discovery.
b. nearby robin was the same robin that seemed far away.
c. writer is not a very reliable observer.
d. garden is filled with many strange creatures.

a ______ 3. We can conclude from the story of the 500-pound robin that **(10)**
a. eyes can play perceptual tricks on you.
b. you never know what to expect.
c. psychologists see many strange things.
d. bird watching can be a surprising activity.

a ______ 4. We can generalize about the relation between sensation and perception that **(11)**
a. they influence each other.
b. they are totally separate processes.
c. perception always precedes sensation.
d. perception is only interpreted sensation.

d ______ 5. We can infer that nineteenth-century psychologists **(8)**
a. understood sensation and perception well.
b. had no experience of perception.
c. did faulty experiments.
d. did not understand the relation between sensation and perception.

b ______ 6. According to constructionist theory, we can predict that **(10)**
a. if we assume we will meet a friend at 7:00 P.M., we will see him then.
b. if we assume that the salt should be on the kitchen counter, we may not notice it sitting in the refrigerator.
c. once we notice that someone has changed the furniture in a room, we do not look for a chair where it used to be.
d. we do not notice anything that is not in its expected place.

a ______ 7. From the experience of looking at Figure 4.3, we are expected to infer that **(4, 8)**
a. people find it difficult to locate unexpected objects.
b. people are not able to find unexpected objects.
c. being tricked by an optical illusion is embarrassing.
d. once we know about perception we cannot be tricked by assumptions.

c ______ 8. From the experience of looking at the picture of the staircase (page 614), we can conclude that **(4, 10)**
a. once you study pictures, you can always make sense of them.
b. the picture is very confused.
c. artists can use conflicting cues to confuse us.
d. the people in the picture are floating in space.

9. Identify the person or persons that hold each of the following opinions, by putting the number of the person or persons from List B in front of each statement in List A. **(12a)**

List A

7 ______ a. We have principles of perceptual inference from birth.

5 ______ b. People overlook things when the things aren't in their expected place.

1 ______ c. Percepts seem real.

8 ______ d. Artists can create impossible worlds by controlling assumptions and cues.

6 ______ e. We learn to infer through experience with the environment.

4 ______ f. Perceptual cues help us build perceptions.

3 ______ g. Perception relies on unconscious inference.

2 ______ h. Perceptions are simply interpretations of sensations.

List B

1. The authors
2. Nineteenth-century psychologists
3. Hermann von Helmholtz
4. Psychologists who believe in constructionist theory
5. Irving Biederman
6. Empiricists
7. Nativists
8. M. C. Escher

a ______ 9. We can generalize about perception that **(11)**
   a. it relies on unconscious processes.
   b. it is rarely reliable.
   c. everything we sense, we wind up perceiving.
   d. perception is just a figment of the imagination.

10. What techniques do the authors use to engage the readers' attention? **(12d) Student responses will vary.**

striking stories; illustrations; personal examples that

refer to students' experience

11. What special techniques do the authors use to help students understand and remember the material in the selection? **(12d) Student responses will vary.**

definitions; headings; a chart; explanatory captions;

a recap

d 12. Based on information presented in the selection, what can you predict about what appears in the next sections of the textbook? **(10)**
   a. Another theory about perception
   b. Information on cognitive processes of information gathering
   c. Information on perceptions of sound, brightness, and depth
   d. All of the above

Vocabulary

Try to determine the meanings of the following words from the selection. Then do the crossword puzzle, filling in the words that best suit the meanings given. **(1)**

cues
empiricists
expectancies
illusion
innate
nativists
percept
perception
perceptions
perceptual
retina
sensory
stimuli

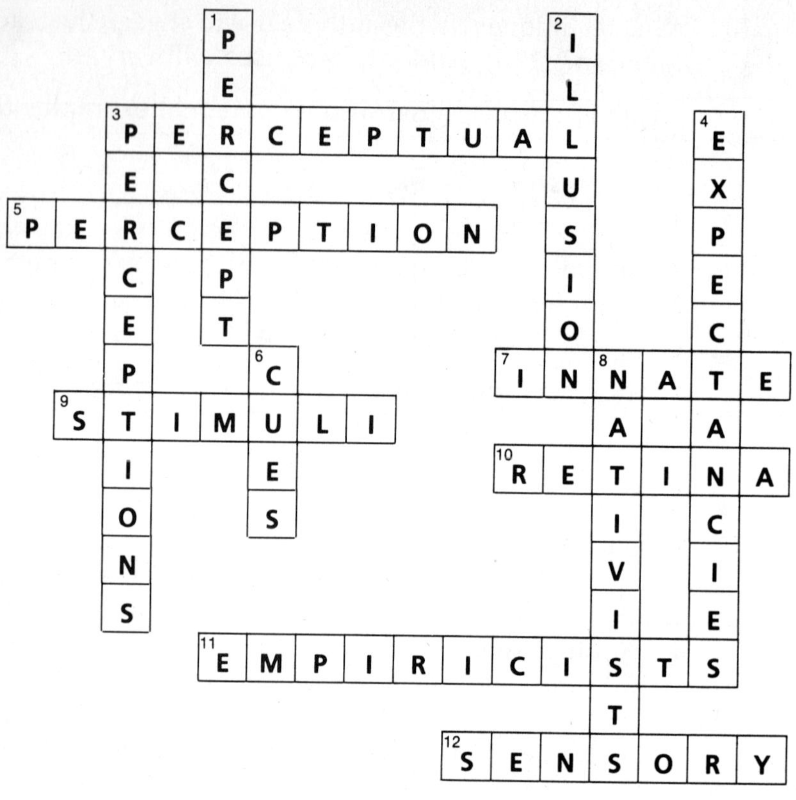

Across

3. Relating to perceptions
5. The process of organizing, interpreting, and integrating sensory information
7. With you from birth
9. Those things that excite the nervous system
10. Where the eye receives sensory data
11. Those who believe inference processes are learned
12. Relating to information collected from the environment

Down

1. The product of perception; the thing we see, feel, or hear
2. A mistaken perception
3. What we experience
4. Assumptions
6. Bits of information
8. Those who believe that we are born with inference processes

WRITING PRACTICE

1. In a paragraph explain the constructionist theory of perception.
2. Write several paragraphs about a time when your perceptions fooled you or left you uncertain about what you saw, felt, or heard. Explain both where the confusion came from and how you corrected or confirmed your perceptions.

Acknowledgments

Text Credits

Alison Lurie, excerpts from *The Language of Clothes* (5/e). Copyright © 1981 by Alison Lurie. Used by permission of Melanie Jackson Agency. Pages 17, 200–201, 206–207.

Phyllis Clark and Robert Lehrman, *Doing Time: A Look at Crime and Prisons*. New York: Hastings House, 1980, pp. 13–14. Reprinted by permission. Page 20.

Courtesy Canon Inc. Page 37.

Courtesy Jaguar Cars Inc. Page 36.

Sherman/Sherman/Russikoff: *Basic Concepts of Chemistry*, Third Edition. Copyright © 1984 Houghton Mifflin Company. Used with permission. Pages 42–43.

Marvin Perry et al., *Western Civilization*. Reprinted by permission of Houghton Mifflin Company. Pages 41–42, 126, 178–179, 210–211.

American Heritage Dictionary. Copyright © 1979 by Houghton Mifflin Company. Reprinted by permission from *The American Heritage Dictionary of the English Language*, paperback edition. Page 47.

James D. Laird and Nicholas S. Thompson, excerpts from *Psychology*, by James D. Laird and Nicholas S. Thompson, copyright © 1992 Houghton Mifflin Company. Reprinted by permission. Pages 60–63, 122, 607–615.

Melvin DeFleur and Everette Dennis, "Scott Joplin and the 'Maple Leaf Rag'." *Understanding Mass Communication*, Fourth Edition, copyright © 1991 Houghton Mifflin Company. Reprinted by permission. Pages 73–75.

Douglas A. Bernstein, Edward J. Roy, Thomas K. Srull, and Christopher D. Wickens, excerpts from *Psychology*, by Douglas A. Bernstein, Edward J. Roy, Thomas K. Srull, and Christopher D. Wickens. Reprinted by permission of Houghton Mifflin Company. Pages 76–78, 147.

William Boyes and Michael Melvin, excerpts from *Economics*, by William Boyes and Michael Melvin, copyright © 1991 Houghton Mifflin Company. Reprinted by permission. Pages 81–85, 123, 149–150.

Gordon McComb and John Cook. Reprinted, with permission, from *Compact Disk Player Maintenance and Repair*, by Gordon McComb and John Cook. Copyright 1987 by TAB Books, a Division of McGraw-Hill Inc., Blue Ridge Summit PA 17294-0850. (1-800-233-1128). Pages 90–92.

David E. Morine. Reprinted with permission from *Good Dirt: Confessions of a Conservationist*, © 1990, by David E. Morine. Published by the Globe Pequot Press, Old Saybrook, CT. Page 93.

Daniel Goleman, "True or False? The Anatomy of a Smile." Copyright © 1987 by The New York Times Company. Reprinted by permission. Pages 99–100.

David Macaulay, excerpts from *The Way Things Work* by David Macaulay. Compilation copyright © 1988 by Dorling Kindersley Limited, London. Illustration copyright © 1988 by David Macaulay. Text copyright © 1988 by David Macaulay and Neil Ardley. Reprinted by permission of Houghton Mifflin Co. All rights reserved. Pages 101, 108.

Desda Moss. Copyright 1991. *USA Today.* Reprinted with permission. Pages 113–115.

Harold Grilliot and Frank Schuber, excerpts from *Introduction to Law and the Legal System,* Fifth Edition by Harold Grilliot and Frank Schuber, copyright © 1992 Houghton Mifflin Company. Reprinted by permission. Pages 124, 208–209.

Bud Getchell, Rusty Pippin, and Jill Varnes, excerpts from *Health* by Bud Getchell, Rusty Pippin, and Jill Varnes. Reprinted by permission of D.C. Heath and Company. Pages 125, 350–354.

Danuta Bukatko and Marvin Daehler, excerpts from *Child Development* by Danuta Bukatko and Marvin Daehler, copyright © 1992 Houghton Mifflin Company. Reprinted by permission. Pages 125–126, 162–163.

Mary Beth Norton et al., *A People and a Nation: A History of the United States,* Second Edition. Reprinted by permission of Houghton Mifflin Company. Pages 148, 187–189, 256.

Seth Mydans, "20th Century Lawsuit Asserts Stone Age Identity." Copyright © 1988 by the New York Times Company. Reprinted by permission. Pages 153–154.

Susan Kraft, "The Heart of the Home." Reprinted with permission © *American Demographics,* June 1992. For subscription information, please call (800) 828-1133. Pages 155–156.

Daniel Boorstin. From *Wilson Quarterly,* Summer 1992. Copyright 1992 by the Woodrow Wilson International Center for Scholars. Pages 160–161.

Kenneth Boulding, *The Image.* Copyright © 1956, University of Michigan Press, Reprinted by permission. Page 176.

Douglas Bennet Lee, "America's Third Coast," *National Geographic,* July 1992, p. 10. Reprinted by permission. Pages 179–180.

Jane Brody. Copyright © 1992 by The New York Times Company. Reprinted by permission. Pages 185–186.

Melvin DeFleur and Everette Dennis, *Understanding Mass Communication,* Fourth Edition, copyright © 1991 Houghton Mifflin Company. Reprinted by permission. Page 197.

Deborah Tannen, *You Just Don't Understand.* Copyright © 1990 by Deborah Tannen, Ph.D. By permission of William Morrow and Company, Inc. Pages 198–199.

Douglas Bennet Lee, "Bolt from the Blue More Likely to Hit Men," *National Geographic,* April 1992, p. iv. Reprinted by permission. Page 205.

Franklin Crawford, "Fried Chicken Still Rules the Roost." Reprinted with permission © *American Demographics,* July 1992. For subscription information, please call (800) 828-1133. Pages 213–214.

Diane Burns, "Sure You Can Ask Me a Personal Question" is reprinted by permission of the author. Pages 232–233.

Colleen McElroy from "Living Under the Wing," in *Winters Without Snow.* Copyright © 1979, I. Reed Books, used by permission of Colleen McElroy and I. Reed Books. Page 241.

Michael Ondaajte, "Letters and Other Words," reprinted by permission. Page 241.

William Everson, *The Residual Years.* Copyright 1948 by New Directions Publishing Corporation. Reprinted by permission of New Directions Publishing Corp. Page 242.

Sandra Cisneros. From *The House on Mango Street.* Copyright © 1989 by Sandra Cisneros. Published in the United States by Vintage Books, a division of Random House, Inc., New York. Originally published, in somewhat different form, by Arte Publico Press in 1984 and revised in 1989. Reprinted by permission of Susan Bergholz Literary Services, New York. Pages 243–244.

Dianne Crispell, "The Brave New World of Men." Reprinted with permission © *American Demographics,* January 1992. For subscription information, please call (800) 828-1133. Pages 252–254.

David Gelman. From *Newsweek,* July 18, 1988. © 1988 Newsweek, Inc. All rights reserved. Reprinted by permission. Pages 261–262.

Bruce Brower and C. Ezzell. Reprinted with permission from *Science News,* the weekly newsmagazine of science, copyright 1992 by Science Service, Inc. Pages 263–264.

Barbara Kerbel, "Schoolwork: The Student's Job." *Newsday,* April 6, 1987, p. 58. Used by permission of the author. Pages 275–277.

Juliet Schor, "Americans Work Too Hard." Copyright © 1991 by The New York Times Company. Reprinted by permission. Pages 281–282.

Robert Ragaini. Reprinted by permission of the author. Pages 287–288.

Oldsmobile. Used by permission of Oldsmobile Division of General Motors. Pages 291–292.

Scott Ober, "International and Intercultural Dimensions," *Contemporary Business Communication,* copyright © 1992 Houghton Mifflin Company. Reprinted by permission. Pages 305–312.

Charles Panati, "Where Does Money Come From?" From *The Browser's Book of Beginnings* by Charles Panati. Copyright © 1984 by Charle Carroll Hudson. Reprinted by permission of Houghton Mifflin Co. All rights reserved. Pages 321–322, 333.

Jay Barney and Ricky Griffin, *The Management of Organizations,* copyright © 1992 by Houghton Mifflin Company. Reprinted by permission. Pages 322–324.

"Does Dating Work?" from *Wilson Quarterly,* Summer 1992. Copyright 1992 by the Woodrow Wilson International Center for Scholars. Pages 329–330.

Patricia Skalka, "Six Keys to Quicker Learning." Reprinted by permission of the author. Pages 359–364.

Rogelio R. Gomez, "Foul Shots." Copyright © 1991 by The New York Times Company. Reprinted by permission. Pages 371–374.

Roberta Israeloff, "Role Reversal," *Woman's Day,* September 13, 1988. Reprinted by permission of the author. Pages 380–383.

Elizabeth Joseph, "My Husband's Nine Wives." Copyright © 1991 by The New York Times Company. Reprinted by permission. Pages 389–391.

John Harrington, "The Beauty of Quantitative Thinking Begins with Counting Things" from DISCOVERING SCIENCE. Reprinted by permission of Houghton Mifflin Company. Pages 396–398.

Susan Perry and Jim Dawson, "What's Your Best Time of Day?" Reprinted with the permission of Rawson Associates, an imprint of Macmillan Publishing Company from *The Secrets Our Body Clocks Reveal* by Susan Perry and Jim Dawson. Copyright © 1988 by Susan Perry and Jim Dawson. Pages 403–406.

Gary Soto, "Looking For Work." From *Living Up the Street,* by Gary Soto. © 1985 by Gary Soto. Used by permission of Strawberry Hill Press, Portland, Oregon. Pages 413–418.

Bruce Shertzer, *Career Planning: Freedom to Choose,* Third Edition. Reprinted by permission of Houghton Mifflin Company. Pages 423–429.

Simon J. Ortiz, "My Father's Song," is reprinted by permission of the author. Pages 435–436.

Thomas V. DiBacco et al., "Organizing Labor." From *History of the United States* by DiBacco et al. Copyright © 1992 by Houghton Mifflin Company. Reprinted by permission of Houghton Mifflin Company. Pages 442–451.

Elizabeth Wong, "The Struggle to Be an All American Girl," *Los Angeles Times*, September 7, 1980. Reprinted by permission of the author. Pages 459–460.

Richard T. Schaefer, "An Introduction to Sociology" from *Sociology*. Copyright © 1983 by McGraw-Hill. Reproduced with permission of McGraw-Hill. Pages 468–475.

Alan R. Gitelson, Robert L. Dudley, and Melvin J. Dubnick, "What Is News?" from *American Government*. Reprinted by permission of Houghton Mifflin Company. Pages 484–486.

Robert DeBlois, "Looking Forward, Looking Back," *Long Island Newsday*, May 25, 1987. Reprinted by permission of the author. Pages 492–494.

Janny Scott, "How They Get You To Do That." Copyright 1992, Los Angeles Times. Reprinted by permission. Pages 501–507.

Lawrence Summers, "The Most Influential Investment." Reprinted with permission. Copyright © 1992 by Scientific American, Inc. All rights reserved. Pages 517–520.

David Sue, Derald Sue, and Stanley Sue, "Crime and Violence" from *Abnormal Psychology*. Reprinted by permission of Houghton Mifflin Company. Pages 528–534.

Charles Whitaker, "The Disappearing Black Teacher," reprinted by permission from *Ebony* Magazine and Johnson Publishing Co., Inc. © 1988. Pages 540–544.

Cassandra Franklin-Barbarjosa, "To Make a DNA Print," *National Geographic*, May 1992, pp. 116–117. Used by permission. Pages 553–555.

Joseph Berger, "Classroom Focus Shifting to the Art of Thinking." Copyright © 1988 by The New York Times Company. Reprinted by permission. Pages 563–568.

Robert A. Dahl, "Conflict and Cooperation" from *Democracy in the United States: A Promise and Performance*, Fourth Edition. Reprinted by permission of Houghton Mifflin Company. Pages 575–578.

George J. Brabb and Gerald W. McKean, "The Computer" from *Business Data Processing*. Reprinted by permission of Houghton Mifflin Company. Pages 586–587.

Richard Rodriguez, "Minority Student," from *Hunger of Memory* by Richard Rodriguez. Copyright © 1982 by Richard Rodriguez. Reprinted by permission of David R. Godine, Publisher. Pages 593–598.

Art Credits

Photo courtesy of Jaguar Cars Inc. Page 36.

"Marathon to Makka," copyright © 1979 by Houghton Mifflin Company. Reprinted by permission from *The American Heritage Dictionary of the English Language*, paperback edition. Page 47.

Dr. Patricia Kuhl, University of Washington. Pages 61–62.

© David R. Frazier Photolibrary. Page 82.

"Four Categories of Resources" from William Boyes and Michael Melvin, *Economics*, copyright © 1991 Houghton Mifflin Company. Reprinted by permission. Page 84.

Copyright Paul Ekman, 1988. Page 100.

"Immigrants Arriving in the United States, 1820–1970," from Getis and Getis, *Geography*. Reprinted by permission of Houghton Mifflin Company. Page 104.

Courtesy of AT&T Archives. Page 107.

"After-School Money" from *Newsweek,* July 18, 1988. Page 111.

"USA Remains Solidly Religious" from "Practicing or Not, Many Identify with Religion" by Desda Moss. Copyright 1991. *USA Today.* Reprinted with permission. Page 114.

"Give Me Something Fried" from "Fried Chicken Still Rules the Roost" by Franklin Crawford. Reprinted with permission © *American Demographics,* July 1992. For subscription information, please call (800) 828-1133. Page 214.

Bohdan Hrynewych. Page 222.

Courtesy of Eaton Corporation. Page 229.

Brown Brothers. Page 444.

"The Business Cycle" from Thomas V. DiBacco et al, "Organizing Labor," in *History of the United States* by DiBacco et al. Copyright © 1992 by Houghton Mifflin Company. Reprinted by permission of Houghton Mifflin Company. Page 444.

Library of Congress. Page 447.

The Granger Collection, New York. Pages 448–449.

Ira Wyman/SYGMA. Page 470.

Jack Fields/Photo Researchers, Inc. Page 472.

Jim McHugh/SYGMA. Page 472.

J.P. Laffont/SYGMA. Page 473.

Stephen Castagneto/NYT Pictures. Page 564.

"Cues, Assumptions, and Principles of Inference" and "The 500-lb. Robin" from James D. Laird and Nicholas S. Thompson, *Psychology,* copyright © 1992 by Houghton Mifflin Company. Reprinted by permission. Page 610.

Irving Biederman et al. Reprinted with permission from *Human Factors, Vol. 23, No. 2, 1981.* Copyright 1981 by the Human Factors and Ergonomics Society, Inc. All rights reserved. Page 612.

Subject Index

Author Index

To the Student:

We hope that you will take a few minutes to fill out this questionnaire. The comments you make will help us plan future editions of *Reading Skills Handbook*. After you have completed the following questions, please mail this sheet to:

College Marketing
Houghton Mifflin Company
222 Berkeley Street
Boston, MA 02116-3764

1. Name of college or university ______________________
2. Did you find the discussion of the specific reading skills easy to understand? ______________________

   Were any sections especially difficult? ______________________

   ____
3. Which chapters in the *Handbook* did you find most helpful?

   ____

   Why? ______________________

   ____
4. Which chapters did you find least helpful? ______________________

   Why? ______________________

   ____
5. Were the exercises in the *Handbook* useful? ______________________

   Were there enough exercises? ______________________
6. Did you find the reading passages used for the examples and in the exercises interesting? ______________________

   Which did you enjoy most? ______________________

   Which did you enjoy least? ______________________
7. Were the exercises that accompanied the *Reading Selections* useful to you? ______________________
8. Did you find the cross-referencing system that keys each question in the *Reading Selections* to the appropriate section in the *Handbook* easy to use?

   ____
9. Which Critical Thinking in Writing activities did you enjoy most? ______________________

   ____

   Which did you enjoy least? ______________________

10. Did your reading improve after using this text? ______________________

____

11. Please rate the *Reading Selections.*

	Excel-lent	*Good*	*Fair*	*Poor*	*Didn't Read*
1. Six Keys to Quicker Learning	____	____	____	____	____
2. Foul Shots	____	____	____	____	____
3. Role Reversal	____	____	____	____	____
4. My Husband's Nine Wives	____	____	____	____	____
5. The Beauty of Quantitative Thinking Begins with Counting Things	____	____	____	____	____
6. What's Your Best Time of Day?	____	____	____	____	____
7. Looking for Work	____	____	____	____	____
8. Career Planning	____	____	____	____	____
9. My Father's Song	____	____	____	____	____
10. Organizing Labor	____	____	____	____	____
11. The Struggle to Be an All American Girl	____	____	____	____	____
12. An Introduction to Sociology	____	____	____	____	____
13. What Is News?	____	____	____	____	____
14. Looking Forward, Looking Back	____	____	____	____	____
15. How They Get You to Do That	____	____	____	____	____
16. The Most Influential Investment	____	____	____	____	____
17. Crime and Violence	____	____	____	____	____
18. The Disappearing Black Teacher	____	____	____	____	____
19. To Make a DNA Print	____	____	____	____	____
20. Classroom Focus Shifting to the Art of Thinking	____	____	____	____	____
21. Conflict and Cooperation	____	____	____	____	____
22. The Computer	____	____	____	____	____
23. Minority Student	____	____	____	____	____
24. Perception	____	____	____	____	____

12. Please make any additional comments that you think might be useful.

____

Thank you very much.

Your name (optional) ______________________________________